Movements in Times of Democratic Transition

Edited by

BERT KLANDERMANS AND
CORNELIS VAN STRALEN

Movements in Times of Democratic Transition

TEMPLE UNIVERSITY PRESS
Philadelphia   Rome   Tokyo

8795 3518

TEMPLE UNIVERSITY PRESS
Philadelphia, Pennsylvania 19122
www.temple.edu/tempress

All reasonable attempts were made to locate the owners of the illustrations published in this book. If you believe you may be one of them, please contact Temple University Press, and the publisher will include appropriate acknowledgment in subsequent editions of the book.

Library of Congress Cataloging-in-Publication Data

Movements in times of democratic transition / edited by Bert
Klandermans and Cornelis van Stralen.
    pages cm
  Includes bibliographical references and index.
   ISBN 978-1-4399-1180-8 (hardback : alk. paper) —
 ISBN 978-1-4399-1181-5 (paper : alk. paper) —
 ISBN 978-1-4399-1182-2 (e-book)   1. Social movements—Political
aspects.   2. Democratization.   3. Political participation.
I. Klandermans, Bert.   II. Stralen, Cornelis J. van.
  HM881.M673 2015
  303.48'4—dc23

                                                  2014018552

∞ The paper used in this publication meets the requirements of the
American National Standard for Information Sciences—Permanence
of Paper for Printed Library Materials, ANSI Z39.48-1992

Printed in the United States of America

2 4 6 8 9 7 5 3 1

Contents

Movements in Times of Democratic Transition

Introduction

BERT KLANDERMANS
CORNELIS VAN STRALEN

In Latin America, on the African continent, in Asia, and in the Northern Hemisphere, movements have struggled for societal change. Once the changes begin to materialize, the movements that fought for them face the question of how to proceed. Quite often there is little room for maneuvering because the constituency abandons the movement or the leadership takes governmental responsibilities on itself. In those situations we see movement organizations struggle with the new reality. Decline, radicalization, and revitalization are possible outcomes.

This book brings together essays on how social movement organizations act in the context of the democratic transition they have been fighting for. It compares movement dynamics in these circumstances and develops theoretical frameworks for the study of movements in times of democratic transition. The plan for this book originated at a workshop held in November 2008 in Belo Horizonte, Brazil. Contributors include participants at the workshop and other scholars from South Africa, Central Europe, and Latin America.

Decline

One trajectory of movements in times of democratic transition is decline. Why would a democratic transition lead to the decline of a movement? One obvious reason is success or failure. Success decreases the demand for movement activity; even partial success reduces the urgency of the movement's cause. As a consequence, the motivation of individual citizens to take part in movement activity declines. Failure implies that the supply of movement activity is flawed or not effective. Why would someone continue to be involved in activities that appear to be ineffective? Because both demand and supply are needed for protest to materialize, movement activity declines when either side is deemed insufficient.

Radicalization

Decline is not the only trajectory a movement can take in response to societal transition. Hanspeter Kriesi and colleagues (1995) distinguish in addition to decline (or "involution," as they call it) three more trajectories: radicalization, institutionalization, and commercialization. Radicalization of a movement usually results in decline as well, because more-moderate supporters can no longer identify with the radicalized movement. Institutionalization and commercialization arguably mean the end of movement activity. The movement has become part of the political or governmental establishment or turned into a commercial enterprise.

Revitalization

Although the literature frequently refers to decline as a movement's fate, we also see a revitalization of the movement sector in response to democratic transition. Indeed, some old movements die, but new movements come into existence. In some countries, such as Brazil and South Africa, the movement sector seems to grow rather than dwindle.

Abeyance

When a movement declines, that does not necessarily mean it disappears altogether. Leila Rupp and Verta Taylor (1987) note that pockets of movement activity continue to exist in so-called abeyance structures. Groups of movement activists, who continue to meet, keep the remainders of the movement alive. It is not unlikely that these pockets become the kernels for starting points of a new cycle of the same or a new movement.

Disengagement

At the individual level, movement decline or demobilization has the appearance of disengagement. Previously active individuals decide to quit active involvement and give up movement activity. Disengagement results from declining levels of satisfaction and commitment. Satisfaction is related to the extent to which movement activity satisfies motives to participate, be they instrumental, identity, or ideological motives. *Commitment* refers to the individual's level of identification with the movement, the expectation that the movement will continue to satisfy the motives to participate, and perceived alternative ways to satisfy the motives. Dissatisfaction and low levels of commitment can coexist without making a person quit. Although disengagement does not necessarily imply movement decline—movements may successfully replenish their numbers when participants quit—movement decline does necessarily imply disengagement.

The Book

The book contains edited, peer-reviewed papers from Latin America, South Africa, and Central Europe preceded by three theoretical contributions. The regional sections each begin with a short introduction by an expert on the region.

Part I contains three chapters on theory relevant in the context of democratic transition. In "Mobilizing for Democracy" Federico Rossi and Donatella della Porta observe that political scientists have paid little attention to the role of social movements in processes of democratization, while social movement scholars have given short shrift to processes of democratization. The authors discuss three perspectives on democratization—structural, historical, and transitional—and formulate an answer to the question of what has been the role of social movements, trade unions, advocacy networks, and cycles of protest in democratization processes. They conclude that their role tends to vary with the different stages of democratization. Olivier Fillieule in "Disengagement from Radical Organizations" elaborates on yet another relevant aspect of the fate of movements in times of democratic transition: disengagement and, consequently, decline. He argues strongly for research on people's life course and the justifications they give for their actions as a means to investigate the complex interplay of factors at micro, meso, and macro levels. But not every activist career ends in disengagement. Alison Crossley and Verta Taylor's "Abeyance Cycles in Social Movements" takes up Taylor's classic argument about movements in abeyance. They show that a movement does not necessarily disappear when it declines. Building on material on feminist mobilization among college-age students during a period of abeyance for the U.S. women's movement, the authors show how the abeyance formulation helps in understanding the complex role of movements during periods of democratic transition.

The four chapters on Latin America in Part II all concern transitions to democracy of authoritarian or dictatorial regimes. Sebastián Pereyra in "Strategies and Mobilization Cycles of the Human Rights Movement in the Democratic Transition in Argentina" describes how that movement, crucial in the struggles against the military dictatorship, gradually institutionalized during the transition to democracy. He shows how human rights organizations became legitimate political players. At the same time, the movement reformulated and widened its demands to encompass recent institutional human rights violations. North of Argentina, in Brazil, the land reform movement Movimento dos Trabalhadores Sem Terra (MST; Landless Rural Workers' Movement) tries to accommodate successive regime changes. Camila Penna in "Social Movement Activity

in the Transition to Partido dos Trabalhadores Government" describes how the
land reform movement coped with the transition to the government of the Partido dos Trabalhadores led by Lula da Silva. Although not exactly a transition to
democracy, it is a transition to a regime that is closely affiliated with the MST.
From the standpoint of the movement sector, the transition to the Partido dos
Trabalhadores government was unprecedented in Brazilian politics. Four years
later a similar transition took place in Bolivia when Evo Morales and his Movimiento al Socialismo took office. Ton Salman in "A Democracy for 'Us'—or for
All?" analyzes the ambivalence of social movements when parties akin to them
win an election. He illustrates how ideological affinities and shared causes are
troubled by the responsibilities of the now-governing standard-bearer. Farther
north, in Central America, between 1980 and 2010 a whole region transitioned
to democracy. Paul Almeida in "Democratization and the Revitalization of
Popular Movements in Central America" describes the two waves of protest
that accompanied the transition. The first wave occurred when the region was
still characterized by authoritarian regimes; the second took place in a more
democratic context. Interestingly, Almeida also highlights the revitalization of
movements as the movement sectors in each country adjusted to the new political economic context of democratization.

   South Africa is the exemplar of a peaceful transition to democracy. It also
proved false the theories holding that movement activity declines during democratic transitions. In his introduction to Part III Stephen Ellis observes that the
country was home to a bewildering number of political and social movements
articulating grievances of one or another sort. The three chapters in this section
all underscore that observation. Ineke van Kessel discusses the demise of the
United Democratic Front (UDF), the most representative movement organization in South Africa's history, in "The United Democratic Front and Its Legacy
after South Africa's Transition to Democracy." Soon after the African National
Congress (ANC) was unbanned, the UDF disbanded itself. Some of its organizations went back to their core business, other member movements merged with
branches of the ANC, and dozens of organizations ceased to exist. Van Kessel
shows how during the honeymoon years of Nelson Mandela's presidency the
relationship between the state and civil society was largely collaborative but that
in recent years civil society organizations increasingly began to protest against
the ANC because it failed to deliver a better life for all. This is exactly what Bert
Klandermans found in surveys conducted in South Africa around the time of
the first two democratic elections (1994 and 1999). In "Movement Politics and
Party Politics in Times of Democratic Transition" he compares engagement in
party politics and movement politics between 1994 and 2000. Data collected
among random samples of the population tell us that many continued to be
actively involved in movement politics. Unlike what is suggested in the literature, the engagement in party politics did cause a decline in movement politics. Indeed, in the election year 1999 the proportion of the citizens who were
involved in both movement politics and party politics increased significantly.

Steven Robins and Christopher Colvin bring the argument down to the ground level of citizens in neighborhoods of Cape Town. Community-based activism in South Africa continues to be dynamic and animated, as their chapter, "Social Movements after Apartheid," illustrates. The authors provide figures that suggest that social activism and community protest are not only alive and well after apartheid but on the upsurge. They refer to the emergence of numerous new social movements, focusing on one, the Treatment Action Campaign (TAC), which during the years of the Thabo Mbeki administration struggled for provision of HIV treatment. The chapter examines the ways TAC and its partner organizations have navigated the postapartheid political landscape.

Meanwhile, in Eastern and Central Europe, former communist countries were experiencing democratization trajectories that impress the observer as more chaotic than those in Latin America and South Africa because of the complexities of attempts by the population to come to terms with the legacy of the communist systems. The two chapters on Poland and the one on Hungary each document processes of institutionalization. In Hungary the former protest organization Fidesz evolved into a conservative, extreme-right party. In Poland two important movement organizations, the labor movement and the farmers' movement, institutionalized into interest organizations, negotiating interests of their constituencies rather than striving for broader political goals. In "From Anticommunist Dissident Movement to Governing Party," Máté Szabó documents the transformation of Fidesz in Hungary. He demonstrates how the experience of being outlawed in the communist system produced long-lasting effects on the leading activists of Fidesz. Describing the transformation of the labor unions in Poland in "From Total Movement to Interest Group," Michał Wenzel similarly alludes to political division, in both elites and masses, between former Solidarity members and former members and supporters of the Communist Party and its allies. Grzegorz Forys and Krzysztof Gorlach, discussing the fate of the Polish farmers' movement in "Defending Interests," draw attention to the creation by the political and economic changes of a visible division between those who took advantage of the completed transformation and those who mostly paid for it, including traditional rural farmers.

Coda

The chapters in this volume evidence that movement organizations have no single trajectory in times of democratic transition. Cessation, continuation, institutionalization, revitalization, and abeyance are all routes movements can take. Obviously, it matters where the political system comes from. Postcommunist societies have different problems to cope with than do postauthoritarian societies. Movements that have long fought the ancien régime must solve different problems than newly formed movements, and movements that take office face again other problems. Rossi and della Porta notice that scholars of democratic transitions neglect movements as actors, while students of social movements neglect processes of democratization. Echoing their observation I call for research of movements in times of democratic transition. This book is meant to stimulate such research.

REFERENCES

Kriesi, Hanspeter, Ruud Koopmans, Jan Willem Duyvendak, and Marco Giugni. 1995. *New Social Movements in Western Europe: A Comparative Analysis.* Minneapolis: University of Minnesota Press.
Rupp, Leila J., and Verta Taylor. 1987. *Survival at the Doldrums: The American Women's Rights Movement, 1945 to the 1960s.* New York: Oxford University Press.

I

Theory

1

Mobilizing for Democracy

Social Movements in Democratization Processes

FEDERICO M. ROSSI
DONATELLA DELLA PORTA

E ven though social movements are more and more recognized, in political and academic debates, as important actors in democracies, interactions between politics and the social sciences have been rare (Rossi and della Porta 2009; della Porta 2014). Social movements have been far from prominent in the literature on democratization, which has mainly focused instead on economic preconditions, elites' behavior, or the geopolitical situation. Modernization theory and the historical class perspective are structural approaches, especially concerned with the preconditions for democracy. They recognize the central role of economic conditions and social classes but disregard the specific role of social movements and contentious politics. The so-called developmental approach after World War II recommended economic supports as a precondition to political democratization. Transitology conceives of democratization as a transactional process among elites; although it presents a more dynamic perspective of democratization, it assigns a limited role to movements, unions, and protest. Most political science approaches privilege parties as main actors in the consolidation of democracy. Even the more dynamic approaches to democratization point to a declining degree of "participation from below" after the first phase of transition and, especially, during the so-called consolidation phase. Similarly, until recently, social movement scholars have paid only limited attention to democratization processes, mostly focusing on established democratic countries, especially the Western European and North American experiences. However, three recent trends brought potential for bridging research on social movements and that on democratization. First, in social movement research, the emergence of the global justice movement pushed social movement scholars to pay more attention to issues of democracy and to the social movements in the

Global South. At the same time, the global justice movements have addressed issues of democratization of more and more powerful international governmental organizations, as well as a "radical democratization" of already-democratic countries faced with the emerging challenges of representative democracy (Avritzer 2009; Baiocchi 2005; Sintomer, Herzeberg, and Roecke 2008). Second, the emergence of transnational advocacy coalitions on human rights and democracy has also been analyzed in research on democratization (in particular, in Latin America; see Brito 1997; Keck and Sikkink 1998). Third, research on the wave of democratization in Eastern Europe since 1989 has started to emphasize the democratizing role of civil society—theoretically located between the state and the market—with a diminishing confidence in political parties as carriers of the democratization process. In some of these interpretations, civil society is conceptualized almost as synonymous for social movements (Cohen and Arato 1992; Kaldor 2003). Within this frame, several programs of civil society promotion have been sponsored by international governmental organizations and individual states (Beichel et al. 2014).

In what follows, we review these different perspectives and then propose an analytic organization of the different roles that social movements, trade unions, advocacy networks, churches, and cycles of protest play in the *dynamic, contingent*, and *contentious* shaping of democracy. In doing this, we are of course not pleading for an exclusive focus on democratization from below; we are convinced that the path and speed of democratization processes are influenced by the strength and characteristics of several social and political actors. The combination of protest and consensus is, in fact, a main challenge for democratization processes. We suggest, however, that social movements are often important actors in all stages of democratization. In our discussion of these topics, we draw examples especially from Latin America, Southern Europe, and Eastern Europe.

The Marginal Concern with Social Movements in Research on Democratization

Studies on democratization have traditionally assigned a limited role to social movements and protest. This is true, although to different extent, within the main approaches to democratization, including structural approaches (modernization theory and the historical class perspective) and the elite transactional process approach (transitology).

Structuralist Approaches to Democratization

The first studies of democratization emerged in the aftermath of the massive destruction produced in Europe by World War II and in the reconfiguration of world politics mainly caused by the expansion of the Soviet Union's area of influence and the decolonization of Africa and Asia. Two predominantly structural perspectives developed with the intention of explaining political regime change in peripheral countries (democratic, authoritarian, or totalitarian). Research mainly focused on the prerequisites necessary for democracy to emerge and survive and on discovering which social class is the key actor in promoting and sustaining a democratic regime.

Within modernization theory, S. M. Lipset's (1959) pioneering work associated the chance for emergence of a democratic regime with economic development. This approach tended to recommend economic supports (such as the Marshall Plan) as a precondition to political democratization and accordingly considered the emergence of democracy in low-income countries improbable and its survival precarious. Sustainable democracy requires structural prerequisites, among them the development of a prodemocratic middle class. Even if studies with large samples have often confirmed a positive and statistically significant correlation between gross domestic product and the presence of democratic institutions,[1] that does not account for agency and thus cannot explain why poorer countries, such as Portugal (1974), Greece (1974), Ecuador (1979), Peru (1980), and Bolivia (1982), democratized before more industrialized countries such as Argentina (1983), Brazil (1985–1990), Chile (1991), and South Korea (1987–1988).[2]

Although powerful in explaining the survival of already-established democracies, modernization theory tends to ignore the role of social actors (social movements among them) in *crafting* democracy and therefore cannot explain the different tempos (i.e., whether decadelong or abrupt transitions) and democratization quality (i.e., whether procedural or substantive democracy) among them. As we argue later, incorporating social movement literature into the study of democratization processes can help bring agency back in.

The most prominent modernization scholar, Samuel Huntington (1965, 1991), rejects mobilization (in particular of the working class) as a source of democratization from below, defining those with high levels of mobilization as "praetorian societies."[3] In his view, the potential for disruption produced by claims for inclusion needs to be limited and controlled, because the assumption is that democracy needs low levels of mobilization and unionization and that even these low levels can be allowed only after a relatively high level of industrialization has been achieved.

Several authors from diverse analytic traditions—for example, N. Bermeo (1997), R. B. Collier (1999), D. McAdam, S. Tarrow, and C. Tilly (2001), and Tilly (2004)—have instead convincingly demonstrated that mobilized actors play a crucial role in the emergence of democracy and in its preservation or expansion. Especially within historical sociology, research singled out the role of the masses in the first and second waves of democratization and in resistance movements in the fall of authoritarian regimes at the end of World War II. A central question became: Which is the democratizing social class? Historical accounts of the first democratization processes in Europe point to the labor movement's part in struggling for civil, political, and social rights. In this regard, Barrington Moore Jr. (1966), although agreeing on the importance of some socioeconomic conditions, stresses the importance of social classes in first democratizations[4] in England (1642–1649), France (1789–1848), and the United States (1861–1865). Similarly, R. Bendix (1964) looks at how the masses entered history during the first European democratization wave; T. H. Marshall (1992) stresses popular mobilization in the struggle for civil, political, and social rights; A. Pizzorno (1996) observes that the socialist and other movements were important in the development of liberal democracy; and Tilly (2007) points to the nationalization and autonomization of protest activities during state and market building.

Moore's hypotheses on the impact of class structures on democratization processes have been cited by scholars looking at the role of different classes in more recent waves of democratization. In pathbreaking work, D. Ruesche-meyer, E. H. Stephens, and J. Stephens (1992) found that—given a certain level of economic development—the working class has been the key actor promoting democratization in the last two waves of democratization in Southern Europe, South America, and the Caribbean.[5] More recently, in another cross-national comparison, Collier (1999) suggests that the working class—although not so important in the nineteenth- and early-twentieth-century transitions in Western Europe as suggested by Rueschemeyer, Stephens, and Stephens—was crucial to the most recent wave of democratization in Southern Europe and South America. Beyond workers' role, C. Boix (2003) and D. Acemoglu and J. Robinson (2006: 38–39), using game theory, argue that democratization is successful when the middle classes do not side with the privileged classes in blocking the working class's demand for political inclusion. And J. Markoff (1996) emphasizes women's movements demanding democratic rights in the first long wave of democratization, starting in the late eighteenth century.

Conjunctural Approaches to Democratization

While the historical class perspective shows more concern for interactive historical paths than does classic modernization theory, both perspectives overlook the agency of contentious actors and the interactive mechanisms associated with democratization.[6] Agency is instead central in the so-called transitologist approach, which, however, did not pay much attention to social movements as potential actors in democratization.

After the 1970s wave of democratization in Southern Europe, political science approaches to the construction of political institutions have privileged political parties as main democratic actors (Higley and Gunther 1992). Even the more dynamic approaches to democratization (O'Donnell and Schmitter 1986; Linz and Stepan 1996) tended to perceive the *reforma pactada–ruptura pactada* (negotiated reform–negotiated break) in Spain (1977) as the model for successful democratization. They stressed a demobilization of "mass politics" (or at least their channeling within institutionalized political parties) as necessary for an effective consolidation of democracy. In the theoretical volume concluding their broad research project, G. O'Donnell and P. Schmitter (1986) dedicate a section to what they call the "resurrection of civil society," meaning the short disruptive moment when movements, unions, churches, and the society in general push for an initial transition of a nondemocratic regime toward democracy. Although this is a moment of great expectations,

> regardless of its intensity and of the background from which it emerges, this popular upsurge is always ephemeral. Selective repression, manipulation, and cooptation by those still in control of the state apparatus, the fatigue induced by frequent demonstrations and "street theatre," the internal conflicts that are bound to emerge over choices about procedures and substantive policies, a sense of ethical disillusionment with the "realistic" compromises imposed by pact-making or by the emergence of oligarchic leadership within its component groups are all factors leading toward the dissolution of the upsurge. The surge and decline of the "people" leaves many dashed hopes and frustrated actors. (1986: 55–56)

The short time civil society is present in the streets is not only inevitable, given the rechanneling of participation through the political parties and the electoral system, but also desirable, to avoid frightening authoritarian softliners into abandoning the negotiation process with the prodemocracy moderates. Elites are thus not only the source of the democratization process but also the ones who control its outcome. If for O'Donnell and Schmitter contentious politics favors the transition of a nondemocratic regime to democracy, for the contributors to J. Higley and R. Gunther's volume (1992) any kind of social movement, protest, or strike must be controlled and demobilized to assure a consolidated procedural democracy. While in O'Donnell and Schmitter's view democratization is made possible by a division between (authoritarian and democratic) elites, in Higley and Gunther's analysis it is the consensus among negotiating elites that allows for consolidation. Transitology, thus, emphasizes the contingent and dynamic nature of the democratization process but tends to reduce it to a bargaining among political elites in a context of uncertainty.

Within transitology, more systematic attention to civil society in democratization processes can be found in J. Linz and A. Stepan's (1996) model of extended transition. They take into account not only the immediate liberalization and transition bargaining process but also the characteristics of the previous nondemocratic regime (i.e., authoritarian, totalitarian, post-totalitarian, sultanistic), the way the nondemocratic elites exit state power, the historical characteristics of the political parties and the elites, and, when it ends, the uncertainty climate. "A robust civil society, with the capacity to generate political alternatives and to monitor government and state[,] can help transitions get started, help resist reversals, help push transitions to their completion, help consolidate, and help deepen democracy" and is necessary to complement the "political society," made of the elites and institutionalized actors. "At all stages of the democratization process, therefore, a lively and independent civil society is invaluable" (9). Even though recognizing its role in theory, the two authors do not give much empirical space to the analysis of civil society.

Reflecting on the relationship between the characteristics of the previous authoritarian regime and the chances for the emergence of prodemocratic mobilizations, Linz and Stepan (1996: chap. 3) suggest that, by eliminating any pluralism, totalitarian regimes jeopardize the development of autonomous organizations and networks that could then be the promoters of democracy. Sultanistic regimes, because of the high personalization of power, manipulate mobilization for ceremonial purposes and through para-state groups, discouraging and repressing any kind of autonomous organization that could sustain resistance networks. Authoritarian regimes, mainly those installed in countries with previous (semi)democratic familiarity, generally experience the most massive mobilizations and face some organized underground resistance based on several networks that either preexisted the regime or formed later, thanks to the higher degree of pluralism. Linz and Stepan add another ideal-typical regime, post-totalitarian, but this seems to be more an intermediate step in the democratization of totalitarian regimes than a regime type. Two subtypes of authoritarianism, not mentioned by these authors, are important for our purposes: (a) bureaucratic-authoritarianism, in which a technocratic civic-military elite commands the depoliticization of a mobilized society for capital accumulation (O'Donnell 1973), and (b) populist-authoritarianism, in which elites mobilize the society from above for legitimating the regime while incorporating the lower classes (see Hinnebusch 2007). While some South American and Southeast Asian countries (Argentina, Brazil, Chile, South Korea, Taiwan, etc.) were bureaucratic-authoritarian, the predominant model in some Middle Eastern and North African countries (Egypt, Algeria, etc.) was populist-authoritarian. Linz and Stepan hypothesize an interesting relationship between the type of nondemocratic regime and the potential for the emergence of movements, protests, strikes, and underground resistance networks that antedate liberalization and accompany democratization. Recent studies have shown the impact of the regime type on the characteristics of contentious politics (Almeida 2003; Ulfelder 2005; Ortiz 2013).

Linz and Stepan (1996: chap. 2) also stress the need to consider multiple simultaneous transitions (e.g., simple, with only regime change; dual, with a change in regime plus economic system; or triple, with change also in the nation-state arrangement). In this sense, it is important not only whether the previous regime was authoritarian or totalitarian but also whether it was capitalist or communist (Stark and Bruszt 1998). Additionally, in a triple transition, nation-state building is complicated when nationalist movements mobilize in the name of contending visions of which movement should be the demos of the future democracy. Thus, although in the Soviet Union in 1991 regional mobilization led to the dissolution of the political unit, in Spain it did not. Basque and Catalan nationalist movements undermined the legitimacy of Francisco Franco's regime but were unsuccessful in achieving independence. Czechoslovakia, for instance, experienced a peaceful dissolution of the polity along with a democratic and capitalist transition in 1989–1992. These changes can be explained only through the intertwined role played by regime elites, democratic elites, mobilized groups, and international pressures. Moderation in claims for autonomy and independence has been mentioned as favoring the transition to democracy and radicalized claims as jeopardizing it (see, e.g., Reinares 1987; Oberschall 2000; Glenn 2003).

Even though the dynamic, agency-focused approach of transitology allowed some interest in the role played by movements in democratization to develop (see Pagnucco 1995), it did not focus attention on them. In addition to its elitist bias, some other assumptions of transitology have been criticized. First, transitologists tend to emphasize individuals over collectives, which reduces the process to strategic instrumental thinking, ignoring class-defined actors such as unions and labor and left-wing parties, and it is state-centric, which subordinates social actors to state actors (Collier and Mahoney 1997). Second, transitology tends to consider movements and protest actors as manipulated by elites and focusing on very instrumentally defined purposes (Baker 1999).[7] Third, while transitologists believed in the inevitability and desirability of "elitization" of the democratization process, research by social movement scholars proved the importance of the interplay between elites and mobilized social actors as the necessary (though not sufficient) condition for a democratization process, questioning the elite-led and elite-ended logic that previously dominated democratization studies. Scholars who have analyzed democratization in nonelitist perspectives generally agree that not even the Spanish transition model is a purely elite-controlled bargaining process. Massive strike waves, terrorist attacks by nationalist movements, and an ascending cycle of protest characterized the transition (see, e.g., Maravall 1978, 1982; Reinares 1987; Foweraker 1989; Tarrow 1995; McAdam, Tarrow, and Tilly 2001: 171–186; Sánchez-Cuenca and Aguilar 2009), better defined as a destabilization and extrication process (Collier 1999: 126–132) or as "a cycle of protest intertwined with elite transaction" (McAdam, Tarrow, and Tilly 2001: 186). In sum, transitology is accused of ignoring the long-term, dynamic, contingent, and contentious process associated with the creation of the conditions for the breakdown of nondemocratic regimes. The next section addresses this process.

Perspectives of Democratization from Social Movement Studies

With few exceptions (e.g., some Latin American scholars), the literature on social movements has traditionally shown little interest in democratization processes (della Porta and Diani 2006). Only recently the concept of contentious politics, as opposed to routine politics, has been proposed to link research on phenomena such as social movements, revolutions, strike waves, nationalisms, and democratization (McAdam, Tarrow, and Tilly 2001).

Moreover, even those who have accorded an importance to social movements disagree on the positive versus negative effects of their intervention. Charles Tilly singles out two opposed conceptions of social movements in the process of democratization. First, a "populist approach to democracy" emphasizes participation from below, where "social movements contribute to the creation of public space—social settings . . . in which consequential deliberation over public affairs take place—as well as sometimes contributing to transfers of power over states" (Tilly 1993–1994: 1). Second, an elitist approach believes that democratization must be a top-down process and that an excess of mobilization leads to new forms of authoritarianism since the elites fear changes that are too much too soon. In this sense, Tilly stresses that, although it is not always straightforward, one can see "a broad correspondence between democratization and social movements" (2004: 125). On the one hand, many of the processes that cause democratization also promote social movements, and "democratization as such further encourages people to form social movements" (131). On the other hand, "under some conditions and in a more limited way, social movements themselves promote democratization" (131).

If democratization promotes social movements via the broadening of citizens' rights and the public accountability of ruling elites, many, but not all, social movements support democracy. Some movements refuse democracy altogether (as do fascist and neofascist ones), others might have the unwanted effect of producing backlash in democratic rights (as have some guerrilla movements in Latin America; see Wickham-Crowley 1992; Brockett 2005). Sometimes people mobilize against democratic regimes, demanding authoritarian solutions to political or economic crisis, providing the nondemocratic actors with a popular source of legitimacy (e.g., middle-class women's protests against Salvador Allende's government in Chile), and some actors seek restrictions of democratic rights in democratic regimes (e.g., European anti-immigration and xenophobic movements).[8] Identity politics, such as in ethnic conflicts, often led to religious war and racial violence (Eder 2003). In other cases, movements trying to promote democratization might have the perverse effect of increasing state repression or facilitating the emergence of undemocratic actors (e.g., the collapse of the Weimar Republic in Germany).

In most cases, however, a positive relation between social movements and the promotion of democracy can be found. By pushing for suffrage enlargement or the recognition of associational rights, many social movements contribute to democratization. As Edwin Amenta and Neal Caren summarize, "Gains in the democratization of state processes are perhaps the most important [gains] that social movements can influence and have the greatest systemic effects" (2004: 465). An incomplete but relevant correspondence between the processes that promote democratization and social movements has been explained this way:

"First, many of the same processes that cause democratization also independently promote social movements. Second, democratization as such further encourages people to form social movements. Third, under some conditions and
in a more limited way social movements themselves promote democratization"
(Tilly 2004: 131).

In sum, social movements contribute to democratization only under certain
conditions. Collective mobilization frequently creates the conditions for a destabilization of authoritarian regimes, but it can also lead to an intensification
of repression or the collapse of weak democratic regimes, particularly when
social movements do not stick to democratic conceptions. Labor, student, and
ethnic movements brought about a crisis in the Franco regime in Spain in the
1960s and 1970s, but the worker and peasant movements and the fascist countermovements contributed to the failure of the process of democratization in
Italy in the 1920s and 1930s (Tarrow 1995).

Because the relationship between social movements and democratization is
not simple, the main question for social movement scholars has been when and
how do movements promote democratization? Two branches in social movement studies have tried to answer this question: the new social movement approach and the political process one. We begin with a brief overview of both
and then analyze the role of social movements in each stage of democratization.

In Europe the new social movement approach has looked at the emergence
of a new actor in postindustrial society. Alain Touraine (1981), the most prominent exponent of this perspective, argues that the capital-labor conflict has
been surpassed by new conflicts related to the self-representation of the society
and the types of actions related to its transformation. Thus, the new conflicts
developed outside the factory and the labor movements, and the claims for taking state power were abandoned by the women's, student, and environmental
movements of Western Europe. Although its original aim was to explain a very
different phenomenon, some authors widely applied the new social movement
approach in the 1980s–1990s Latin American transitions, emphasizing the cultural and social democratization produced by movements, decentering the state
as their main interlocutor (Slater 1985; Jelin 1987; Escobar and Álvarez 1992),
which is what ultimately caused these authors to ignore the elite-movement interaction as crucial for democratization (for example, see Arato 1981).

As interest in Latin American democratizations and the new social movement approach decreased, the political process approach became more prominent in studies of regime transformation as a result of the emergence of new
democracies in Eastern Europe and the former Soviet Union. Trying to eluci-
date what favors emergence of contention in liberal democracies, the political
process approach devotes more systematic attention to the institutional context
than the new social movement approach does, highlighting the interrelation-
ship of governmental actors, political parties, social movements, and protest.
Scholars taking this perspective have observed a curvilinear relationship between the emergence of protest and the openness of political opportunities

(Eisinger 1973). Recently, some have proposed the reformulation of transitology's perspective, accounting for contentious politics (McAdam, Tarrow, and Tilly 2001; Schock 2005; Tilly 2004).

Both approaches converge in suggesting that, if it is true that social movements are not necessarily promoters of democracy, neither does the elitist dynamic model fully explain democratization processes. Social movements play different roles in each specific stage of the democratization process. The rest of this chapter looks at social movements and contentious politics in the different stages of the democratization process (resistance, liberalization, transition, and expansion).

Resistance to Nondemocratic Regimes

Democratization as a process starts much earlier than transitologists generally suggest. The elites begin a bargaining process because something happens that pushes some of them to withdraw their support from the nondemocratic regime. A trigger might be a prodemocratic cycle of protest and an increasingly massive and nonsyndical wave of strikes (see, e.g., Foweraker and Landman 1997; Collier 1999; McAdam, Tarrow, and Tilly 2001). If "democratic transitions express a wide variety of trajectories and outcomes, it is suggested that 'the role of social movements within them is conditioned by the specific rhythm of the "protest cycle," the shape of the political opportunity structure, and the contingency of strategic choice'" (Foweraker 1995: 90n2). In Spain, Brazil, and Peru, for instance, strike waves were very important during part of the democratization process if not the entire process (Maravall 1982; Sandoval 1998; Collier 1999). So Peru's democratization process was very much influenced by a strike wave (1977–1980) against a highly unpopular authoritarian regime (Collier 1999: 115–119), and Brazil experienced a strike wave (1974–1979), followed by a cycle of protest (1978–1982) mainly mobilized by urban movements (Mainwaring 1987). If sometimes cycles of protest and strike waves converge, more often strike waves are stronger in the first resistance stages, decline later, and then reemerge during liberalization and transition in coordination with the upsurge of a cycle of protest originating from underground resistance networks.

Whatever the relevance of these contentious processes, most important in undermining the legitimacy of the regime and the (national and international) support for it are the underground networks of resistance. Latin American new social movement scholars (Jelin 1987; Corradi, Fagen, and Garretón 1992; Escobar and Álvarez 1992) studied the cultural and political resistance to the authoritarian regimes and the construction of alternative democratic networks. Human rights movements, trade unions, and churches often promote delegitimation of authoritarian regimes at international forums such as the United Nations and in clandestine or open resistance to an authoritarian regime at the national level. The resilience of resistance networks under repression is decisive at this stage, because these networks can lead to splits in the ruling authoritarian or totalitarian elites and force even unwilling elites to initiate liberalization (Schock 2005). For instance, whereas the Catholic high hierarchy was often part of the elites that supported the authoritarian regime, in some countries church-related actors played a prodemocratic role.[9] So the Vicaría de la Solidaridad (Vicariate of Solidarity) in Chile condemned the repression, persecution, and assassinations ordered by Augusto Pinochet and helped coordinate the unions, parties, and grassroots activists that organized protests against the regime in the 1980s (Lowden 1996). In Brazil, with the incorporation of liberation theology, the church helped create grassroots empowering spaces through the Comunidades Eclesiais de Base (CEB; Christian-based Communities; see Burdick 1992; Levine and Mainwaring 2001). The CEB was central to the struggle for democratization, and Catholic groups worked as a broker in a prodemocratic coalition with the trade unions and urban movements. Similarly, in the Basque countries, the local clergy supported the opposition to the Francoist regime, helping preserve the Euskera language (della Porta and Mattina 1986). In Poland a prodemocratic alliance developed between the Catholic Church and Solidarność (Solidarity) union, which proved crucial in the network of resistance that helped create the necessary resources for the massive mobilizations during liberalization and transition (Glenn 2003; Osa 2003). And in Lithuania, the Catholic Church in cooperation with the Lithuanian diaspora in the United States and intellectuals in Russia were the main organizers of the resistance to Moscow's policies of sovietization (Lane 2001: 89–92).

In other countries, such as Argentina, the Catholic Church was a supportive bystander to state terrorism and in some cases even actively participated (Mignone 1988; Obregón 2005; Verbitsky 2005). Civic networks played delegitimizing roles: the Madres de Plaza de Mayo (Mothers of the Plaza de Mayo), Servicio de Paz y Justicia (Peace and Justice Service), and Asamblea Permanente por los Derechos Humanos (Permanent Assembly for Human Rights), among other organizations of the human rights movement, in coordination with human rights transnational advocacy networks initiated national and transnational campaigns for truth and justice to learn the fate of the thousands of disappeared—those kidnapped and killed by the military of Argentina (Brysk 1994; Wright 2007; Chapter 8). By naming and shaming, social movement organizations damage the image of authoritarian regimes in international forums such as the United Nations and the Organization of American States (Brysk 1993; Brito 1997; Sikkink 1996; Keck and Sikkink 1998: chap. 3). Although authoritarian regimes are closed to political opposition, M. Keck and K. Sikkink have shown that a boomerang effect develops when human rights networks sensitize other countries and intergovernmental organizations to generate political pressure on an authoritarian regime:

> Governments are the primary "guarantors" of rights, but also their primary violators. When government violates or refuses to recognize rights, individuals and domestic groups often have no recourse within

domestic political and judicial arenas. They may seek international con-nections finally to express their concerns and even to protect their lives. When channels between the state and its domestic actors are blocked, the boomerang pattern of influence characteristic of inter-national networks may occur: domestic NGOs bypass their state and directly search out international allies to try to bring pressure on their states from outside. (Keck and Sikkink 1998: 12)

Resistance to authoritarian regimes also developed inside (nonreligious) cultural groups. In the Czech Republic, for instance, the main organization in the democratization movement, the Civic Forum, emerged from the action of a network of artists and theaters constructing a space for autonomy and expres-sion after strong state repression of student protests (Glenn 2003). Also in Asia and Africa, intellectuals and students often formed circles in which a critique of the regime developed (Parsa 2000).[10]

In particular, during the resistance stage, the labor movement and its allies may be effective promoters of democratic values and understandings that erode a nondemocratic regime and set the necessary conditions for liberalization to take place. Especially in Latin America and Southern Europe, workers' organi-zations but also other social movements have often developed strong ties with left-wing political organizations (Collier 1999). In a comparative study of wom-en's movements in Southern European countries, D. della Porta, C. Valiente, and M. Kousis (forthcoming) stress the importance of women's organizations in the resistance against fascist regimes and the effect that their alliance had on the characteristics of the women's movement in those countries. The struggle against fascism represented, for instance, an important political experience for many Italian women: "If fascism . . . restricted women to a narrow, passive, limited existence as baby-makers, the antifascist democratic front created a new and active model for women" (Hellman 1987: 32–33). In 1943, the Gruppi di Difesa della Donna e di Assistenza ai Combattenti della Libertà (Groups for the Defense of Women and for Aid to the Volunteers for Liberty) were formed as part of the Resistance (Beckwith 1985: 22). These units, depending on the all-party Comitato di Liberazione Nazionale (Committee for National Libera-tion), were in charge of food and weapon supply and assisted wounded partisans and partisans' families. Although only a few women of the seventy thousand or so who participated in the Resistance actually took up arms against fascism, their support role was essential. Similarly, feminism developed in authoritar-ian Spain mainly in a milieu of opposition to the dictatorship. Feminists were very active in general political and syndical clandestine work and in gender equality issues. In Greece, during the early 1960s, new organizing efforts led to the reemergence of a militant women's movement in the popular struggle for radical social change. The well-organized Pan-Hellenic Union of Greek Women was formed by women who were active participants of the national resistance and members of the Greek Communist Party. A Coordinating Committee of Working Women was organized by communist and other progressive women.

Sometimes multisectoral coalitions were built to turn resistance into a liberalization process under control of the democratizing sectors. In Estonia, Latvia, and Lithuania, Popular Fronts were the main coalitions in the struggle for independence from the USSR, and—as a by-product—for democratization. The Popular Fronts were coalitions of environmental and cultural social movement organizations, religious groups, the Catholic Church, neocommunist elites, and dissident groups organized by local intelligentsia profiting from Mikhail Gorbachev's glasnost policies. They were later imitated in Ukraine, Armenia, and Georgia, coordinating their actions for independence from the USSR (Beissinger 2002).

Liberalization and the Upsurge of Mobilization

Democratization needs an acceleration of certain dynamics in order to occur. This acceleration spreads the perception among the authoritarian elites that there is no other way than to open the regime if they want to avoid civil war or violent takeover of power by democratic or revolutionary actors. This was the case, for instance, with the civic-military socialist revolution in Portugal in 1974 that started the transition to a democratic (although capitalist) regime and the protracted insurgency in El Salvador (1994) and in South Africa (1994) (Wood 2000). The intensity of the protests and strikes affected the elite choices of pursuing a long and controlled transition or a short extrication from state power.

During the liberalization stage, organized society becomes more visible: easing restrictions on meeting and demonstration rights develops in what has been called a "resurrection of civil society" (O'Donnell and Schmitter 1986: 26). During this stage movements may push toward effective democracy or resist the democratization process. Trade unions, labor/left-wing parties, and urban movements, mainly in shantytowns and industrial districts, have been presented as main actors seeking democracy (Slater 1985; Collier 1999; Silver 2003). In Chile, shantytown movements organized by members of the Communist Party in Santiago were among the main promoters of a 1983–1987 cycle of protest that pushed Augusto Pinochet to seek legitimacy through a referendum whose results triggered a controlled transition (Schneider 1992, 1995; Hipsher 1998). In Southern Europe women's organizations exercised pressure from below during the phases of liberalization, pushing regimes to open up. In fact, the few women's organizations that were tolerated by the authoritarian regimes provided the organizational resources for informal oppositional networks to develop. In particular, in Spain, during the wave of popular protest that accompanied the liberalization of Francoism, women took part in a sort of a resurrection of civil society. In the struggle against fascist regimes, some women's organizations were influenced by the dominant frames that emphasized civil and political rights, participating in the common struggles for liberalization.

On some occasions, during phases of liberalization, boomerang effects are produced by social movement alliances with transnational actors. In Latin America and in Eastern Europe these alliances were crucial for the push from regime liberalization to an actual transition to procedural democracy (Keck and Sikkink 1998; Glenn 2003).

Transition to Procedural Democracy

During the transition to democracy, social movements may push for social justice and the elimination of the reserved powers that limit the emerging democracy. Although political opportunities for mobilization open up because of the high uncertainty that characterizes this stage, cycles of protest may push in opposite directions. "Mobilization strengthens the ability of challengers and elites to make claims yet also limits the range of acceptable outcomes because of the conditional nature of popular support" (Glenn 2003: 104). Old (labor, ethnic) movements and new (women's, urban) movements participate in large coalitions asking for democratic rights (Jelin 1987; Tarrow 1995; della Porta, Valiente, and Kousis, forthcoming; Chapter 10).

Often the transition stage is characterized by mobilization of a prodemocracy coalition of trade unions, political parties, churches, and social movements. Without this coalition democracy is usually not achieved because contending countermovements are likely to push for restoration of the authoritarian or totalitarian regimes. Some right-wing or military networks might also resist transition or try to violently produce a democratic breakdown. This is exemplified by the Carapitanda (Face-painted) military group in Argentina in 1987, 1988, and 1990, which tried to end the trials of the military who had tortured and assassinated during the 1976–1983 authoritarian regime (Payne 2000: chap. 3). In other cases the reaction comes from the regime *nomenklatura* (those in positions of power in governmental, industrial, and other spheres, usually members of the Communist Party), with an increase in repression, as in the case of the 1989 crackdown on the Chinese student movement or the state of emergency against unions in Poland (Zhao 2000; Ekiert and Kubik 2001). In double transitions, we can also find protests and movements that resist the transformations of the economic system. This was the case of the 1989–1993 wave of farmers' protest in Poland following promarket reforms (see Chapter 15).

The bargaining dynamic among elites and the increased radicalization of contention in the streets intensify the relationship between elites and movements (Casper and Taylor 1996: 9–10). J. Glenn (2003: 104) argues that the logic of the transition is manifold: (a) mobilizations affect elite negotiations by introducing new actors to the political arena, altering the power relationships among the contending parties, and inserting new demands into the process reshaping the course of action, and (b) elites' negotiation affects mobilizations by itself changing the degree of openness of the political opportunities for movements by modifying part of the claims and acceptable interlocutors of the process.

The moment at which the society is demobilized and politics is channeled into party politics is considered by transitologists as the end of the transition period. This outcome, however, is only one of many possible outcomes in actual transitions. Although demobilization did not occur after the transition in Argentina, Bolivia, Ecuador, and Central America, in countries such as Uruguay and Chile politics was quickly institutionalized through the party system (Canel 1992; Schneider 1992; Hipsher 1998; Chapter 5; Chapter 7; Chapter 8). Latin America was not unique in this regard. For instance, in South Africa mobilization did not decrease after the transition (Klandermans, Roefs, and Olivier 1998; Chapter 11), and the same is true in Egypt and Tunisia after the Arab Spring (della Porta 2014). Demobilization does not seem essential to consolidation, being instead linked to specific characteristics of the party system (Rossi 2006: 262). In general, continuous popular pressures after transition can be a major means for a successful consolidation (Karatnycky and Ackerman 2005).

Certainly, social movement organizations mobilized during liberalization and transition do not totally disband. As soon as the institutions of representative democracy start to work, many activists dedicate themselves to building organizations capable of interacting with these institutions. In Southern Europe, women who had mobilized in the struggle for democracy participated in building new institutions. Even though the need to construct democratic institutions reduced the space for autonomous women's movements, women's groups emerged and reemerged. True, the very characteristics that had helped movements during liberalization and transition—an informal and flexible organizational structure, an emphasis on the society against the state, a focus on the unifying target of the struggle against the old regime—are likely to jeopardize their capacity to adapt to democratic politics. Social movements do not disappear, however. In Southern European countries, democratization helped a large number of women's organizations to flourish, even though they had different organizational structures, political and cultural aims, and propensity to use protest forms of action. In fact, the women's movements of the 1990s in Southern Europe were more similar than they had been in the 1980s to those in other Western democracies. In particular in Spain, Portugal, and Greece, the women's movements seem to have leap-frogged the radical phase that in other Western democracies has characterized the construction of a new feminist identity but are still ready to play a role in the consolidated democracies using routine as well as contentious forms of political participation.

The characteristics of the previous regime and the specific path of the transition seem to affect the ability of social movement organizations to adapt to democratization processes. Demobilization can be particularly difficult if democratic consolidation does not happen easily. This was the case in Portugal, complicated as it was by the involvement of the military and a mass insurgency that was not the expression of a strong and well-organized social movement

sector. To the contrary, as the analysis of the women's movement seems to indicate, a long-lasting authoritarian regime, with no previous experience with
mass democracy and only a timid liberalization in the 1970s, had destroyed the
organized society to the point that the democratic state had to actively intervene
to build up civic associations (della Porta, Valiente, and Kousis, forthcoming).
The reconstruction of civic participation seems to have been easier in Spain,
where social movements had developed in the 1960s and 1970s that pushed for
and took advantage of the liberalization of the regime. In Greece and Italy, with
relatively shorter-lived authoritarian regimes, the nucleus of future social movement organizations was formed by the well-organized and armed Resistance,
although in Italy the repression of the labor movement in the 1950s brought
about a demobilization of social movements.

A tradition for mobilization and support for movements by political parties,
unions, and religious institutions facilitate a high level of protest, as happened
with the Communist Party promotion of shantytown dwellers' protests in Chile
(Hipsher 1998; Schneider 1992, 1995); with the Partido dos Trabalhadores (PT;
Workers' Party) and part of the Roman Catholic Church support of the rural
movements and unions in Brazil (Branford and Rocha 2002; Burdik 2004); and
with the environmental movements in Eastern Europe (Koulov 1988; Beissinger
2002; Petrova 2004).

The role of social movement organizations and nongovernmental organizations (NGOs) has been particularly stressed for the last wave of democratization. In particular, the transition in Eastern Europe beginning in the late 1980s
brought about a new paradigm for the democratization of politics and policies:
democracy needs a civically active collection of social organizations, prefer-
ably with some autonomy from the state. In recent democratization processes in
Eastern Europe, the availability of public and private funds for NGOs contributed to an early institutionalization of movement organizations, showing that
the weakness of civil society is often exaggerated (Flam 2001).

Consolidation of a Procedural (or Substantive?) Democracy

In the political science literature, consolidation is generally defined as coming
at the completion of the democratization process as signaled by the first free
and open elections, the end of the uncertainty period, and/or the implementation of a minimum substantive democracy (O'Donnell 1993, 1994; Linz and
Stepan 1996). Democracy, however, cannot be consolidated without the universal and effective application of citizenship rights, which transcend voting.
At this stage, movements in many countries claim rights for those excluded by
low-intensity democracies and ask for a more inclusive democracy (e.g., land
reform, employment, and indigenous and women's rights) and the end of the
authoritarian legacies (Eckstein 2001; Hite and Cesarini 2004; Rossi, forthcoming; della Porta, Valiente, and Kousis, forthcoming). Claims framed by movements in the name of rights, citizenship, and their political practices are crucial

in creating citizenry (Foweraker and Landman 1997; Eckstein and Wickham-Crowley 2003). As Joe Foweraker observes, "The struggle for rights has more than a merely rhetorical impact. The insistence on the rights of free speech and assembly is a precondition of the kind of collective (and democratic) decision-making that educates citizens" (1995: 98). In brief, social movements usually produce long-term effects that are not only institutional but also cultural and social. These transformations are developed through the movements' alternative practices and values that help sustain and expand democracy (Rossi 2005a; Santos 2005). Furthermore, movements' networks are important in mobilizing against persistent exclusionary patterns and authoritarian legacies (Hagopian 1990; Yashar 2005; Chapter 8).

Expansion to Postrepresentative Democracy

Finally, social movements may influence the expansion of democracy (a not-yet fully studied stage in democratization)[11] by addressing both democratic reform of the international system of governance and transcendence of representative democracy at the national level, through experiments of participatory and deliberative democracy (Baiocchi 2005; Santos 2005; della Porta 2013).[12]

The global civil society perspective (Kaldor 2003; Keane 2003) emphasizes the democratizing effect of a worldwide organized civil society (Cohen and Arato 1992) in democratization at a supranational scale. Moreover, research on global justice movements (della Porta and Tarrow 2005; della Porta 2009a, 2009b) and transnational advocacy networks (Keck and Sikkink 1998) notes the role of human rights, indigenous, women's and alter-globalization groups in the promotion and expansion of national democratic regimes and in the reformulation of the not-so-democratic procedures of international governmental organizations such as the World Bank and the International Monetary Fund. In the case of the global justice movements, proposals for reform are especially oriented toward a broader transparency of decision making in international governmental organizations, increased controls by national parliaments, and opening of channels of access for social movement organizations (della Porta 2005; Grimson and Pereyra 2008).

Conclusion

Social movements have long been omitted from analysis of democratization. Modernization approaches have given little attention to agency (in general) and social movements in particular, focusing on the economic conditions for democratic stability. Scholars taking other approaches have studied the social classes that led democratization processes, focusing, however, more on their structural conditions than their mobilization. The dynamic study of democratization in so-called transitology considers social movements to be short-lived relevant actors in only the liberalization stage, focusing research on the institutional actors especially when addressing transition and consolidation. Even though some authors mention a robust civil society as facilitating democratization processes, transitologists have traditionally paid little empirical attention to its characteristics and development. Social movement studies until recently have tended to focus on advanced democracies, remaining broadly unconcerned about social movements in authoritarian regimes and social movements in processes of democratization.

This lack of reciprocal attention is all the more concerning because protest cycles and waves of strikes are important in democratization processes, in both the forms of eventful democratization, driven by protest, and participatory pacts, in which civil society organizations invest their resources on the negotiation table (della Porta 2014). Emerging research shows that social movements tend to vary in the different stages of democratization:

1. Underground networks of resistance undermine internal and international supports for authoritarian regimes.
2. The intensity of the protest might accelerate processes of liberalization.
3. Social movements are often important allies of political parties and other collective actors in prodemocracy coalitions during the transition phase.
4. During and after democratic consolidation, alternative praxes of democracy within social movements might promote a procedural and/or substantive expansion of democracy.

Though movements have promoted democracy, they have not always been effective. Several factors are necessary for effective democratization to take place. One is the need for a combination of perspectives from above and from below, because "the 'mode of transition,' the context of the democratization process, the types of actors involved in the process, and their strategic interactions, all influence the kind of democracy that is established" (Pagnucco 1995: 151). Elements that favor democratization include a nonsyndical strike wave or a prodemocracy cycle of protest, increased political organization in urban areas and a relatively dense resistance network, a church that is actively involved in the struggle for democratization, international pressure from human rights advocacy networks, divisions within the elites concerning whether to continue the nondemocratic regime, and the existence of prodemocratic elites able to integrate the demands for democracy coming from below (at least until transition is well initiated). Difficulties emerge when the transition must deal with contending movements demanding national independence and alternative exclusionary demos views or when terrorist attacks or guerrilla movements develop during the democratization process rejecting democracy as a plausible immediate outcome. These two elements do not make democratization impossible but may put it at risk of never consolidating or of bringing only limited liberalization of authoritarianism.

NOTES

Acknowledgments: In this chapter we build on and expand the ideas we present in Rossi and della Porta 2009, 2011. We thank Amr Adly, Patrick Bernhagen, Christian Haerpfer, Bert Klandermans, Leonardo Morlino, Ronald Inglehart, Philippe Schmitter, Juan Carlos Torre, Christian Welzel, and two anonymous reviewers for their useful comments on previous versions of this chapter. Donatella della Porta acknowledges the support of the European Research Council, AG 269136, "Mobilizing for Democracy."

1. Democracy, despite breaks and irregularities, has in general been correlated with decreasing poverty and inequality (Przeworski et al. 2000; Houle 2009).

2. For comparison of gross domestic product and Gini index (when available) for these countries in the years of the transitions to democracy, we consulted the World Bank's database at http://data.worldbank.org.

3. According to Huntington, "In a praetorian society groups become mobilized into politics without becoming socialized by politics" (1965: 83). This "politicization of social forces" (195) has several implications; the author emphasizes one: "The stability of a praetorian society varies inversely with the scope of political participation" (198).

4. Moore stresses in particular the presence of an urban bourgeoisie that is not allied with the aristocracy in repressing the emerging working class, allowing the latter to expand its claims.

5. On the working class and unions in democratization processes, see also Silver 2003.

6. Collier (1999) develops a dynamic analysis of democratization processes but concentrates her analysis in the working class (i.e., unions and labor or left-wing parties) with the intention of finding empirical answers to Moore's puzzle.

7. A. Przeworski (1991: 57), for example, considers movements important in the creation of the conditions for liberalization, but they are a tool of an elite-led process.

8. For nondemocratic movements in Latin America, see Payne 2000; for Western Europe, see Klandermans and Mayer 2005.

9. In Orthodox countries, like Romania, the churches played different roles. The majoritarian Romanian Orthodox Church was co-opted by the regime, and the 2,500 buildings of the Greek Orthodox Church were expropriated and all the assets given to the Romanian Orthodox Church. The smaller Hungarian Reformed Church was crucial in the first phase of the transition to democracy (Siani-Davies 2005: chap. 5; Deletant 2006).

10. For a comparison of the role played by resistance movements and state repression in the struggles for democratization in the authoritarian regimes of Ne Win (1958–1981) in Burma (Myanmar), Ferdinand Marcos (1965–1986) in the Philippines, and Thojib (Raden) Suharto (1967–1998) in Indonesia, see Boudreau 2004.

11. Chapter 5 analyzes expansion of democracy in Bolivia following accession to power of the Movimiento al Socialismo (MAS; Movement toward Socialism).

12. Pearce 2010 offers several interesting examples of city-level experiments of direct democracy in Brazil, Colombia, Great Britain, and Venezuela. For the case of the assemblies movement of Buenos Aires, see Rossi 2005b.

REFERENCES

Acemoglu, D., and J. Robinson. 2006. *Economic Origins of Dictatorship and Democracy.* Cambridge: Cambridge University Press.

Almeida, Paul D. 2003. "Opportunity Organizations and Threat-Induced Contention: Protest Waves in Authoritarian Settings." *American Journal of Sociology* 109 (2): 345–400.

Amenta, Edwin, and Neal Caren. 2004. "The Legislative, Organizational, and Beneficiary Consequences of State Oriented Challengers." In *The Blackwell Companion to Social Movements*, edited by D. Snow, S. Soule, and H. Kriesi, 461–488. Oxford, UK: Blackwell.

Arato, A. 1981. "Civil Society against the State: Poland 1980–81." *Telos* 42:23–47.

Avritzer, L. 2009. *Participatory Institutions in Democratic Brazil.* Baltimore: Johns Hopkins University Press.

Baiocchi, G. 2005. *Militants and Citizens: The Politics of Participatory Democracy in Porto Alegre.* Stanford, CA: Stanford University Press.

Baker, G. 1999. "The Taming Idea of Civil Society." *Democratization* 6 (3): 1–29.

Beckwith, K. 1985. "Feminism and Leftist Politics in Italy: The Case of UDI-PCI Relationships." *West European Politics* 8 (4): 19–37.

Beichel, T., I. Hahn, F. Schimmelfennig, and S. Worschech, eds. 2014. *Civil Society and Democracy Promotion.* Basingstoke, UK: Palgrave Macmillan.

Beissinger, M. 2002. *Nationalist Mobilization and the Collapse of the Soviet State.* Cambridge: Cambridge University Press.

Bendix, R. 1964. *Nation Building and Citizenship.* New York: Wiley and Sons.

Bermeo, N. 1997. "Myths of Moderation: Confrontation and Conflict during Democratic Transition." *Comparative Politics* 29 (2): 205–322.

Boix, C. 2003. *Democracy and Redistribution.* Cambridge: Cambridge University Press.

Boudreau, V. 2004. *Resisting Dictatorship: Repression and Protest in Southeast Asia.* Cambridge: Cambridge University Press.

Branford, S., and J. Rocha. 2002. *Cutting the Wire: The Story of the Landless Movement in Brazil.* London: Latin American Bureau.

Brito, A. 1997. *Human Rights and Democratization in Latin America: Uruguay and Chile.* Oxford: Oxford University Press.

Brockett, C. 2005. *Political Movements and Violence in Central America.* New York: Cambridge University Press.

Brysk, A. 1993. "From Above and Below: Social Movements, the International System, and Human Rights in Argentina." *Comparative Political Studies* 26 (3): 259–285.

———. 1994. *The Politics of Human Rights in Argentina: Protest, Change, and Democratization.* Stanford, CA: Stanford University Press.

Burdick, J. 1992. "Rethinking the Study of Social Movements: The Case of Christian Base Communities in Urban Brazil." In *The Making of Social Movements in Latin America: Identity, Strategy and Democracy*, edited by A. Escobar and S. Álvarez, 171–184. Boulder, CO: Westview.

———. 2004. *Legacies of Liberation: The Progressive Catholic Church in Brazil at the Start of a New Millennium.* Aldershot, UK: Ashgate.

Canel, E. 1992. "Democratization and the Decline of Urban Social Movements in Uruguay: A Political-Institutional Account." In *The Making of Social Movements in Latin America*, edited by A. Escobar and S. Álvarez, 276–290. Boulder, CO: Westview.

Casper, G., and M. Taylor. 1996. *Negotiating Democracy: Transitions from Authoritarian Rule.* Pittsburgh, PA: University of Pittsburgh Press.

Cohen, J., and A. Arato. 1992. *Civil Society and Political Theory.* Cambridge, MA: MIT Press.

Collier, R. B. 1999. *Paths toward Democracy: The Working Class and Elites in Western Europe and South America.* New York: Cambridge University Press.

Collier, R. B., and J. Mahoney. 1997. "Adding Collective Actors to Collective Outcomes: Labor and Recent Democratization in South America and Southern Europe." *Comparative Politics* 29 (3): 285–303.

Corradi, J., P. W. Fagen, and M. A. Garretón, eds. 1992. *Fear at the Edge: State Terror and Resistance in Latin America.* Berkeley: University of California Press.

Deletant, D. 2006. "Romania, 1945–89: Resistance, Protest and Dissent." In *Revolution and Resistance in Eastern Europe,* edited by K. McDermott and M. Stibbe, 81–99. Oxford: Berg.

della Porta, D. 2005. "Globalization and Democracy." *Democratization* 5 (12): 668–685.

———, ed. 2009a. *Another Europe.* London: Routledge.

———, ed. 2009b. *Democracy in Social Movements.* Basingstoke, UK: Palgrave Macmillan.

———. 2013. *Can Democracy Be Saved?* Oxford: Polity.

———. 2014. *Mobilizing for Democracy. Comparing 1989 and 2011.* Oxford: Oxford University Press.

della Porta, D., and M. Diani. 2006. *Social Movements: An Introduction.* Oxford: Blackwell.

della Porta, D., and L. Mattina. 1986. "Ciclos políticos y movilización étnica: El caso Vasco" [Political Cycle and Ethnic Mobilization: The Basque Case]. *Revista Española de Investigaciones Sociológicas* [Spanish Journal of Sociological Research] 35: 123–148.

della Porta, D., and S. Tarrow, eds. 2005. *Transnational Protest and Global Activism.* Lanham, MD: Rowman and Littlefield.

della Porta, D., C. Valiente, and M. Kousis. Forthcoming. "Sisters of the South: The Women's Movement and Democratization." In *Democratic Consolidation in Southern Europe: The Cultural Dimension,* edited by R. Gunther, P. Diamandouros, and H. Puhle. Baltimore: Johns Hopkins University Press.

Eckstein, S., ed. 2001. *Power and Popular Protest: Latin American Social Movements,* 2nd ed. Berkeley: University of California Press.

Eckstein, S., and T. Wickham-Crowley. 2003. *What Justice? Whose Justice? Fighting for Fairness in Latin America.* Berkeley: University of California Press.

Eder, K. 2003. "Identity Mobilization and Democracy: An Ambivalent relation." In *Social Movements and Democracy,* edited by P. Ibarra, 61–80. New York: Palgrave.

Eisinger, P. 1973. "The Conditions of Protest Behavior in American Cities." *American Journal of Political Science* 67:11–28.

Ekiert, G., and J. Kubik. 2001. *Popular Protest and Democratic Consolidation in Poland, 1989–1993.* Ann Harbor: University of Michigan Press.

Escobar, A., and S. Álvarez, eds. 1992. *The Making of Social Movements in Latin America: Identity, Strategy and Democracy.* Boulder, CO: Westview.

Flam, H. 2001. *Pink, Purple, Green: Women's, Religious, Environmental and Gay/Lesbian Movements in Central Europe Today.* New York: Columbia University Press.

Foweraker, J. 1989. *Making Democracy in Spain: Grassroots Struggle in the South, 1955–1975.* Cambridge: Cambridge University Press.

———. 1995. *Theorizing Social Movements.* London: Pluto Press.

Foweraker, J., and T. Landman. 1997. *Citizenship Rights and Social Movements: A Comparative and Statistical Analysis.* Oxford: Oxford University Press.

Glenn, J. 2003. "Contentious Politics and Democratization: Comparing the Impact of Social Movements on the Fall of Communism in Eastern Europe." *Political Studies* 55:103–120.

Grimson, A., and S. Pereyra, eds. 2008. *Conflictos globales, voces locales: Movilización y activismo en clave transnacional* [Global Conflicts, Local Voices: Mobilization and Activism in a Transnational Logic]. Buenos Aires: Prometeo.

Hagopian, F. 1990. "Democracy by Undemocratic Means? Elites, Political Pacts and Regime Transition in Brazil." *Comparative Political Studies* 23 (2): 147–170.

Hellman, J. 1987. *Journeys among Women: Feminism in Five Italian Cities.* Oxford: Oxford University Press.

Higley, J., and R. Gunther. 1992. *Elites and Democratic Consolidation in Latin America and Southern Europe.* New York: Cambridge University Press.

Hinnebusch, R. 2007. "Authoritarian Persistence, Democratization Theory and the Middle East: An Overview and Critique." In *Democratization in the Muslim World: Changing Patterns of Power and Authority,* edited by F. Volpi and F. Cavatorta, 11–33. London: Routledge.

Hipsher, P. 1998. "Democratic Transitions as Protest Cycles: Social Movements Dynamics in Democratizing Latin America." In *The Social Movement Society: Contentious Politics for a New Century,* edited by D. Meyer and S. Tarrow, 153–172. Lanham, MD: Rowman and Littlefield.

Hite, K., and P. Cesarini. 2004. *Authoritarian Legacies and Democracy in Latin America and Southern Europe.* Notre Dame, IN: University of Notre Dame Press.

Houle, C. 2009. "Inequality and Democracy: Why Inequality Harms Consolidation but Does Not Affect Democratization." *World Politics* 61 (4): 589–622.

Huntington, S. 1965. *Political Order in Changing Societies* New Haven, CT: Yale University Press.

———. 1991. *The Third Wave: Democratization in the Late Twentieth Century.* Norman: University of Oklahoma Press.

Jelin, E., ed. 1987. *Movimientos sociales y democracia emergente* [Social Movements and the Emergent Democracy]. 2 vols. Buenos Aires: Latin American Press Center.

Kaldor, M. 2003. *Global Civil Society: An Answer to War.* Cambridge, UK: Polity Press.

Karatnycky, A., and P. Ackerman. 2005. *How Freedom Is Won: From Civic Resistance to Durable Democracy.* New York: Freedom House.

Keane, J. 2003. *Global Civil Society?* Cambridge: Cambridge University Press.

Keck, M., and K. Sikkink. 1998. *Activists beyond Borders: Advocacy Networks in International Politics.* Ithaca, NY: Cornell University Press.

Klandermans, B., and N. Mayer, ed. 2005. *Extreme Right and Activists in Europe: Through the Magnifying Glass.* New York: Routledge.

Klandermans, B., M. Roefs, and J. Olivier. 1998. "A Movement Takes Office." In *The Social Movement Society: Contentious Politics for a New Century,* edited by D. Meyer and S. Tarrow, 173–194. Lanham, MD: Rowman and Littlefield.

Koulov, B. 1998. "Political Change and Environmental Policy." In *Bulgaria in Transition: Politics, Economics, Society and Culture after Communism,* edited by J. Bell, 143–161. Boulder, CO: Westview.

Lane, T. 2001. *Lithuania: Stepping Westward.* London: Routledge.

Levine, D. H., and S. Mainwaring. 2001. "Religion and Popular Protest in Latin America: Contrasting Experiences." In *Power and Popular Protest,* edited by S. Eckstein, 203–240. Berkeley: University of California Press.

Linz, J., and A. Stepan. 1996. *Problems of Democratic Transition and Consolidation: Southern Europe, South America, and Post-Communist Europe.* Baltimore: Johns Hopkins University Press.

Lipset, S. M. 1959. "Some Social Requisites to Democracy: Economic Development and Political Legitimacy." *American Political Science Review* 55:69–105.

Lowden, P. 1996. *Moral Opposition to Authoritarian Rule in Chile, 1973–1990*. London: Macmillan.

Mainwaring, S. 1987. "Urban Popular Movements, Identity, and Democratization in Brazil." *Comparative Political Studies* 20 (2): 131–159.

Maravall, J. M. 1978. *Dictatorship and Political Dissent: Workers and Students in Franco's Spain*. New York: St. Martin's Press.

———. 1982. *The Transition to Democracy in Spain*. London: Croom Helm.

Markoff, J. 1996. *Waves of Democracy: Social Movements and Political Change*. Thousand Oaks, CA: Pine Forge Press.

Marshall, T. H. 1992. "Citizenship and Social Class (1950)." In *Citizenship and Social Class*, edited by T. H. Marshall and T. Bottomore, 3–51. London: Pluto Press.

McAdam, D., S. Tarrow, and C. Tilly. 2001. *Dynamics of Contention*. New York: Cambridge University Press.

Mignone, E. 1988. *Witness to the Truth: The Complicity of Church and Dictatorship in Argentina, 1976–1983*. New York: Orbis.

Moore, B., Jr. 1966. *Social Origins of Dictatorship and Democracy: Lord and Peasant in the Making of the Modern World*. Boston: Beacon Press.

Oberschall, A. 2000. "Social Movements and the Transitions to Democracy." *Democratization* 7 (3): 25–45.

Obregón, M. 2005. *Entre la cruz y la espada: La Iglesia Católica durante los primeros años del "Proceso"* [In Between the Cross and the Sword: The Catholic Church during the First Years of the "Proceso"]. Buenos Aires: Universidad Nacional de Quilmes.

O'Donnell, G. 1973. *Modernization and Bureaucratic-Authoritarianism: Studies in South American Politics*. Berkeley: University of California Press.

———. 1993. "On the State, Democratization, and Some Conceptual Problems (A Latin American View with Glances at Some Post-Communist Countries)." Working Paper Series No. 192. Helen Kellogg Institute for International Studies, University of Notre Dame, Notre Dame, IN.

———. 1994. "Delegative Democracy?" *Journal of Democracy* 5:56–69.

O'Donnell, G., and P. Schmitter. 1986. *Transitions from Authoritarian Rule: Tentative Conclusions about Uncertain Democracies*. Baltimore: Johns Hopkins University Press.

Ortiz, David G. 2013. "Rocks, Bottles, and Weak Autocracies: The Role of Political Regime Settings on Contention-Repression Interactions." *Mobilization* 18 (3): 289–312.

Osa, M. 2003. "Networks in Opposition: Linking Organizations through Activists in the Polish People's Republic." In *Social Movements and Networks: Relational Approaches to Collective Action*, edited by M. Diani and D. McAdam, 77–104. Oxford: Oxford University Press.

Pagnucco, R. 1995. "The Comparative Study of Social Movements and Democratization: Political Interaction and Political Process Approaches." In *Research in Social Movements, Conflicts and Change*, vol. 18, edited by M. Dobkowski, I. Wallimann, and C. Stojanov, 145–183. London: JAI Press.

Parsa, M. 2000. *States, Ideologies and Social Revolutions: A Comparative Analysis of Iran, Nicaragua and the Philippines*. Cambridge: Cambridge University Press.

Payne, L. 2000. *Uncivil Movements: The Armed Right Wing and Democracy in Latin America*. Baltimore: Johns Hopkins University Press.

Pearce, A., ed. 2010. *Participation and Democracy in the Twenty-First Century City.* Basingstoke, UK: Palgrave Macmillan.

Petrova, D. 2004. "Bulgaria." In *Dissent and Opposition in Communist Eastern Europe: Origins of Civil Society and Democratic Transition,* D. Pollack and J. Wielgohs, 161–184. Aldershot, UK: Ashgate.

Pizzorno, A. 1996. "Mutamenti nelle istituzioni rappresentative e sviluppo dei partiti politici" [Metamorphosis in the Representative Institutions and the Development of Political Parties]. In *La storia dell'Europa contemporanea* [History of Contemporary Europe], edited by P. Bairoch and E. J. Hobsbawm, 961–1031. Turin: Einaudi.

Przeworski, A. 1991. *Democracy and the Market: Political and Economic Reforms in Eastern Europe and Latin America.* Cambridge: Cambridge University Press.

Przeworski, A., M. Alvarez, J. Cheibub, and F. Limongi. 2000. *Democracy and Development: Political Institutions and Well-Being in the World, 1950–1990.* Cambridge: Cambridge University Press.

Reinares, F. 1987. "The Dynamics of Terrorism during the Transition to Democracy in Spain." In *Contemporary Research on Terrorism,* edited by P. Wilkinson and A. Stewart, 121–129. Aberdeen, UK: Aberdeen University Press.

Rossi, F. M. 2005a. "Crisis de la República Delegativa: La constitución de nuevos actores políticos en la Argentina (2001–2003); las asambleas vecinales y populares" [Crisis of the Delegative Republic: The Constitution of New Political Actors in Argentina; the Neighborhood and Popular Assemblies]. *América Latina Hoy* [Latin America Today] 39:195–216.

———. 2005b. "Las asambleas vecinales y populares en la Argentina: Las particularidades organizativas de la acción colectiva contenciosa" [The Neighborhood and Popular Assemblies in Argentina: The Organizational Specificities of Contentious Collective Action]. *Sociológica* [Sociological] 19 (57): 113–145.

———. 2006. "Movimientos sociales" [Social Movements]. In *Política: Cuestiones y Problemas* [Politics: Questions and Problems], edited by L. Aznar and M. De Luca, 235–274. Buenos Aires: Editorial Ariel.

———. Forthcoming. "Beyond Clientelism: The Piquetero Movement and the State in Argentina." In *Handbook of Social Movements across Latin America,* edited by P. Almeida and A. Cordero. New York: Springer.

Rossi, F. M., and D. della Porta. 2009. "Social Movement, Trade Unions and Advocacy Networks." In *Democratization,* edited by C. Haerpfer, P. Bernhagen, R. Inglehart, and R. Welzel, 172–185. Oxford: Oxford University Press.

———. 2011. "Acerca del rol de los movimientos sociales, sindicatos y redes de activistas en los procesos de democratización" [About the Role of Social Movements, Trade Unions and Advocacy Networks in Democratization Processes]. *Desarrollo Económico* [Economic Development] 50 (200): 521–545.

Rueschemeyer, D., E. H. Stephens, and J. Stephens. 1992. *Capitalist Development and Democracy.* Chicago: University of Chicago Press.

Sánchez-Cuenca, I., and P. Aguilar. 2009. "Terrorist Violence and Popular Mobilization: The Case of the Spanish Transition to Democracy." *Politics and Society* 37 (3): 428–453.

Sandoval, S. 1998. "Social Movements and Democratization: The Case of Brazil and the Latin Countries." In *From Contention to Democracy,* edited by M. Giugni, D. McAdam, and C. Tilly, 169–201. Lanham, MD: Rowman and Littlefield.

Santos, B. S., ed. 2005. *Democratizing Democracy: Beyond the Liberal Democratic Canon.* London: Verso.

Schneider, C. 1992. "Radical Opposition Parties and Squatter Movements in Pinochet's Chile." In *The Making of Social Movements in Latin America*, edited by A. Escobar and S. Álvarez, 60–75. Boulder, CO: Westview.

———. 1995. *Shantytown Protests in Pinochet's Chile*. Philadelphia: Temple University Press.

Schock, K. 2005. *Unarmed Insurrections: People Power Movements in Nondemocracies*. Minneapolis: University of Minnesota Press.

Siani-Davies, P. 2005. *The Romanian Revolution of December 1989*. Ithaca, NY: Cornell University Press.

Sikkink, K. 1996. "The Emergence, Evolution, and Effectiveness of the Latin American Human Rights Network." In *Constructing Democracy: Human Rights, Citizenship, and Society in Latin America*, edited by E. Jelin and E. Hershberg, 59–84. Boulder, CO: Westview.

Silver, B. 2003. *Forces of Labor*. New York: Cambridge University Press.

Sintomer, Y., C. Herzeberg, and A. Roecke. 2008. *Les budgets participatifs en Europe* [Participatory Budgets in Europe]. Paris: La Découverte.

Slater, D. 1985. *New Social Movements and the State in Latin America*. Amsterdam: Center for Latin American Research and Documentation.

Stark, D., and L. Bruszt. 1998. *Postsocialist Pathways: Transforming Politics and Property in East Central Europe*. Cambridge: Cambridge University Press.

Tarrow, S. 1995. "Mass Mobilization and Regime Change: Pacts, Reform and Popular Power in Italy (1918–1922) and Spain (1975–1978)." In *Democratic Consolidation in Southern Europe*, edited by R. Gunther, P. Diamandouros, and H. Puhle, 204–230. Baltimore: Johns Hopkins University Press.

Tilly, C. 1993–1994. "Social Movements as Historically Specific Clusters of Political Performance." *Berkeley Journal of Sociology* 38:1–31.

———. 2001. "When Do (and Don't) Social Movements Promote Democratization?" In *Social Movements and Democracy*, edited by P. Ibarra, 21–45. New York: Palgrave Macmillan.

———. 2004. *Social Movements, 1768–2004*. Boulder, CO: Paradigm.

———. 2007. *Democracy*. Cambridge: Cambridge University Press.

Touraine, A. 1981. *The Voice and the Eye: An Analysis of Social Movements*. Cambridge: Cambridge University Press.

Ulfelder, J. 2005. "Contentious Collective Action and the Breakdown of Authoritarian Regimes." *International Political Science Review* 26 (3): 311–334.

Verbitsky, H. 2005. *El Silencio: De Paulo VI a Bergoglio; las Relaciones Secretas de la Iglesia con la ESMA* [The Silence: From Paulo VI to Bergoglio; the Secret Relations of the Church with the ESMA]. Buenos Aires: Sudamericana.

Wickham-Crowley, T. 1992. *Guerrillas and Revolution in Latin America: A Comparative Study of Insurgents and Regimes since 1956*. Princeton, NJ: Princeton University Press.

Wood, E. 2000. *Forging Democracy from Below: Insurgent Transitions in South Africa and El Salvador*. New York: Cambridge University Press.

Wright, T. 2007. *State Terrorism in Latin America: Chile, Argentina and International Human Rights*. Lanham, MD: Rowman and Littlefield.

Yashar, D. 2005. *Contesting Citizenship in Latin America: The Rise of Indigenous Movements and the Postliberal Challenge*. New York: Cambridge University Press.

Zhao, D. 2000. *The Power of Tiananmen*. Chicago: University of Chicago Press.

2

Disengagement from Radical Organizations

A Process and Multilevel Model of Analysis

OLIVIER FILLIEULE

Their behavior has been blamed on all kinds of social and
psychological factors. . . . [A] social common denominator
seems out of the question, but it is true that psychologically
this generation seems everywhere characterized by sheer
courage, an astounding will to action, and by no less astounding confidence in the possibility of change. But these
qualities are not causes.

—HANNAH ARENDT, *On Violence*

While research on political activism has raised the essential question of
how activists are recruited and enrolled, it has said very little until
recently on their defection and disengagement. Many factors explain
this situation. For example, activism itself has been studied less from microsociological perspectives than through analysis of the organizations encompassing it, which naturally leads to reasoning in terms of current assets rather than
flux. Moreover, microsociological approaches to individual behavior, except the
economists' version of rational choice theory, have long been dismissed in the
name of collective behavior theory and also because of the scarcity of available sources for those interested in activist engagement and disengagement. By
definition, ex-activists are no longer there at the time of study, and very often organizations do not keep or make readily available the membership files
needed to find people who have left. Further, there is the difficulty in moving from snapshots of reality to a process perspective, which in cases of this
sort requires longitudinal studies, whether retrospective or, ideally, prospective
(Fillieule 2001).

However, in broadening the range of literature to related fields, the spectrum of potentially relevant research widens. If we exclude the autobiographi-
cal works of priests, terrorists, and communist activists, literature that more or

less directly broaches the question of disengagement emerges from the sociology of roles, in the Mertonian or interactionist tradition, especially in literature on churches and cults but also divorce and professions (Vaughan 1986; Fuchs-Ebaugh 1988). In the same theoretical vein, a number of studies address various aspects of how individuals join and leave different types of clandestine, reclusive, and stigmatized groups by describing several stages in the disaffiliation process. A research tradition in psychosociology focuses on group dynamics within terrorist groups (Wasmund 1986; Jamieson 1990; Crenshaw 1991; Taylor and Horgan 2006; Horgan 2009) and also on members' reasons for leaving racist and right-wing movements (Fangen 1999; Klandermans and Mayer 2006). Lastly, from the field of criminology and deviance theory we have research on desistance from criminal lifestyle and the theory of differential association and the rich literature on criminal youth gangs, which provides a significant source of insight to understand the links between life course and disengagement from violent or criminal activities (Vigil 1988; Klein 1995; Decker and Lauritsen 1996; and see Grenne and Pravis 2007 for a review).

More recently, some scholars have turned to disengagement process in social movements, with a dominant focus on radical movements (e.g., della Porta 1992, 1995; Klandermans 1997; Bennani-Chraïbi and Fillieule 2003; Fillieule 2005, 2010; Leclercq 2008). Indeed, more and more social movement scholars maintain that there is no difference in reasoning and determinants between conventional law-abiding political protests and illegal and violent forms of action. They contend that a social movement approach toward radical organizations and violent political action that considers them forms of contentious politics and analyzable with the existing conceptual tools of social movement theory would be fruitful (Bennani-Chraïbi and Fillieule 2003; see also della Porta 1992, 1995; Goodwin 2004, 2006; and Beck 2008).

At the same time, research specifically dedicated to radical organizations, in the broad field of terrorism studies, distances itself more and more with outdated theoretical models that borrow their structure from studies on relative deprivation and collective behavior (e.g., Testas 2004; Gurr and Björgo 2005)[1] or, worse still, from a psychopathology depicting radical activists as abnormal (see Silke 2003 for a critical review). Actually, these renewed approaches take a route closer to contemporary social movement theory and produce extremely interesting results (Taylor and Horgan 2006; Horgan 2005; Gayer and Jaffrelot 2008; Björgo and Horgan 2009; Horgan 2009; Gayer 2009; Bosi 2012).

In this chapter I propose an interactionist model of activist withdrawal that is based on both the sociology of social movements and contemporary studies on terrorism. I discuss this theoretical model elsewhere (Fillieule 2005; Fillieule and Broqua 2005; Fillieule 2010) and do not address all its elements here. My aim is twofold here: first, I argue that such an approach offers a solid basis for building a process and multilevel model of disengagement; second, I contend that it is particularly well suited to understanding the peculiarities of disengagement from radical organizations.[2]

In what follows I start by explicating a process and multilevel approach of disengagement from activist careers, using an interactionist and configurational approach. I then explore the intrication of the macro, meso, and micro levels in understanding disengagement. To do this, one must abandon macro-level theories and focus on the complex interplay between the activists' motivations for involvement and disengagement and organizational dynamics, structural factors and political opportunities being considered only at a second step to contextualize micro- and mesodynamics. Only some research has focused on individual activists, their motives, and how their motives are tightly linked to organizational dynamics.[3] To untangle the web of relations between micro-level, or individual, dynamics of commitment and meso-level, or organizational, factors, I focus on two central dimensions: the complex effects of organizational modeling on individuals and the contradictory effects of repression on organizations. I show that organizational molding is key to understanding meso- and microinteractions and that exploring the effects of repression on individuals is a good entry point for grasping the complex web of interactions between macro and micro levels (the individual effects of repression) and between macro and meso levels (effects of repression on organizational forms and strategies).

Leaving Militantism Behind: Some Answers, More Questions

Literature that has considered disengagement is mostly interested in total institutions, high-risk activism, and extralegal activities, suggesting that we should pause and recognize the diversity of phenomena to which *disengagement* refers. Indeed, the process of disengagement is highly likely to vary as a function of what provokes it, the cost of defection, the manner in which it takes place, and therefore what becomes of those who leave.

Disengagement as a Multifaceted Phenomenon

Defection is not always voluntary. It may result from the dissolution of a collective; decline of a movement, producing orphans in a cycle of mobilization, as Verta Taylor illustrates with regard to postwar American feminism (1989); exclusion; extraction or deprogramming (Beckford 1978); or even a forced exit through exile or, for example, a prison sentence. To these situations one must add revolutionary movements that lead to a change of regime, as in most democratic transitions, and therefore a conversion and institutionalization of protest organizations.

The cost of leaving relates primarily to the manner in which organizations frame defection through various constraints. As I and a colleague have emphasized elsewhere:

> The psychic or material cost of defection, and therefore its probability, is
> a result of a number of factors, among them the extent of the sacrifices

accepted to enter the group (initiation rites, trials, hierarchization and isolation of collectives); weaker or stronger group socialization, which translates especially into the reinforcement of emotional attachment and which varies as a function of the degree of renunciation of social relations external to the group (networks of family and friends); and finally the rules in place at the time of the defection, which is sometimes rendered impossible by material dependence or the threat of being pursued as a traitor. (Fillieule and Bennani-Chraïbi 2003: 123; my translation)

To these barriers to defection I must also add the existence of lateral possibilities (the opportunities to reconvert acquired resources, the possibility of reconnecting with alternative networks of sociability, and so on) and, finally, the degree of social legitimacy of defection.

Forms of defections are extremely variable. They may be isolated or take place collectively, such as when a group splinters or an entire affinity group leaves. M. Introvigne distinguishes among defectors, who leave their organization in a negotiated fashion and by agreement; apostates, who become their organization's professional enemies; and ordinary leave-takers, who disappear quietly and whose disengagement carries no apparent notable cost for either themselves or the organization (1999: 62, 67). Yet this is a rather cursory typology lacking various types of passive defections—withdrawal without leaving an organization—and different scenarios in which disengagement from an organization is followed, and sometimes provoked, by joining another organization or cause.

A Process Model of Disengagement

A process model of disengagement strikes me as particularly useful today for bridging terrorism studies and recent trends in contentious politics studies. It is also one of the most promising routes to a multilevel model of disengagement.

Until recently, little research has been directly interested in disengagement per se, as a process rather than a moment in time. Research has centered on the determinants of defection or the future of ex-activists and only rarely on the disengagement process and what happens within organizations. However, two recent edited volumes have paved the way for new developments: one on the disengagement process in conventional political organizations like unions, parties, and social movement organizations (Fillieule 2005) and the other on individual and collective disengagement from terrorism (Björgo and Horgan 2009). J. Horgan's model is quite similar to the perspective I am advocating, despite quite different theoretical underpinnings and epistemological foundations.[4] We share four basic methodological and epistemological principles.

1. One should move from "analysis of *profiles* to *pathways*, and from roots (as in 'root causes') to *routes*" (Horgan 2009: xxiii; see also Horgan 2008; Crenshaw 2000).

2. One should abandon a logic of causal explanation, solely attached to sin-
   gling out the determinants of violent trajectories, to concentrate on the
   process by which people join radical organizations and remain involved
   or disengage.
3. We must first investigate the individuals and their life story and then
   question the manner in which their existence is partly determined by
   structural factors at the meso and macro levels, which means adopting
   the framework of a comprehensive sociology, attentive to the justifications of the actors.[5]
4. Activist trajectories can be understood only through a multilevel
   analysis that articulates the micro-level role of the individual in the
   group and the broader network and sociopolitical context in which he
   or she belongs (see also Hairgrove and McLeod 2008).

However, while I share this perspective on the appropriate objectives and the
ways to attain them, I am considerably less convinced by the theoretical foundations of an approach that I consider much too eclectic and that, in the field
of social psychology, borrows simultaneously from deviant behavior theories
(Sutherland and Cressey 1966), social learning theory (Hundeide 2003), and
Merton's role theory (Fuchs-Ebaugh 1988). In particular, it seems to me that one
should find a clearer delineation of the three levels of idiosyncrasies, organizations, and contexts. More precisely, the notion of a community of practice that
is at the core of Horgan's model (Taylor and Horgan 2006; Horgan 2009), referring to the shared exercise of social learning and the related social and cultural
practices that develop between and within groups, seems far less heuristic for
analyzing one fundamental aspect of militant trajectories: secondary socialization, or what we call "organizational modeling." In my own conception, two
elements are central.

First, violent commitments, as well as disengagement from radical organizations, should be understood as the result of a process more than the product
of a precipitating event. Approaches that are based on an analysis of deep psychological motivations or stick to the simplifications of rational choice theory
cannot understand the process of commitment. Indeed, people often act on
purpose but without a fully formed intention, in the sense of a balanced appreciation of the possible costs and consequences of their actions. As John Searle
(1983) states, "intention-in-action" is not equivalent to "intention to act." The
analytical language of motivations, which is polluted by intentionalism, is too
often used as a substitute for thick description of what actually happened. In
fact, people are often forced to act violently because of explicit (e.g., physical
tying devices) or implicit (e.g., the strength of role taking in a close-knit group)
pressures, which means that actors are not always purposeful agents but can be
subjects, as brilliantly illustrated by Dipesh Chakrabarty (2000) in his critique
of Ranjit Guha's analysis of a peasant revolt in colonial India (1983).[6]

These remarks are well in line with the "hypothesis of continuity" suggested by Annie Collovald and Brigitte Gaïti (2006: 39–42) to take account of the process by which radicalization and, therefore, the eventual deradicalization of individuals works. In this they draw on the fascinating study that T. Tackett (1996) devoted to how deputies to the Estates General progressively became revolutionaries at the start of the French Revolution and the analysis produced by C. Browning (1992) on how ordinary German soldiers progressively came to systematically eliminate thousands of Polish Jews, by shooting them.[7] This brings us back to one of the strongest principles of the Howard Becker approach—that is, that one must stop reasoning in terms of *why* it happened and shift to *how* (in other words, to the chain of facts that result from specific contemporary causes and are reconfigured as events unfold). In sum,

> the principle of continuity involves hypotheses about the times experienced, comprised of small disjunctions, changes to routine, disparate initiatives, and events perceived as heterogeneous, ephemeral, anecdotal, and rationalized in the patchwork reality of the moment, brought back to familiar phenomena over which one is in relative control. We see this, the temporality of experience as distinct from the temporality of the process of radicalization, reconstructed and homogenized after the fact around "origins," "turning points," and "causes and effects." (Collovald and Gaïti 2006: 35; see also Dobry 1986, 2010)

In the second central element, the process of disengagement is explained as well by idiosyncratic as by structural and contextual factors (i.e., the dialectic between dispositions and motives of the actors and their structural positions). Such an approach means that one should articulate micro-level (dispositions, socialization), meso-level (secondary socialization in protest groups, organizational modeling, strength of role taking, and dependence on the activist group, etc.), and macro-level (political context, repression, and opportunities) analysis—in other words, a multilevel approach to political commitment and disengagement. Calls for multilevel approaches are more and more frequent in the literature. However, scholars often content themselves with making an analytical distinction among three types of factors of commitment or withdrawal at the macro, meso, and micro levels, without offering a convincing explanation of their joint occurrence over time. In my opinion, symbolic interactionism, particularly the version articulated by Hans Gerth and Charles Wright Mills (1954) and Howard Becker (1960, 1966), offers a powerful tool for resituating the commitment process diachronically, within the totality of individual life stories and helps contextualize individual engagements and exits synchronically at both organizational level and macro level, rejecting the scholastic opposition between agency and structure.[8] In such a model, activism is conceived of as a long-lasting social activity articulated by phases of joining, commitment, and defection.

A term coined by Herbert Blumer in 1937, *symbolic interactionism* is closely linked to the social behaviorism of George Herbert Mead (1934). Its subsequent usage belongs less to a school of thought than to a wide array of research sharing two standpoints: a common conception of the individual and his or her relation to society and a way of doing research inherited from the Chicago School of Sociology (i.e., field work and qualitative methodologies). More precisely, symbolic interactionism can be defined as a microsociological and process approach that *systematically* links the individual and the study of situations to broader contextual factors and social order rules and norms. In this perspective, individuals and society not only are interdependent but also mutually construct each other. I contend that recent research on activism based on the interactionist concept of career developed by Everett Hughes (1958), Anselm Strauss (1959), and Howard Becker (1960, 1966)—what I refer to as the sociology of activist careers (Fillieule 2001, 2005, 2010)—is particularly suited to proposing a theoretical account of the disengagement process as a multilevel phenomenon.

The notion of career initially developed by Everett Hughes casts the stages of access to and exercise of a profession as a series of objective changes of position and an associated series of subjective upheavals. As Howard Becker stresses, quoting Hughes, the concept of career comes back to two dimensions:

> In its objective dimension, a career is "a series of statuses and clearly defined offices . . . typical sequences of position, achievement, responsibility, and even of adventure. . . . Subjectively, a career is the moving perspective in which the person sees his life as a whole and interprets the meaning of his various attributes, actions, and the things which happen to him." (Becker 1966: 102, quoting Hughes 1937: 409–410)

This powerful concept allows us to focus on the process and permanent dialectic between individual history, social institutions, and more generally, context. The outcome is less prediction of a state (activism, disengagement, and so on) than rebuilding a sequence of steps, of changes in the individual's behavior and perspectives, to understand the phenomenon.

> Each step requires explanation, and what may operate as a cause at one step in the sequence may be of negligible importance at another step. . . . In a sense, each explanation constitutes a necessary cause of the behavior. . . . The explanation of each step is thus part of the explanation of the resulting behavior. (Becker 1966: 23)

A career approach consequently involves considering the two essential dimensions of social identity: from a diachronic perspective, the transformation of identities and the social mechanisms at work in these transformations, and from a synchronic perspective, the plurality of life spheres in which social actors may be involved:

Identity shifts: In *Mirrors and Masks* (1959), Strauss analyzes how identities are liable to change permanently, as a function of modifications of the social structure and actors' successive positions in this structure, with all that this means for different stages of actor biography in terms of the subjective interpretation of the changes experienced. Strauss thus analyzes what he calls "institutionalized changes" (changes in status provoked, for example, by entrance into the workforce or marriage) and "biographical accidents" (crises, failures, losses, and so forth), placing particular emphasis on the processes of disidentification and initiation that may produce lasting and irreversible changes in identity, such as in representations, attitudes, and motives.

Plurality of subworlds: In Strauss's work, plurality is a fundamental characteristic of contemporary social life and refers to social actors being embedded in multiple social worlds and subworlds that may on occasion conflict. Activists are also individuals, inserted in a multiplicity of life spheres and therefore permanently subjected to the obligation to submit to different norms, rules, and logics that at times may conflict. In other words, individuals' political memberships are in tension with their other involvements. Owing to this plurality of social worlds, individuals are governed by heterogeneous and sometimes even contradictory principles of socialization that they internalize. We may thus hypothesize that each actor incorporates a multiplicity of behavior patterns and habits, organized as repertoires, and relevant social contexts that the actor learns to distinguish through the totality of previous socializing experiences.

The link between social contexts and systems of disposition significantly reduces the value of analyses of the determinants of commitment or disengagement that are based on multivariate treatments that correlate the dependent variable with individuals' social characteristics. The explanatory power of social characteristics is established and varies in conjunction with the system of competitive interrelations in which they are found. This system may be interpreted at three levels.

First, there is the *macro* level of the political field and social arenas. Depending on the social valuation, at a particular time and in a particular sector, of a particular model of a good activist, certain social characteristics and aptitudes will be devalued or privileged. Second, there is the *micro* level of biography. As noted above, it is in the succession of encounters of social characteristics and variable socialization contexts that aptitudes are created. Third, the system of competitive interrelations must also be observed at the *meso* level of organizations. This means understanding how organizations, structurally, socially, and politically, select and orient individual activities, to grasp how they differentially relate to their members' social attributes. R. M. Kanter (1968) confirms this when she places commitment at the intersection of organizational requirements and individual experiences, necessitating consideration of the logics of commitment and keeping in mind the social context of practical involvement.

Such a conception of the micro-meso-macro linkage is in line with a configurational approach, which denotes a dynamic pattern in articulating different scales of analysis and used by Norbert Elias (1939, 1970) to describe certain patterns of relations between human beings as "configuration" (*figuration* in German).[9] Such a concept contrasts deliberately with the dominant explanations of social action that is motivated by the aims and strategies of the actors, as an expression of weltanschauung, or by mere interest.

In the next two sections, rather than following the usual analytical route by describing successively ideological, identity, and instrumental factors of commitment and disengagement at the macro, meso, and micro levels, I explore two crucial series of mechanisms to determine their effects on individual reasons for withdrawal: the complex effects of organizational molding on individuals caught up in radical groups and the conflicting effects of repression and the criminalization of radical activities. To put it clearly, my intention is not to offer a general model of disengagement. Such an ambition would be contradictory with a configurational approach that can only suggest mechanisms, the combination of which always depends on situated contexts. However, by examining the effects of organizational molding on individuals, we embrace the essence of meso- and micro-level interactions, and by studying the effects of repression on individuals, we are at the very heart of the complex web of interactions between macro and micro levels (the individual effects of repression) and between macro and meso levels (effects of repression on organizational forms and strategies). Last, in what follows, although the discussion is primarily at an abstract level, I use numerous empirical illustrations.

The Complex Effects of Organizational Molding

Forget the profiles, understand the cells.
—Frank Hairgrove and Douglas McLeod,
"Circles Drawing toward High Risk Activism"

Nobody familiar with the literature would attempt to understand involvement in terrorism without looking at group and organizational dynamics. But we have become increasingly confused about how to understand the individual (and individual issues) within a multiple level analysis of terrorism.
—J. Horgan, *Walking Away from Terrorism*

Obviously, radical organizations vary widely, and I do not intend to minimize these differences. Nevertheless, three broad characteristics reveal certain permanent traits of these organizations: first, their illegal character and the repression they undergo; second, their clandestine and reclusive structure; and finally, their refusal to participate in the legitimate space of social and political struggles and the organizations involved in these battles. I offer the hypothesis that these three common attributes determine modalities of involvement at the individual level, the forms of its maintenance, and *at the end* the possibilities and means of leaving the organization. Indeed, these three characteristics suppose very strong and peculiar forms of secondary socialization and organizational modeling that may have the potential to deeply transform a person's biography, by a logic similar to what M. Zeitlin calls the "independent psychological effects of activism" (1967: 241).[10]

It is precisely these socializing mechanisms that Horgan attempts to capture in the phrase "community of practice" (2009: 13) in order to take account of a learning process that occurs through repeated social and psychological interactions with an ideology and related social and cultural practices. Within the interactionist framework, Hans Gerth and Charles Wright Mills offer a more sociological conceptual toolkit to examine the relationships between individuals and institutions (1954: 165–191). They define an institution as an organization with distinct hierarchical roles to which members must conform. The internalization of such roles occurs through secondary socialization, the strength of which needs to be studied—from conversion and alternation, in the sense used by P. L. Berger and T. Luckmann (1966), to strategic and limited adaptations—along with durability, from the viewpoint of biographical consequences in all spheres of life.

This model places at the center of the analysis of activism the Goffmanian notion of moral career, referring to *selection of people* (the incentives and barriers to joining and the orientations of activities) and *organizational modeling* (the multiple socializing effects of activism, which are in part determined by organizational rules and modes of operation and understood as a set of constraints—status, proposed or reserved activities, leadership, and so on).

Organizations do a lot of work in socializing their members, understood as role taking, which allows individuals to identify their different roles and fulfill their customary tasks. This secondary socialization can, at times, assume the form of explicit inculcations, the goal of which is to homogenize activists' categories of thought and their way of acting within and in the name of the organization. However, know-how and activist wisdom also frequently amount to a practical sense, what P. Bourdieu refers to as "the anticipated adjustment to the requirements of a field, what the language of sports calls the 'sense of the game' (like 'sense of place', 'the art of anticipation', etc.)," acquired over the course of a "long dialectical process, often described as a 'vocation', by which 'we make ourselves' according to what is making us and we 'choose' that by which we are 'chosen'" (1980: 111–112). This process takes place outside our conscious awareness. If, then, an institution "leaves its mark" on social actors who are part of it "by modifying their external conduct as well as their private life" (Gerth and Mills 1954: 173), we need to examine both the content and the methods of the process of institutional socialization to understand the individual disengagement process.

Three different effects of the interactions between meso and micro levels may be distinguished: the acquisition of a vision of the world (ideology), the

acquisition of know-how and wisdom (resources), and the restructuring of sociability networks in relation to the construction of individual and collective
identities (social networks and identities). It is at these three levels that we may
discern factors explaining disengagement from radical organizations.

Ideology

Socialization within organizations may bear on the internalization of a vision
of the world, of the place of the group in this world, and an individual's place in
the group. From the outset, it is vital to stress that the strength of an ideology
is rarely the driving force behind radical involvement but that it becomes important in the course of militant activities, under the effect of varied processes
of indoctrination and sometimes even programming. In other words, the adop-
tion of a political line and especially a visceral attachment to the cause rarely
preceded involvement, and they are acquired only gradually.

It is in the observation of everyday activist practices that one can see how
institutions legitimize certain types of discourse and practices to the detriment
of others, and how, faced with these constraints, members do not all have the
same resources to modify or renew the dominant ideologies. Here, institutional
resources (such as the exercise of a formal or informal leadership function, a
proximity to or membership in leadership circles, and an activist legitimacy
based on seniority or battle scars) and those beyond the rewards offered by the
organization (expert ability or moral authority linked, for example, to a profession such as religious responsibility, university scholar, or elected politician)
determine the capacity to resist and eventually contest the ideologies imposed
by the organization.

Therefore, for us to understand disengagement, we must also examine the
erosion of this aspect of activist socialization. How do we explain the weakening of the organization's ideological power, which may lead to a lessening of the
sacrifices one is willing to make for the cause? We may distinguish two possible
levels of determination.

First, the strength of beliefs may decline after a change of political climate,
whether caused by historical exhaustion of a model of commitment or by a
backlash and a return to order because of erosion of belief in the imminence
of the revolution. For example, J. Whalen and R. Flacks (1989) show that after
the Vietnam War ended and the repression of leftist movements intensified
in the United States, militant groups began to reevaluate the chances of success
of the revolutionary project and the cost of commitment. As a result, for young
activists the question of the personal versus the political became more important than any other consideration.

Second, ideological conviction may also be lost because of a rupture of the
consensus within a movement, the appearance of factions, and eventually a
splitting. The causes may vary, and on this point social psychology has produced
a great number of fascinating results, especially from the study of small groups

showing which conditions foster group loyalty. Historical examples abound. For example, in Italy, in the failed Red Brigades kidnapping of Aldo Moro in 1977, conflicts emerged between the groups of prisoners and the external management of the movement at the same time that the state was creating a special category for those who left the organization and agreed to collaborate with the state, thus providing opportunities for withdrawal and treason (Moretti 2004).

Resources

Participation in a protest group may enable the acquisition of multiple resources, which obviously vary as a function of the social resources acquired in other life spheres and before commitment, and which I refer to by the generic term *rewards* and define as the material or symbolic benefits individuals think they receive from their commitment. Rewards have four main characteristics. First, rewards include both objective and subjective dimensions; in other words, they are not always perceived by actors. Second, they may be both expected before commitment and pursued afterward, but also, and perhaps especially for grassroots activists who do not always expect to acquire significant and tangible rewards, they may be discovered in the course of action, produced in some way by the activist experience. Third, rewards vary according to the evolution of contexts and individual experiences. Fourth, costs are often confused with benefits.

Such a definition of rewards makes it difficult to link withdrawal from radical organizations to a simple disappearance of expected benefits. Since sacrifice is an integral part of the mechanism of attachment, then, as Kanter (1968) argues, the more that is sacrificed to enter the group and remain a member, the higher the cost of defection. In other words, the cost of activism somehow determines its price. Following a mechanism close to the one identified in the concept of cognitive dissonance, the more intense the efforts, the more difficult it is to recognize the futility of these efforts.

This draws attention to a certain deficiency in classic explanations of diminishing rewards that refer only to the evolution of radical organizations, such as the increased life constraints from the strengthening of repression or loss of faith in the triumph of the cause. By excluding everything not directly related to the area of protest activities (which typically are not further explored), it is difficult, for example, to take into account individual defections or the crumbling of groups in contexts in which the functioning of the organization and the economy of rewards on offer do not change.

Beyond organizational reasons, we need first to add factors that are linked to the public image of the group, its social legitimacy, and the accepted justification of violence. This is because the value accorded to rewards in a particular life sphere is also related to the value that other beneficiaries and society as a whole accord them. As a matter of fact, the social value of a cause, as well as ways of contributing to it, may vary as a function of the cultural context and its possible transformations. Specifically, social sectors initially assenting to a radical movement that employs targeted or random violence may turn against the movement, which has an effect on the group's trajectory, forcing it to retrench and rely on an increasingly restricted and vanishing social base. The Egyptian Al-Gama'a al-Islamiyya (GAI) experienced this after killing sixty-two people in Luxor. G. Zwerman and P. Steinhoff (2005) illustrate the process with respect to leftist movements in the 1970s, especially in Germany and Japan (also see Crenshaw 1991 and Gupta 2008 on these trajectories of decline).

Most importantly, keep in mind what I established previously: individuals are involved in a number of social spaces and the perceived returns from these different life spheres in themselves vary. In each of these spaces, individuals are led to adopt specific roles in which they are more or less stuck and which define various contexts of socialization. With time, significant changes may intervene in different spheres of life, constituting bifurcations in which certain roles are redistributed and identities transformed. This is why analysis of the logic of disengagement must proceed through identification, in different life spheres, of critical moments that can translate into a new valuation of the expected rewards, knowing that their value in a sphere covaries with the value attributed to them in all other spheres.

This point is particularly important in understanding withdrawal from radical organizations to the extent that organizations, because of the repression they experience and, therefore, their often clandestine and exclusive character, tend to compartmentalize, to a greater or lesser degree, different spheres of life and encourage activists to focus on a single field of militancy. This double process of compartmentalization and focus may cause divergent effects. First, because it encourages a personal housecleaning and withdrawal from social ties within the militant milieu, it contributes to cohesion. Yet this retreat to an increasingly confined world can lead at the same time to burnout and a degeneration of personal relationships (Ross and Gurr 1989; della Porta 2009). The literature on small and exclusive groups is useful to understand to specificities of most radical organizations in this respect. For example, Lewis Coser (1974) argues that exclusive groups require total commitment from their members, which makes conflicts more explosive, since they are quite likely to take on an emotional and unrealistic cast. As a result, individuals tend to ignore potential conflicts, and thus tensions accumulate. Protesting and defection, therefore, become more difficult and tend to be put off, but they develop more rapidly and intensely: "The intensity of the conflict grows when unrealistic elements are introduced into a realistic conflict. Thus, the conflict grows in intensity when participants are led to suppress their emotions of hostility and, in return, the accumulation of these feelings will aggravate the conflict if they burst out" (48).

Also, how and according to what logic do individuals manage their commitment once the rewards it yields are exhausted, whether through psychological repression, distancing from or attempts to transform their role, or defection?

When rewards are gone, the institutional setups facilitating or inhibiting defection (Hechter 1987; Taylor 1988a) and the strength of the dependence on the role and the existence of lateral possibilities, determined notably by the degree of autonomy of life spheres, describe a world of constraints making defection easier or more difficult. And it is as much the socializing force of the role that one is leaving as the manner in which one leaves, once the departure is finalized or even many years later, that best reflects the shift in trajectories and the degree to which the biographical consequences of commitment are sustained.

Social Networks and Identities

It is pretty clear now that socialization within organizations also occurs through the degree of redistribution of activists' relationship networks, in the activist sphere, and in other social subworlds. Above all, belonging to an organization is belonging to a group, with its borders and world of meaning, participating in its illusion. It is interacting with other members, at varying degrees of regularity; therefore, to belong is to construct a place or an identity for oneself.

Becker's approach in his article on the notion of commitment (1960) constitutes a valuable point of departure for exploring the interindividual dynamics of radical groups. One may simply define this concept as a psychological state that pushes an individual to remain caught up in an organization (sustained participation). Attachment both exists before involvement and is the *product* of the latter, suggesting that beyond the motivations for joining, we should focus on the work of the institution in producing this attachment. At the end of the 1960s, Kanter proposed a typology of specific elements likely to encourage attachment within groups. She distinguishes three aspects of attachment: maintenance, cohesion, and control, the mechanisms of some of which we have already seen.

The maintenance of attachment is based on *sacrifice*, already discussed, and *investment*. This brings us back to the existence of alternatives. The more that individuals are caught up in a system that is the only one to distribute rewards and costs, the more committed they remain: "When individuals invest their resources in one system rather than in other potential paths, they tie their rewards and the future usefulness of their resources, in effect, to the success of the system, burning other bridges, cutting themselves off [from] other ways to allocate resources" (Kanter 1968: 506).

The notion of cohesion designates the affective links between individuals and emotional attachment. As C. McCauley and his colleagues write, "Devotion to comrades is not only a force for joining a radical group, it is equally or more a barrier to leaving the group" (2008: 422). Two mechanisms are at play in this case: renunciation and communion (Kanter 1968, 1972). Renunciation refers to a withdrawal from all social relationships outside the group, with the goal of ensuring a maximum of internal cohesion (see also Bittner 1963; Coser 1974). Communion, the "we" feeling, is characteristic of the establishment of a unanimity-exclusion dialectic. R. H. Turner and L. M. Killian's very

Durkheimian observations with respect to the importance of camaraderie and the role of ceremonies and rituals in the cohesion of social movements (1957: 399, 442) are useful here (see also Linden and Klandermans 2003 on the importance of conformity to the peer group in far-right organizations).

Cohesion is also assured through means and techniques of control, from the most subtle to the most extreme, such as mortification and denial. Mortification brings us back to renunciation of one's desires and interests, to the abandonment of a private identity in favor of identification with a group, which Goffman develops in his discussion of the total institution and the notion of mortification of the self—that is, the loss of individuals' sense of self-determination when subject to such institutions as the army or religious communities. It shows how the practice of confession, self-criticism, the notion of the sin of pride, and so on, serve this function of mortification and the "effacement of the sense of individual autonomy" (Hoffer 1963: 66). Denial, for its part, brings us back to unconditional dedication to an authority, to members' internalization of what the group says and wants, what Catherine Leclercq (2005) calls adherence in the double sense of a merging (sticking to) and a continued allegiance.

Overall, it is the manner in which groups structure sociability relations, both internally and externally, as much as the placement of individuals in the group, that suggests a series of important factors underpinning the logics of disengagement.

The Conflicting Effects of Repression on the Disengagement Process

Despite its proliferation, research on repression's effects on protest, at the level of social movement organizations and at the micro level of individual commitment and disengagement, has produced largely inconsistent results. For some, repression would have a positive effect on mobilization for a number of reasons (Olivier 1991; Rasler 1996; Khawaja 1993; Bayat 1997; Bennani-Chraïbi and Fillieule 2003; Hafez 2003; Bianco 2005; Francisco 2005; Okión 2006), all stemming from more or less explicit mechanisms of radicalization, such as the provocation of moral shocks and the generation of incidents of emotional mobilization (Karklins and Peterson 1993; Kurzman 2004; Gayer 2009). The level of repression exercised seems crucial if the effect is positive. Some scholars suggest a curvilinear relation, proposing that semirepressive regimes are those that generate the most violence, while for others, the engines of radicalization are extremely repressive situations (Goodwin 2001; Einwohner 2003). Yet many studies stress that repression may decapitate a movement, slowing activist efforts and putting an end to protests (Gupta and Vinieris 1981; Lichbach and Gurr 1981; De Nardo 1985; Mueller and Weede 1990; Francisco 1996). The picture that emerges from the literature is very confusing. At most, we can suggest that, for those proposing different versions of the theory of frustration, repression tends to radicalize protesters, while from the perspective of the mobilization of resources, it tends to be dissuasive because of an imbalance in the costs, risks, and advantages of taking action.

As I argue above, a method for dealing seriously with the question of individual effects of repression consists of articulating the individual trajectories to organizational strategies and contexts (multilevel analysis) and considering the gradual unfolding of the course of the interactions (process analysis). In this way, we may hope to determine the precise effects (specification of relations) and the particular conditions at play (contextualization of relations).

Macro- and Mesoeffects of Repression on the Micro Level of Disengagement

At the contextual level, reinforcement of activism or withdrawal in the face of repression must be related to repression's specific or indiscriminate character (Mason and Krane 1989). When only the most active leaders and militants in a movement are repression's focus, demobilization of occasional militants and simple sympathizers is more likely. In contrast, indiscriminate repression of all activists, sympathizers, and even the population suspected of supporting them makes the spread of mobilization, even radicalization, more probable. France is a good illustration of this; the policy of "collective responsibility" confronting the Front de Libération National (National Liberation Front) has undoubtedly been a major influence in the commitment of broad sectors of the population to the liberation war between Algeria and France or, more recently, in Algeria in the context of Islamist movements:

> Reactive and indiscriminate repression of Islamists in Algeria in the context of political exclusion contributed to widespread rebellion. The perceived injustice of the coup gave Islamist violence legitimacy. The mortal threat posed by state repression against Islamist organizations and cadres gave supporters of the FIS [Front Islamique du Salut] additional incentive to fight back. The indiscriminate application of repression meant that FIS sympathizers could not guarantee their security through neutrality. (Hafez 2003: 82)

Still, at the contextual level, the individual effects of repression on withdrawal partially depend on how, in a particular time and place, this is socially perceived (notably with reference to the memory of past events), both in the population at large, in a specific area of social space, and in connection to the way individuals are variously caught up in preexisting relations (clans and community networks). Thus, in societies in which clan or caste solidarity is strongly rooted, rather than encouraging withdrawal, repression may lead to *bloc recruitment*, while offering the material means to proceed to action (mentoring, learning about violence and modes of action, armaments) and drastically reducing the domain of what is mentally conceivable (see Post, Sprinzak, and Denny 2003 on the importance of social settings in terrorist careers). G. Dorronsoro and O. Grojean (2004) demonstrate this well for Partiya Karkerên Kurdistan (PKK) and Kurdish Hezbollah, organizations in which trajectories of involvement occur in blocs, mobilizing entire families from the same villages and associations. This is not far removed from Dorronsoro's approach (2001) with respect to Afghanistan and the role of *qawm*.[11] In the same way, research on the Irish Republican Army (Bosi 2012) and Euskadi Ta Askatasuna (ETA) (Crettiez 2006) often shows how commitment to these organizations takes place within the context of a family tradition, fathers frequently playing the role of mentors to enroll their sons, and sons often motivated to be involved in the memory of relatives who died in combat or were imprisoned.

At the meso level of organizations, the literature effectively demonstrates the multiple effects of repression on the internal functioning of radical organizations. Repression automatically encourages the development of clandestine and exclusive organizations (Zald and Ash-Gardner 1987: 125–126; Hafez 2003). Faced with the risk of infiltration, arrest, and the dismantling of militant networks, organizations progressively cut themselves off from the outside world and adopt strict models of behavior, very often leading to an isolation propitious for building tightly knit emotional communities (Crenshaw 1981; Laqueur 1987; della Porta 1995). R. Alvarez (2003) demonstrates this effectively in an analysis of the repression of the Chilean Communist Party after Pinochet's coup. Militants went underground and created a group prepared for armed struggle, the Frente Patriotico Manuel Rodriguez. Alvarez concludes that

> the subjectivity of clandestineness was an indispensable condition for "naming" a new way of being a communist militant, from then on, increasingly linked to the military theme. . . . The principal characteristics of clandestineness have incurred a tendency towards external control and disciplinary vigilance with respect to the party's operational behavior, perceived to be the only way to resist the new "scientific" methods of the dictatorship's repression. (Alvarez 2003: 16, 23)

Another central effect of repression on radical organizations is the way it redefines their place within militant spaces, with consequences for the opportunities to leave and the constraints affecting withdrawal. The trajectories of revolutionary movements in the 1970s in Italy, Germany, or even Japan provide many such examples. Thus, I. Sommier reminds us that the competition between leftist organizations was a determining factor in the Italian escalation, with the militaristic watershed of Potere Operaio and Lotta Continua starting in 1972 and then the game of higher and higher stakes between the Red Brigades and independent actors:

The process of radicalization that characterizes the Italian cycle (and leads to its exhaustion through defection and a rise in the cost of involvement) is largely linked to competitions between groups on the extreme left, as well as their confrontation on the street with militants of the extreme right, who will, moreover, also be used as part of the strategy of tension to help in the counter-mobilization by a fringe group of military secret service people. (Sommier 2010: 74; see also della Porta 1995; Sommier 1996)

In Japan, competition assumes an even more critical form, to such a degree that internal struggles (the *uchigeba*) give way to more deaths than the repression (Steinhoff 1992; Zwerman, Steinhoff, and della Porta 2000; Zwerman and Steinhoff 2005; *United Red Army* 2007).

The Effects of Repression in a Process Model: The Continuity Hypothesis

Interactions between different actors, and therefore the temporal development of the relationships between repression and protest, have been mainly studied at macro and meso levels, focusing especially on cycles of mobilization. Thus, S. Tarrow (1989) shows that in the mid-1960s Italy's circumstances were especially favorable to the emergence of protest movements, giving rise to an ascendant phase of revolt (from 1966 to mid-1968) and a phase of radicalization (from mid-1968 to 1972), following which the state unleashed a wave of repression that marked the end of the cycle. In this latter phase, new, much more radical organizations detached themselves from the reform groups that had joined forces with them, and it is there that withdrawal first appeared.[12]

However, scant research has examined the succession of "micro cohorts" (Whittier 1997) of militants who join and leave organizations at various stages of repressive policies. Research on the trajectories of radicalization of revolutionary movements in the 1970s under the effect of repression has found that radicalization more readily affects those who did not experience the initial phase but joined the movement later, at the peak of the cycle of mobilization. This seems to be corroborated by a rise in the levels of violence with the second or even third generation of militants (della Porta 1995; Sommier 2010). The reasons are legion. Research of Zwerman and Steinhoff (2005) demonstrates that in Japan and in the United States the first generations of extreme left militants withdraw generally at the moment when repression leads to development of clandestine armed struggle; they are replaced by others, younger and with quite a different profile. In the United States, the second cohort includes more African Americans, a substantial proportion of working-class members, and various minorities, recruited from public and community colleges, organizations fighting poverty, and gangs. In Japan, while the 1968 movement started among university-educated elites, it has spread to young workers, marginalized members of society, and Korean residents born in Japan, who are deprived of their civil rights. For Zwerman and Steinhoff, these social differences explain some of the waves of withdrawal and radicalization.

More generally, this illustrates that, contrary to a homogeneous vision of collectives, it is necessary to pay attention to two interconnected dimensions to understand the diversity of demobilizing effects of repression within a single movement: on one hand, the succession of militant generations at the center of the analysis of the internal dynamics of recruitment and selection, the transformations of collective identities, and the organizational and ideological changes that result (Fillieule 2001). On the other hand, this ebb and flow of militants must be correlated with a historical period that includes a succession of repressive events. Traumatic episodes, such as the killings of Fred Hampton and Mark Clark by the Chicago police in December 1969 or the battle of Valle Giulia in Rome March 1, 1967, constitute "socializing events," the weight and individual consequences of which depend, in fact, on earlier socializing events and the particular generation of militants (Bosi 2012). Furthermore, the specific forms the repression takes for a given cohort translate into a whole series of socializing effects that lay the foundation for generational phenomena. So analysts often consider the experience of prison and torture crucial, as incubators of militancy, serving as intense forms of socialization and indeed a manner of redefining identities (see Kepel 1994 and Haenni 2001 on Egypt; Bucaille 1996 on Palestine; Martinez 2000 and Labat 1995 on Algeria; and Larzillière 2003 on Chechnya). Finally, the importance of the succession of militant generations in understanding the individual effects of repression also raises questions about transmission of the memory of struggles, which could be disrupted and facilitate withdrawal when repression decimates an entire generation, as M. Bennani-Chraïbi (2003) shows with respect to the disappearance of militants of the left and the extreme left from Moroccan campuses in the 1970s.

It is essential here to recognize that individual changes of attitude and conduct under the effect of repression do not follow the model of action-reaction but are rather part of a long and complex process, leading us to the interactionist approach in terms of career and the continuity hypothesis, which helps us sociologize and historicize the disruption in individual trajectories through restoring the time periods and the sequences of these transformations.

To sum up, an interactionist approach to the processes of involvement in and withdrawal from radical organizations also means that it is fruitless to try to construct a model for these changes in individual conduct within the framework of a rational conception of action. Cost-benefit analyses that are used to build models of individual effects of repression prove to be particularly inadequate to sufficiently take account of the convergences of decisions that only a comprehensive approach attentive to the motives advanced by the actors, in association with their structural positions at each stage of their trajectory, can help understand. To the extent that involvement in radical activity is usually marked by what D. Gupta (2008) calls acts of selfish altruism and "self-sacrifice," it is impossible to understand withdrawal by merely invoking exhaustion of rewards or modification in the perception of the chances of success, as, for example, E. Berman and D. Laitin (2006) do. The examples of suicide terrorism (Gambetta 2005; Pape 2003, 2005; Brym and Araj 2006) and voluntary immolations (Pettigrew 1997; Kim 2002; Bozarslan 2004; Biggs 2005; Grojean 2006, 2007; see Crenshaw 2007 for a review) show this quite clearly. We can only agree here with J. Elster (2009) who, in a recent book on the disinterest and the dead ends of the rational action theory, explores all the explanations produced on the rationality of suicide missions and concludes that, at each stage of individual trajectories, the complexity of mobilized individuals and institutional setups can lead militants to become involved in such actions. (See also Merari 2005 on the importance of temporal factors in suicide bombings.)

Conclusion

In this chapter, I offer a number of conceptual and methodological tools to develop a process and multilevel model of disengagement. I illustrate this model by bringing out characteristics that may be involved in the complex web of interactions between individuals, organizations, and contexts. I now summarize these characteristics.

First, at the *macro* level, specific contexts and transformations in the structure of commitment and disengagement opportunities are important. The sociopolitical environment constrains organizational evolution at the meso level and shapes activists' expectations at the micro level. These elements are particularly visible in a diachronic perspective when one considers the observable differences between cohorts or generations of activists (Reinares 2001; Roy 2004; Zwerman and Steinhoff 2005; Viterna 2006). Characteristics include the state of the commitment offer, the nature of state intervention (or the lack of it) in the public policy domain addressed by the mobilized network, and the public image of the cause.

Second, at the *meso* level of organizations, one must study the extent of the development of the mobilized network (territorial spread and numerical growth, including recruitment through personal connections), the degree of homogeneity or heterogeneity of the group in terms of sociobiological and ideological characteristics (which also constrain the nature and range of acquaintance networks), and the degree of openness of the groupings studied (the voluntary recruitment policy, ways of integrating newcomers into the group, and so on). All these organizational factors must be factored into an analysis of moral career, the combination of the effects of selection and organizational modeling on the long-term commitment of individuals, in the orientation of their activities within the group, and in the forms (the practical modalities and the reasons they cite) that eventual disengagement will assume. This last point emphasizes not only the well-known collective incentives (be they positive or negative) that enhance or discourage individual participation but also the great importance of institutional socialization and its libidinal dimension, a dimension that is increasingly stressed by contemporary studies in the field of social movements.

Finally, at the *micro* level of the individual, we have institutionalized changes and biographical ruptures at different career stages. The pivotal nature of the plurality of life spheres underlines that activist organizations comprise individuals who are inserted in a variety of social space locations. Activists are thus permanently subject to the obligation to comply with different norms, rules, and logic that may conflict. These different levels of experience may proceed simultaneously or successively; for the observer, the difficulty lies in studying simultaneously the succession of events within each order of experience (the structure of each order) and the influence of each level on all the others, and consequently, of course, in studying the dependent variable: activist commitment.

Obviously, this interactionist and configurational approach does not aim to offer a definitive conclusion about which factors or combination of factors might universally determine disengagement from a radical organization. I fully agree with Horgan when he writes that

> while we might aspire to developing a scientific study of terrorist behavior, exploration (let alone description) might be a more noble and realistic achievement than true explanation at this point. The nature of this exploration may be empirical, but it is important to accurately reflect on the scientific limitations of our enquiry, at whatever level we operate as academic researchers. (2009: xxii)

However, I propose a set of methodological recommendations for those whose ambition is to implement a process and multilevel model of commitment and disengagement. These recommendations boil down to five components:

1. Move away from reasoning in terms of independent and dependent variables, in favor of a thick description of the observed phenomena. This does not mean that we must renounce any causal explanation but that this can be achieved only after an analysis of a series of mechanisms whose composition (in time and space) produces observable effects (e.g., disengagement).[13]
2. Move away from monocausal explanations by discerning factors that explain individual behavior at the three interrelated micro-meso, micro-macro, and meso-macro levels of observation.
3. Move away from synchronic mechanisms toward diachronic variations with regard to context change, organizational transformations, and individual life course.
4. Move away from models that suggest that individuals are either always strategic and rational or the mere plaything of psychological

or structural forces. One should try to overcome the far-too-simplistic analytical distinction between instrumental, solidarity, or ideological motives. If such incentives are obviously at play in commitment and disengagement processes, they certainly cannot be used as a classification for characterizing individuals' different paths toward activism or, even worse, for building movements' typologies. The complex way interactionist sociology and configurational approach define individual entities and the links between agency and structure are of great help here.

5. Focus research on the individual level—that is, the person's life course and the justifications he or she gives for his or her actions—as a means to investigate the complex interplay among micro, meso, and macro levels. If such a recommendation implies that the biographical material is the most suitable source to relate the meso- and macroconditions to individuals' motives, it remains that activists are always caught in social ties and organizational bounds at the meso level, which means that it is virtually impossible to isolate the micro level of the meso level.

These five recommendations should help us go further than the structural functionalist generalizations of much of the sociology of social movements and the normative approximations of many psychosociological approaches.

NOTES

1. See Asel, Fair, and Shellman 2008 for an approach that focuses more on reasons behind relative frustration than on objective indicators of frustration. Nonetheless, Fair 2008, on Pakistani activists, and Roy 2008 develop well-supported critiques of all the attempts to associate the terrorist commitment of jihadis to socioeconomic factors.

2. By "radical organization," I mean any form of organization willing to operate outside the legal framework and resort to violence, whether because it believes that conventional forms of action are ineffective or because repression leaves no other alternative than violence or the dissolution of the group. By "violent" action, I mean a vast array of more or less long-lasting or extreme forms of commitment, including violence against oneself (e.g., immolation, suicide attacks) or against others (e.g., assassination, so-called terrorist acts, guerrilla warfare). Disengagement from radical organizations is certainly one of the central social phenomena that take place in postrevolutionary situations and democratic transitions.

3. Klandermans (1997, 2004; Klandermans and Mayer 2006) and others introduced the supply and demand metaphor to explain participation in movement organizations, distinguishing between identity, ideological, and rational motives. However, such distinctions are far too simple to account for the complex interrelations between organizations and individuals and fall short of establishing how the three motives are produced and coexist. See, for example, Tilly and Tarrow 2007 for a critique of the lack of a theoretical model that summarizes and links micro- and meso-level factors.

4. This model is discussed in Taylor and Horgan 2006. The basic ideas of this model are the following: "1. There is never one route to terrorism, but rather there are individual

routes, and furthermore those routes and activities as experienced by the individual change over time (hence the idea of a process); 2. Terrorism works at both an individual and political level, through behaviour acting on the environment sustained and focused by ideology, and the effect of that on subsequent behaviour; 3. The significant element in strengthening engagement with terrorism and giving it direction is the increased role of the social-political-organisational context (and especially as expressed through ideology) in exerting control over behaviour" (597).

5. This point is crucial in the field of terrorism studies, in which it is often falsely assumed that not talking to terrorists is a guarantee and a source of scholarly authority.

6. Chakrabarty criticizes Guha for sticking to an orthodox Marxist explanation of the revolt, which led him to explain people's acts in purely strategic terms, when the actors themselves declared to the police that they were acted on by supernatural forces and did not understand retrospectively what happened to them.

7. For another illustration of the continuity hypothesis, see the contemporary revision of the usual explanations given for individual engagement in the extreme violence of World War I: the culture of war, the brutalization of societies, and the soldiers' consent or their constraint (e.g., Mariot 2003; Loez and Mariot 2008).

8. I do not have the scope here to discuss at length the reasons why we privilege such a theoretical approach to the link between agency and structure and why it seems more appropriate to us in this context than other conceptual tools, like those elaborated by Pierre Bourdieu, Anthony Giddens, or Marshall Sahlins.

9. The concept of configuration is key to Elias's sociology of civilization. He defines these configurations as the changing pattern that players form with each other, relations of suspense, interdependence of players, *and* the fluctuating balance of suspense, the to-and-fro of a balance of power ("das sich wandelnde Muster, das die Spieler miteinander bilden, Spannungsgefüge, Interdependenz der Spieler, *und* das fluktuierende Spannungsgleichgewicht, das Hin und Her einer Machtbalance") (Elias 1939: 139).

10. This importance of secondary socialization within radical organizations has typically been neglected because of the structuralist orientation adopted by the sociology of social movements, even if periodically some authors underscored the imbalance between research on recruitment by movements and that studying the effect of the institution on militants (e.g., Keniston 1968: 353–354; Killian 1973: 36; McAdam 1989: 123).

11. This Afghan word refers to any form of solidarity based on kinship, residence, or occupation. Afghans identify themselves by *qwam* rather than by tribe or nationality. A *qawm* is usually governed by *jirga* or *shura* ("council" or "assembly of elder males").

12. See Sommier 2010 and Zwerman and Steinhoff 2005, on leftist movements in the 1960s in France, the United States, and Japan, and Brockett 2005, on the cycles of repression in Guatemala and El Salvador.

13. For more on this conception of causality, see Bennani-Chraïbi and Fillieule 2013.

REFERENCES

Alvarez, R. 2003. *Desde las sombras: Una historia de la clandestinidad comunista 1973–1980* [From the Shadows: A History of the Communist Underground, 1973–1980]. Santiago: Ediciones Lom.

Asel, V., C. Fair, and S. Shellman. 2008. "Consenting to a Child's Decision to Join a Jihad: Insights from a Survey of Militant Families in Pakistan." *Studies in Conflict and Terrorism* 31: 973–994.

Bayat, A. 1997. *Street Politics: Poor People's Movements in Iran*. New York: Columbia University Press.

Beck, C. 2008. "The Contribution of Social Movement Theory to Understanding Terrorism." *Sociological Compass* 2 (5): 1565–1581.

Becker, H. 1960. "Notes on the Concept of Commitment." *American Journal of Sociology* 66 (1): 32–40.

———. 1966. *Outsiders*. Glencoe, IL: Free Press.

Beckford, J. A. 1978. "Through the Looking-Glass and Out the Other Side: Withdrawal from Rev. Moon's Unification Church." *Archives de Sciences Sociales des Religions* [Archives of Social Sciences of Religion] 45 (1): 95–116.

Bennani-Chraïbi, M. 2003. "Parcours, cercles et médiations à Casablanca: Tous les chemins mènent à l'action associative de quartier" [Itineraries, Circles and Mediations in Casablanca: All Roads Lead to Associative Neighborhood Action]. In *Résistances et protestations dans les sociétés musulmanes* [Resistance and Protests in Muslim Societies], edited by M. Bennani-Chraïbi and O. Fillieule, 293–352. Paris: Presses de Sciences Po.

Bennani-Chraïbi, M., and O. Fillieule, eds. 2003. *Résistances et protestations dans les sociétés musulmanes* [Resistance and Protests in Muslim Societies]. Paris: Presses de Sciences Po.

———. 2012. "Towards a Sociology of Revolutionary Situations: Reflections on the Arab Uprisings." *Revue Française de Science Politique* [French Journal of Political Science] 62 (5–6): 767–796.

Berger, P. L., and T. Luckmann. 1966. *The Social Construction of Reality: A Treatise in the Sociology of Knowledge*. New York: Anchor Books.

Berman, E., and Laitin, D. 2006. "Hard Targets: Theory and Evidence on Suicide Attacks." Working paper. Available at http://econweb.ucsd.edu/~elib/Hardtargets.pdf.

Bianco, L. 2005. *Jacqueries et révolution dans la Chine du xxᵉ siècle* [Peasant Protest and Revolution in 20th-Century China]. Paris: La Martinière.

Biggs, M. 2005. "Dying without Killing: Self-Immolations, 1963–2002." In *Making Sense of Suicide Missions*, edited by Diego Gambetta, 173–208. Oxford: Oxford University Press.

Bittner, E. 1963. "Radicalism and the Organization of Radical Movements." *American Sociological Review* 28 (6): 928–940.

Björgo, T., and J. Horgan, eds. 2009. *Leaving Terrorism Behind: Individual and Collective Disengagement*. London: Routledge.

Blumer, H. 1937. "Social Psychology." In *Man and Society*, edited by E. P. Schmidt, 144–198. New York: Prentice-Hall.

Bosi, L. 2012. "Explaining Pathways to Armed Activism in the Provisional IRA, 1969–1972." In "Cultures of Radicalization: Discourses and Practices of Political Violence and Terrorism," edited by C. Verhouven and M. Tokic. Special issue, *Social Science History* 36 (3): 347–390.

Bourdieu, P. 1980. *Le sens pratique* [Practical Reason]. Paris: Minuit.

Bozarslan, H. 2004. *Violence in the Middle-East: From Political Struggle to Self-Sacrifice*. Princeton, NJ: Markus Wiener.

Brockett, C. 2005. *Political Movements and Violence in Central America*. Cambridge: Cambridge University Press.

Browning, C. 1992. *Ordinary Men: Reserve Police Battalion 101 and the Final Solution in Poland*. New York: Harper Collins.

Brym, R. J., and B. Araj. 2006. "Suicide Bombing as Strategy and Interaction: The Case of the Second Intifada." *Social Forces* 84 (4): 1969–1986.

Bucaille, L. 1996. *Génération Intifada* [Intifada Offspring]. Paris: Hachette.

Chakrabarty, D. 2000. *Provincializing Europe: Postcolonial Thought and Historical Difference.* Princeton, NJ: Princeton University Press.

Collovald, A., and B. Gaïti. 2006. "Questions sur une radicalisation politique" [Some Questions about Political Radicalization]. In *La démocratie aux extremes* [Democracy Facing Extremism], edited by A. Collovald and B. Gaïti. Paris: La Dispute.

Coser, L., 1974. *Greedy Institutions: Patterns of Undivided Commitment.* New York: Free Press.

Crenshaw, M. 1981. "The Causes of Terrorism." *Comparative Politics* 13 (4): 379–399.

———. 1991. "How Terrorism Declines." *Terrorism and Political Violence* 3 (1): 69–87.

———. 2000. "The Psychology of Terrorism: An Agenda for the 21st Century." *Political Psychology* 21 (2): 405–420.

———. 2007. "Explaining Suicide Terrorism." *Security Studies* 16 (1): 133–162.

Crettiez, X. 2006. *Violence et nationalism* [Violence and Nationalism]. Paris: Odile Jacob.

De Nardo, J. 1985. *Power in Numbers.* Princeton, NJ: Princeton University Press.

Decker, S., and J. Lauritsen. 1996. "Breaking the Bonds: Leaving the Gang." In *Gangs in America*, 2nd ed., edited by C. R. Huff, 103–122. Newbury Park, CA: Sage.

della Porta, D., ed. 1992. *Social Movements and Violence: Participation in Underground Organizations.* Greenwich, CT: Jai Press.

———. 1995. *Social Movements, Political Violence, and the State: A Comparative Analysis of Italy and Germany.* New York: Cambridge University Press.

———. 2009. "Leaving Underground Organizations: A Sociological Analysis of the Italian Case." In *Leaving Terrorism Behind: Individual and Collective Disengagement*, edited by T. Björgo and J. Horgan, 49–65. London: Routledge.

Dobry, M. 1986. *Sociologie des crises politiques* [Sociology of Political Crisis]. Paris: Presses de Sciences Po.

———. 2010. "Le politique dans ses états critiques: retour sur quelques aspects de l'hypothèse de continuité" [On Some Aspects of the Continuity Hypothesis]. In *Bifurcations: Les sciences sociales face aux ruptures et à l'événement* [Turning Points: Social Science Facing Turning Points and Events], edited by M. Bessin, C. Bidart, and M. Grosseti, 64–88. Paris: La Découverte.

Dorronsoro, G. 2001. *La révolution afghane* [Revolution in Afghanistan]. Paris: Khartala.

Dorronsoro, G., and O. Grojean. 2004. "Engagement militant et phénomènes de radicalisation chez les kurdes de Turquie" [Commitment and Radicalization among Kurds in Turkey]. *European Journal of Turkish Studies*, August. Available at http://ejts.revues.org/198.

Einwohner, R. L. 2003. "Opportunity, Honor, and Action in the Warsaw Ghetto Uprising of 1943." *American Journal of Sociology* 109:650–675.

Elias, N. 1939. *Über den Prozess der Zivilisation: Soziogenetische und psychogenetische Untersuchungen* [The Civilizing Process: Sociogenetic and Psychogenetic Investigations]. Frankfurt: Suhrkamp.

———. 1970. *Was ist Soziologie?* [What Is Sociology?]. Munich: Juventa.

Elster, J. 2009. *Le désintéressement* [Disinterest]. Paris: Seuil.

Fair, C. 2008. "Who Are Pakistan's Militants and Their Families?" *Terrorism and Political Violence*, no. 1: 49–65.

Fangen, K. 1999. "Pride and Power: A Sociological Interpretation of the Norwegian Radical Nationalist Underground Movement." Ph.D. diss., University of Oslo.

Fillieule, O. 2001. "Propositions pour une analyse processuelle de l'engagement individual" [Proposal for a Process Analysis of Disengagement]. *Revue française de science politique* [French Journal of Political Science] 51 (1–2): 199–215.

———, ed. 2005. *Le désengagement militant* [Political Disengagement]. Paris: Belin.

Fillieule, O. 2010. "Some Elements of an Interactionist Approach to Political Disengagement." *Social Movement Studies* 9 (1): 1–15.

Fillieule, O., and M. Bennani-Chraïbi. 2003. "Exit, voice, loyalty et bien d'autres choses encore . . ." [Exit, Voice, Loyalty and Many Other Things . . .]. In *Résistances et protestations dans les sociétés musulmanes* [Resistance and Protests in Muslim Societies], edited by M. Bennani-Chraibi and O. Fillieule, 43–126. Paris: Presses de Sciences Po.

Fillieule, O., and C. Broqua. 2005. "La défection dans deux associations de lutte contre le sida: Act Up et AIDES" [Defectors in Two Anti-AIDS Organizations: Act Up and AIDES]. In *Le désengagement militant* [Political Disengagement], edited by O. Fillieule, 189–228. Paris: Belin.

Francisco, R. A. 1996. "Coercion and Protest: An Empirical Test in Two Democratic States." *American Journal of Political Science* 40 (4): 1179–1204.

———. 2005. "The Dictator's Dilemma." In *Repression and Mobilization*, edited by C. Davenport, H. Johnston, and C. Mueller, 58–81. Minneapolis: University of Minnesota Press.

Fuchs-Ebaugh, H. R. 1988. *Becoming an Ex: The Process of Role Exit*. Chicago: University of Chicago Press.

Gambetta, D. 2005. *Making Sense of Suicide Missions*. Oxford: Oxford University Press.

Gayer, L. 2009. "Le parcours du combattant: Une approche biographique des militants sikhs du Khalistan" [A Warrior Life Course: A Biographical Analysis of Sikhs Militants from Khalistan]. CERI Working Paper 28, Sciences Po, Paris.

Gayer, L., and C. Jaffrelot, eds. 2008. *Milices armées d'Asie du Sud: Privatisation de la violence et implication des Etats* [Armed Militias of South Asia: Privatization of Violence and Involvement of the States]. Paris: Presses de Sciences Po.

Gerth, H., C. Wright Mills. 1954. *Character and Social Structure: The Psychology of Social Institutions*. London: Routledge and Kegan Paul.

Goodwin, J. 2001. *No Other Way Out: States and Revolutionary Movements, 1945–1991*. Cambridge: Cambridge University Press.

———. 2004. "What Must We Explain to Explain Terrorism?" *Social Movement Studies* 3:259–265.

———. 2006. "A Theory of Categorical Terrorism." *Social Forces* 84:2027–2046.

Grenne, J., and K. Pravis. 2007. *Gang Wars: The Failure of Enforcement Tactics and the Need for Effective Public Safety Strategies*. Washington, DC: Justice Police Institute.

Grojean, O. 2006. "Investissement militant et violence contre soi au sein du Parti des Travailleurs du Kurdistan" [Militant Violence against the Self in the Kurdistan Workers Party]. *Cultures et Conflits* [Cultures and Conflicts] 63:101–112.

———. 2007. "Violence against the Self: The Case of a Kurdish Non-Islamist Group." In *The Enigma of Islamist Violence*, edited by Amélie Blom, Laetitia Bucaille, and Luis Martinez, 105–120. London: Columbia University Press.

Guha, R. 1983. *Elementary Aspects of Peasant Insurgency in Colonial India*. Delhi: Oxford University Press.

Gupta, D. 2008. *Understanding Terrorism and Political Violence: The Life Cycle of Birth, Growth, Transformation and Demise*. Abingdon, UK: Routledge.

Gupta, D., and Y. P. Vinieris. 1981. "Introducing New Dimensions in Macro Models: The Socio-Political and Institutional Environment." *Economic Development and Cultural Change* 30 (1): 31–58.

Gurr, T. R., and T. Björgo. 2005. "Economic Factors that Contribute to Terrorism in Social and Political Context: Final Report, May 1, 2005." Paper presented at the International Summit on Democracy, Terrorism and Security, Club de Madrid, March 8–11.

Haenni, P. 2001. "Banlieues indociles: Sur la politisation des quartiers périphériques du Caire" [Rebellious Suburbs: On the Politicization of the Suburbs of Cairo]. Ph.D. diss., Institut d'Etudes Politiques, Paris.

Hafez, M. M. 2003. *Why Muslims Rebel: Repression and Resistance in the Islamic World.* Boulder, CO: Lynne Rienner.

Hairgrove, F., and D. McLeod. 2008. "Circles Drawing toward High Risk Activism." *Studies in Conflict and Terrorism*, no. 31: 399–411.

Hechter, M. 1987. *Principles of Group Solidarity.* Berkeley: University of California Press.

Hoffer, E. 1963. *The True Believer: Thoughts on the Nature of Mass Movements.* New York: Time.

Horgan, J. 2005. *The Psychology of Terrorism.* London: Routledge.

———. 2008. "From Profiles to *Pathways* and Roots to *Routes*: Perspectives from Psychology on Radicalization into Terrorism." *Annals of the American Academy of Political and Social Science* 618 (1): 80–94.

———. 2009. *Walking Away from Terrorism.* London: Routledge.

Hughes, E. C. 1937. "Institutional Office and the Person." *American Journal of Sociology* 43:404–413.

———. 1958. *Men and Their Work.* Glencoe, IL: Free Press.

Hundeide, K. 2003. "Becoming a Committed Insider." *Culture and Psychology* 9:107–127.

Introvigne, M. 1999. "Defectors, Ordinary Leave-Takers, and Apostates: A Quantitative Study of Former Members of New Acropolis in France." *Nova Religio: The Journal of Alternative and Emergent Religions* 3 (1): 83–99.

Jamieson, A. 1990. "Entry, Discipline and Exit in the Italian Red Brigades." *Terrorism and Political Violence* 2 (1): 1–20.

Kanter, R. M. 1968. "Commitment and Social Organization: A Study of Commitment Mechanisms in Utopian Communities." *American Sociological Review* 33 (4): 499–517.

———. 1972. *Commitment and Community: Communes and Utopias in Sociological Perspective.* Cambridge, MA: Harvard University Press.

Karklins, R., and R. Peterson. 1993. "Decision Calculus of Protesters and Regimes: Eastern Europe 1989." *Journal of Politics* 55 (August): 588–614.

Keniston, K. 1968. *Young Radicals.* New York: Harcourt, Brace.

Kepel, G. 1994. *Exils et royaumes* [Exiles and Kingdoms]. Paris: Presses de la FNSP.

Khawaja, M. 1993. "Repression and Popular Collective Action: Evidence from the West Bank." *Sociological Forum* 8:47–71.

Killian, L. M. 1973. "Social Movements: A Review of the Field." In *Social Movements: A Reader and a Source Book*, edited by R. R. Evans, 124–138. Chicago: Rand McNally.

Kim, H. 2002. "Shame, Anger, and Love in Collective Action: Emotional Consequences of Suicide Protest in South Korea, 1991." *Mobilization* 7 (2): 159–176.

Klandermans, B. 1997. *The Social Psychology of Protest.* Cambridge, UK: Blackwell.

———. 2004. "The Demand and Supply of Participation: Social-Psychological Correlates of Participation in Social Movements." In *The Blackwell Companion to Social*

Movements, edited by D. A. Snow, S. A. Soule, and H. Kriesi, 360–379. Oxford: Blackwell.

Klandermans, B., and N. Mayer. 2006. *Extreme Right Activists in Europe: Through the Magnifying Glass*. Abingdon, UK: Routledge.

Klein, M. W. 1995. *The American Street Gang*. Oxford: Oxford University Press.

Kurzman, C. 2004. *The Unthinkable Revolution in Iran*. Cambridge, MA: Harvard University Press.

Labat, S. 1995. *Les islamistes algériens* [Algerian Islamists]. Paris: Le Seuil.

Laqueur, W. 1987. *The Age of Terrorism*. Boston: Little, Brown.

Larzillière, P. 2003. "Tchétchénie: Le djihad reterritorialisé" [Chechnya: The Jihad Reterritorialized]. *Critique internationale* [International Critic], no. 20: 151–164.

Leclercq, C. 2005. "'Raisons de sortir': Le désengagement des militants du Parti communiste français" ["Motives for Exiting": Disengagement from the French Communist Party]. In *Le désengagement militant* [Political Disengagement], edited by O. Fillieule, 131–154. Paris: Belin.

———. 2008. "Histoires d' 'ex': Une approche socio-biographique du désengagement des militants du parti communiste français" [Becoming an Ex: A Socio-biographical Approach of Disengagement from the French Communist Party]. Ph.D. diss., Institute of Political Science of Paris.

Lichbach, M., and T. Gurr. 1981. "The Conflict Process: A Formal Model." *Journal of Conflict Resolution* 25 (1): 700–714.

Linden, A., and B. Klandermans. 2003. "Stigmatization and Repression of Extreme Right Activism in the Netherland." *Mobilization: An International Journal*, no. 2: 213–228.

Loez, A., and N. Mariot, eds. 2008. *Obéir/désobéir: Les mutineries de 1917 en perspective* [Obey/Disobey: The 1917 Mutinies in Perspective]. Paris: La Découverte.

Mariot, N. 2003. "Faut-il être motivé pour tuer? Sur quelques explications aux violences de guerre" [Do We Need to Be Motivated to Kill? On Some Explanations of War Violences]. *Genèses: Sciences sociales et histoire* [Genesis: Social Sciences and History] 53:154–177.

Martinez, L. 2000. *The Algerian Civil War, 1990–1998*. London: Hurst.

Mason, T. David, and D. A. Krane. 1989. "The Political Economy of Death Squads: Toward a Theory of the Impact of State-Sanctioned Terror." *International Studies Quarterly* 33:175–198.

McAdam, D. 1989. *Freedom Summer*. Oxford: Oxford University Press.

McCauley, C., and S. Moskalenko. 2008. "Mechanisms of Political Radicalization: Pathways toward Terrorism." *Terrorism and Political Violence* 20 (3): 415–433.

Mead, G. H. 1934. *Mind, Self and Society from the Standpoint of a Social Behaviorist*. Chicago: University of Chicago Press.

Merari, A. 2005. "Social, Organisational and Psychological Factors in Suicide Terrorism." In *Root Causes of Terrorism: Myths, Realities, Ways Forward*, edited by Tore Björgo, 70–84. London: Routledge.

Moretti, M. 2004. *Brigate Rosse* [Red Brigade]. Milan: Baldini Castoldi Dalai.

Mueller, E. N., and E. Weede. 1990. "Cross-national Variation in Political Violence: A Rational Action Approach." *Journal of Conflict Resolution* 34 (4): 624–651.

Okión Solano, V. 2006. "El movimiento de acción revolucionaria: Una historia de radicalización política" [The Movement of Revolutionary Action: A History of Political Radicalization]. In *Movimientos armados en México, siglo XX* [Armed Movements in Mexico, 20th Century], edited by Verónica Okión Solano and Marta García Ugarte, 123–143. Tlalpan, Mexico: El Colegio de Michoacán.

Olivier, J. 1991. "State Repression and Collective Action in South Africa, 1970–84." *South African Journal of Sociology* 22:109–117.

Pape, R. A. 2003. "The Strategic Logic of Suicide Terrorism." *American Political Science Review* 97:343–361.

———. 2005. *Dying to Win: The Strategic Logic of Suicide Terrorism*. New York: Random House.

Pettigrew, J., ed. 1997. *Martyrdom and Political Resistance: Essays from Asia and Europe*. Comparative Asian Studies 18. Amsterdam: VU University Press.

Post, J. M., E. Sprinzak, and L. M. Denny. 2003. "The Terrorists in Their Own Words: Interviews with Thirty-Five Incarcerated Middle Eastern Terrorists." *Terrorism and Political Violence* 15 (1): 171–184.

Rasler, K. 1996. "Concessions, Repression, and Political Protest in the Iranian Revolution." *American Sociological Review* 61:132–152.

Reinares, F. 2001. *Patriotas de la Muerte: Quiénes han militado en ETA y por qué* [Patriots of Death: Who Have Fought in ETA and Why]. Madrid: Taurus.

Ross, J. I., and T. R. Gurr. 1989. "Why Terrorism Subsides: A Comparative Study of Canada and the United States." *Comparative Politics* 21 (4): 405–426.

Roy, O. 2004. *Globalized Islam: The Search for a New Ummah*. New York: Columbia University Press.

———. 2008. "Islamic Terrorist Radicalization in Europe." In *European Islam*, edited by Samir Amghar, Amel Boubekeur, and Michael Emerson, 52–60. Brussels: Centre for European Policy Studies.

Searle, John. 1983. *Intentionality: An Essay in the Philosophy of Mind*. Vol. 9. Cambridge: Cambridge University Press.

Silke, A., ed. 2003, *Terrorists, Victims and Society: Psychological Perspectives on Terrorism and Its Consequences*. Chichester, UK: John Wiley.

Sommier, I. 1996. *La violence politique et son deuil: L'après 68 en France et en Italie* [Political Violence and Its Mourning: After the 1968 in France and Italy]. Rennes, France: Presses Universitaires de Rennes.

———. 2010. *La violence révolutionnaire* [Revolutionary Violence]. Paris: Presses de Sciences Po.

Steinhoff, P. G. 1992. "Death by Defeatism and Other Fables: The Social Dynamics of the Rengo Sekigun Purge." In *Japanese Social Organization*, edited by T. S. Lebra, 195–224. Honolulu: University of Hawaii Press.

Strauss, A. 1959. *Mirrors and Masks: The Search for Identity*. Glencoe, IL: Free Press.

Sutherland, E. D., and D. Cressey. 1966. *Principles of Criminology*. Chicago: J. B. Lippincott.

Tackett, T. 1996. *Becoming a Revolutionary: The Deputies of the French National Assembly and the Emergence of a Revolutionary Culture*. Princeton, NJ: Princeton University Press.

Tarrow, S. 1989. *Democracy and Disorder: Protest and Politics in Italy, 1965–1975*. Oxford: Clarendon Press.

Taylor, V. 1989. "Social Movement Continuity: The Women's Movement in Abeyance." *American Sociological Review* 54 (5): 761–775.

Taylor, M., and J. Horgan. 2006. "A Conceptual Framework for Addressing Psychological Process in the Development of the Terrorist." *Terrorism and Political Violence* 18 (4): 585–601.

Testas, A. 2004. "Determinants of Terrorism in the Muslim World: An Empirical Cross-Sectional Analysis." *Terrorism and Political Violence* 16:252–273.

Tilly, C., and S. Tarrow. 2007. *Contentious Politics*. Boulder, CO: Paradigm.

Turner, R. H., and L. M. Killian. 1957. *Collective Behavior*. Englewood Cliffs, NJ: Prentice Hall.

United Red Army. 2007. Directed by K. Wakamatsu. Skhole Co. and Wakamatsu Production.

Vaughan, D. 1986. *Uncoupling: Turning Points in Intimate Relationships*. Oxford: Oxford University Press.

Vigil, J. D. 1988. "Group Processes and Street Identity: Adolescent Chicano Gang Members." *Ethos* 16 (4): 421–445.

Viterna, J. 2006. "Pulled, Pushed, and Persuaded: Explaining Women's Mobilization into Salvadoran Guerrilla Army." *American Journal of Sociology* 112 (1): 1–45.

Wasmund, K. 1986. "The Political Socialization of West German Terrorists." In *Political Violence and Terror: Motifs and Motivations*, edited by P. H. Merkl, 191–213. Berkeley: University of California Press.

Whalen, J., and R. Flacks. 1989. *Beyond the Barricades: The Sixties Generation Grows Up*. Philadelphia: Temple University Press.

Whittier, N. 1997. "Political Generations, Micro Cohorts and the Transformation of Social Movements." *American Sociological Review* 62 (5): 760–778.

Zald, M. N., and R. Ash-Gardner. 1987. "Social Movement Organizations: Growth, Decay and Change." In *Social Movements in an Organizational Society: Collected Essays*, edited by J. B. McCarthy and M. N. Zald, 327–341. New Brunswick, NJ: Transaction Books.

Zeitlin, M. 1967. *Revolutionary Politics and the Cuban Working Class*. Princeton, NJ: Princeton University Press.

Zwerman, G., and P. Steinhoff. 2005. "When Activists Ask for Trouble: State-Dissident Interactions and the New Left Cycle of Resistance in the United States and Japan." In *Repression and Mobilization*, edited by C. Davenport, H. Johnston, and C. Mueller, 85–107. Minneapolis: University of Minnesota Press.

Zwerman, G., P. G. Steinhoff, and D. della Porta. 2000. "Disappearing Social Movements: Clandestinity in the Cycle of New Left Protest in the U.S., Japan, Germany, and Italy." *Mobilization* 5 (1): 85–104.

3

Abeyance Cycles in Social Movements

ALISON DAHL CROSSLEY
VERTA TAYLOR

S ocial movements, protest campaigns, demonstrations, and other forms of contentious politics play an important part in democratic transitions. Some scholars have argued that grassroots activism is so central to the civic engagement on which democracies depend that social movements are a form of "people's politics" that exists alongside and contrasts with routine or elite politics (Blee 2012; Johnston 2011). In authoritarian societies, decades-long political mobilization often precedes transition to democracy, resulting in numerous activist groups that sustain the legacy of the challenge (Wood 2000). In democratic societies, popular protest and disruption tend to occur in waves, or cycles, of *political opportunity* and *threat* (Almeida 2008; Tarrow 1989). The creation of civic groups, social organizations, and new identities and practices is often the most important outcome of democratization and regime liberalization. Among scholars of social movements, political opportunity variables have received far more attention than threat in explanations of movement emergence and decline. Researchers interested in how repressive conditions and threat affect political contention and social protest find that organizational holdovers, civic associations, and social justice groups that manage to survive continued state repression are significant in both sustaining a wave of collective action and facilitating future mobilization (Almeida 2008; Van Dyke 1998; Meyer and Whittier 1994; Taylor 1989).

What happens to social movements when the democratic transition they have been fighting for stalls or even fails? How do movements operate in a hostile political environment that is bereft of opportunities and in which the actions of the government and other authorities seek to exclude or repress oppositional voices? How do activists sustain commitment in the face of apathy and even opposition? When a movement declines, it does not necessarily disappear. Rather, pockets of movement activity, or free spaces, continue to exist and can become the starting points of a new cycle of the same movement or a new movement at a future time (Taylor 1989). It may be that the path and speed of democratization are influenced, at least in part, by the strength and characteristics of the free spaces, or small-scale settings and indigenous networks within a community, that nurture counterhegemonic frames and oppositional identities during the doldrums, or unfavorable political conditions that promote movement decline (Tilly 2000; Reed and Foran 2002). These free spaces have been referred to variously as "cultures of solidarity," "safe spaces," "submerged networks," "social movement communities," "movement halfway houses," "political cultures of opposition," "beloved communities," and "abeyance structures" (Taylor 1989). As Francesca Polletta (1999) notes, free spaces are important not only for the distinct roles they play in maintaining democratic practices but also as enduring outcomes of protest that can serve as pipelines to future mobilization.

The expansion of women's legal, property, and marital rights was essential to the process of democratization in the nineteenth-century United States and in many Western societies. Women's movements have been instrumental in the transition to democracy and have had an impact on democratization through adopting distinctive practices and forms of activism suited to different and shifting political contexts. Women suffragists mobilized for citizenship rights, including the vote, across North America and Europe in the late nineteenth and early twentieth centuries (Chafetz and Dworkin 1986). Other women's democratization movements include the U.S. women's right-to-jury movement, which persisted from the late nineteenth century to 1968, when Mississippi became the final U.S. state to allow women the right to serve on juries (McCammon 2012). Because citizenship rights are pivotal to democracy, these examples illuminate how women's movements have been instrumental to democratization and to the creation of significant changes in political structures. In all democratic societies, the advancement of women's position in society has been fundamental to democratization. While previous analyses of democratic transition have tended to emphasize social class as the "master key" (Rueschemeyer, Stephens, and Stephens 1992: 5) to democratization processes, attention to women's mobilization reveals the significance of gender in democratization.

In a study completed in the early 1980s, Janet Saltzman Chafetz and Anthony Gary Dworkin (1986) divided women's movements into two waves (1850–1950 and 1960–mid-1980s) after analyzing forty-eight movements from around the world, including India, Latin America, the Caribbean, North and South America, Europe, Australia, and New Zealand. Since that study, women's movements have continued to mobilize in these countries, as well as in Eastern Europe, Central and South America, sub-Saharan Africa, the Middle East, and elsewhere. Women's mobilizations have been heterogeneous and have varied widely on the basis of national context and the racial, ethnic, and sexual composition and the ideas and practices of indigenous groups and societies. During the 1970s and 1980s, for example, Argentinian mothers and grandmothers organized a movement for human rights that deployed motherhood and family as forms of symbolic capital (Brysk 1994). In the United States, women's movements peaked during two periods of political liberalization that provided fertile ground for protest: the 1830s–1920s, which gave rise first to the abolitionist and then the suffrage movements, and the 1960s and 1970s, which spawned the civil rights, antiwar, and women's and gay liberation movements (Costain 1992; Katzenstein and Mueller 1987; Reger 2005).

Verta Taylor (1989) introduced the concept of abeyance to understand what happened to feminist activists and organizations between these two waves of activism, and the concept of abeyance has changed scholars' interpretation of the history of the U.S. women's movement (Reger 2005; A. Crossley 2014). Abeyance theory delineates the organizational and cultural processes that explain how the women's movement managed to survive the post–World War II period in spite of widespread opposition to women's rights that emerged in the larger society after suffragists won the voting rights campaign. For scholars of social movements, one of the most lasting contributions of the abeyance framework is to uncover previously overlooked or unrecognized pockets of feminist activism between peak cycles of mobilization (Weigand 2001; Rupp and Taylor 1987). Abeyance depicts a holding process by which social movements try to sustain themselves under unfavorable political conditions and provide continuity from one stage of mobilization to the next. The abeyance formulation calls attention to previously unexplored phases of social movement development when it is difficult to mobilize large masses of participants, allowing scholars to understand the "carry-overs and carry-ons" between movements (Gusfield 1981: 324).

In a comparative study of women's movements and democratic transitions, Jocelyn Viterna and Kathleen M. Fallon found that one important factor in the success of women's mobilization during periods of democratic transition is that "women's past activism legitimates present-day feminist demands" (2008: 686). Their findings regarding the significance of organizational holdovers and abeyance structures for movement continuity suggest the potential applicability of the abeyance formulation for understanding the complex role of movements during periods of democratic transition. Thus far, scholars have identified abeyance processes in the American New Left (Weigand 2001), agrarian mobilization in the United States (Mooney and Majka 1995), French socialism (Fillieule 2004), the American civil rights movement (Rojas 2007), Australian feminism (Grey and Sawer 2008), the transnational homophile movement (Rupp 2011), grassroots community organizing (Holland and Cable 2002), and peace movements (Kendrick 2000; Edwards and Marullo 1995; Klandermans 2010).

In this chapter, we discuss the concept of abeyance to understand one of the ways that social movement networks contribute to democratization processes, especially under conditions of threat and repression. We draw on new research on the contemporary U.S. women's movement to present an extension of the initial abeyance formulation (Taylor 1989) that accounts for different movement trajectories during periods of abeyance (A. Crossley 2014). Our analysis points to some of the ways abeyance shapes a challenging group's field of contention, collective identity, and tactical repertoires. After outlining our data sources, we briefly discuss the abeyance framework and then propose three variables that help us understand different movement trajectories during periods of abeyance. We have two main objectives in this chapter. The first is to extend the abeyance framework to reflect the characteristics of movements as they relate specifically to regime-movement interaction. The second is to broaden our understanding of different movement trajectories during times of abeyance.

Data

The case we discuss here is feminist mobilization among college-age students during a period of abeyance for the U.S. women's movement (see A. Crossley 2014; A. Crossley, forthcoming). Feminist scholars frequently have looked to college students to understand whether feminist mobilizations persist, although to date there has been very little research on feminist organizing among college women (for exceptions, see Reger 2005, 2012). Data for this study are based on in-depth interviews with contemporary feminists and observation of feminist student groups at three U.S. institutions of higher education: the University of California at Santa Barbara (UCSB), a midsize public university in California; the University of Minnesota, a large Big Ten public university in St. Paul and Minneapolis; and Smith College, a small, women's liberal arts college in Northampton, Massachusetts. By employing a multicampus study, we are able to compare meanings of feminist mobilization in different regions of the country and in different institutional contexts with distinct student demographics. Each campus also has a distinctive activist culture.

Respondents were recruited through snowball procedures: first, through the participant observation portion of research; second, through announcements made in undergraduate classes; and third, through posting and distributing fliers in high-traffic areas of each campus. Alison Crossley conducted seventy-five interviews with undergraduate college students, primarily between the ages of eighteen and twenty-one. Participants self-identified as white (forty-two), Latina/o (eight), mixed race/other (thirteen), Asian American (six), African American (five), and American Indian (one); heterosexual (forty-six), queer (nine), bisexual (nine), gay/lesbian (seven), queer and bisexual (one), and nonspecified sexuality (three); and women (sixty-eight) and men (seven), including a transgender male. Many were first-generation college students, and twenty-seven self-identified as poor, working class, or lower-middle class and forty-eight as in middle class. Approximately a third of the interview participants belonged to feminist organizations and also served as key informants about their communities. The remaining participants were involved in social-justice-oriented organizations or expressed interest in feminist, gender, or social justice issues. The interviews were tape recorded and transcribed and analyzed.

The Abeyance Formulation

As C. Tilly (1995) noted, the ways that people act together in pursuit of shared interests varies considerably. The factors that promote movement abeyance are both structural and cultural, as well as internal and external to a movement. Taylor's initial theory of abeyance (1989) drew on political-process assumptions about the significance of political opportunity and resource mobilization precepts regarding the importance of organizational factors for understanding movement emergence, strength, and decline. Changing political, cultural, and institutional contexts steer activist networks and social movement organizations toward alteration of repertoires of contention during periods of abeyance. Although early versions of the formulation emphasized the political and structural context that contributes to abeyance, Taylor and her collaborators increasingly recognized the significance of culture in abeyance. Culture is central to abeyance cycles not just as ideology, practices, and shared discourse in a particular activist community but as both the discursive context for mobilization and the foundation for the ties—that is, the identities and emotional investments—that make up the free spaces that challenging groups use to combat their disadvantages (Taylor and Rupp 1993; Taylor 2010). Mapping structural relationships between collective actors without understanding the meaning of those relations will not aid understanding the form and timing of collective action. Identity and emotion, for example, both foster and impede mobilization (Taylor and Leitz 2010). The promise of abeyance as a concept rests on its integration of structural characteristics of the free space (e.g., isolation, centralization) with the meanings attached to participation in the free space (e.g., identity, solidarity).

The abeyance concept acknowledges that the oppressed are not without free spaces, which provide indigenous resources, frames of meaning, and strategies to combat their oppression (Morris 1986; Polletta 1999; Rupp and Taylor 2003; Evans and Boyte 1992). For example, the black church has historically been such a space for at least some African Americans, and gay bars and lesbian feminist communities have filled a similar function for the gay and lesbian movement. The abeyance formulation calls attention to free spaces that derive specifically from prior phases of mobilization and collection action; they often are former movement organizations, such as the League of Women Voters, the National Association for the Advancement of Colored People, the National Woman's Party, the Women's International League for Peace and Freedom, and the National Rifle Association, that have evolved into civic organizations. In their study of the women's movement, Leila Rupp and Verta Taylor (1987; Taylor 1989; Taylor and Rupp 1993) found that the following organizational factors allowed feminist groups to survive and continue during a period of abeyance: *longevity of attachment* to movement organizations, intense levels of individual *commit-*

ment to movement goals and tactics, *exclusiveness* in terms of membership, *centralization* that ensures organizational stability and sustained action among a small group of highly committed activists, and a rich political *culture* that promotes solidarity, oppositional consciousness, and continued involvement in the movement. It is in the dense interactive network of indigenous groups and institutions where people imagine alternative visions, plot strategies for overcoming obstacles to reaching their goals, and form identities, solidarities, and interests that facilitate mobilization (Brysk 2000). As Eric Hirsh explains, "Havens insulate the challenging group from the rationalizing ideologies normally disseminated by the society's dominant group" (1990: 206).

What scholars tended to overlook before the abeyance formulation is the critical importance of movement-to-movement influence in explaining the survival and long-term endurance of movements to promote democratization, such as feminism, peace activism, civil rights and antiracist movements, gay and lesbian movements, labor movements, and socialism. For example, although the U.S. women's movement of the late 1960s and 1970s emerged at the height of the 1960s cycle of protest, women had been organizing on their own behalf for at least a century, and these predecessors made important organizational, ideological, and tactical contributions to the emerging mass feminist mobilization (Rupp and Taylor 1987; Weigand 2001). Similarly, women's movements influenced the larger movements of the New Left with a broad-based critique of male dominance that linked sexism with racism, capitalism, and militarism (Whittier 1995; Meyer and Whittier 1994; Roth 2004). On a global scale, human rights organizing ebbs and flows depending on global and local networks composed of participants from a variety of social movements, including women's movements, peace movements, and environmental movements (Brysk 2000; Keck and Sikkink 1998). Preexisting movements provide free spaces that foster the construction of identities and relationships that can be mobilized by future collective actors (Taylor et al. 2009).

Taylor identified three principal ways that abeyance structures contribute to subsequent rounds of mobilization. First, because of the strong bonds that form between activists struggling to maintain their commitment against heavy odds, abeyance structures provide a preexisting *activist network* with the activist capital (i.e., network ties, activist identities, injustice frames, etc.) to sustain the challenge until the political and social context becomes amenable to mobilization. Second, for a movement to survive periods of relative hiatus, activists must alter their goals to include *tactical repertoires* that are modular and low cost and that can be deployed by a relatively smaller number of activists. This increases the collective action repertoires available to a challenging group. Third, a group of relatively isolated activists struggling to maintain a political community can be held together only by solidarity, shared commitment, a deep sense of purpose, or a *collective identity* that can then become an important symbolic resource for subsequent mobilizations (Taylor 1989; Rupp and Taylor 1999; Taylor et al. 2009).

In an abeyance phase, social movements largely rely on internally oriented activities, often of a cultural nature, to maintain their identity and political vision (Taylor and Rupp 1993; Staggenborg and Lecomte 2009). Nevertheless, a movement can be highly influential on subsequent movements, even if it fails to achieve its intended aims, through its discourses and frames, collective identity, and tactics. Consider, for example, the phrase, "the personal is political," which emerged out of the women's consciousness-raising movement as a way of linking private experiences to gender domination. The use of coming out as a tactic has spilled over to the gay and lesbian movement (Whittier 2012). Equality Florida's Refuse to Lie campaign encourages legally married same-sex couples to refuse to check "single" on their federal tax forms as a political act.

Scholars agree that women's movements in many Western societies, such as the United States, Canada, Australia, New Zealand, England, and Japan, are currently in stages of abeyance (Grey and Sawer 2008). In the United States, several interconnected factors have created a period of feminist abeyance. Women's movement participants, nevertheless, have found supportive environments inside the state, church, and military (Katzenstein 1998), which some scholars argue is a marker of abeyance (Bagguley 2002). Feminism inside institutions of higher education, in the form of women's studies departments, women's centers, and women-friendly policies, on the one hand, is a sign of movement success, since access to education was one of the major goals of the women's movement. On the other hand, educational institutions have also created numerous opportunities for feminist contention and mobilization (A. Crossley 2014; A. Crossley, forthcoming). Institutional embeddedness also has important consequences for the transmission of feminist knowledge and ideas to college students during periods of abeyance. Indeed, individual social movement participation varies significantly over a lifetime, depending on biographical availability and changes in a life course (Corrigall-Brown 2012a, 2012b). Most scholars, however, consider one of the main cultural causes of abeyance to be the perpetuation of popular discourses that stigmatize and vilify feminists and assert that gender equality in the United States has been achieved (A. Crossley 2010). Historically, college students have been the prime participants in movements for social change, and our findings confirm Jo Reger's analysis that "feminism is everywhere and nowhere" (2012: 186)—that is, that women's mobilizations and feminist protest continue to exist on college campuses in the United States but in myriad forms and variations (A. Crossley, forthcoming).

Fields of Contention, Collective Identities, and Tactical Repertoires

Drawing from our research on feminist mobilization on campus and the existing literature on women's movements, we extend abeyance theory by proposing three factors that influence social movement trajectories during periods of abeyance. First, when the political environment takes a more politically repressive trajectory and challenging groups lose access to the political and electoral process, they may redirect their actions away from the state or government entities previously receptive to mobilization to locate new targets in more open and receptive *fields of contention*. Social movements and protests typically occur within democratic states, and their targets are typically state, government, and other authorities in a position to implement the demands of collective actors. However, protestors also challenge nonstate institutions, such as religious denominations, universities and their administrations, and medical authorities and health care institutions (Van Dyke, Soule, and Taylor 2004). When the state is not receptive to democratic protest, social movements and other collective challengers may redirect claim making to other institutional contexts. While the opportunities afforded by these contexts vary, in democratic societies power is diffuse and rests in multiple institutional arenas (Armstrong and Bernstein 2008). A field of contention is a structured arena of conflict that includes all relevant actors to whom a social movement might be connected in pursuing its claims (Taylor and Zald 2010; Brown 2007; N. Crossley 2006). Thus, when political elites and alignments are not receptive to feminist claim making, social movements and other challenging groups frequently turn to educational, religious, health, or other institutions to stake their claims.

Second, a considerable body of scholarship demonstrates that *collective identity* is crucial in social movement abeyance both as an antecedent or motive of participants and as an outcome or achievement of protest (Taylor 2010; Taylor et al. 2009; Whittier 1995; Taylor and Whittier 1992). *Collective identity* is the shared definition of a group that derives from members' common interests and solidarity (Taylor and Whittier 1992). In social movements based on fundamental cleavages, such as gender, race and ethnicity, and class, and in movements with a long life span, many different collective identities exist over the course of the movement's history (Whittier 1995), and these different collective identities often simultaneously compete for salience (Ghaziani 2008) and may in turn influence other movements (Meyer and Whittier 1994; Taylor et al. 2009). We find that contemporary abeyance structures in the women's movement foster wide-ranging, multiple, and inclusive collective identities that stimulate movement-to-movement influence.

Finally, one of the principle ways that collective actors form solidarity and common purpose is through contentious performances or protest tactics. *Tactical repertoires* are intentional and strategic forms of claim making linking social movement actors to each other, opponents, and authorities (Taylor, Rupp, and Gamson 2004; Tilly 1986; Taylor and Van Dyke 2004). When mass support for a challenging group's claim declines significantly, as is the case in abeyance cycles, we find that tactical repertoires shift and movement participants often turn to everyday actions and Internet mobilization, in addition to traditional forms of protest. Below, we further develop each of these concepts, presenting preliminary data from our study of feminism among U.S. college women (see A. Crossley 2014).

Fields of Contention

Although most social movements target the state (McAdam, Tarrow, and Tilly 2001), all institutional complexes are potentially subject to the pressures of social movements (Taylor and Zald 2010; Snow 2004; Van Dyke, Soule, and Taylor 2004). The structure of power in families; inequalities in the workplace; the operation of the military; the limit or expansion of religious authority; the regulation of the media and entertainment; the system of local, state, and federal taxation; the acquisition of human capital in education; and medical authority and practice—in other words, the exercise of power in any institutional arena—become sites of political and movement contestation. In the past, social movements were explicitly understood as extrainstitutional, and scholars have only recently begun to analyze the dynamics of social movements inside institutions (Katzenstein 1998; Rojas 2007; Banaszak-Holl, Levitsky, and Zald 2010; Raeburn 2004). Elizabeth A. Armstrong and Mary Bernstein (2008) recently proposed a "multi-institutional politics approach" to social movements that extends the insights of state-centered approaches by directing attention to the distinctive institutional fields in which a social movement mobilizes and to the ways they influence mobilization processes.

Institutions become particularly receptive locations or fields of contention during periods of abeyance (Grey and Sawer 2008). Paul Bagguley argues that the British women's movement is in abeyance primarily because the tactics and targets have changed from public protest to institutional contexts (2002: 173) and describes abeyance as "the shift of activism from mobilizing people, from public protest to bureaucratic struggles to obtain funding to maintain organizations that provide services" (181).

Not all scholars of the women's movement find that mobilization is diminished by institutional embeddedness, however (Staggenborg 1998). In her research on feminist mobilization in the Catholic Church and military, Mary Fainsod Katzenstein found that opportunities existed for protest and other forms of claim making that challenged the male-dominated church hierarchy (1998; see also Staggenborg and Taylor 2005).

Similarly, we found that contemporary feminist mobilization by college students included planning public protests and confronting objectionable institutional policies and that tactics were not relegated to bureaucratic participation or service provision (A. Crossley 2014). Students with feminist organizational affiliations mobilized their peers around a host of social justice issues. They protested at their university's administration building and at the state capital against rising fees and tuition, against the repression of antiwar activists by the FBI, and against increasing restrictions on women's reproductive rights. They were supported by a variety of institutional entities, such as the student government, national women's organizations, and nationally chartered multicultural sororities. This broad base of support afforded the organizations significant resources for mobilization, although support varied by institutional context.

One organization employed its own staff member-advisor, and another hosted a large dinner banquet with a famous feminist scholar as speaker. At UCSB, students reported that their campus nourished feminism. Lisa said, "I think there's a general climate among UCSB faculty and students where it's very inviting toward feminism. I feel like feminism could be a difficult thing, and it might even be shunned. But on this campus it's very encouraged." These examples underscore the institutional opportunities for mobilization and the development of a movement culture among feminists on college campuses.

However, very little research on feminism is performed today within institutions of higher education other than in the women's centers and women's studies departments created by feminists in the 1960s and 1970s. Our analysis suggests that there are organized pockets or feminist free spaces in other areas of the university. Multicultural sororities, which in our case included predominantly Latina and African American women, were an important location for feminist mobilization. UCSB student Summer, who is a member of a historically black sorority and a non-Greek student organization, both of which she described as feminist, stated that "Greek affairs is very, very, very supportive" of her activism, as is the student government. These sororities created feminist networks and contributed to a larger feminist social movement community on campus. Members of multicultural sororities, such as Summer, reported that feminism was implicit in the collective identities of their organizations, which worked to empower members, provide professional and social opportunities, and serve their community through volunteer work and outreach. Members also spoke about how their sororities articulated feminist goals and cosponsored events with other feminist organizations, which demonstrates the extent to which feminist networks have diffused in institutional settings.

Supporting Traci M. Sawyers and David S. Meyer's (1999) claim that movements in periods of abeyance often miss valuable opportunities for mobilization, women's movement participants in this research were also limited by their institutional contexts. Although the universities provided numerous benefits to student organizations, even during severe budget cuts in recent years, each campus also imposed restrictions that curtailed movement participation. For example, UCSB student Isabela explained that her group's affiliation with student government restricted them from mobilizing around any topic related to abortion. She explained that the group was prohibited from mentioning "any political ideologies or anything to do with politics. So that's why, a lot of times, our organization has to step back. Like with the whole Planned Parenthood controversy, we can only take a certain stance on it. We can't endorse Planned Parenthood." Since funding depended on following the rules, the students took these restrictions seriously, despite their concern, even outrage, over the accessibility of women's health care and reproductive health services and the national threats to Planned Parenthood (A. Crossley, forthcoming).

Institutional surveillance of student organizations ensured compliance with university policies. The weekly meetings of a student-government-funded women's organization at UCSB included the attendance of a long-time university administrator who clarified rules, decision-making procedures, and funding restrictions. Although her presence as a university official initially seemed out of place at the casual meetings, the students in the organization expressed appreciation for her guidance, because they had to negotiate numerous university policies. At the University of Minnesota, the feminist collective had a large resource center, lounge, and office in the student union and also employed a part-time staff member of their choosing. While they experienced no direct oversight, members believed that the university administration was not receptive to feminist claims making. Lauren said, "It's really frustrating, and I don't feel supported by the university at all. I think that my professors, absolutely, they support my activism, but I think the university, in general, doesn't." This was hardly surprising given the anti-institutional and radical positions for which the feminist collective was known. During our interviews and observation, members of the feminist collective along with other campus activists organized an impressive campaign and all-day event that questioned the university's policy on diversity and accessibility to underrepresented populations.

Scholars caution that institutional arms of social movements may become polarized from grassroots or radical wings (Sawyers and Meyer 1999) and that without the support of grassroots activists, women's movements are "vulnerable to backlash, state control, or merely a lack of resources" (Gray 2008: 74). Our findings suggest, however, that during periods of abeyance, institutions may provide a variety of unexpected opportunities for mobilization (Staggenborg 1996). While the institutional context did sometimes constrain mobilization, participants found numerous chances to mobilize, forge, and sustain feminist culture and to engage in protest and other forms of contentious claim making (see A. Crossley 2014).

Collective Identity

Collective identities are transient in the sense that they change over the life cycle of a movement as a result of historical context (Klandermans 1994; Whittier 1995; Bernstein 1997), the organizational characteristics of movements (Reger 2002), internal identity disputes (Taylor and Rupp 1993; J. Gamson 1995a, 1995b), and a movement's targets (Bernstein 1997; Einwohner 2002; Rupp and Taylor 2003; Leitz and Taylor 2010). Collective identities are generally constructed by interacting layers of social movement organizations and individuals with personal and social identities that at times conflict with each other (Rupp and Taylor 1999), and movements may have numerous collective identities coexisting simultaneously (Stryker, Owens, and White 2000). In the original abeyance formulation, Taylor (1989) argued that feminist organizations survived the post–World War II backlash by using internally oriented cultural activities and building deep emotional connections. These allowed activists to maintain a feminist collective identity and political vision that was crucial to the resurgence of the women's movement in the mid-1960s. Our research suggests that contemporary abeyance structures are more likely to foster open and permeable collective identities that emphasize inclusivity based on race, class, gender, and sexuality. These collective identities are created and sustained through both internally oriented activities and the diffusion of collective identities to other movements and networks (A. Crossley 2014).

The U.S. women's movement has never had a coherent collective identity, although feminist organizations, despite being composed of women of diverse backgrounds, sometimes organized around similar injustices (Taylor and Rupp 1993; Whittier 1995; Roth 2004, 2010; Breines 2006). It is not surprising that the feminist collective identities in this study varied considerably by institution. Smith College is an elite institution where feminism is a common topic of discussion both inside and outside the classroom, and students possess a strong sense of political efficacy (Van Dyke 1998). Student Bette said that while at Smith she did not need to "be a super feminist" or wear her "feminist cape," because it is a place where women and feminists are already empowered. Smith students spoke comfortably about queer feminisms and the importance of transinclusion in feminist communities, and the largest feminist organization on campus was a transgender group. Smith students were adept with the language of queer theory, used terms such as "heteronormativity" and "cisgender" when discussing the complexities of feminism, and spoke more uniformly and articulately about feminism than did students on the other two campuses. The level of assumed feminism at Smith was so striking that some students admitted to defining their feminist identities and perceptions of feminism differently according to whether they were on the Smith campus or in the real world. Nearly all Smith interviewees described their college in terms of its feminist culture and encouragement of strong women.

In contrast, feminism did not emerge as an important element in students' descriptions of the two other schools, where feminism was neither engrained in the campus cultures nor embraced by the majority of students. The University of Minnesota and UCSB had considerably larger student bodies and lacked an established feminist culture, but feminist communities on campus appeared more tightly knit and their collective identities more monolithic than those at Smith. For example, University of Minnesota students used strong language to affirm the importance of being a member of a feminist organization. University of Minnesota student Sophia said that participation in her feminist organization was "hugely important" to her feminism. Many students believed their feminist organization helped integrate them into a "feminist community" at the university. The term *feminist community* was not used as frequently by students on the other two campuses. We speculate that this is because feminist students on the larger campuses are distinguished and to some extent isolated and stigmatized from the rest of the student body as a result of their feminist consciousness and its influence on their everyday lives. Students at Smith were assumed to be feminists, and the lack of a need for identity validation seemed to curtail their motivation to express a sense of feminist solidarity or to educate their peers about feminism.

The feminist collective identity at UCSB was more cohesive and unified than at the other two research sites, exhibited by numerous campus feminist organizations in which coalitions and overlapping networks created a large feminist social movement community (A. Crossley 2014). These networks appeared to be facilitated primarily by Latina students, reflecting the demographic makeup of UCSB, recently named a Hispanic-Serving Institution. One event that highlights the cohesiveness of feminists at UCSB is an annual banquet to celebrate women's groups on campus. This year's theme, "Building a Collective Consciousness through Creating Community," drew over 250 attendees for a lecture on women of color feminism by Cherríe Moraga.

Despite institutional and local differences, we found some cross-institutional commonalities in collective identities. Students at all three campuses had grievances about sexual assault and reproductive rights, and each campus had a student chapter of a national women's organization, such as the National Organization for Women or Planned Parenthood. Most striking, however, was the expansiveness of the collective identities at each school. This was vividly illustrated in Northampton, where a feminist organization at Smith hosted a cupcake social. The purpose of the event, according to Gabrielle, an organizer, was to "show students that feminism is broader than the issues they think it includes" and to create feminist community. Participating organizations included Transcending Gender (focusing on transgender inclusion and education and represented with a sign reading "Feminists are concerned with all people"), the National Organization for Women, Radical Catholic Feminists of Smith (a spiritual organization that also advocates for women to participate more actively in the Catholic Church), Afternoon Tea (a social group that hosts period movie nights and teas), Smith Republicans (sporting a sign at their table reading "Republicans Can Be Feminist Too"), Smith Democrats, STAND (a group that advocates for human rights and fair labor practices), and Body Talk (a body acceptance organization). A student at the STAND table said that issues of genocide and conflict minerals are feminist. Several students explained that their organizations qualified as feminist because the social inequalities with which they were most concerned disproportionately affected women.

A large yellow banner hung in the Smith campus center to advertise this event, with the slogan SPREAD FEMINISM in multicolored letters. This theme reflected that individuals and organizations at each campus sought to promote feminist identities and ideologies throughout their campus networks. Even the members of organizations that did not explicitly present themselves as feminist in their names or mission statements explained the incorporation of feminist values and solidarity in their organizing. The students who belonged to explicitly feminist organizations described the significance of feminism to their organizations; referred to their grievances in intersectional terms, noting the interactions of race, class, gender, and sexuality; and participated in cross-movement coalitions (W. Gamson [1975] 1990; Van Dyke 2003; Van Dyke and McCammon 2010).

The collective identities of these feminist social movement communities were far more inclusive than those of campus feminist organizations in the 1970s and early 1980s (Freeman 1975), reflecting self-definitions that embraced multiple and intersecting identities of race, class, gender, and sexuality, and many students emphasized the importance of an intersectional understanding of feminism (A. Crossley, forthcoming). Camille, a UCSB student who identified as a woman of color feminist, spoke of the importance of intersectionality in feminism:

> Women of color are embracing feminism more as it becomes more inclusive. The feminist framework is very specific. It's talking about intersections. I don't think any other framework is talking about intersections. I think that's why feminism is going to be successful. That's what our generation is going to add to it, you know. It's not about women—it's about gender, and class and race, and nationality, and ability. So many identities. That's what I love!

To Camille and many other students, the greatest strength of feminism was the inclusivity and intersectionality of the movement, exhibited in the group's embrace of the "we-ness" of feminism and in the feminist organization's activities, which included cooperation with other social justice groups on campus. For example, a UCSB feminist student organization hosted an event with a black student organization about domestic violence and sexual assault in African American communities, and likewise a University of Minnesota feminist organization hosted events with the queer student organization and the disabled student center (A. Crossley 2014).

In contrast to Taylor's original abeyance formulation, which emphasized the exclusive and internal orientation of feminist collective identity in the post–World War II period (Taylor 1989), we found that the collective identities of young contemporary feminists are more inclusive and externally oriented (Staggenborg and Taylor 2005). Further, the collective identities supported and sustained by feminist organizations and networks on each of the campuses spilled over to other movements and participants, blurring the boundaries between which elements of feminist collective identity are internal and which are external to the movement (Meyer and Whittier 1994). Movement participants extended feminist frames to immigrant rights movements, antiwar movements, and movements fighting for accessible public education (Benford and Snow 2000; Snow et al. 1986). This kind of identity work makes it hard to distinguish between who is inside and who is outside the movement, reflecting recent perspectives on the intersectional nature of collective identity construction (Reger, Myers, and Einwohner 2008). Such a collective identity may also foster resurgence in feminist mobilization as a result of inter- and intramovement solidarity (Taylor 1989; Melucci 1995; Rupp and Taylor 1999).

Tactical Repertoires

Gender and social movement scholars have expanded theories of tactical repertoires and goals to understand the distinctively gendered forms of activism deployed by women's movements that have contributed to their endurance (Taft 2010; Taylor 1996; Taylor and Van Dyke 2004; A. Crossley, forthcoming). A large body of scholarship demonstrates that repertoires of contention change during periods of abeyance, and in particular, movements tend to focus on cultural events that ensure the maintenance of collective identity and promote movement continuity (Staggenborg 1998; Taylor and Rupp 1993; Staggenborg and Taylor 2005; Staggenborg and Lang 2007). We found that feminist groups on college campuses rely heavily on cultural events for mobilization. Tactical similarities also exist between campuses, demonstrating both continuity from previous phases of feminist mobilization and tactical diffusion between movement organizations across universities (Soule 1997).

Women's movement scholars have analyzed how the incorporation of feminist principles in everyday life and interaction sustains movements during inhospitable periods, and it remains an important feature of contemporary feminist culture (Whittier 1995; Taylor and Whittier 1992; Staggenborg 1996). It is important, as Pam Oliver (1989) points out, to keep in mind that the concept of movement includes millions of everyday actions by individuals, some of whom never belonged to a movement organization. Everyday activism, which does not involve the same kind of conscious coordination that organized actions do, is often provoked by the emotion of the moment. Given the centrality of the concept of the "personal as political" to the women's movement, it should come as no surprise that a recent study by Jane Mansbridge and Katherine Flaster (2008) finds that women who reported having called someone a male chauvinist pig were motivated, in most cases, by feminist identity and solidarity. Everyday feminism, or taken-for-granted actions and behaviors in the realm of appearance, dress, consumption habits, and social relationships, expresses movement ideologies and goals. Feminist students connected their feminist consciousness to where they chose to shop, their resistance to beauty rituals, their relationship dynamics, and their career aspirations. Anne W., a Smith student, reported having "a mental framework that is engrained with feminism." University of Minnesota student Sophia said, "Feminism really is very much about the lens with which I look at the world. It impacts my daily life just in the ways that I see things and the ways that I problematize the things that I see." UCSB student Elsa said, "[My feminism is exhibited by] standing up for myself. By me being independent, by me . . . pointing out gender inequality within my workplace, amongst my circle of friends, [and] womanizing, degrading of women—I do speak up about it." Students described the influence of feminism on their everyday interactions with peers, friends, family, and even on dates, and they noted the ways feminism shaped their participation in various student organizations on campus.

Tactical repertoires during periods of abeyance may shift because challenging groups typically face a reduction in numbers and resources (Taylor 1989; A. Crossley, forthcoming). The students in this research employed a variety of innovative techniques. Students at the University of Minnesota, for example, made stencils to write feminist messages in mud that so that they would wash away in the rain. Also at the University of Minnesota, a community organizer presented an Activism 101 training, during which the facilitator provided practical advice about effectively using social media as well as how to conduct meetings and plan events. All of the organizations in this study used the Internet to further their organizational goals and, in particular, social networking sites to communicate grievances and advertise events (A. Crossley, forthcoming). A UCSB antirape organization devoted one meeting to stalking and how it is perpetuated through texting and participating on Facebook. Lisa, a member of the organization, told me that she posted numerous status updates about the seriousness of Facebook stalking and the dangers it poses. She reported receiving mostly positive feedback, and many Facebook friends inquired further about stalking and sexual assault awareness months. Many students also reported posting Facebook status updates or news articles related to feminism, social justice issues, and organizational events (A. Crossley, forthcoming). The Smith College feminist organization, which was allocated only seventeen dollars for one semester, could not afford to copy flyers, make posters, or even chalk the sidewalks on campus with notices of an upcoming event. Instead, they relied on a free Facebook event page, highlighting the utility of the Internet when faced with limited resources and support (A. Crossley, forthcoming).

Feminist blogs served as a valuable means of disseminating feminist information and creating feminist communities (Crossley et al. 2011; A Crossley, forthcoming). The most frequently accessed blog was Feministing.com, which features original commentary and links to feminist or gender-related news articles around the web. The University of Minnesota feminist collective, at a recent event, hosted the blog contributors, who have published books and become feminist fixtures in the popular media (Martin 2010; Valenti 2007, 2009). Many of the students reported that they discussed what they read on feminist blogs with roommates and friends and forwarded links to their high school and college friends via Facebook, demonstrating the potential for blogs to reach wide audiences (A. Crossley, forthcoming). Smith student Liz described blogs as "good because they also connect you with a group of people who generally have the same interest as you do, and you get a lot of meaningful and insightful information from them." Although scholars find that online debates may be more polarizing than those that take place offline (Van Stekelenburg, Oegema, and Klandermans 2010), the accessibility of computers and ease of blogging and website creation augments existing social movement organizations and allows movement participants to communicate their messages and create communities and solidarities when other resources are unavailable (McCaughey and Ayers 2003; Rowe 2008; A. Crossley, forthcoming).

Our analysis illuminates how cultural tactics remain consistent over time in some respects but also shift according to changes in communication technology and the availability of resources. The tactical repertoires of campus feminists are particularly appropriate during periods of abeyance, but they also function in a manner similar to the letter-writing campaigns of the nineteenth century or consciousness-raising groups of the 1970s. In all cases, tactics provide opportunities for communication and transmission of information, community building, and personal transformation. As earlier formulations of abeyance have demonstrated, these expanded repertoires of contention benefit subsequent mobilization even if a movement does not realize its goals (Taylor 1989).

Conclusion

The abeyance formulation has been an influential theory in the field of social movements for its attention to the ways movements manage to survive and sustain themselves in inhospitable climates or even in times of threat. Democratic transitions do take place, despite the tendency of authoritarian and repressive governments to decrease the potential for social movement activity because of restricted access to the state, lack of democratic freedoms, and state repression (Almeida 2008). Similarly, democratic states vary in their openness to challenges, making abeyance theory useful for understanding the role of social protest and social movement communities during challenges.

In this chapter, we apply and extend theories of abeyance to understand the continuity and changes in feminist mobilization over time. Drawing from new data and recent scholarship on women's movements, we use the case of feminist mobilization among U.S. college students to show how abeyance can affect a movement's field of contention, collective identity, and tactical repertoire (A. Crossley 2014). We discuss each of these elements as though they operate in isolation from one another, yet each element influences the other. First, we describe how, during periods of abeyance, institutional locations are important sites for feminist mobilization and everyday feminism. Once we recognize the ways that fields of contention affect the location and nature of movements in periods of abeyance, we find feminist organizing happening in unexpected places, such as within multicultural sororities and in organizations funded by student government, and we open our eyes to feminists' use of obtrusive and unobtrusive tactics. Depending on the context, we find that educational institutions provide opportunities for, as well as constraints on, student mobilizing (see A. Crossley 2014).

Second, we find on each campus cohesive feminist collective identities and the usual identity disputes involved in mobilization. Feminist identities vary according to campus feminist cultures and the racial/ethnic, class, and sexual/

gender compositions of activist groups. At each campus, feminist collective identities spilled over to other organizations and movements, such as antiwar, global justice, antiracist, immigrant rights, and queer, demonstrating how college students link feminism and gender inequality to a wide variety of other social injustice issues. This reflects the movement-to-movement influence that has always been important to the long-term continuity of feminism.

Third, we find that contemporary women's movement tactics remain consistent with those used by previous eras of feminist mobilization, including education, lobbying and petitioning, consciousness raising, everyday feminism, and community building. However, the use of social media and blogging appear to be key tactics during periods when organizations received little funding and when a movement lacks mass appeal (A. Crossley, forthcoming). Students' focus on "social justice," a key component of democratization, is also a divergence from earlier forms of women's movement organizing that tended to concentrate on legal rights.

Our research also joins that of recent scholars who argue for the continued existence of the contemporary U.S. women's movement (Reger 2012; Staggenborg and Taylor 2005; Gilmore 2008; Rupp and Taylor 2005; A. Crossley 2014), even as pundits continue to write its obituary, and it highlights a range of feminist free spaces in which democratic possibilities and feminism are still spoken, long after the decline of the second wave of mass feminism. Participants in women's movements have secured numerous citizen rights and have been important actors in protest waves that have led to democratization in all regions of the world. While the significance of working-class mobilization to democratic transitions has been documented in numerous world regions (Rueschemeyer, Stephens, and Stephens 1992), less attention has been paid to the role of women's movements in processes of democratization.

Research documenting abeyance structures has found that during periods of abeyance, feminist protest moves into unexpected institutional locations—for example, medicine and health care in the United States (Taylor and Zald 2010)—and the institutional context influences the evolution of collective identities and tactical repertoires (A. Crossley 2014). The revised abeyance framework presented in this chapter allows scholars to understand how different movement trajectories during abeyance are linked to the institutional context of activism and variations in political regimes (e.g., whether they are authoritarian or democratic). The abeyance formulation also has implications for understanding movement resurgence. Our analysis suggests that during periods of abeyance, expanded collective identities may create movement-to-movement coalitions and widespread activist networks, which are critical for movement resurgence (Taylor 1989; Taylor et al. 2009). Coalitions have also been found to be essential for the successful mobilization of women's movements in new democracies (Viterna and Fallon 2008).

Attention to abeyance cycles leads to a rethinking of such fundamental questions as what counts as a movement, what counts as social protest, and when does an episode of contention begin and end. The abeyance framework has facilitated our understanding of movement-to-movement influence between different periods of mobilization and different movements, as well as our understanding of transnational feminism by tracing links between oppositional groups across political and geographical boundaries (Rupp 2011). As scholars continue to study movements in cycles of abeyance, remaining issues that should be addressed include the relationship between personal and collective identities, the role of new media in collective identity formation, how the strength of connections between different movement organizations in different phases of mobilization affects movement continuity, and the multiple collective identities that characterize and sometimes divide mature movements. Abeyance has not yet been used widely to understand social movements in times of democratic transition, but as illustrated in this chapter, it holds potential to shed light on the dynamics of mobilization over time.

REFERENCES

Almeida, Paul D. 2008. *Waves of Protest: Popular Struggle in El Salvador, 1925–2005.* Minneapolis: University of Minnesota Press.

Armstrong, Elizabeth A., and Mary Bernstein. 2008. "Culture, Power, and Institutions: A Multi-institutional Politics Approach to Social Movements." *Sociological Theory* 26:74–99.

Bagguley, Paul. 2002. "Contemporary British Feminism: A Social Movement in Abeyance?" *Social Movement Studies* 1:169–185.

Banaszak-Holl, Jane, Sandra R. Levitsky, and Mayer N. Zald. 2010. *Social Movements and the Transformation of American Health Care.* Oxford: Oxford University Press.

Benford, Robert D., and David A. Snow. 2000. "Framing Processes and Social Movements: An Overview and Assessment." *Annual Review of Sociology* 26:611–639.

Bernstein, Mary. 1997. "Celebration and Suppression: The Strategic Uses of Identity by the Lesbian and Gay Movement." *American Journal of Sociology* 103:531–565.

Blee, Kathleen. 2012. *Democracy in the Making: How Activist Groups Form.* Oxford: Oxford University Press.

Breines, Winifred. 2006. *The Trouble between Us: An Uneasy History of White and Black Women in the Feminist Movement.* New York: Oxford University Press.

Brown, Phil. 2007. *Contested Illnesses and the Environmental Health Movement.* New York: Columbia University Press.

Brysk, Alison. 1994. *The Politics of Human Rights in Argentina: Protest, Change, and Democratization.* Stanford, CA: Stanford University Press.

———. 2000. *From Tribal Village to Global Village: Indian Rights and International Relations in Latin America.* Stanford, CA: Stanford University Press.

Chafetz, Janet Saltzman, and Anthony Gary Dworkin. 1986. *Female Revolt: Women's Movements in World and Historical Perspective.* Totowa, NJ: Rowman and Allanheld.

Corrigall-Brown, Catherine. 2012a. "From the Balconies to the Barricades, and Back? Trajectories of Participation in Contentious Politics." *Journal of Civil Society* 8 (1): 17–38.

———. 2012b. *Patterns of Protest: Trajectories of Participation in Social Movements.* Stanford, CA: Stanford University Press.

Costain, Anne. 1992. *Inviting Women's Rebellion: A Political Process Interpretation of the Women's Movement*. Baltimore: Johns Hopkins University Press.

Crossley, Alison Dahl. 2010. "'When It Suits Me, I'm a Feminist': International Students Negotiating Feminist Representations." *Women's Studies International Forum* 33 (2): 125–133.

———. 2014. "Social Movement Continuity and Abeyance: Feminist Mobilization on U.S. College Campuses." Ph.D. diss., University of California, Santa Barbara.

———. Forthcoming. "Facebook Feminism: Social Media, Blogs, and New Technologies of Contemporary U.S. Feminism." *Mobilization*.

Crossley, Alison Dahl, Verta Taylor, Nancy Whittier, and Cynthia Pelak. 2011. "Forever Feminism: The Persistence of the U.S. Women's Movement, 1960–2011." In *Feminist Frontiers*, 9th ed., edited by Verta Taylor, Leila J. Rupp, and Nancy Whittier, 498–516. New York: McGraw-Hill.

Crossley, Nick. 2006. *Contesting Psychiatry: Social Movements in Mental Health*. New York: Routledge.

Edwards, Bob, and Sam Marullo. 1995. "Organizational Mortality in a Declining Social Movement: The Demise of Peace Movement Organizations in the End of the Cold War Era." *American Sociological Review* 60:908–927.

Einwohner, Rachel L. 2002. "Motivational Framing and Efficacy Maintenance: Animal Rights Activists' Use of Four Fortifying Strategies." *Sociological Quarterly* 43:509–526.

Evans, Sara M., and Harry C. Boyte. 1992. *Free Spaces: The Sources of Democratic Change in America*. Chicago: University of Chicago Press.

Fillieule, Olivier. 2004. *Devenirs militants: Approches sociologiques du desengagment* [Becoming Militant: Sociological Approaches to Disengagement]. Paris: Belin.

Freeman, Jo. 1975. *The Politics of Women's Liberation*. New York: Longman.

Gamson, Joshua. 1995a. "Must Identity Movements Self-Destruct? A Queer Dilemma." *Social Problems* 42:390–407.

———. 1995b. "The Organizational Shaping of Collective Identity: The Case of Lesbian and Gay Film Festivals in New York." *Sociological Forum* 11 (2): 231–261.

Gamson, William A. (1975) 1990. *The Strategy of Social Protest*, 2nd ed. Homewood, IL: Dorsey Press.

Ghaziani, Amin. 2008. *The Dividends of Dissent: How Conflict and Culture Work in Lesbian and Gay Marches on Washington*. Chicago: University of Chicago.

Gilmore, Stephanie, ed. 2008. *Feminist Coalitions: Historical Perspectives on Second-Wave Feminism in the United States*." Urbana: University of Illinois Press.

Gray, Gwendolyn. 2008. "Institutional, Incremental and Enduring: Women's Health Action in Canada and Australia." In *Women's Movements: Flourishing or in Abeyance?*, edited by Sandra Grey and Marian Sawer, 49–64. New York: Routledge.

Grey, Sandra, and Marian Sawer, eds. 2008. *Women's Movements: Flourishing or in Abeyance?* Routledge: New York.

Gusfield, Joseph R. 1981. "Social Movements and Social Change: Perspectives of Linearity and Fluidity." In *Research in Social Movements, Conflict and Change*, vol. 4, edited by Louis Kriesberg, 317–339. Greenwich, CT: JAI Press.

Hirsch, Eric L. 1990. *Urban Revolt: Ethnic Politics in the Nineteenth-Century Chicago Labor Movement*. Berkeley: University of California Press.

Holland, Laurel, and Sherry Cable. 2002. "Reconceptualizing Social Movement Abeyance: The Role of Internal Processes and Culture in Cycles of Movement Abeyance and Resurgence." *Sociological Focus* 35:297–314.

Johnston, Hank. 2011. *States and Social Movements*. Boston: Polity.

Katzenstein, Mary Fainsod. 1998. *Faithful and Fearless: Moving Feminist Protest inside the Church and Military*. Princeton, NJ: Princeton University Press.

Katzenstein, Mary Fainsod, and Carol McClurg Mueller, eds. 1987. *The Women's Movements of the United States and Western Europe*. Philadelphia: Temple University Press.

Keck, M. E., and K. Sikkink. 1998. *Activists beyond Borders: Advocacy Networks in International Politics*. Ithaca, NY: Cornell University Press.

Kendrick, Richard. 2000. "Swimming against the Tide: Peace Movement Recruitment in an Abeyance Environment." In *Social Conflicts and Collective Identities*, edited by Patrick G. Coy and Lynne M. Woehrle, 189–206. Lanham, MD: Rowman and Littlefield.

Klandermans, Bert. 1994. "Transient Identities: Changes in Collective Identity in the Dutch Peace Movement." In *New Social Movements: From Ideology to Identity*, edited by Hank Johnston, Joseph Gusfield, and Enrique Llarana, 168–185. Philadelphia: Temple University Press.

———. 2010. "Legacies from the Past: Eight Cycles of Peace Protest." *The World Says No to War: Demonstrations against the War on Iraq*, edited by Stefaan Walgrave and Dieter Rucht, 61–77. Minneapolis: University of Minnesota Press.

Mansbridge, Jane, and Katherine Flaster. 2008. "The Cultural Politics of Everyday Discourse: The Case of 'Male Chauvinist.'" *Critical Sociology* 33:627–660.

Martin, Courtney E. 2010. *Do It Anyway: The New Generation of Activists*. Boston: Beacon Press.

McAdam, Doug, Sidney Tarrow, and Charles Tilly. 2001. *Dynamics of Contention*. Cambridge: Cambridge University Press.

McCammon, Holly. 2012. *The U.S. Women's Jury Movements and Strategic Adaptation*. New York: Cambridge University Press.

McCaughey, Martha, and Michael D. Ayers. 2003. *Cyberactivism: Online Activism in Theory and Practice*. New York: Routledge.

Melucci, Alberto. 1995. "The Process of Collective Identity." In *Social Movements and Culture*, edited by Hank Johnston and Bert Klandermans, 41–63. Minneapolis: University of Minnesota Press.

Meyer, David S., and Nancy Whittier. 1994. "Social Movement Spillover." *Social Problems* 41 (2): 277–298.

Mooney, Patrick, and T. J. Majka. 1995. *Farmers' and Farm Workers' Movements: Social Protest in American Agriculture*. New York: Twane.

Morris, Aldon D. 1986. *The Origins of the Civil Rights Movement: Black Communities Organizing for Change*. New York: Free Press.

Oliver, Pamela. 1989. "Bringing the Crowd Back In: The Nonorganizational Elements of Social Movements." *Research in Social Movements, Conflict and Change* 11:1–30.

Polletta, Francesca. 1999. "Free Spaces in Collective Action." *Theory and Society* 28:1–38.

Raeburn, Nicole C. 2004. *Changing Corporate America from Inside Out: Lesbian and Gay Workplace Rights*. Minneapolis: University of Minnesota Press.

Reed, Jean-Pierre, and John Foran. 2002. "Political Cultures of Opposition: Exploring Idioms, Ideologies, and Revolutionary Agency." *Critical Sociology* 28 (3): 335–370.

Reger, Jo. 2002. "Organizational Dynamics and the Construction of Multiple Feminist Identities in the National Organization for Women." *Gender and Society* 16 (5): 710–727.

————, ed. 2005. *Different Wavelengths: Studies of the Contemporary Women's Movement.* Routledge: New York.

————. 2012. *Everywhere and Nowhere: Contemporary Feminism in the United States.* New York: Oxford University Press.

Reger, Jo, Daniel J. Myers, and Rachel Einwohner, eds. 2008. *Identity Work in Social Movements.* Minneapolis: University of Minnesota Press.

Rojas, Fabio. 2007. *From Black Power to Black Studies: How a Radical Social Movement Became an Academic Discipline.* Baltimore: Johns Hopkins University Press.

Roth, Benita. 2004. *Separate Roads to Feminism: Black, Chicana, and White Feminist Movements in America's Second Wave.* Cambridge: Cambridge University Press.

————. 2010. "'Organizing One's Own' as Good Politics: Second Wave Feminists and the Meaning of Coalition." In *Strategic Alliances: Coalition Building and Social Movements,* edited by Nella Van Dyke and Holly J. McCammon, 99–118. Minneapolis: University of Minnesota Press.

Rowe, C. J. 2008. "Cyberfeminism in Action: Claiming Women's Space in Cyberspace." In *Women's Movements: Flourishing or in Abeyance?,* edited by Sandra Grey and Marian Sawer, 128–139. London: Routledge.

Rueschemeyer, Dietrich, Evelyne Huber Stephens, and John D. Stephens. 1992. *Capitalist Development and Democracy.* Chicago: University of Chicago Press.

Rupp, Leila J. 2011. "The Persistence of Transnational Organizing: The Case of the Homophile Movement." *American Historical Review* 116 (4): 1014–1039.

Rupp, Leila J., and Verta Taylor. 1987. *Survival in the Doldrums: The American Women's Rights Movement, 1945–1960s.* New York: Oxford University Press.

————. 1999. "Forging Feminist Identity in an International Movement: A Collective Identity Approach to Twentieth-Century Feminism." *Signs* 24 (2): 363–386.

————. 2003. *Drag Queens at the 801 Cabaret.* Chicago: University of Chicago Press.

————. 2005. Foreword to *Different Wavelengths: Studies of the Contemporary Women's Movement,* edited by Jo Reger, xi–xiv. New York: Routledge.

Sawyers, Traci M., and David S. Meyer. 1999. "Missed Opportunities: Social Movement Abeyance and Public Policy." *Social Problems* 46 (2): 187–206.

Snow, David, B. Rochford, S. Worden, and R. Benford. 1986. "Frame Alignment Processes, Micromobilization, and Movement Participation." *American Sociological Review* 51 (4): 464–481.

Soule, Sarah A. 1997. "The Student Divestment Movement in the United States and Tactical Diffusion: The Shantytown Protest." *Social Forces* 75:855–883.

Staggenborg, Suzanne. 1996. "The Survival of the Women's Movement: Turnover and Continuity in Indiana." *Mobilization* 1:143–158.

————. 1998. "Social Movement Communities and Cycles of Protest: The Emergence and Maintenance of a Local Women's Movement." *Social Problems* 45 (2): 180–204.

Staggenborg, Suzanne, and Amy Lang. 2007. "Culture and Ritual in the Montreal Women's Movement." *Social Movement Studies* 6 (2): 177–194.

Staggenborg, Suzanne, and Josée Lecomte. 2009. "Social Movement Campaigns: Mobilization and Outcomes in the Montreal Women's Movement." *Mobilization* 14 (2): 405–422.

Staggenborg, Suzanne, and Verta Taylor. 2005. "Whatever Happened to the Women's Movement?" *Mobilization* 10 (1): 37–52.

Stryker, Sheldon, Timothy J. Owens, and Robert W. White, eds. 2000. *Self, Identity, and Social Movements.* Minneapolis: University of Minnesota Press.

Taft, Jessica. 2010. *Rebel Girls: Youth Activism and Social Change across the Americas.* New York: New York University Press.

Tarrow, Sidney G. 1989. *Democracy and Disorder: Protest and Politics in Italy, 1965–1975.* Oxford: Clarendon Press.

Taylor, Verta. 1989. "Social Movement Continuity: The Women's Movement in Abeyance." *American Sociological Review* 54 (5): 761–775.

———. 1996. *Rock-a-by Baby: Feminism, Self-Help, and Postpartum Depression.* New York: Routledge.

———. 2010. "Culture, Identity, and Social Movements: Studying Protest as if People Really Matter." *Mobilization* 15 (2): 113–134.

Taylor, Verta, Katrina Kimport, Nella Van Dyke, and Ellen Andersen. 2009. "Culture and Mobilization: Tactical Repertoires, Same-Sex Weddings, and the Impact on Gay Activism." *American Sociological Review* 74:865–890.

Taylor, Verta, and Lisa Leitz. 2010. "From Infanticide to Activism: Emotions and Identity in Self-Help Movements." In *Social Movements and the Transformation of American Health Care*, edited by Jane Banaszak-Holl, Sandra Levitsky, and Mayer N. Zald, 446–475. New York: Oxford University Press.

Taylor, Verta, and Leila J. Rupp. 1993. "Women's Culture and Lesbian Feminist Activism: A Reconsideration of Cultural Feminism." *Signs* 19 (1): 32–61.

Taylor, Verta, Leila J. Rupp, and Joshua Gamson. 2004. "Performing Protest: Drag Shows as Tactical Repertoires of the Gay and Lesbian Movement." *Research in Social Movements, Conflict and Change* 25:105–137.

Taylor, Verta, and Nella Van Dyke. 2004. "'Get Up, Stand Up': Tactical Repertoires of Social Movements." In *The Blackwell Companion to Social Movements*, edited by David A. Snow, Sarah A. Soule, and Hanspeter Kriesi, 262–293. Oxford: Blackwell.

Taylor, Verta, and Nancy Whittier. 1992. "Collective Identity in Social Movement Communities: Lesbian Feminist Mobilization." In *Frontiers in Social Movement Theory*, edited by Aldon D. Morris and Carole McClurg Mueller, 104–129. New Haven, CT: Yale University Press.

Taylor, Verta, and Mayer N. Zald. 2010. "Conclusion: The Shape of Collective Action in the U.S. Health Sector." In *Social Movements and the Transformation of American Health Care*, edited by Jane Banaszak-Holl, Sandra Levitsky, and Mayer N. Zald, 300–317. Oxford: Oxford University Press.

Tilly, Charles. 1986. *The Contentious French.* Cambridge, MA: Belknap Press.

———. 1995. *Popular Contention in Great Britain.* Cambridge, MA: Harvard University Press.

———. 2000. "Spaces of Contention." *Mobilization* 5 (2): 135–159.

Valenti, Jessica. 2007. *Full Frontal Feminism: A Young Woman's Guide to Why Feminism Matters.* Berkeley, CA: Seal Press.

———. 2009. *The Purity Myth: How America's Obsession with Virginity Is Hurting Young Women.* Berkeley, CA: Seal Press.

Van Dyke, Nella. 1998. "Hotbeds of Activism: Locations of Student Protest." *Social Problems* 45 (2): 205–220.

———. 2003. "Crossing Movement Boundaries: Factors that Facilitate Coalition Protest by American College Students, 1930–1990." *Social Problems* 50 (2): 226–250.

Van Dyke, Nella, and Holly McCammon, eds. 2010. *Strategic Alliances: Coalition Building and Social Movements.* Minneapolis: University of Minnesota Press.

Van Dyke, Nella, Sarah A. Soule, and Verta Taylor. 2004. "The Targets of Social Movements: Beyond a Focus on the State." In *Authority in Contention*, edited by Daniel J. Meyers and Daniel M. Cress, 27–51. Oxford: JAI Press.

Van Stekelenburg, Jacquelien, Dirk Oegema, and Bert Klandermans. 2010. "No Radicalization without Identification: How Ethnic Dutch and Dutch Muslim Web Forums Radicalize over Time." In *Identity and Participation in Culturally Diverse Societies*, edited by Assaad Azzi, Xenia Chryssochoou, Bert Klandermans, and Bernd Simon, 256–274. Hoboken, NJ: Wiley Blackwell.

Viterna, Jocelyn, and Kathleen M. Fallon. 2008. "Democratization, Women's Movements, and Gender-Equitable States: A Framework for Comparison." *American Sociological Review* 73:668–689.

Weigand, Kate. 2001. *Red Feminism: American Communism and the Making of Women's Liberation*. Baltimore: Johns Hopkins University Press.

Whittier, Nancy. 1995. *Feminist Generations: The Persistence of the Radical Women's Movement*. Philadelphia: Temple University Press.

———. 2012. "The Politics of Coming Out: Visibility and Identity in Activism against Child Sexual Abuse." In *Strategies for Social Change*, edited by Gregory M. Maney, Rachel V. Kutz-Flamenbaum, Deana A. Rohlinger, and Jeff Goodwin, 145–169. Minneapolis: University of Minnesota Press.

Wood, Elisabeth Jean. 2000. *Forging Democracy from Below: Insurgent Transitions in South Africa and El Salvador*. Cambridge: Cambridge University Press.

II

Latin America

4

Introduction

CORNELIS VAN STRALEN

Recent decades have witnessed radical alterations of the political landscape in Latin America. Leaving dictatorial regimes behind, most Latin American countries advanced to democratic regimes, and the open and competitive presidential elections that Brazil and Chile held in 1989 marked the first time that all Latin American countries, nineteen excluding Cuba, simultaneously enjoyed elected constitutional governments. The transition from authoritarian rule, however, was far from uniform, varying from a long, gradual transition (Brazil) to an abrupt one (Argentina). The outcomes, too, were a kaleidoscope of "uncertain democracies" (O'Donnell and Schmitter 1986); subtypes of democracy, such as "authoritarian democracy," "neopatrimonial democracy," "military-dominated democracy," and "protodemocracy" (Collier and Levitsky 1997); or "levels of democracy" (Pérez-Liñan and Mainwaring 2013).

The turn of the century marked another important process of transition in Latin America, because left or center-left governments were elected in some of the most developed countries. This electoral shift started with the election of President Hugo Chávez in Venezuela in 1998, followed by the 1999–2000 election in Chile of President Ricardo Lagos, a member of the Socialist Party of Chile and the Concertación de Partidos por la Democracia (Coalition of Parties for Democracy). Luiz Inácio da Silva (Lula) of the Partido dos Trabalhadores (the Workers' Party) won the elections in Brazil in 2002, left-wing Peronist leader Néstor Kirchner of the Justicialist Party was elected in 2003, and Tabaré Vásquez, supported by the Frente Amplio (Broad Front) in Uruguay won that country's 2004 elections.

The leftward shift continued with the 2005 election of Evo Morales and his 2009 reelection in Bolivia. In 2006 Lula was reelected for a second term and

Rafael Correa was elected president of Ecuador. In Argentina Christina Kirchner, the wife of Néstor Kirchner, was elected president in 2007. Fernando Lugo, former bishop of Paraguay's poorest diocese, was elected president in 2008 but then ousted by the Paraguayan Congress in 2012. José Mujica, former guerrilla fighter, was elected president of Uruguay in 2009. In Brazil Dilma Rousseff, former member of Marxist urban guerrilla groups who had been captured and jailed from 1970 to 1972, was elected president in 2010. In Chile Michelle Bachelet, president from 2006 to 2010, was again elected president in 2013. As a result, the second decade of the twenty-first century found Latin America with clear right-leaning governments only in Paraguay and some small countries of Central America.

Although the shift to the left seems obvious, it is not clear what the left stands for, as Benjamin Arditi (2008) points out. By no means is there a monolithic political bloc, and there are important differences in matters of trade policies and relations with the United States, political reforms, and socioeconomic conditions. While Bolivia, Ecuador, Nicaragua, and Venezuela remain contestatory leftist and reject the market economy, other countries moved to the center left following in the footsteps of Lula, who changed from an icon of the left to a model of the responsible left, as his 2001 campaign Letter to the Brazilian People put it. Leftist governments continue to support private-capital and market reforms while protecting domestic industries and intervening strongly in the economy. Admittedly, power is concentrated in the hands of elected presidents in several countries, particularly the most leftist, in which constituent assemblies were used to increase presidential power and to augment the mandate of the elected president or allow reelections and in which populism continues to be the most important political strategy. However, participatory mechanisms are arising, such as popular councils and plebiscites, although they are often used tentatively or lack representativeness. Bribery and corruption of politicians and public officials is still widespread, but the traditional ambivalence of society toward corruption is waning, and social movements and nongovernmental organizations (NGOs) have started to denounce corrupt politicians and suspect business dealings. Recognition of political and civil rights is still uneven, but discourses on citizenship and human rights are becoming more widespread even as violations of them continue.

The transition from authoritarian rule originated the academic field of transitology, which best can be traced to the four-volume work of Guillermo O'Donnell, Philippe C. Schmitter, and Laurence Whitehead on transitions from authoritarian rule (1986). In the last volume of this seminal work, O'Donnell and Schmitter define transition somewhat loosely as "the interval between one political regime and another" (1986: 6). Transition begins with the breakdown among civil or military elites, and it ends with elections or at least the return to normality, though other outcomes are possible too, such as the return to some form of authoritarian rule or a revolutionary alternative. The process goes through several stages: liberalization, or opening of the authoritarian regime;

negotiating and renegotiating of formal or informal pacts between military, political party, and employer and trade union elites; and social mobilization, or the revival of civil society.

O'Donnell and Schmitter highlight the uncertainty and indeterminacy of the transition process, arguing that the factors that were necessary and sufficient for provoking the collapse or self-transformation of an authoritarian regime, such as conflicts between hard- and soft-liners or the institutional decay of the military, are made irrelevant by the mobilization of new actors and by the rules change and may be neither necessary nor sufficient to ensure the instauration of another regime (1986: 65). They illustrate this through the metaphor of a multilayered chess game with its infinite combinations and permutations and with unexpected victories or defeats (66).

Outcomes vary because of the indeterminate nature of the process and because of the effect of each country's previous experience with democracy and the continuity or discontinuity of political institutions during the authoritarian regime. While some countries, such as Argentina, Chile, and Uruguay, had an important legacy of democratic institutions and a relatively stable party system, others, especially Central American countries, with the exception of Costa Rica, had little or no previous experience. These foregoing conditions, combined with other factors, such as the role of the army, the style of political leadership, the presence of patrimonial parties, and the degree of social inequalities, are more decisive than the characteristics of the authoritarian regime or the process of transition, as O'Donnell states (1994).

The installation of a democratically elected government opens the way for a second transition, from a democratically elected government to an institutionalized, consolidated democratic regime, but that second transition does not necessarily occur (O'Donnell 1994). However, it is not easy to define which form of democracy is being installed and assess when it will be consolidated. Thus, the second transition is often longer and more complex than the transition from authoritarian rule. The efforts to capture the diversity lead to the already mentioned proliferation of subtypes of democracy, noted in the title of A. P. Spanakos's review of eight books on democracy in Latin America: "Adjectives, Asterisks and Qualifications, or How to Address Democracy in Contemporary Latin America" (2007).

The indeterminacy of the democratic transition called into doubt the transitology approach itself. The debate on transitology began with Thomas Carothers's much-cited article "The End of the Transition Paradigm" (2002), in which he questioned the assumptions of what he calls the transition paradigm, or the "analytic model of democratic transition" derived principally from the interpretations of democratic change made by the democracy promotion community but "also to a lesser degree from the early works of the field of 'transitology,' above all the seminal work of Guillermo O'Donnell and Philippe Schmitter" (6). For Carothers, one of the core assumptions of the transition paradigm is that "any country moving away from dictatorial rule can be considered a country in transition toward democracy" (2002: 6). This implies that the transition has a teleological orientation and follows a sequence of stages: first, the opening, a period of liberalization, and then the breakthrough, the collapse of the regime and the establishment of a democratic system with national elections and democratic institutions, followed by consolidation, "a slow but purposeful process in which democratic forms are transformed into democratic substance through the reform of state institutions, the regularization of elections, the strengthening of civil society and the habituation of the society to the new democratic rules" (2002: 7). Carothers admits that during a time of momentous political upheavals the paradigm was useful but that it is increasingly clear that reality is no longer conforming to the model, because countries do not go through a regular sequence of stages, and there is not a clear outcome. Most countries enter a gray zone that has some attributes of democracy but also serious democratic deficits.

Carothers's criticism corresponds with much of O'Donnell's view of the transition paradigm. However, O'Donnell points out that the transition paradigm has nothing to do with the viewpoints he and Schmitter present in their work on transition and that Carothers largely ignores what the scholarly literature says on the transition process (O'Donnell 2002). Apparently, Carothers's criticism related more to the political and ideological discourse of U.S. democracy promoters than the academic literature. Be that as it may, Carothers's criticism did not lead to the demise of transitology but provoked a rethinking. It became clear that to understand political transition it is necessary to include not only the transition from authoritarian rule but also the subsequent routes to democracy (Smith and Kearney 2010). Furthermore, political transition is a complex process with successive and overlapping stages during which different groups of actors come to the fore.

Social movements have been prominent in political transitions. Their role differed according to the nature of the authoritarian regime and the form and the timing of their insertion into the political process (Foweraker 1995: 92–93). In the beginning of the transition from authoritarian rule, when liberalization favored the eruption of mass movement, strikes, and popular demands, the convergence of the trade unions, ecclesiastical base communities, neighborhood organizations, and professional associations helped in several countries to delegitimize the regimes and to accelerate the breakdown of authoritarian rule and the pact making between outgoing rulers and oppositional forces. However, in the aftermath of the transition from authoritarian rule, at the turn of the twentieth century and in the first decade of the twenty-first, social movements intervened more directly in political processes. For instance, Evo Morales owes his election to years of organizing social movements and taking part in their struggles to control land, water, and petroleum resources and opposing eradication of coca crops. Lula owes his victory to the Workers' Party, whose foundation is the labor movement and church-related grassroots movements, albeit in coalition with right-wing parties. Some scholars even argue that social movements are the new face of political power because "citizens across the world have shifted from older and traditional forms of representation, such as political parties and unions, to 'newer' modes, such as social movements, informal citizen groups and non-governmental organizations" (Chandoke 2005: 308). Other scholars emphasize that "[political] parties are among the least credible institutions in Latin America, yet democracy is nearly inconceivable without them" (Levitsky and Cameron 2009: 358).

Because Latin American countries encompass diverse social conditions and political dynamics, the battlefields of social movements are very different. Hence, the variety of social movement is enormous, with an overwhelming multiplicity of activists, issues, conflicts, and orientations. Besides the traditional unions, they include the so-called new social movements, loosely composed of two large groups: (1) broad social and protest movements, such as the Movement of Landless Workers (MST) in Brazil, the *piqueteros* (unemployed workers who hold protest actions involving blocking of roads) of Argentina, the Zapatistas in Mexico, the *cocaleros* (coca growers) in Bolivia, and the Indigenous Confederation in Ecuador, and (2) myriad smaller but interacting groups and organizations, such as feminist organizations, LGBT (lesbian, gay, bisexual, and transgender) movements, human rights committees, environmental movements, cultural and artistic groups for the defense of regional traditions, Afro-Brazilian and Afro-Colombian groups, the Mothers of Disappeared Children in Chile, the Mothers of the Plaza de Mayo in Argentina, and Christian base communities. Many of these movements emerged during the era of military dictatorship, some of them in direct opposition to the military rulers, but most flourished after the return to political democracy. They resulted from a mix of local conditions but also from international factors, such as changes in the Roman Catholic Church, the second wave of feminism, the black power movement in the United States, and the hemispheric gathering of indigenous people.

Many scholars distinguish the old social movements from the new social movements on grounds of identity references, objectives, ways of organizing and mobilizing, methods of action, cultural contents, values, and antiparty trends. However, some scholars argue that the issues are the same and the methods of action and demands are not so new; they just occur in a new political and economic context characterized by neoliberalism (Galvão 2008). Other scholars point out that new social movements are not as isolated from class and partisan struggles as some have asserted. For instance, in Brazil during the prolonged transition to democracy, the most interesting and significant struggles took place precisely at the point of intersection between trade unions and social movements (the strikes of metalworkers with support of neighborhood associations, the links between unions and the Christian base communities) (Hellman 1995). This suggests that it is more useful to look at the dynamic process of movements adapting to the changing forms of state and market than to categorize them as new or traditional.

Although Latin American social movements are heterogeneous and follow different tracks, it is possible to map them onto more general categories based on a series of criteria, such as the profile of the activists, the issues, the pattern of actions, and the territories. However, these elements do not reveal the meaning of collective actions and social protest. Thus, it is necessary to consider their historical embeddedness and their relationship with their opponents and the state, because these not only are results of collective actions but also trigger the social construction of protest issues. In the last quarter of the last century and the first decade of this century, three struggles affected the dynamics of social movements: against authoritarian rule, against neoliberalism, and for human rights, social justice, and citizenship.

The Struggle against Authoritarian Rule

Studies of Latin American social movements initially focused on the relationship between social movements and the transition to democracy. This complex relationship involves a twofold question: What part did social movements have in the transition from authoritarian military regimes, and how did they affect the aftermath of the transition process? Although the consensus is that social movements were important in the breakdown of authoritarian regimes in several countries, interpretations of their role vary, depending on what phase of the transition process the interpretation focuses on and on the methodological approach used, whether top-down or bottom-up. Both the focus on a phase and the approach used can lead to different or even misleading interpretations.

It is generally supposed that the life cycle of social movements depends on the timing and insertion in political processes. For instance, social movements that emerge during liberalization show a tendency to decline during consolidation because of the high cost of maintaining them. However, as I mentioned earlier, a transition has no predetermined outcome and varies according to the points of departure, directions of change, and long-term political processes. The choice of a top-down or bottom-up approach implies a selective view because the first approach tends to emphasize the autonomy and collective action of grassroots movements and the second the actions of and interactions with opponents exercising pressures, organizing protest actions, and lobbying or bargaining with decision-making authorities such as the government. They thus draw attention to different dimensions of democratic transition and can help to better qualify the political actors and their interrelationships. However, both approaches risk misjudging the relationships with the state and political institutions.

The role social movements played in the democratic transition of Latin American countries was far from unilinear. In the most developed countries, particularly the countries of the Southern Cone, social movements contributed to the end of the authoritarian military regime, mainly through delegitimization of these regimes and pressure to democratize. In these countries the modern middle classes often played a crucial role as catalysts or as resources (Assies 1992: 35). Sometimes this interaction temporarily resulted in high degrees of mobilization, such as the 1983 mobilization of the middle class and the popular sector in Chile for democracy or the 1984 campaign for direct presidential elections in Brazil. Lasting interactions emerged above all in local contexts with the proliferation of urban social movements, professional associations, and Christian base communities and with priests, university students, social workers, and architects and other professionals becoming articulators and mediators of social demands. In other countries, such as in Central America, groups of insurgents, supported to greater or lesser extent by civil groups and organizations, drove away the military dictatorship.

While their transitions followed a variety of roads, by the early 1990s nearly all Latin American countries had embraced some form of democracy. The largest differences between countries came from each's previous experiences with democratic regimes and who the initiators of the transition from authoritarian rule had been. Countries such as Chile, Uruguay, and to a lesser extent, Argentina and Brazil, had a democratic past, with more or less consolidated party systems, but countries such as Bolivia, the Dominican Republic, Ecuador, El Salvador, Guatemala, Honduras, Nicaragua, and Paraguay had poor or almost nonexistent previous experiences with democracy. Despite the considerable differences among countries, democracy overall progressed. Even so, the term *consolidation* used by some transitologists is misleading because it suggests that the outcome is known, which can lead to underestimating the degree of change in the transition and the diversity of democratic regimes (Pickvance 1999: 354).

Initially, the opening up of democratic regimes, the upsurge of a variety of new social movements, and the creation of new participatory political institutions nurtured expectations among middle-class activists and left-wing academics for political change and democratization. Social experimentation did flourish in several countries, such as the introduction of participatory budgeting, participatory policy councils, policy forums, and conferences, but in general did not support the "faith in the transformative potential of popular organizations" (Roberts 1997: 138). Though democratization brought new access to the government, the demise of the dictatorial and authoritarian regimes against which opposition forces had unified and mobilized their struggles resulted in a decline or fragmentation of several movements that had been important in the transition. Groups returned to their original issues, and new groups pushed other demands. Moreover, the old politics and institutional hybridism between formal liberal democracy and informal particularism still maintain restrictions and obstacles to collective action and prodemocratic mobilization. It is no surprise that, on the whole, Latin Americans do not believe they have a functioning democracy. In the 2013 Latinobarómetro survey, only 8 percent of adult Latin Americans believed that there is full democracy in their country, 46 percent believed that there is democracy with major problems, and 9 percent said that there is no democracy (Corporación Latinobarómetro 2013: 32).

Support for democracy, measured by positive responses to the statement "Democracy is preferable to any other kind of government," has not shown major changes since 1995. In 2013, the percentage of Latin Americans who agreed with this statement was 56 percent, only 2 percentage points below the percentage in 1996 (30). However, there were larger variances in individual countries and a difference of 11 percentage points between Central America (49 percent) and South America and Mexico (60 percent) (21). Nevertheless, 79 percent of Latin Americans agreed in 2013 with the statement "Democracy may have problems but is the best system." This suggests that "democracy is increasingly seen as the only alternative in Latina America" (31).

The emergence of left-wing governments raised new expectations. However, while not ignoring the prominent contribution of social movements to the election of left-wing governments, it is important to realize that governments often take the initiative for participatory democracy themselves. This move of left-wing governments raises the already classic question: Does their accommodation of social movement demands lead to convergence or to co-optation?

The Struggle against Neoliberalism

In most Latin American countries, the process of democratization coincided with the upsurge of neoliberalism. Latin American political elites became major advocates for neoliberal policies, using a free-trade and free-market rhetoric and demanding modernization of the national economy through major integration with the world economy. Through wide support of the media, they were able to convince large segments of the middle class to support a shift to the neoliberal model. Chile, during the dictatorship of Augusto Pinochet, was one of the first to push radical market reforms, and in the course of the 1990s, a large number of Latin American democracies also carried out painful market reforms, forced by international agencies. The neoliberal model became hegemonic in almost all Latin American countries.

At the end of the 1990s, the failure of some experiments with certain neo-Keynesian economic policies and the profound transformations of the international economy paved the way for strengthening neoliberal economic policies. The economic restructuring included painful changes felt by vast sectors of the population: weakening labor laws and dismantling job guarantees, withdrawing price and wage supports, diminishing or eliminating aid to farmers, cutting public health care and other social policies, decreasing public infrastructure investments, and privatizing state-owned industries and social agencies. These caused a new wave of protest, triggered protest actions, and promoted large social movements.

While the loss of momentum by many human rights organizations and the fragmentation of social organizations in the aftermath of the breakdown of military dictatorships reduced social upheaval, the neoliberal reforms gave rise to new forms of struggle. Spearheaded by peasants and indigenous people, new social movements include the Confederación de Nacionalidades Indígenas del Ecuador; the Afro-Colombians; the *cocaleros*; groups mobilizing against water privatization and gas pipeline investments in Bolivia; the Zapatistas in Mexico; the broad, community organized *piqueteros* of Argentina; and the MST in Brazil. They contest the political and economic systems, protest the privatization of state-owned industries and services, challenge traditional rural ownership, and call for new forms of citizenship, democracy, and participation (Stahler-Sholk, Vanden, and Kuecker 2007).

The upsurge of these movements introduced a new cycle of protests and struggles against neoliberalism, which spilled over to labor organizations, university student movements, and other groups. Toward the end of the 1990s, Latin American mobilization against neoliberal policies converged with movements and protest actions on other continents, taking its most iconic shape at the battle of Seattle in 1999, where thousands of students, ecologists, feminists, peasants, farmers, and human rights activists protested the World Trade Organization's policies and disrupted the inaugural ceremony of the WTO ministerial conference (Seoane and Taddei 2002).

The battle of Seattle showed consolidation and internationalization of coordination among different organizations and movements. Protests intensified, especially in Latin America, and spread to every continent, giving rise to the first World Social Forum in Porto Alegre, Brazil, in January 2001, which attracted participants from 117 countries representing a wide range of social and political organizations and movements, ranging from feminist groups and environmentalist organizations to anarchist movements and leftist parties. In principle, they all resisted neoliberal ideology and policies. The World Social Forum was planned as a counterweight to the World Economic Forum annually held in Davos, Switzerland, and was driven by broad consensus that capitalist globalization is destructive and that international institutions such as the International Monetary Fund, World Bank, and WTO are part of a worldwide structure of power representing the interests of financial and transnational powers (Seoane and Taddei 2002).

While the majority of Latin American social movements do not fundamentally strive for seizing state power and are eager to maintain autonomy, they have contributed to destabilizing and, in some cases, ousting governments (e.g., Bolivia, Argentina, and Ecuador), and they coexist in awkward relationships with leftist parties (Brazil's Workers' Party [PT] and Mexico's Party of the Democratic Revolution [PDR]). Mainstream attention also focuses on these social movements to explain the apparent ascendance of the electoral left. However, as intense as social mobilization can be, it does not always engender effective changes linearly, and the overthrow of neoliberal governments (not always of neoliberal policies) was also favored by the relatively weakened state of American political and economic leadership.

According to R. Stahler-Sholk and H. E. Vanden (2011) Latin American social movements continue to have a positive impact through their fundamental role in the expansion of citizenship, extension of public spaces, and strengthening of democratic participation. Social movements disrupted the Washington Consensus (ten economic policies recommended by the U.S. government and financial institutions based in Washington that are nowadays often seen as synonymous with neoliberalism and globalization) and became transnational. They have experimented with ways of engaging with political parties and governments without losing their autonomy. They were instrumental in electing new progressive governments in Ecuador and Bolivia and put continuous pressure on the governments of Argentina, Brazil, and Mexico for much-needed reform. And they changed the way ordinary citizens think about politics and political participation.

A crucial question, mentioned above, is what happens to the relationship of social movements with the state. Are the movements co-opted in support of public policies, or do they maintain a critical stance? Particularly with left or center-left governments, social movement leadership often has been incorporated into government institutions, and mobilization of the movements has declined as a result. However, some movements maintain a critical stance even when they receive political and financial support from the government, such as the Brazilian MST. Either way, social movements cannot expect that all their demands will be met; almost inevitably there will be disappointment and conflicting relations. Furthermore, the international context creates or kills opportunities. The overthrow of neoliberal governments and the relative weakening of American political and economic leadership in the late 1990s and early 2000s facilitated alternative policies and regional integration (Alianza Bolivariana para los Pueblos de Nuestra América [ALBA; Bolivarian Alliance for the Peoples of the Americas], Mercado Común del Sur [Mercosur; Common Market of the South], and Unión de Naciones Suramericanas [UNASUR; Union of South American Nations]). However, the current financial crisis and the North American recession could result in a new interest in co-optation by Washington, working with its traditional allies Colombia and Mexico, plus Peru, and moving the center-left governments of Brazil, Argentina, and Uruguay out of the bloc of regional integration consisting of Venezuela, Bolivia, Ecuador, and Cuba (Sader 2008: 30). The restructuring of international and internal relations between political and social actors could again encourage protest and resistance movements but also contribute to their decline according to regional circumstances and long- or middle-term political processes.

The Struggle for Human Rights, Social Justice, and Citizenship

Latin American organizations and entities emerged in a different moment from their European counterparts. Latin American social movements were shaped first by the experience of military dictatorship and then by the democratic transition and the struggle against neoliberal reforms. The process of meaning making that forged their identities and influenced collective action resulted from discourses that were not only context dependent but also framed through political and religious discourses introduced by several other social actors—above all the Catholic Church.

In the 1970s and the 1980s, urban social movements addressed human rights in addition to combating poverty. The greater the violation of human rights, the more prominent became the struggle for it, as the human rights movement in Argentina makes clear. With the rise of the democratic transition, focus moved to citizenship rights, meaning not only women's and ethnic rights but, above all, the right to rights. Urban movements increasingly formulated demands in terms of rights, and eventually, political participation and citizenship discourse gained prominence in countries with left-wing governments as well as in countries with neoliberal governments, because both participatory democracy and neoliberalism presuppose an active civil society—the first, to increase social control on the government and to participate in the formulation and the management of public policies, and the latter, to shift state responsibilities to civil society.

As mentioned earlier, the rise of democracy tended to weaken or demobilize traditional urban movements, such as neighborhood associations, for several, often context-dependent reasons. While the struggle against authoritarian regimes had unified and coalesced movements, claims for rights fragmented them or favored the emergence of competing movements with specific demands. In other cases movements simply lost their constituencies. Furthermore, relationships with government changed. Political parties started to compete for the movements' support to increase their bargaining power in deals with political authorities, whereas community leaders tried to bypass the parties by directly contacting local and regional authorities. In this context, movements have not infrequently been reduced to small leadership groups. However, some became more organized and even more effective by reorganizing as NGOs and taking part in advocacy networks. This process was fostered by the rise of NGOs from the 1980s onward with funding from churches or international agencies.

The early development of the NGOs was marked by polarization and antagonism and by the presence of popular movements. Many of them envisaged education for all and "conscientization" (critical consciousness) and were heavily influenced by scholars and educationalists such as Paulo Freire and Fals Borda and by liberation theology. However, as political polarization waned and formal democracy rose, NGOs became a replacement for social movements. According to various scholars, they became increasingly professionalized and depoliticized insofar as they emphasized projects and not movements (Petras 1997). However, some NGOs are linked with social movements, such as the MST in Brazil, the *piquetero* movement in Argentina, and the Zapatistas in Mexico. This suggests that it is impossible to treat NGOs equally and that none can be taken out of their political, social, and historical context.

The dynamics of indigenous and rural movements had been somewhat different. They emerged as political actors in the last decades, claiming rights on the basis of their ethnic identity or their ties with their territory. Salvador Martí i Puig differentiates them into two large categories: (1) the "tribal" or "self-defense" movements that make up only a tiny percentage of the population of Latin America and (2) the large movements and organizations made up of indigenous peasants (2010: 84). The first category has been mainly mobilized from the outside by a sector of the Latin American Bishop Conference (CELAM) and the World Council of Churches (WCC), anthropologists, and various networks of humanitarian-aid NGOs. Although these movements have had little effect on national political agendas, they have made their demands visible and received delimited territories and recognition of their existence as original peoples. The people of the second category, who have suffered from considerable assimilation, have developed a type of ethnogenesis that gave a new meaning to their socioeconomic demands. Although they have had fewer links with international networks and obtained less response from governments, they have had a definite impact on the national political agenda, particularly in Bolivia with the victory of the Movimiento al Socialismo (MAS; Movement for Socialism) and in Ecuador and Mexico (Martí i Puig 2010: 77–79, 84–85). The Brazilian MST is made up of peasants, many already driven from their land, and has had strong support from sectors of the Catholic Church. With the rise of democracy, these peasants have been successful in strengthening a collective identity and making their demands for agrarian reform and opposition to neoliberal policies visible through land occupation and occupation of public buildings in the Brazilian state capitals. More recently, the movement has lost momentum because of opposition from conservative political elites and agribusiness and the loss of the solidarity of the urban middle classes. The government has continued to distribute land and create settlements but at an increasingly slow pace.

All in all, the political landscape in Latin America is populated by a multiplicity of social movements and in a state of permanent flux. I have described some general trends that make a first approximation but cloud any definition as well. It will be necessary to look for differences behind the similarities and for similarities behind the differences. We will possibly discover that it is not useful to examine Latin America as a unit of analysis, a choice influenced by the legacy of the past. The chapters in Part II discuss democratic transitions in Latin American countries and regions and highlight issues that provide insights into processes of transition to democracy and the contribution of social movements to democracy.

The first chapter, by Ton Salman, focuses on a central issue in the debate on the transition to democracy: the relationship between social movements and democracy. While this relationship arises in almost all Latin American experiences of democratic transition and even in those of the Global North as a result of the crisis of liberal democracy and the search for new models of democracy, Bolivia is emblematic to the extent that the MAS is a mixture of a political party and a federation of social movements that originated out of the movement of *cocaleros*. It brought Evo Morales to power in the midst of the fragmentation and then collapse of the party system. It also fostered the upsurge of a lot of local, regional, and national ethnic movements that filled the void left by the traditional parties. Salman stresses the ambivalence of the MAS that arises from being the governing party, which acts in terms of inclusive citizenship, and a coalition of ethnic movements, which have their own specific identities and interests.

Apparently, the duality of the MAS in efforts at reinventing democracy represents a specific Bolivian problem. However, it shares with several other Latin American countries the challenge of how to institutionalize a participatory and multiethnic democracy. Furthermore, it puts forward key questions for democratic experiments that introduce participatory or cogovernance structures alongside the traditional representative institutions, such as the Brazilian management councils in which representatives of both government and civil society formulate, manage, and monitor public policies. The civil society representatives of social movements and organizations each have specific interests.

The Brazilian MST shares characteristics with indigenous movements, all having been established in a wave of rural activism and becoming sociopolitical movements that took center stage in the 1990s and the first decade of the twenty-first century, all strongly rejecting neoliberal policies and capitalism. The mobilizing capacity of urban and labor movements declined with the democratic transition but went on to dominate popular struggles for social change in the 1990s and the beginning of the twenty-first century.

Camila Penna analyzes the MST during the last years of the government of Fernando Henrique Cardoso and the first years of Lula's government. Cardoso carried out land reforms, moved by the growing strength of the MST, and tried to preserve his image as a progressive political leader. However, he ended his term with less tolerance for the MST and land occupations, and conservative calls to restrain or eliminate the MST had increased. Penna stresses that the election of Lula was true political change, despite his alliance with center-right parties. However, she observes that the Workers' Party took a different position toward the government when it became clear that the government had put aside the left project and sought a third road, neither socialist nor neoliberal. The party's left and movements such as the MST pressured the government to take a more leftist stance through mass mobilizations in order to overcome the influence of the right in the government coalition. The MST increased land occupations as well as occupations of public buildings, mainly buildings of the National Institute for Colonization and Agrarian Reform (INCRA). At the same time, the Lula government increased land distribution. From 2003 to 2009, the Lula government settled 416,014 families, compared with 393,842 families settled by the Cardoso government. Lula's government also aided the MST through support for cooperatives and social projects by transferring funds to NGOs related to the MST. However, on the whole, the agrarian reforms were rather conservative.

In contrast with other social movements and labor organizations, MST leaders did not accept positions in Lula's government, and therefore the MST preserved its autonomy and critical stance toward the government. However, the movement did not isolate itself from the government, because it took part in local election processes and supported progressive candidates. While criticizing Lula's agrarian policies, the MST gave its support to Lula in his 2006 election run, albeit at the last minute. Other factors contribute to the MST's autonomous dynamic, particularly its strong collective identity nurtured by a rich symbolic repertoire, extensive collective actions, and education strategies and network of schools in the settlements.

The MST has also contributed to democracy, as Miguel Carter (2010) argues, in contrast to some Brazilian scholars who consider the MST a threat to democracy. The movement has contributed to the rise of democracy in several ways, such as public activism in building political capacities, broadening the scope of the public agenda, extending civil rights, and raising new hopes through its ideals.

Penna discusses a long-lasting grassroots movement, whereas Paul Almeida compares two waves of popular movement activity in Central America during the transition to democracy; the first during a period of violent conflict when the region was still characterized by authoritarian regimes and civil conflicts and the second in a more democratic context. Taking into account the second wave's coordinated actions between oppositional political parties, NGOs, and new social movements with more traditional social sectors, such as urban labor organizations and agricultural cooperatives, he argues that the processes of democratization and the economic threats associated with globalization add to popular mobilization. Almeida's country-by-country analysis of the two protest waves brings two interrelated issues into discussion: the decline of social movements after democratic transition and the decline of social movements as a result of competition between political parties and social movements. Although there are a lot of examples of decline of social movements after democratic transitions, particularly when urban social movements are involved, Almeida convincingly argues that, just as authoritarian regimes can unify social movements in a struggle, so can worsening economic conditions revitalize social movements. He bases his argument on data showing that democratization provides an organizational basis in civil society to launch campaigns of collective opposition when faced with new economic threats and shrinking of feeble welfare states. He adds that democratization does not simply institutionalize earlier social struggles but provides an organizational basis for even larger campaigns of collective opposition. This argument apparently refutes the supposition that social movement mobilizations decline as they become more institutionalized actors, such as political parties and state agencies, which reduces the need for mass collective actions. However, what is the strength of these institutionalized actors, and to what extent can they take over the role of social movements?

The combination of democratic transitions with economic threats can increase the possibility of collective action with an alliance between traditional movements, NGOs, new social movements, and political parties. However, this alliance can also be influenced by feeble representations of all parties, considering that the history of Central America is much more marked by repression than by structured political parties and social movements. In any case, it is worthwhile to consider Almeida's observation that, even though the entire region has witnessed massive campaigns against neoliberal reforms organized by NGOs, labor unions, new social movements, and oppositional political parties with a variety of outcomes, significant differences remain between countries in terms of political social sectors and mobilized groups.

In the last chapter of this part, Sebastián Pereyra analyzes the dynamics involved in the development of the human rights movement in Argentina throughout the transition to democracy, focusing on the political institutionalization of the movement. In all countries with military dictatorship and political violence, human rights became an important issue, but the scope has varied just as the constituency of human rights movements varied according to the victims of violence and the social groups that supported them. It is no surprise that the dramatic experience of state terrorism in Argentina with its massive number of victims gave rise to a human rights movement formed by organizations with different strategies, some of which are very well known, like the Mothers of the Plaza de Mayo. Several organizations started to enlarge their scope to also include relatives of victims and all victims of police brutality, of bad detention conditions, with mental health problems, and of economic and social rights violations. In this perspective the human rights movement introduced concerns for rights and the rule of law into the political culture. Pereyra examines the cycle of the human rights movements during the first decades of the return to democracy and the development of several public discourses. Subsequently, he examines the impact of the human rights discourses and the extension to violations of human rights in times of democracy. His chapter invites reflection on why the human rights issue is less prominent in other countries and how discourses on human rights can move to concerns with contemporary crime and police brutality, which paves the way for reflection on citizenship rights as well.

These four chapters together ask questions important to the understanding of social movements in Latin America. They improve our understanding of the dynamics of social movements: how they change according to political circumstances, how they are determined by their structure and the style of their leadership, how the relationship with democracy is shaped by long- and short-term political processes, and how they influence other political spheres. Furthermore, the great variety of social movements, the complexity of their dynamics, and the different links with democracy invite us to work out new theories. However, this effort probably will require a larger number of case studies.

REFERENCES

Arditi, B. 2008. "Arguments about the Left Turns in Latin America: A Post-liberal Politics?" *Latin American Research Review* 43 (3): 59–81.

Assies, W. 1992. *To Get Out of the Mud: Neighborhood Associativism in Recife, 1964–1988.* Amsterdam: Centre for Latin American Research and Documentation.

Carothers, T. 2002. "The End of the Transition Paradigm." *Journal of Democracy* 13 (1): 5–21.

Carter, M. 2010. "The Landless Rural Workers Movement and Democracy in Brazil." *Latin American Research Review* 45:186–217.

Chandoke, N. 2005. "Revisiting the Crisis of Representation Thesis: The Indian Context." *Democratization* 12 (3): 308–330.

Collier, D., and S. Levitsky. 1997. "Democracy with Adjectives: Conceptual Innovations in Comparative Research." *World Politics* 49:430–451.

Corporación Latinobarómetro. 2013. "2013 Report." Available at http://www.latinobaro metro.org/latContents.jsp.

Foweraker, J. 1995. *Theorizing Social Movements.* London: Pluto Press.

Galvão, A. 2008. "Os movimentos sociais da América Latina em Questão" [The Social Movements of Latin America in Question]. *Revista Debates* [Journal of Debates] 2 (2): 8–24.

Hellman, J. A. 1995. "The Riddle of New Social Movements: Who They Are and What They Do." In *Capital, Power and Inequality in Latin America*, edited by S. Halebsky and R. L. Harris, 165–184. Boulder, CO: Westview.

Levitsky, S., and M. Cameron. 2009. "Democracy without Parties? Political Parties and Regime Change in Fujimori's Peru." In *Latin American Democratic Transformations: Institutions, Actors and Processes*, edited by William C. Smith, 339–363. Oxford: John Wiley.

Martí i Puig, S. 2010. "The Emergence of Indigenous Movements in Latin America and Their Impact on the Latin American Scene." *Latin American Perspectives* 37 (6): 74–92.

O'Donnell, G. 1994. "Delegative Democracy." *Journal of Democracy* 5 (1): 55–69.

———. 2002. "In Partial Defense of an Evanescent Paradigm." *Journal of Democracy* 13 (3): 6–12.

O'Donnell, G., and P. C. Schmitter. 1986. *Tentative Conclusions about Uncertain Democracies.* Vol. 4 of *Transitions from Authoritarian Rule.* Baltimore: Johns Hopkins University Press.

O'Donnell, G., P. C. Schmitter, and L. Whitehead, eds. 1986. *Transitions from Authoritarian Rule: Prospects for Democracy.* 4 vols. Baltimore: Johns Hopkins University Press.

Pérez-Liñan, A., and S. Mainwaring. 2013. "Regime Legacies and Levels of Democracy: Evidence from Latin America." *Comparative Politics* 45 (4): 379–397.

Petras, J. 1997. "Imperialism and NGOs in Latin America." *Monthly Review* 49 (7): 10–27.

Pickvance, C. G. 1999. "The Democratization and the Decline of Social Movements: The Effects of Regime Change on Collective Action in Eastern Europe, Southern Europe and Latin America." *Sociology* 33 (2): 353–372.

Roberts, K. 1997. "Beyond Romanticism: Social Movements and the Study of Political Change in Latin America." *Latin American Research Review* 32 (2): 137–151.

Sader, E. 2008. "The Weakest Link?" *New Left Review* 52 (July–August): 5–31.

Seoane, José, and Emilio E. Taddei. 2002. "From Seattle to Porto Alegre: The Anti-neoliberal Globalization." *Current Sociology* 50 (1): 99–122.

Smith, P. H., and M. C. Kearney. 2010. "Transitions, Interrupted: Routes toward Democracy in Latin America." *Taiwan Journal of Democracy* 6 (1): 137–163.

Spanakos, A. P. 2007. "Adjectives, Asterisks and Qualifications, or How to Address Democracy in Contemporary Latin America." *Latin American Research Review* 42 (2): 225–237.

Stahler-Sholk, R., and H. E. Vanden. 2011. "A Second Look at Latin American Social Movements: Globalizing Resistance to the Neoliberal Paradigm." *Latin American Perspective* 38 (5): 5–13.

Stahler-Sholk, R., H. E. Vanden, and D. Kuecker. 2007. "The New Politics of Social Movements in Latin America." *Latin American Perspectives* 34 (2): 5–16.

5

A Democracy for "Us"—or for All?

The Ambivalences of Bolivia's Social Movements since Their Triumph

TON SALMAN

On the evening of February 4, 2010, Felix Patzi—the governing party's candidate in the upcoming election for governor in the department of La Paz, Bolivia—was stopped by police while driving through the city of La Paz and found to be under the influence of alcohol. Patzi is one of the most important intellectuals and leading figures in the cluster of social movements that are either wholly or largely supported by the Aymara indigenous people.[1] In turn, this cluster is part of the group of social movements that support the Movimiento al Socialismo (MAS; Movement toward Socialism),[2] which currently governs Bolivia. Patzi is an important ideologue of the MAS, the party that fused the demands of all these indigenous and other social movements and that in 2006 brought to power the country's first indigenous president, Evo Morales.

Patzi, that particular night, first tried to escape from the police, but he was caught a few blocks away. He failed the breath test, was charged, and was told he would have to go on trial. The police then released him, whereupon he declared to the journalists and television cameramen who in the meantime had gathered at the spot that, because of what had happened, he was stepping down and would no longer be a candidate for governor. He urged Bolivian drivers not to make his mistake, to "honor human life," and to submit to the law in the case of any transgression (see the February 5, 2010, editions of *La Prensa*, *La Razón*, and *El Diario*).

This seemingly simple event had ramifications. To begin with, the very day before the event, a decree had been proclaimed stipulating that from then on, all drunk drivers would lose their driver's license for life. This decision had been taken because that January had been exceptionally dramatic in Bolivia in terms of loss of life related to driving under the influence. Nevertheless, according to later press reports (see, e.g., the May 6, 2011, edition of *La Razón*), although Patzi handed in his license, it was returned to him a year later.

Second, this was the not the first time that Patzi had been caught driving while inebriated. Less than a year earlier, he had crashed his car. He was still drunk after a medical checkup in a hospital following the collision when he cheerfully declared in front of television cameras, which had just taken shots of his crushed car, "[I was] lucky because thank God I did not cause an accident." This made him the country's laughingstock for many days to come.

Third, Patzi initially claimed that he had been returning from a relative's wake, a ritual that in Aymara tradition needs to be accompanied by substantial alcohol consumption. This could have counted as an extenuating circumstance—had it not been an outright lie. Patzi had been celebrating with friends, and according to comments in the newspapers, "there were also women there," implying that he might have participated in inappropriate sexual activities.

Fourth, and most important for our story, Patzi retracted his declaration that he was stepping down as a candidate in the election. Although President Morales had declared that the MAS would not back him as a candidate, the day after the accident Patzi announced that he would put his fate in the hands of the social movements that had supported him throughout his career as a politician and now backed his candidacy. That, he stated, would be the right thing to do (see *La Prensa*, May 2, 2010) and would be in agreement with the new constitution, which had been in place since early 2009. Most of these movements had a predominantly Aymara composition and support base, and the current constitution acknowledges traditional indigenous' administration of justice. It also stipulates that social movements ought ideally to have a substantial say in the selection of candidates for a host of public offices. Social movements today should cogovern. A spokesperson for one of these movements—the women's section of the national peasants' confederation, Federación de Mujeres Campesinas (Federation of Peasant Women), Bartolina Sisa—even declared that Patzi did not have the right to unilaterally renounce his candidacy, since he had been appointed by the movements and therefore these movements should decide his fate (see *La Prensa*, July 2, 2010). A spokesperson for an affiliated movement declared that Patzi's mandate was given to him "by the social bases" and only these could exempt him from his duty.

As one so closely connected to his social movements, Patzi, not surprisingly, received a verdict from the social movement tribunal that judged him a couple of days later that did not affect his candidacy. Instead, Patzi was sentenced to produce a thousand blocks of adobe, the traditional Andean building material of loam fortified with straw. Patzi complied with the sentence and handed over 1,020 adobe blocks on February 11 to the indigenous authorities' tribunal representing the social movements that had convicted him. Next, he was absolved of his wrongdoing through a small ritual with the result that the damage was restored in the eyes of the tribunal.

In the meantime, his relationship with the MAS leadership had deteriorated. MAS denounced his lies, irresponsibility, and undisciplined behavior and
reiterated that he could no longer be an MAS candidate. The most important
social movements that had been behind Patzi had meanwhile become divided
over the affair. Some had absolved him; others had not. Among those that had
not were Consejo Nacional de Ayllus y Markas del Qullasuyu (CONAMAQ;
National Council of Ayllus and Markas of Qullasuyu), the council of indigenous hamlets and administrative units of the former southeastern quarter (Col-
lasuyu) of the four quarters of the Inca Empire (Tawantinsuyu); the militant
peasant group Ponchos Rojos (Red Ponchos); and Confederación Sindical Única
de Trabajadores Campesinos de Bolivia (CSUTCB; Unified Syndical Confederation of Peasant Workers of Bolivia). But the Federación de Campesinos del
Departamento de La Paz (Federation of Peasants of the La Paz Department),
including various important social movement representatives, insisted that the
verdict was legitimate. They even accused the MAS of racism and disrespect
for communitarian justice and for the social movements' prerogatives. Eventually, because the MAS would not give in, they decided to establish a new political party that would present Patzi as candidate for governor (see the February
10–16, 2010, editions of *La Prensa*, *El Diario*, and *Jornada*).[3]

Although the Patzi affair lends itself to an analysis of "community justice,"[4]
currently a hot issue in Bolivia, in what follows I concentrate more specifically
on the intricacies of the social movements' attitudes and positions in the matter. The affair lays bare the conflicted situation in which social movements and
their electoral vehicle (the MAS) ended up after their victory. It illustrates how
ideological affinities and shared causes—apparently promising a smooth collaboration—will nevertheless be troubled by the responsibilities of the now governing standard-bearer. Although I argue that this is an inevitable outcome of
situations like the Bolivian one, specific circumstances and backgrounds color
the precise evolution of this process. I show how this affects movements' part in
democratization, a part often thought to be a side effect of a revolution like the
Bolivian one. I also address the role of ethnicity.

The social movements directly involved in the Patzi affair, and many others besides, were the backbone of the MAS (and still are), contributing to the
MAS's first electoral victory in December 2005. Many of them have an explicit,
or at least a mixed, ethnic identity. In addition, the MAS recognizes the social
movements as the mainstays of its legitimacy. In the new constitution, the social movements, representing "organized civil society," are assigned a specific
task: "The organized civil society will exercise social control over public policy
at all levels of the state, and over public, mixed and private companies and institutions that manage fiscal funds" (*Nueva Constitución Política del Estado*,
article 241, II; my translation). Although the precise mechanisms and scope of
this control are largely still to be defined in lower-level legislation, it was this
article that factions within the social movements supporting Patzi were referring to when they denounced the MAS's position on Patzi's candidacy. And

this reference contains, in a condensed way, the clue to the matter. In calling on article 241, the movements claim to have a special position in state affairs since "their" standard-bearer, the MAS, became the governing party. Consequentially, they suggest that pro-MAS social movements are entitled to a decisive say on governmental measures and positions. This, of course, problematizes the classic view that a polity, whatever its ideological stand and policies, once in government, ought to guarantee citizen equality.[5] In effect, the movements' stand meant they would be favorites on an institutionalized unequal playing field, a democratic edifice that would benefit some over others. And that, in turn, would be an ironic finale to their struggle against the deficient and exclusionary democracy that was in place until the MAS's victory (Rojas Ortuste 1994; *Bolivia* 2008; Seoanne and Nacci 2007; Assies and Salman 2003; also see below). It would mean that an earlier democracy that tacitly but effectively benefited some people (e.g., nonindigenous, wealthy, or powerful) over other people (e.g., indigenous or poor) would now be replaced by a democracy that was explicitly and openly "for us," as it was phrased by an MAS supporter (*Bolivia* 2008: 127). That would hardly be in accordance with the democracy-enhancing nature often attributed to social movements (see, e.g., Foweraker and Landman 1997: 225–243; Palmer 2003: 246–249; Diamond 1996: 228–234; Sall 2004; Cohen and Arato 1992: 492–563; Ibarra 2002; Chapter 1; and—with some qualifications—Tilly 2002). The relationship between social movements' actions and democracy (especially after a victory) is more complicated than allowing for a credulous and naive cheer (Salman 2009).

In the following sections, I first explore some of the more theoretical ideas on the relationship between social movements and democracy. I then briefly sketch Bolivia's recent history and social movements' role therein and in the MAS's victory. After that, I address the situation in which the MAS and its supporting social movements find themselves today. I then explore from both a skeptical and a more benevolent viewpoint how social movements' contribution to Bolivia's democracy can be evaluated. I end with a brief discussion of the findings.

Social Movements and Democratization: Visions and Viewpoints

Many have argued that the tidal wave of social movement protests that arose in Bolivia in the 1990s and peaked between 2000 and 2005 should be interpreted as a cry for more, for true, for sincere democracy and as a denunciation of the treacherous and phony democracy in place at the time (García Linera et al. 2008; Rojas Ortuste 1994; *Bolivia* 2008; Seoanne and Nacci 2007; Crabtree 2005; Assies and Salman 2003; Grey Postero 2009; Prats 2009; Zegada, Tórrez, and Cámara 2008; Kohl and Farthing 2006; Salman 2006, 2007, 2008). Alvaro García Linera and colleagues even called these movements "democratization machines of civil society" that would undermine "the structuring schemes of the institutionalized political field" (2008: 19). Such assertions are in accordance with much of the literature on the subject. Various authors have argued that social movements might be able to repair, or at least begin to correct, deficient democratic systems and may keep the adequate ones on the democratic path. Social movements are a good, and possibly even a necessary, element of democracy. Larry Diamond, for instance, states that "by enhancing the accountability, responsiveness, inclusiveness, effectiveness, and hence legitimacy of the political system, a vigorous civil society gives citizens respect for the state and positive engagement with it. In the end, this improves the ability of the state to govern" (1996: 234). It is not hard to see social movements as an exemplary manifestation of such a "vigorous civil society."

However, the relatively undisputed capacity *in principle* of social movements to enliven or improve democracy becomes much more complex once the concrete mechanisms for that goal come into play and once the situation after an electoral (or revolutionary or even military) triumph comes under scrutiny. It is, of course, plausible that social movements often act in favor of subaltern, discriminated, or socially invisible groups. They could in a way mend flaws in democratic mechanisms (and even more, repressive and discriminating ones) to give such groups a voice. That, no doubt, *is* taking democracy forward. But that is only the beginning.

The very conceptualization of what democracy is, or should be, makes a key difference. For the sake of argument, I choose two amid the plethora of definitions and distinctions (Held 2006; Axtmann 2003; Diamond 1999, 2008; Van Beek 2005): one for a more formal, institutionalized, and representative democracy (often called a liberal democracy) and one for a more participatory and direct democracy. Those favoring the representative form (see, e.g., Bobbio 1990; Molina 2007) argue that a set of minimum guarantees—such as the broadest possible participation in elections, equality, free political competition, and rights for minorities—is the best possible way to do democracy. This form entails "certain institutions and practices, above all the uses of more or less free elections in which citizens of a country are entitled to vote to choose those who will govern them, with their consent, for a limited period: their representatives" (Saward 2003: 52).

In even plainer style, Joseph Schumpeter asserts that "democracy means only that the people have the opportunity of accepting or refusing the men who are to rule them" (1976: 284). These authors argue that more direct forms of democratic participation, although appealing, will in the end not work, because of problems of scale, complexity, and unequal living conditions resulting in asymmetrical opportunities for such participation. Additionally, Norberto Bobbio (1990) argues against a narrow sector-bound representation based on, for instance, class, region, or ethnic background and against a directly revocable mandate; instead, citizens ought to be represented by citizens on a fiduciary basis. Representatives should be chosen on the basis of ideas and ideologies, not on the basis of who they are (women, indigenous, gay, or whatever) or where they come from (my region, hometown, or district). Finally, Bobbio makes a plea for a democracy that is primarily a formal, not a "substantial," one: democracy does not include, for instance, the goal of complete and full equality, or a socialist or an Islamic society, or an indigenous cosmology's primacy. Democracy should be about agreed mechanisms for governance, compromise, and conflict resolution. It should be obvious that although social movements can doubtlessly contribute to the birth of such democracies, their very movement characteristics do not sit easy with such an interpretation of democracy (Szasz 1995: 150). It is a movement's very nature to pressure, frame political ideals, actively and interferingly engage in decision-making processes on the basis of concrete identities and interests and not as any citizen. Movements concern political substance, not upholding formal democratic procedures.

The affinity of social movements with direct democracy is clearly much stronger than with representative democracy. In general, and despite their heterogeneity, the gamut of thinkers on direct and participatory democracy do agree on a couple of issues: They believe the formal existence of rights and equality to be an insufficient basis for genuine and fair influence on politics. They believe state institutions are neither impartial nor neutral and tend to reproduce the "asymmetries of power and resources [that] impinge upon the meaning of liberty and equality" (Held 2006: 209–210). This distorts the ideal of equal access. For more effective control and influence, parliament, bureaucracies, and political parties ought to be more accountable and accessible. And smaller-scale entities, such as neighborhoods and factories, ought to be ruled by the stakeholders themselves and be "self-managed organizations" (212). Direct and continuous involvement in political affairs ought to be fostered, and "democratic rights need to be extended from the state to the economic enterprise and the other central organizations of society" (212). Only in such a manner can concern for the public cause be fostered, capable and knowledgeable citizens emerge, identities be acknowledged, and the system remain open for experimentation with political forms (210–216). It would involve an "assembly democracy" (Saward 2003: 54), entailing as much face-to-face gathering and decision making without formal mediation as possible.

In addition, the referendum is often mentioned as one of the more institutionalized forms of direct democracy. When participatory democracy, "also about self-organization and protest and action at all sorts of different levels and layers of national and international political life" (Saward 2003: 56), surfaces, social movements are obviously not far away. It seems uncontroversial, therefore, to suggest that social movements' impact on democracy might entail both the empowerment and the legitimation of specific groups or categories of people that "real" representative democracy tends to neglect or marginalize and thus amplify democratic participation. Also, movements, even those against the system's repression or reluctance to include all sectors of society, can and should broaden the range of methods and channels of political involvement.

Movements tend to distrust, or deem insufficient, voting and instead use public opinion campaigns, petitions, and street protests and in some cases also blockades, strikes, and violence to make themselves heard. That may arguably be called an enrichment and enlivenment of democratic mores. As Joan Prats writes, a real democrat

> believes and hopes that in the democratic polis all people have an equal right to political participation and can exercise it in real and effective freedom. . . . [And this real democrat] will fight all forms of discrimination. And as a democrat, he will fight poverty and inequality, because these cause some people to be the instrument of others and open the terrain for clientelism, populisms and exclusionary elite democracies. (2009: 10; my translation)

The claim is that democracy is possibly made up of procedures but that it *also* concerns humanitarian values, and social movements introduce this normative and "substantial" element into democracies—albeit sometimes by unconventional means.

However, others will argue that such methods weaken the democratic equilibrium: Social movements might acquire a disproportionate influence compared to the numbers of supporters they speak for and may outmatch groups that are less effective in disrupting routine decision-making mechanisms. In addition, movements often have a "substantial" view on politics and democracy: Rather than concerns about a fair and give-and-take procedure, they stress their ideals and demands. They are challengers, and sometimes reckless ones, in the arena of democratic struggles rather than formal democracy's custodian or keeper (Molina 2007).

Finally, a consideration might be that social movements can either foster alleged common goods and interests (the environment, disarmament, economic fairness) or fight for the emancipation of, or specific rights for, specific subaltern groups. In the latter case, social movements often bring the voice of specific groups or minorities to the fore. Instead of intervening as citizens, they intervene as ethnic, religious, or gendered populations that feel discriminated against or marginalized. This might lead to a political particularism that is criticized by, among others, Bobbio (1990). And it might, in some cases, lead to such effects as fear (Tilly 2002: 23) and a feeling of new exclusions among those who were formerly in privileged, or at least visible, positions. In Tilly's view, that would be a situation in which the contribution of social movements to democratization is negative. Relatively little, however, has been written about the potentially difficult relationship, *should the movements be called to govern,* between the intrinsic demand-focused nature of movements and democracy's need for checks and balances and equality. This is a central issue in what follows.

We may thus suspect that the relationship between social movements and democracy is often a multilayered and thorny one (see Chapter 1). But the

situation in Bolivia calls for the introduction of yet another aspect of the relationship between social movements and democracy. According to Luis Tapia,
one of the things social movements do, and emphatically so in Bolivia, is un-
settle and "question the order" (2009: 110). They enact a sort of "wild politics . . .
beyond the positions that the [given] social order distributed and around which
it constitutes subjects and relations of subordination, inequality, discrimination
and exploitation" (112–113).

Thus, social movements question in a fundamental way the structure of
things, the given order, the established formal democratic system, because they
experience their exclusion from it (Salman 2009). This would mean that they
not only aim to expand and make more inclusive the given democratic system
but also criticize its very groundwork. "A social movement generally emerges
when the mechanisms of mediation and representation, and of inclusion in the
social order through representative mediation, have failed or have been exclusionary" (Tapia 2009: 115). Here, the link between social movements and democracy is not merely the model of democracy in which the movements best fit
or that includes a hitherto neglected category of people in a given democratic
system. Instead, it is the rejection of the system, depicted as a dysfunctional
or even hypocritical democracy. Or alternatively, it is the right they claim to
participate in the very design of the national democracy (Chapter 1). Instead
of portraying social movements as an object of academic reflection on the link
between their actions and democracy, Tapia makes a plea to give social movements a protagonist's role in the very conceptualization of what democracy is
and should be.

This is a valid point, but the Bolivian case shows that attaining this role
is difficult when a social movement's party obtains electoral victory, largely
becoming the government's mainstay, and is tempted to focus on supporters'
ethnic difference. In such cases, identity politics rather than inclusive dialogue
threatens to characterize a movement's attitude after emerging victorious in
a democratic transition. And as a consequence, the movement might want to
annex this thing called "democracy" because members believe that, in earlier
times, it had been taken from them. Therefore, the discussion needs to go beyond the mere compatibility between social movements and given ideas of democracy and question the very groundwork of common democratic structures.
But before we turn to this question and analyze Bolivia's current developments,
let us briefly look at Bolivia's recent history.

Bolivian Turbulence, 1982–2005

In 1982, Bolivia, the poorest country in South America, regained democracy
after almost two decades of authoritarian rule. However, raging inflation and
protests over long-neglected social welfare programs prematurely ended the
left-wing government's term in 1985. The center-right coalition that assumed
power in 1985 implemented a series of neoliberal reforms, including measures

to reduce the fiscal deficit, reform the monetary system, dismantle state enterprises, slim down the state bureaucracy with massive layoffs, liberalize markets, and foster exports. It is estimated that, since then, over 65 percent of the Bolivian workforce has been unemployed, underemployed, or informally employed (Tokman 2007). The traditional correlation between poverty and ethnic background (the indigenous are thought to form the majority of the Bolivian population) remained largely intact.

Although there were various coalitions made up of various parties, there was, in general terms, a consistency in these neoliberal policies. The result was some slow, uneven, and fragile macroeconomic growth but also persistent poverty, high unemployment, and a lack of substantial progress in such areas as health care and education (the latter, however, making progress in the second half of the 1990s). Because of its clanlike nature, deafness to protest, and inaccessibility, Bolivia's political system gradually lost credibility, as did the democratic system as such (Latinobarómetro 2004). According to José Antonio Lucero (2008: 12), political parties were no more than "ideologically thin electoral vehicles." Identification with parties weakened, as did the feeling that formal politics in general mattered and deserved commitment. Instead, social organizations and movements—such as recovering trade unions and increasingly newer social movements like civic committees, federations of neighborhood councils, peasant unions, *cocaleros* (coca leaf growers), and ethnic organizations—became "the primary organizations expressing the interests of society" (Gamarra and Malloy 1995, quoted in Lucero 2008: 42). Moreover, in Tapia's words, it was a time in which "society surpassed the [state] institutionality, imposing an agenda of transformations with the banners of deepening and broadening democracy" (2008: 33).

The country's daily routine became characterized by uncountable protests that started in the 1990s and peaked in 2000–2005. They were the response to an exclusionary political system unable and unwilling to change economic policies (Assies and Salman 2003; McNeish 2006) and unable and unwilling to change the petrified and dysfunctional democratic mores. The movements that emerged in the 1990s and came into full bloom from 2000 to 2005 are those of the coca growers (Coca Trópico); the Federación de Juntas de Vecinos (FEJUVEs; Federation of Neighborhood Councils) in various cities, especially El Alto; the Coordinación, a group of water consumers in and around Cochabamba and other cities; the migrating peasants looking for new land in the east (Confederación de Colonizadores [Confederation of Colonizers]); and miners, both salaried and those in cooperatives and holding mining concessions. Additionally, there were the indigenous movements like those mentioned earlier: CONAMAQ, Confederación de Pueblos Indígenas del Oriente (CIDOB; Eastern Indigenous Peoples Confederation), Coordinadora de Pueblos Étnicos del Oriente (CPESC; Eastern Ethnic People's Coordination), and Movimiento de los Trabajadores Rurales sin Tierra (MST; Landless Rural Workers' Movement). The indigenous also gained prominence as peasant-cum-ethnic person, as in the CSUTCB and its women's section, Federación de Mujeres Campesinas, Bartolina Sisa, or in *sindicatos* (rural unions) or *ayllus*. *Ayllus* are the traditional Andes community organizational form, combining territory and symbolic kinship. Furthermore, there were actions by transporters, teachers, health workers, students, pensioners, street vendors, organizations opposing free-trade treaties and other outcomes of globalization (Mayorga and Córdova 2008), and many others.

Not all the above represent consolidated social movements, and there is much overlap among them. And, conspicuously, the once-powerful labor confederation Central Obrera Boliviana (COB; Bolivian Workers' Center) had little influence, having suffered severe weakening in the 1980s and 1990s. Nevertheless, the protests were massive, often in the form of street rallies, blockades, gatherings, ensembles, and *cabildos* (plenary street manifestations). Thus, according to García Linera and colleagues, they were "mechanisms that were projected as political systems, complementary or alternative, able to comply more efficiently and democratically than parties and the 'aggregation of wills' through liberal representation" (2008: 19; see also Lucero 2008). It was often more than merely the concrete protest issue that was at stake. Protest alluded to a comprehensive alternative to the ruinous liberal democratic legacy, a new democracy in which these social movements had an important voice. As a consequence, many came to feel that they were represented, to a greater or lesser extent, in the MAS, the movement and party that brought Evo Morales to power in 2005.

The MAS developed as a movement party or party of movements (Zegada, Tórrez, and Cámara 2008: 43). It won over many movements by combining class and socioeconomic terms with ethnic terms. It synthesized national-popular, leftist Marxist, and indigenist inspirations. It represented the popular and the indigenous, all those suffering the consequences of the politics of "elites, imperialists, neoliberals, *vendepatrias*" (land sellers), as protest slogans denounced them. It was the embodiment of the *real* democratic will of Bolivia, according to Tapia (2008) and García Linera (2008). The outcome, the victory of Morales and the MAS in December 2005, was unprecedented. First, these elections signaled the end of the old party system. The level of trust in politicians and parties is traditionally low in Latin America (see Camp 2001), but in Bolivia it had reached dramatic depths (Latinobarómetro 2004; Salman 2007). The victory of the MAS crushed a consolidated but failing and inept party system, and the movement party assumed power. But the minority sectors that had been represented by the old polity had not, of course, disappeared and would in the future search for new ways of articulation.

Second, and often highlighted, this was the first time a candidate of indigenous descent had won the presidency of Bolivia. It confirmed the emancipation processes that had been taking place in earlier decades (Van Cott 2008: 1). The awakening indigenous self-awareness of Bolivia's alleged majority, facilitated in a paradoxical way by the "un-traditionalizing" shifts in indigenous habitat and access to city life (De Munter and Salman 2009: 444), contributed to an increasing awareness of the systematic exclusion of indigenous representation from previous governing coalitions.

Third, and closely related to the above, a novel political configuration emerged out of the frustration with the defective party system, the indigenous exclusion, and the neoliberal policies that had been pursued in the country since 1985. The MAS's proposals combined ethnic ingredients referring to governing ethics (alleged indigenous traditions, such as subservient authorities, continuous deliberation, and close contact with the community as a whole; see Van Cott 2008: 13) with ingredients alluding to the ideological rejection of greed, indifference toward the environment and *Pachamama*,[6] the sellout of national sovereignty (Albro 2005: 445–448), and financial gain above well-being (*vivir bien*; "living well" instead of avariciously). The revival of indigenous self-awareness thus merged with a criticism of white imperialism and harsh, neoliberal capitalism. It made the political shift more than a routine exchange of power positions and change in ideology; this was, in the words of MAS supporters, a revolution. Note that the MAS was considered an antisystemic party (Assies and Salman 2005); it allegedly reinvented democracy outside the realm of the given democratic and political framework (Tapia 2008: 23).

Fourth, reiterating, Morales's victory was possible partly because a sustained and massive series of protests, on themes that many Bolivians were concerned or angered about, had delegitimized and dented the incumbent party and electoral system. These themes were the exclusion of the indigenous and the poor, neoliberalism, privatizations, corruption, the misuse of the country's natural resources, the lack of economic growth and employment, and a "treacherous democracy" (De Munter and Salman 2009: 448). These movements now shifted positions from being challengers, as they are often called, to members (Tilly 1978; McAdam et al. 2001). Hence, not only the political and polity makeup but also the social movement landscape in Bolivia radically changed.

Movements on the Throne

The above sketch clearly suggests that the ambitions manifested in the social movements and articulated in the MAS comprised much more than new socioeconomic directions or a specific group's inclusion. Largely shaped by ethnic discourses, the goal was nothing less than to refound the country, reshuffle traditional sociocultural relationships, reinvent state institutions and democracy, and give an explicit and large role to *el pueblo* (the people), purportedly personalized in the social movements. Consequentially, something remarkable happened to the new administration during the transition process: Morales, the MAS, and subsequently also the media and even the opposition began to refer to "the" social movements as though they were a clearly identifiable, addressable entity. It is now very common to hear Evo Morales say, "I will ask the social movements to defend our democratic revolution" or "to support the new

constitution" (see, e.g., *Ultimas Noticias*, August 22, 2008), or to hear a critical journalist say, "The social movements have hijacked Evo's administration"
(see, e.g., *La Prensa*, November 10, 2009). A spokesperson of one movement
said, "We, the social movements, will closely watch the current process" (see *La
Prensa*, March 6, 2009, September 13, 2009).

The social movements, as a whole and strategically portrayed as united,
seem to have acquired a sort of name tag. The new constitution formulates an
explicit and legal role for them. The current ministerial cabinet has a *vicemin-
istro de coordinación con movimientos sociales* (vice-minister for coordination
with social movements). Title VI, article 141, section 2 of the constitution states,
"Organized civil society will control public administration at all state levels"
(my translation). Here, social movements are not only recognized as legitimate
defenders of interest but also integrated into the legislation process and in state
affairs in such a way that they are almost part of the state institution. Through
the social movements, *el pueblo* is now given the task to watch over democracy.
In his speeches, Morales often calls on the movements to participate in his administration (Mayorga 2007). Movements are addressed as though they could
be employed, or at least called on, to achieve specific political goals or be at
the service of specific political actors. Additionally, the government established
Coordinadora Nacional para el Cambio (CONALCAM; National Coordinator
for the Change), a coalition of national movements that allegedly guarantee the
administration's compliance with its promises.

Social movements[7] are in an awkward and complex position. First, the new
constitution is ambivalent about their position. Although they are called on to
guard the processes of change the current administration is realizing, in the
constitution they are referred to as "organized civil society." There is no clear
and unequivocal reference to specific entities and, in theory, staunch supporters, lukewarm sympathizers, and head-on opposition movements are included.
In practice, however, this is not the case.

Second, the government makes no secret of its intention to have the final
word. Decisions are often taken in parliament, and even more often by the president or his cabinet, without consulting civil society representatives. The over-
ruling of the position of the social movements involved in Patzi's "communal
trial" is just one example. The originally proclaimed regular meetings between
the president and CONALCAM are little more than occasional encounters during which little time is reserved for questioning of Morales. In fact, the monitoring to which Morales often refers is not much more than a token discourse
(Atahuichi 2010).

Third, the government is attempting to co-opt "the" social movements.
Cloaked in discourses of dialogue, participation, and unity, the administration
is trying to transform the movements into supporters and followers by asking them to critically review the government's actions but establishing only a
few, hazy channels for them. The government also tends to put carefully selected movement leaders in governmental positions, hence suggesting that the

movements are a governing power parallel to parliament and the constitutional assembly; in reality, however, their presence at decision-making tables is an exception.

Fourth, the movements are a heterogeneous group. Some of them are, or believe they are, a real constitutive part of the MAS. They show up at progovernment rallies and express their trust in the polity. Others sympathize with the current administration but continue to focus on their particular interests. They demand decisions, and if necessary criticize them, albeit in soft words. Yet others insist they are independent and provide critical counteranalyses and counterproposals to government doings. And then there are those who take a more radical position on policies than the government is willing to take. In these cases, a stern indigenist discourse is often part of this distancing between the two—even though in the eyes of many nonindigenous the government itself is already too ethnic in its expressions. Still, especially with regard to indigenous, local, and departmental autonomy; indigenous justice; genuine communal democracy; and decolonization, harsh words are often uttered against the MAS (Saavedra 2009).

The position that some movements (or parts thereof) took in the Patzi affair illustrates this. In a way, they claim a big say in government affairs because they consider themselves authorized participants in it and feel entitled to disagree with the government's stance because they are in a position to interpret the new rules just as much as the government is. They claim, moreover, that the indigenous voice should now (at long last!) prevail (Mamani 2008: 102; Saavedra 2009). Each backs a style of governing that would make its views and prerogatives decisive, shoving aside competing positions. They claim *their* democracy and insist that the government—*their* government—should do the same. Other views on the workings of democracy are more inclusive. For instance, a newspaper columnist insists that the "plural citizenry," not just a selected group, should have a voice (Torrico 2010: 4). Fernando Campero, Gonzalo Mendieta, and Fernando Molina urge Bolivia to acknowledge that "all ideas in the game have the right to compete and none of them can attribute to itself a substantive superiority" (2009: 6). But that is precisely the conundrum of social movements, particularly the more radical indigenist ones. Besides that, the MAS is obviously both unwilling and unable to govern as a movement.

For all the social movement positions referred to above, the ambiguities with regard to being a critical independent entity or a government mainstay are valid in varying degrees. And all the movements are haunted by the conflict between wholehearted support (especially when opposition is fierce or parliament obstructionist) and the self-image of autonomy with its ongoing struggle for group interests. The scale and intensity of antigovernment protests initially diminished when the MAS took power.[8] According to reports from the UNIR,[9] protests against the government peaked in 2006–2008, but these were mainly incited by antigovernment movements in the eastern half of the country, which at the time were struggling for departmental autonomies. After 2009, the number of conflicts tended to rise, but they were less serious; only a small minority related to ideological issues or questioned local or national authorities.[10] Most were over economic or salary issues or reflected internal conflicts in society or between pro-MAS social movements.[11] In the second half of 2009, only 20 percent of the protests related to public and political administration or the legitimacy of the polity. Protests concerned various topics and regions, and often had local, particular, and specific causes. Although the UNIR concludes that distrust between society and the polity persisted, it also seems that protests directly beleaguering state policy directions or legitimacy diminished after the lowland-opposition conglomerate (a series of right-wing social movements) fragmented in late 2008. Protests challenged the state on concrete measures, such as its forsaking mediation between opposing groups, providing deficient services, and responding to demands too slowly, but not its legitimacy or ideology.

This, however, has changed since late 2010. The impression emerges that social movements have become less hesitant to challenge "their" government. It began with a governmental decree announcing an increase in gasoline prices of up to 70 percent, to accord with international levels, and thus put an end to gasoline smuggling to neighboring countries and to subsidies that were costing the government around USD 660 million a year. Some movement leaders initially defended the measure, while admitting that they knew it would be painful for everybody. After all, it would affect food prices, transport costs, and so on—which, of course, is exactly what it did. The government also announced measures to compensate for the public's increased costs, and went to great efforts to explain the necessity of the measure. But this was to no avail. In the last week of December, protests mounted, leading to a remarkable moment: At 10:00 P.M. on the last day of the month, Evo Morales appeared on television and declared that he was revoking the decree. But prices failed to return to previous levels. In the following months, Morales's popularity plummeted.[12] His announcement that wages in 2011 would be increased by 10 percent did not convince the apparently recuperating COB or various other social movement sectors, such as those of health care workers and teachers.[13] Protests in March and April forced the government to grant concessions. Hence, in early 2011, it seemed that social movements were losing their reluctance to confront the government and that relations between the movements and the government were normalizing.

All this being the case, in what way can we say that democracy has improved? That social movements lived up to their promise that they would revive a failing democracy? Rubén D. Atahuichi (2010) concluded in *La Prensa* that the social movements had become merely "functional" for the MAS administration—that is, they simply obeyed MAS instructions and were no longer autonomous. According to Atahuichi, MAS representatives in parliament were explicitly forbidden to form alliances to pursue specific issues; they were allowed to operate only as a unanimous MAS squadron. But protests that flared in early 2011 seem to belie his diagnosis. Critics of the social movements' "big mouth," on the other hand, point to the current asymmetrical access to the polity. But here, too, the big mouth not only boasts about movements' privileged access and programmatic closeness to "their" government but also defies that government. In both cases, the claim that democracy has contracted as a result of collusion between specific movements and the polity no longer seems tenable. Additionally, others note the vigor and legitimacy with which formerly marginalized population sectors now speak out. In their view, democracy has expanded. Moreover, other developments belie the idea that the government controls the movements. Measures that would have affected specific movements' social bases or the poorer population in general have been abrogated thanks to the movements' protests.

Bolivian developments thus seem to provide support for social movements both enhancing democracy by fighting for the vulnerable and, in the end, obstructing rather than contributing to a fair, equal, and unprejudiced democratic playing field. In the following two sections, I explore support and arguments for both positions.

Social Movements: Their Alleged Contribution to an Uneven Democratic Arena

If democracy is first and foremost a procedural arrangement, an institutional edifice guaranteeing equality, liberty, and civil and political rights, then social movements, especially after victory, are unlikely to contribute to a better democracy. Bolivia is full of examples. First, the government made a clear distinction between the social movements whose presence it will accept, and even help, and those that it will not take into account, will ignore, and even will deprive of the now very prestigious denomination of *being* a social movement. In favoring some segments of "organized civil society" over others, the MAS is a movement rather than a government. The very right of social movements to manifest themselves is thus affected; they are placed in unequal conditions with regard to their access to the government, and political rights are violated—albeit the media in Bolivia tend to favor them and denounce this governmental marginalization.

Second, the pro-MAS movements tend to assume a radical "substantial" position in today's political debates in Bolivia: They put goals before procedures. Hence, they will often proclaim—as the government does but less categorically—that they aim for "communal justice," "giving priority to rights for *Pachamama* over human rights,"[14] or that they dream of a "communitarian democracy," without mentioning minority rights or the opposition's views or the possibility of a future electoral defeat. As far as they are concerned, the era of the neoliberals is over.[15] In their view, the processes and changes currently being implemented cannot and will not be reversed, by whatever democratic outcome

But here again they seem to call on the MAS as a movement rather than a governing party, which is, in principle, electorally defeatable. Moreover, according to some, the changes are not radical or fast enough, and the movements foment protests that do not seem to take into consideration that it is *their* government. And yet others protest because changes are not sufficiently ethnic. In a February 14, 2010, interview in *La Prensa*, Patzi himself criticized the government for rejecting his "communal trial," for "talking about a [state, democratic] institutionality [that would be] more important than an indigenous society," a stand he rejected. Felipe Quispe, a radical indigenous leader, stated that "[Evo] should act differently, like the indigenous think; that would really be a contribution for the new generations, a revolution, a real change, and if he doesn't, it is no good for anything" (see *La Prensa*, January 21, 2010). Silvia Rivera, a Bolivian social scientist, said in a recent interview that, in her view, "the Indian hegemony implies the 'indianization' of the whole of society" (Rivera Cusicanqui 2009: 133; see also Saavedra 2009: 121). And when the MAS was selecting candidates for parliamentary seats in August 2009, the FEJUVE of El Alto demanded that the MAS incorporate a quota of their representatives: "Last year we were not heard; this time we'll make our petition prevail" (see *La Prensa*, July 26, 2009). And in late 2006, when the constituent assembly was stalled by grim debates and not making any progress, a nationwide mobilization was announced, with the support of the MAS. The *curac mallku* (an Andean honorary title bestowed on Daniel Miranda of the Consejo de Ayllus Originarios de Potosí [CAOP; Council of Indigenous Ayllus of Potosí]) confirmed the possibility that the *pueblos originarios* (indigenous peoples) might mobilize to prod the constituent assembly to start working again.

Institutionalized and formal democratic processes seem to be monitored by the social movements (and even to some degree by the MAS itself) and forced to present the outcome the movements want (as happened on a few occasions when parliament or the *asamblea constitutional* [constitutional assembly] was beleaguered by protesters) *or else*. Such voices and attitudes, it could be argued, are those of maximalists who put irreversible results above the rights of opponents. But the government itself often expresses itself in terms of specific goals that *will* be achieved, irrespective of whatever opposition.

Nonsupporters of the MAS regard this as impinging on their rights and their equality. In early 2010, the MAS proposed a bill on administration of justice, in which it stated that indigenous justice—because of its specific tradition and because the MAS wanted to establish nonhierarchical relations between "ordinary" and indigenous justice—would not include a right to appeal. The government thus affirmed that justice would be applied differently to different categories of citizens.[16] The MAS has also been criticized for inaugurating Morales for a second time, in Tiwanaku, an archeological site near La Paz that is important to the highland indigenous but with which many Bolivians cannot identify, thus violating the "lay" and neutral nature of the state. Moreover, in the eyes of many nonindigenous, the frequent use of words like *decolonization* and *communal democracy*, the categorical refutation of the "Occident's neoliberalism," the claim that all Bolivia's nations constitute the "plurinational state" to substitute for the old "colonial" one, and the like, are exclusionary and not representative of a government that is "for all Bolivians." The "plurinational state," in the words of Jorge Lazarte Rojas, forsakes the republic, and "the modern republic is of the citizens, whereas the plurinational state is of the ethnic groups" (2009).

Such words are therefore interpreted as belonging to a vocabulary that underscores the division between indigenous and nonindigenous Bolivians and signals a state preference for the former over the latter.[17] In their embodiment as social movements, they are seen as saboteurs rather than promoters of democracy. But in their own or the MAS's terms, they are the correction, or undoing, of former exclusion and discrimination; they are now setting things right. This might be interpreted as a continuation of the sort of toil and struggle the MAS embodied when it was still a social movement and is unable to tone down now that it is the governing party. And thus, in the eyes of critics, the MAS is bad for democracy and the rule of law. Fernando Cuellar Nuñez, president of the Santa Cruz Colegio de Abogados (Santa Cruz College of Attorneys), stated, "The state of law has broken down, and that is dangerous because we could relapse into a state of barbarity where the law of the strongest rules" (quoted in "Defenderemos al estado" 2008).[18] That may be an exaggeration, but it expresses the concerns many feel about how stringently the rule of law is still applied in Bolivia.[19] And according to many, the social movements and the preference for "communal and collective logics" behind them play a prime role in the weakening of state law. Jorge Romero fulminates:

> Since when, in a democratic society, can people of a neighborhood, a community or a village demand that all their inhabitants think, feel, and act unanimously in themes that are debated in public space? By what right do they try the dissident opinion and punish it? Is there a law against having an opinion? (2009; my translation)

Romero states that not only the current hegemonic position of the pro-MAS social movements and their viewpoints but also the collectivism or communalism that is hailed as truly indigenous make the opposition (and various academics and journalists) concerned about such values as individual sovereignty, secrecy of the vote, and societal tolerance. Doubts can also be raised about a number of other issues. For example, beyond the social movements, chances for participation in government by citizens are minimal, and attempts by the government to co-opt the movements will hardly help their internal democracy or independence, but it will restrict their ability to raise more fundamental questions.[20] Molina called the MAS's adherence to democracy a "conversion without faith" (2007).

The concerns of all these skeptics were reaffirmed by the president's speech March 7, 2010, during the campaign for departmental and municipal elections scheduled for April 4 of that year. In that speech Morales stated he would not allow "cross-voting"—for example, voting for the MAS candidate for depart-mental governor and for another party's candidate for mayor. He was impelled to make this statement because some popular candidates had lost the backing of the MAS, switched to another party, and were now leading in the polls. People even merely considering the possibility of sticking with their candidate rather than their party were called traitors and defectors by Morales (see *La Razón*, March 8, 2010).

All these examples clearly suggest that social movements, and the MAS in its movement's cloak, might be good critics of elitist or exclusionary democra-cies and might be good at giving a more prominent position to sectors of the population that were traditionally discriminated against or ignored[21] but that they, once in power, are unlikely to stand up for a democracy that will include others—namely, former opponents or simply the less well organized layers of civil society. Movements' loyalty to and dependence on the government might suffocate their ability to pose fundamental questions and limit their room for internal dissidence, although this danger in Bolivia in the early months of 2011 seemed to be subsiding. The governing party, on the other hand, once a move-ment itself, is discouraged from taking the edge off its movementist attitude and will therefore be tempted to haggle over its governing responsibilities. The pursuit of the movements' goals and interests is likely to prevail over the gov-ernment's guardianship of democracy as an even-handed arena of dialogue, in-clusiveness, and respect for minorities or those without a voice. The MAS seems to be inclined toward such a position. But is this account of the troubled rela-tionship between social movements and democratization really the whole story?

Social Movements: Their Alleged Contribution to a Better Democracy

The demand for an inclusive system, more direct participation, the acknowledg-ment of indigenous governing traditions and values (Rojas Ortuste 1994: 81–82), and genuine national sovereignty—in short, for a better democracy—was part and parcel of the MAS's strategies and campaigns. The philosophy underlying this claim concerned more than just inappropriate operation of the incumbent democratic system by some corrupt parties and politicians. It also included the groundwork of the system, one that many claimed had been imposed on Bo-livia. It did not reflect the indigenous majority's cultures and traditions, and the indigenous had never been asked to participate in the political give-and-take that led to the decisions on what political system, democracy being one of the choices, would suit these cultures.

The social movements' case, therefore, was not merely about being allowed access to the political system; it was about the demand to radically amend that system and to postulate new criteria for a fair, appropriate, and culturally suit-able system to govern the country. Thus, it would be wrong to subject current efforts to make changes to the criteria and standards of liberal democracy, with its mantras about equality, representation, fair and transparent elections, secret voting, checks and balances, individualism, and blindness to particular identities. After all, Bolivia's process of change goes beyond the optimalization of the given structure of democracy. Instead, it could open up new criteria as to what democracy could and should be, given Bolivia's sociocultural makeup.

Severe criticisms of the Western imposition on Bolivia and other former colonies have been articulated in recent decades. For a situation in which alien criteria for distinguishing between right and wrong, realistic and unrealistic, or modern and backward have come to prevail over even *thinking* about reality, the term *epistemological violence* has been suggested (Nandy 1988; see also Lins Ribeiro and Escobar 2006). Mary Louise Pratt states that "on the periphery . . . the price of living by the ideological compass of modernity has been to live one's own reality in terms of lack, fragmentation, partiality, imitativeness, and unfulfillment" (2002: 31). Javier Sanjinés, talking about the "asymmetric times" produced in a sociocultural setting by an imposed modernity, adds:

> It is impossible to talk about democracy if no public spheres are construed that promote the acknowledgement of inequitable subjectivities, that try to overcome the time-asymmetries (contemporaneities that are not contemporary are often rejected for being anachronistic), through debate and dialogue. Only by liberating the subjectivities of the anachronism in which they are incarcerated by the rhetoric of modernity will we be able to re-establish the much-needed symmetry between the past and the present. (2009: 43; my translation)

On a somewhat more political level, Deborah Yashar writes:

> Indigenous movements generally argue that the individual should not be the only unit of representation, nor should it be privileged. They demand that the state uphold equal rights and responsibilities for Indians as individuals and in this sense are calling for the fulfillment of liberal ideals. But they argue as well that the state should recognize indigenous communities as a historically prior and autonomous sphere of political rights, jurisdiction and autonomy. (2005: 292; see also Assies, van der Haar, and Hoekema 2000; Sieder 2002; Cadena 2006; Van Cott 2008)

If the issue is not merely becoming inserted into given political systems, which are backed by specific traditions of thought and logic, but instead fundamentally questioning these traditions of thought and logic and the concomitant institutionalization of politics, then we need to evaluate the contribution of the (mostly ethnic) social movements in Bolivia in a different way. We should not only look at the degree to which the MAS and the social movements enrich or threaten the habitual democratic edifice but also question the criteria and modes of thought that this edifice inculcated us with to judge, and often adhere to, its qualities. If we start to question the epistemological and conceptual groundwork of the democratic institutions that have been handed down, we need to ask, for instance, about the veneration of representation as the hard nucleus of democracy: Are other ways of seeking embodiment and advocacy of interests, such as designation through deliberation and consensus, possibly equally valid and worthy—at least in specific situations? Is the independence of the judicial sphere really the only way to obtain fairness, impartiality, and equality, or might plenary communal administration of justice also be able to do that? Or do it even better, because damage restoration will be part of the outcome? If harmony with nature and ancestors is crucial in a given cultural setting, should *Pachamama* not also be a title holder of rights—instead of only the individual?

In an effort to reveal some aspects of the Andino cosmological paradigm and the ways its contradictions are mastered, Javier Medina (2010: 157–162) mentions some interesting elements that could be explored here to speculative on the prospects of alternative political designs and solutions. Departing from the idea of an asymmetrical Andean cosmological order of complementary elements, he mentions first, an "asymmetrical triangle" or "compensation" as a social or political correcting element. The intention here is to rectify inequality: The wealthier, stronger, or more powerful need to recompense for that position by granting an extra portion to the subaltern. They need to do so for their own sake; if not, harmony will be broken and both will pay. The ritual of suspending a triangle in the house on which hang a pair of pants from the top angle and a skirt from each of the two lower angles symbolizes the intention. As do practices in which the elder of two brothers recompenses for his physical strength primacy and age advantage by granting a communal leadership position to the younger one or in which the higher hierarchical position of two brothers-in-law is given to the one who married the sister, but in redistribution the first is obliged to help out the other with his work.

A second mechanism is the *tinku*: the ritual fight between two halves to enable full integration. The third is mediation: a third party standing above and between two antagonists is entitled to decide on and monitor recompense for inequalities. Finally, there is the *kuti*: an ongoing inversion, restitution, and return, guiding the course of time, which is seen as cyclical rather than linear. It is rash, but tempting, to see such principles embodied in indigenous practices in Bolivia's current political arena: not abstract equality but compensation for (historical?) inequality; not sterile equilibrium but evenhandedness; not concentration of power but its diffusion; not punishment by independent strangers but a restoration of harmony, a redistribution of harm done, and a lesson given by one's peers (Medina 2008: 41); not only checks and balances but also a moral obligation for the ruler to heed the vulnerable and, if need be, end up poorer himself. Hence, social justice and expressing collective preferences, or obtaining what is right and democratic, can be imagined in ways other than through the familiar tune of determining the people's will through the secret ballot and professional administration of justice.

But such ideas touch on the most fundamental assumptions of preceptorial thinking about democracy, rights, and justice. Accepting their legitimacy means acknowledging that the impulsive indignation that often crops up whenever these assumptions are put in doubt or basic rights are allegedly violated might no longer be appropriate. In Bolivia, the Western tradition is summoned to think with another logic, to skip (or at least bracket) its routine judgments and assumptions about what is democratic and procedurally correct and what citizen equality is. It is in this sphere that the pressures from and the interventions of the social movements, and some of the measures of the MAS administration, try to improve democracy or make it more culturally appropriate. And in the current phase, it should not be a surprise that those efforts are experimental, that cases, examples, and solutions surge ad hoc, and that some incidents cause frowns among the defenders of canonic democracy. However, instead of reading into those incidents the demise of democracy (as we know it), the reaction should perhaps be one of entering into dialogue, a dialogue in which the standards and considerations of different viewpoints should be clarified.

In addition, there are a couple of significant aspects to current developments. First, the MAS is attempting to live up to its promise to bring about a new democracy, by searching for mechanisms for direct participation. The invitations to CONALCAM to put forward its observations, no matter how biased and tedious the meetings may have become; the decision on several occasions to put referenda up for a vote (all of which were won by the MAS); and the submission of the new constitutional text to a popular verdict suggest the government takes democracy seriously. Also the insistence on naming state organs (parliament, judicial courts, the electoral court) *plurinacional* (plurinational), the decision to have the supreme judicial authorities chosen by popular vote instead of appointed by the president,[22] the policy to promote decentralization and admit various levels of autonomy, and the—albeit somewhat whimsical—willingness to enter into negotiations with most organizations and movements that express discontent all suggest that democracy does matter to the administration. Furthermore, trust in democracy in the country has conspicuously increased since Morales's first election (Seligson et al. 2006).

The unresolved issue of how a new democratic institutionality should be framed apparently did not negatively influence people's perception of its advancement, although more recent figures are pending. But at least initially, a majority seemed to celebrate the end of the former, corrupt model. In most Latin American countries, the perceptions of how democracy works and how it may (or may not) be put to use to obtain certain results are also saturated with the idiosyncrasies of the respective societal compositions and histories. Why should Bolivia, with its indigenous majority and the concomitant traditions that are often still very much alive, have to be different? This underlines the need for an analysis that includes grass roots' and ethnic groups' perceptions and practices with regard to democracy.

Admittedly, many of the MAS's measures and attitudes are dubious, considering Bolivia's current political turbulence. But perhaps we should allow things to take their time; democracy as we currently know it also took its time, and remains (rightly so) an experiment and process rather than a consolidated procedural formality.

Discussion

There seem to be good reasons to be skeptical about the social movements' and the MAS's role in current developments of Bolivia's democracy, as well as good reasons to be optimistic. Some current developments—such as the presence of a biased or even prejudiced state, the pressure to make the state abide by indigenous customary law, the inclination to rank goals and substance over procedural and institutional equilibriums, and the tendency to politicize the judiciary—suggest that the inherently selfish nature of social movements (and the MAS) prevents them from bringing about or upholding the so much treasured formal, fair, inclusive democracies.

Other developments, however—like the official acknowledgment of different forms of local political organization and the administration of justice, extra state efforts for the poor and vulnerable, the stronger presence of formerly marginalized sectors in the polity, and the improved accessibility of state institutions combined with what, in general, are positive assessments from the outside about individual liberties, freedom of press, and a nonrepressive state[23]—suggest that the social movements' rise to power brought good things to Bolivian democracy.

It remains important to keep in mind that Evo Morales's election signified, at least to a certain degree, a rejection of the traditional, liberal-representative democratic practices that in the eyes of many had lost legitimacy. The question of whether these problems were only the result of a distortion of what, in principle, is an adequate and good model, or whether, alongside changes in socioeconomic policies and stronger state intervention in economic affairs, substantial changes in the democratic system are desired, needed, and possible in Bolivia has in a way been answered by the two successive victories of the MAS: something more radical than just an adjustment or minor correction of the canonic democratic edifice is in order.

Among the key dimensions of this reinvention of democracy is that the current administration creates trust and self-recognition, and thus self-esteem, in hitherto largely excluded sectors of the population and guarantees genuine access to state institutions. And among its positive accomplishments is its sympathetic, and hence more open, stance toward population sectors that have often been marginalized and excluded from sources of information and from decision making. This might be the first time in Bolivian history that poor and ethnically distinct sectors of Bolivian society with little education feel that the government is not (at best) indifferent to or (at worst) hostile toward them. For those sectors, there is now more transparency and democracy.

This is democratic renewal–cum-consolidation: it embodies a process through which effective societal control and the capable participation of civil society (vigilance and loyalty) interact with a generally decisive, inspired, and transparent state and its institutions (Diamond 1996). Moreover, César Rojas Ríos stresses that strengthening democracy is the only way out of controversies and out of a threatening escalation scenario: "Democracy allows, and does not repress, people's wishes to express their discontent, . . . it should adapt to and institutionalize a new socio-political configuration" (2007: 278–279). Democracy, in his view, should be a process, an activity of "making, unmaking, and remaking" (279). The process Bolivia is currently undergoing attests to democracy not being exclusively a formal mechanism to reach outcomes supported by various majorities; it should, as procedure, be part of the continuous effort to institutionalize the ways that people from all walks of life aspire to be represented and to participate.

That, however, is only part of the story. It does not sufficiently cover the transition of social movements from demanders to established members of the governing league and does not make a sufficiently clear distinction between the role and obligations of the governing entity and those of the supporting movements. According to Jean L. Cohen and Andrew Arato (1992: 502), social movements should, in normal circumstances, have civil society as their terrain, as the site where they assemble, organize, and mobilize, even if their targets are the economy and the state. They add that this duality is crucial: social movements concern not only identity, emancipation, democracy, and presence in the civil society sphere but also influence. Social movements, in varying ways, aim for insertion into and bearing on the political and economic institutions, to democratize them, to secure the goals these movements had set. In this sense, there is nothing strange about the possibility of a social movement obtaining a share of state power and pursuing "the democratization of values, norms and institutions"; if "part of the achievement of movements is the institutionalization of rights, then the end of a social movement . . . does not mean the end of the context of the generation and constitution of social movements" (562).

This helps in understanding the ambivalent nature of Bolivia's social movements since 2005: the translation of their goals and ideals into concrete institutional and policy changes does not make superfluous the presence in civil society of rallies, organization, and mobilization; on the contrary, their aims continue to combine "the double political task . . . of . . . acquisition of influence by publics, associations, and organizations on political society, and the institutionalization of their gains" (Cohen and Arato 1992: 555). But that double task is now, in part, distributed over the two spheres: the MAS needs to secure the gains, while the movements need to continue to organize and mobilize and to search for both societal support and political influence.

But this also means that we should acknowledge the key difference in position between the MAS as governing party and personification of the state and the social movements that constitute it. Tensions arise especially when the ethnic dimension comes in: social movements representing the identities and interests of specific ethnic groups are unlikely to think in terms of inclusive citizenship—a category the state should under all circumstances privilege even if its policies are, justifiably, aimed at benefiting specific, historically excluded ethnic sectors and honoring their interventions in the debate on democracy and the political system. When and wherever the state loses sight of the citizen, its affinities with ethnic or other social movements might be an obstacle rather than an asset. In this respect, the MAS has made mistakes, and it continues to make them. Movements, including ethnic movements, may act as social movements. They may struggle on the free terrain of civil society for their identities, interests, and further inclusion and try to influence the state. The state, on the other hand, may show its affinity with and responsiveness to these movements, but it has the vital obligation to defend the rights and the equality of all possible voices that the civil society may produce. The MAS is still in the process of discovering how to do that.

NOTES

Acknowledgments: I thank Gonzalo Rojas, Ricardo Calla, María Soledad Quiroga, and anonymous readers for their valuable comments.

1. But Bolivia, according to anthropologist Ricardo Calla (personal conversation, May 2012), is *diverse in its diversity,* including when it comes to ethnicities and their boundaries: there are Aymara who speak Quechua, Quechua who live in predominantly Aymara regions, Guaraní who married Moxeño and live in Chiquitanía territories, and Aymara urban youngsters who are into gothic and hardly speak their parents' language. The "Aymara indigenous people" is therefore a debatable denomination. This is not the place to elaborate on the issue (see Zavaleta 2008), but it is good to keep in mind.

2. The MAS is often referred to as a party-movement and combines in its discourse ideological and ethnic elements.

3. This never did materialize.

4. In David R. Karp and Todd R. Clear's definition, "Community justice broadly refers to all variants of crime prevention and justice activities that explicitly include the community in their processes and set the enhancement of community quality of life as a goal. Recent initiatives include community crime prevention, community policing, community defense, community prosecution, community courts, and restorative justice sanctioning systems" (2000: 323). In Bolivia, community justice is acknowledged in the new constitution, but the law detailing its scope (passed in December 2010) substantially restricts its application, to the disappointment of more radical indigenous groups.

5. Obviously, the Latin American custom of patronage, or clientelism, often violated this principle. But this tradition was exactly the sort of thing the MAS had been rallying

against: dirty politics. In that sense, the MAS was obliged to do better. But as elaborated below, various circumstances made this difficult: the MAS's debt to the social movements that had supported its campaign, the MAS's not always categorical defense of liberal democracy, and the stubbornness of clientelistic cultures.

6. *Pachamama* is usually translated as "Mother Earth." But it really refers to the world and the universe as a whole and, in today's parlance, is often invoked to refer to the indigenous cosmology, in which all things are connected: humankind, ancestors, the natural environment, the supernatural, and so on. It therefore highlights interdependencies among all these and, consequently the need for a respectful, reciprocal, and thankful interaction with others and with nature.

7. I, regretfully, largely omit in this chapter the social movements that emerged opposing Morales's administration. They are important, and they deserve analysis (see Peña 2009; Assies 2006; Zegada, Tórrez, and Cámara 2008: 169–178) but not in this chapter's discussion of social movements and transitions (and in Bolivia's case, after victory). Other movements, like employers' and entrepreneurs' *gremios* (guilds) and feminist movements, also receive only tangential mention.

8. However, they increased in the eastern region of the country, where the opposition has its stronghold.

9. The UNIR is a Bolivian nongovernmental organization dedicated to promoting democracy, dialogue, negotiation, and information. It does research, training, and intervention. See the UNIR's website at http://unirbolivia.org/nuevo.

10. Some serious protests took place in March and April 2011, mainly by the COB, on issues of salary increases. This suggests that the government-friendly attitude of the pro-MAS social movements is weakening.

11. The conflicts included those between sectors and social movements that support the MAS, like the conflicts between peasants (often also of indigenous origin) demanding land and indigenous people struggling for territorial autonomy, or between miners and peasants, or between salaried and cooperative miners, or between small-scale clothing industries and importers of used clothing from the United States or Europe.

12. Since 2013 it has been on the rise again.

13. A striking detail is how both sides fling the accusation of being "neoliberal." The protesters call the diffident expressions of support for the government "neoliberal," the supporting movements return the accusation, and the government often uses the word to discredit protests whose views it rejects. People apparently believe the label discredits those it is used on, but they disagree about what it means and its applicability. Also interesting is that CONALCAM declared that it did not support the protests (see *La Prensa*, April 15, 2011) and said that COB did not represent all the social movements. A day later, CSUTCB and Federación de Mujeres Campesinas Bartolina Sisa agreed with CONALCAM (see *La Razón*, April 17, 2011).

14. Evo Morales used this phrase in his speech accepting the presidency in January 2010; since then, it has been a subject of controversy in the country.

15. In a speech on October 22, 2008, Morales said, "Digan lo que digan y hagan lo que hagan, no volverá el neoliberalismo a Bolivia. (They may say whatever they say, do whatever they do, but neoliberalism will not return to Bolivia)."

16. The law that was finally approved, in December 2010, is much more moderate.

17. In fact, many indigenous movements are quite unhappy with the way the government often treats them.

18. Interestingly, these words about "the law of the strongest" were also used by Minister Alfredo Rada in a television interview on April 14, 2011, to criticize the

attitude of the protesters. In this way the government refers to the rule of law to discredit strength-testing protests—the government's own very way to power.

19. The government's inclination to file lawsuits (often alleging corruption) against former non-MAS politicians or current opposition politicians is seen as proof of this.

20. However, as explained above, movements have tended to protest more openly since late 2010.

21. An aspect barely touched on in this chapter is the question of internal democracy in these social movements. Critics have questioned Bolivian social movements on this point, because "collective logics" supposedly do not foster individual dissidence or equal rights to speak. However, we also ought to acknowledge that traditional forms of decision making, even if they do not comply with canonic beliefs on democracy, might be just as good as others and might express local identities and value systems better than voting would. Irrespective of the degree of internal democracy in movements before they won their election, they need to change their logic once they assume governing positions.

22. For the time being, and much to the anger of many, the president *has* (temporarily) appointed judicial authorities, and in 2011 a row developed over the procedure to elect these authorities.

23. For Amnesty International's 2011 report on Bolivia, see http://www.amnestyusa .org/research/state-of-the-world-2011?id=ar&yr=2009&c=BOL. In the report, mention is made of aggression toward journalists, children and women trafficking, discrimination of indigenous people, and the like, but the government is not accused of such acts. See also the Human Rights Watch page on Bolivia at http://www.hrw.org/americas/bolivia. In 2011, the UN High Commissioner on Human Rights was also positive about developments in Bolivia, albeit with some qualifications (see United Nations General Assembly 2011).

REFERENCES

Albro, Robert. 2005. "The Indigenous in the Plural in Bolivian Oppositional Politics." *Bulletin of Latin American Research* 24 (4): 433–453.

Assies, Willem. 2006. "La 'media luna' sobre Bolivia: Nación, región, etnia y clase social" [Half Moon over Bolivia: Nation, Region, Ethnicity and Social Class]. *América Latina Hoy* [Latin America Today] 43:87–105.

Assies, Willem, and Ton Salman. 2003. Bolivian Democracy: Consolidating or Disintegrating? *Focaal—European Journal of Anthropology* 42:141–160.

———. 2005. "Ethnicity and Politics in Bolivia." *Ethnopolitics* 4 (3): 269–297.

Assies, Willem, Gemma van der Haar, and André Hoekema, eds. 2000. *The Challenge of Diversity: Indigenous Peoples and Reform of the State in Latin America.* Amsterdam: Thela Thesis Press.

Atahuichi, Rubén D. 2010. Editorial. *La Prensa* [The Press], February 22.

Axtmann, Roland, ed. 2003. *Understanding Democratic Politics.* London: Sage.

Bobbio, Norberto. 1990. *Liberalism and Democracy.* London: Verso Books.

Bolivia, 25 años construyendo la democracia: Visiones sobre el proceso democrático en Bolivia 1982–2007. 2008. La Paz: Vicepresidencia de la República, CIDES/UMSA, fBDM, FES-ILDIS, PADEP/GTZ, Idea Internacional, PNUD-Bolivia.

Cadena, Marisol de la. 2006. "The Production of Other Knowledges and Its Tensions: From Andeanist Anthropology to *Interculuralidad?*" In *World Anthropologies: Disciplinary Transformations within Systems of Power,* edited by Gustavo Lins Ribeiro and Arturo Escobar, 201–224. Oxford: Berg.

Camp, Roderick Ai, ed. 2001. *Citizen Views of Democracy in Latin America*. Pittsburgh: University of Pittsburgh Press.

Campero, Fernando, Gonzalo Mendieta, and Fernando Molina. 2009. "La creación de una nueva dirigencia boliviana" [The Creation of a New Bolivian Leadership]. *Pulso Semanario* [Weekly Seminar], August 11, pp. 5–7.

Cohen, Jean L., and Andrew Arato. 1992. *Civil Society and Political Theory*. Cambridge, MA: MIT Press.

Crabtree, John. 2005. *Patterns of Protest: Politics and Social Movements in Bolivia*. London: Latin America Bureau.

"Defenderemos al estado de derecho en Bolivia" [Defend the Rule of Law in Bolivia]. 2008. *Lex*, September.

De Munter, Koen, and Ton Salman. 2009. "Extending Political Participation and Citizenship: Pluricultural Civil Practices in Contemporary Bolivia." *Journal of Latin American and Caribbean Anthropology* 14 (2): 432–456.

Diamond, Larry. 1996. "Toward Democratic Consolidation." In *The Global Resurgence of Democracy*, 2nd ed., edited by Larry Diamond and Marx F. Plattner, 227–240. Baltimore: Johns Hopkins University Press.

———. 1999. *Developing Democracy: Toward Consolidation*. Baltimore: Johns Hopkins University Press.

———. 2008. *The Spirit of Democracy*. New York: Times Books.

Foweraker, Joe, and Todd Landman. 1997. *Citizenship Rights and Social Movements: A Comparative and Statistical Analysis*. Oxford: Oxford University Press.

García Linera, Alvaro, Marxa Chávez León, and Patricia Costas Monje. 2008. *Sociología de los movimientos sociales en Bolivia: Estructuras de movilización, repertorios culturales y acción política* [Sociology of Social Movements in Bolivia: Structures of Mobilization, Cultural Repertoires and Political Action]. La Paz: Plural Editores.

Grey Postero, Nancy. 2009. *Ahora somos ciudadanos* [Now We Are Citizens]. La Paz: Muela del Diablo Editores.

Held, David. 2006. *Models of Democracy*. 3rd ed. Cambridge, UK: Polity Press.

Ibarra, Pedro. 2002. "The Social Movements: From Promoters to Protagonists of Democracy." In *Social Movements and Democracy*, edited by Pedro Ibarra, 1–20. New York: Palgrave Macmillan.

Karp, David R., and Todd R. Clear. 2000. "Community Justice: A Conceptual Framework." *Criminal Justice* 2:323–368.

Kohl, Benjamin, and Linda Farthing. 2006. *Impasse in Bolivia: Neoliberal Hegemony and Popular Resistance*. London: ZED Books.

Latinobarómetro. 2004. "Summary Report: Latinobarómetro 2004; A Decade of Measurements." Available at http://www.latinobarometro.org/latContents.jsp.

Lazarte Rojas, Jorge. 2009. "Reacción contra la republica" [Reaction against the Republic]. *La Prensa Domingo* [The Press Sunday], February 8.

Lins Ribeiro, Gustavo, and Arturo Escobar. 2006. "World Anthropologies: Disciplinary Transformations within Systems of Power." In *World Anthropologies: Disciplinary Transformations within Systems of Power*, edited by Gustavo Lins Ribeiro and Arturo Escobar, 1–25. Oxford: Berg.

Lucero, José Antonio. 2008. *Struggles of Voice: The Politics of Indigenous Representation in the Andes*. Pittsburgh: Pittsburgh University Press.

Mamani, Pablo. 2008. "Bolivia: Posibilidades históricas de la autodeterminación indígena o reforma criolla" [Bolivia: Historical Possibilities for Indigenous Self-Determination or Criollo Reform]. In *Identidades, etnicidad y racismo en América*

Latina [Identities, Ethnicity and Racism in Latin America], edited by Fernando García, 87–104. Quito, Ecuador: Facultad Latinoamericana de Ciencias Sociales.

Mayorga, Fernando. 2007. "Movimientos sociales, política y estado" [Social Movements, Politics and the State]. In *Temas de coyuntura nacional* [Themes of the Nation Today], vol. 2, 33–62. Opiniones y Análisis [Opinions and Analysis] 85. La Paz: Fundemos/Hans Seidel Stiftung.

Mayorga, Fernando, and Eduardo Córdova. 2008. *El movimiento antiglobalización en Bolivia: Procesos globales e iniciativas locales en tiempo de crisis y cambio* [The Antiglobalization Movement in Bolivia: Global Processes and Local Initiatives in Time of Crisis and Change]. La Paz: United Nations Research Institute for Social Development/Centro de Estudios Superiores Universitarios–Universidad Mayor de San Simon/Plural Editores.

McAdam, Doug, Sidney Tarrow, and Charles Tilly. 2001. *Dynamics of Contention.* Cambridge: Cambridge University Press.

McNeish, John. 2006. "Stones on the Road: Reflections on the Crisis and Politics of Poverty in Bolivia." *Bulletin of Latin American Research* 25 (2): 220–240.

Medina, Javier. 2008. *Ch'ulla y Yanantin: Las dos matrices de civilización que constituyen a Bolivia* [Ch'ulla and Yanantin: The Two Civilization Matrices That Constitute Bolivia]. La Paz: Garza Azul Editores.

———. 2010. *Mirar con los dos ojos, gobernar con los dos cetros: Insumos para profundizar el proceso de cambio como un diálogo de matrices civilizatorias* [Looking with Two Eyes, Governing with Two Scepters: Inputs to Deepen the Process of Change as a Dialogue between Two Civilization Matrices]. La Paz: Garza Azul Editores.

Molina, Fernando. 2007. *Conversión sin fe: El MAS y la democracia* [Conversion without Faith: The MAS and Democracy]. La Paz: Eureka Ediciones.

Nandy, Asnis, ed. 1988. *Science, Hegemony and Violence: A Requiem for Modernity.* Oxford: Oxford University Press.

Palmer, David Scott. 2003. "Citizen Responses to Conflict and Political Crisis in Peru: Informal Politics in Ayacucho." In *What Justice? Whose Justice? Fighting for Fairness in Latin America*, edited by Susan Eva Eckstein and Timothy P. Wickham-Crowley, 233–254. Berkeley: University of California Press.

Peña, Claudia. 2009. "Un pueblo eminente: El populismo autonomista en Santa Cruz, Bolivia" [An Eminent People: The Autonomist Populism in Santa Cruz, Bolivia]. In *Democracia y teoría política en movimiento* [Democracy and Policy Theory in Movement], edited by Luis Tapia, 159–184. La Paz: Muela del Diablo Editores/ Ciencias de Desarrollo–Universidad Mayor San Andrés.

Prats, Joan. 2009. *Por una izquierda democrática: Escritos pensando en Bolivia* [For a Democratic Left: Writings Thinking of Bolivia]. La Paz: Plural Editores.

Pratt, Mary Louise. 2002. "Modernity and Periphery: Toward a Global and Relational Analysis." In *Beyond Dichotomies: Histories, Identities, Cultures, and the Challenge of Globalization*, edited by Elizabeth Mundimbe-Boyi, 21–48. Albany: State University of New York Press.

Rivera, Silvia. 2009. "Indianizar el país" [To Indianize the Country]. In *Subversión: Para pensar el presente más allá del capital y la colonia; la etnicidad en Bolivia* [Subversion: To Think about the Present beyond Capital and the Colony; Ethnicity in Bolivia], 127–136. Cochabamba: Fundación Gandhi/Centro de Ecología y Pueblos Andinos.

Rojas Ortuste, Gonzalo. 1994. *Democracia en Bolivia, hoy y mañana* [Democracy in Bolivia, Today and Tomorrow]. La Paz: Centro de Investigación y Promoción del Campesinado.

Rojas Ríos, César. 2007. *Democracia de alta tensión: Conflictividad y cambio social en la Bolivia del siglo XXI* [Democracy of High Tension: Conflict and Social Change in Twenty-First-Century Bolivia]. La Paz: Plural Editores.

Romero, Jorge. 2009. Editorial. *La Razón* [The Reason], March 19.

Saavedra, José Luis. 2009. "Los derechos de los pueblos indígenas" [The Rights of the Indigenous People]. In *Subversión: Para pensar el presente más allá del capital y la colonia; la etnicidad en Bolivia* [Subversion: To Think about the Present beyond Capital and the Colony; Ethnicity in Bolivia], 111–124. Cochabamba: Fundación Gandhi/CEPA.

Sall, Ebrima. 2004. "Social Movements in the Renegotiation of the Bases for Citizenship in West Africa." *Current Sociology* 52 (4): 595–614.

Salman, Ton. 2006. "The Jammed Democracy: Bolivia's Troubled Political Learning Process." *Bulletin of Latin American Research* 25 (2): 163–182.

———. 2007. "Bolivia and the Paradoxes of Democratic Consolidation." *Latin American Perspectives* 34 (6): 111–130.

———. 2008. "Reinventing Democracy in Bolivia and Latin America." *European Review of Latin American and Caribbean Studies* 84:87–99.

———. 2009. "'We Want a Democracy for *Us!*' Representation and Democracy: Current Debates in and on Bolivia." *European Review of Latin American and Caribbean Studies* 87:121–132.

Sanjinés, Javier. 2009. *Rescoldos del pasado: Conflictos culturales en sociedades postcoloniales* [Embers of the Past: Cultural Conflicts en Postcolonial Societies]. La Paz: Programa de Investigación Estratégica de Bolivia.

Saward, Michael. 2003. "Representative and Direct Democracy." In *Understanding Democratic Politics: An Introduction*, edited by Roland Axtmann, 52–60. London: Sage.

Schumpeter, Joseph. 1976. *Capitalism, Socialism and Democracy.* London: Allen and Unwin.

Seligson, Mitchell, Abby Córdova, Juan Carlos Donoso, Daniel Moreno, Dania Orcés, and Vivian Schwarz. 2006. "Democracy Audit: Bolivia, 2006 Report." Available at http://www.vanderbilt.edu/lapop/bolivia/2006-audit.pdf.

Seoanne, José A., and María José Nacci. 2007. "Movimientos Sociales y democracia en América Latina, frente al 'neoliberalismo de guerra'" [Social Movements and Democracy in Latin America, vis-à-vis "Neoliberalism on the Warpath"]. In *Movimientos sociales y ciudadanía* [Social Movements and Citizenship], edited by Manuel de la Fuente and Marc Hufty, 85–125. La Paz: Plural Editores.

Sieder, Rachel, ed. 2002. *Multiculturalism in Latin America: Indigenous Rights, Diversity and Democracy.* New York: Palgrave Macmillan.

Szasz, Andrew. 1995. "Progress through Mischief: The Social Movement Alternative to Secondary Associations." In *Associations and Democracy*, edited by Joshua Cohen and Joel Rogers, 148–156. London: Verso Books.

Tapia, Luis. 2008. "Las olas de expansión y contracción de la democracia en Bolivia" [The Waves of Expansion and Contraction of Democracy in Bolivia]. In *Bolivia, 25 años construyendo la democracia: Visiones sobre el proceso democrático en Bolivia 1982–2007* [Bolivia, 25 Years Building Democracy: Views on the Democratic Process in Bolivia, 1982–2007], 11–25. La Paz: Vicepresidencia de la República, CIDES/UMSA, fBDM, FES-ILDIS, PADEP/GTZ. Idea Internacional, PNUD-Bolivia.

———. 2009. "Lo politico y lo democrático en los movimientos sociales" [The Political and the Democratic in Social Movements]. In *Democracia y teoría política en movimiento* [Democracy and Policy Theory in Movement], edited by Luis Tapia, 109–122. La Paz: Muela del Diablo Editores/CIDES-UMSA.

Tilly, Charles. 1978. *From Mobilization to Revolution*. Reading, MA: Addison-Wesley.

———. 2002. "When Do (and Don't) Social Movements Promote Democratization?" In *Social Movements and Democracy*, edited by Pedro Ibarra, 21–46. New York: Palgrave Macmillan.

Tokman, Victor. 2007. "The Informal Economy, Insecurity and Social Cohesion in Latin America." *International Labour Review* 146 (1–2): 81–107.

Torrico, Erick. 2010. "Defender la democracia plural" [Defend the Plural Democracy]. *La Prensa* [The Press], February 20, p. 4.

United Nations General Assembly. 2011. "Report of the United Nations High Commissioner for Human Rights." Available at http://www2.ohchr.org/english/bodies/hrcouncil/docs/16session/A.HRC.16.20.Add.2_en.pdf.

Van Beek, Ursula J., ed. 2005. *Democracy under Construction: Patterns from Four Continents*. Pretoria: Van Schaik.

Van Cott, Donna Lee. 2008. *Radical Democracy in the Andes*. Cambridge: Cambridge University Press.

Yashar, Deborah. 2005. *Contesting Citizenship in Latin America: The Rise of Indigenous Movements and the Postliberal Challenge*. Cambridge: Cambridge University Press.

Zavaleta, Diego. 2008. "Oversimplifying Identities: The Debate over What Is *Indigena* and What Is *Mestizo*." In *Unresolved Tensions, Bolivia Past and Present*, edited by John Crabtree and Laurence Whitehead, 51–60. Pittsburgh: University of Pittsburgh Press.

Zegada, María Teresa, Yuri Tórrez, and Gloria Cámara. 2008. *Movimientos sociales en tiempos de poder: Articulaciones y campos de conflicto en el gobierno del MAS* [Social Movements in Times of Power: Articulations and Conflict Zones of the MAS Government]. La Paz: Centro Cuarto Intermedio/Plural Editores.

6

Social Movement Activity in the Transition to Partido dos Trabalhadores Government

The Case of the MST in Brazil

CAMILA PENNA

In 2002 the Partido dos Trabalhadores (PT; Workers' Party) won its first presidential election in Brazil. Members of social movements that had been historical allies of the party began in 2003 to receive administrative posts in governmental agencies. The political transition to a leftist government that took place in Brazil, as well as in most South American countries during the first decade of the twenty-first century, had consequences for the process of democratization—not so much in terms of changing the procedural representative democracy rules but in opening opportunities for social rights amplification, hence contributing to the consolidation of democracy's substantive character, or to the democratization of the democracy (Santos 2002). This chapter analyzes the actions of the Movimento dos Trabalhadores Rurais sem Terra (MST; Landless Rural Workers' Movement) during the transition to the PT government of Luiz Inácio Lula da Silva to assess the movement's trajectory and the extent it contributed to the process of democratic consolidation. In this chapter, I use "political transition" and "transition process" to refer to the transition from the Fernando Henrique Cardoso (FHC) government to Lula's government. My analysis is based on protest data from the last three years of the FHC government and the first three years of the Lula government.

To understand the role of social movements in this political transition I analyze their collective actions and the justifications for the actions. A case study of the MST provides a more in-depth analysis to qualitatively assess leaders' justifications and interpretations of the movements' actions during the transition process. During the last three years of FHC's government and the first three years of Lula's government, the MST engaged in more collective actions than any other movement, trade union, or social organization in Brazil, according to data published by the Observatório Social da América Latina (OSAL [Social Observatory of Latin America] 2000–2006).

Besides being the most mobilized social movement in the political transition period, the MST is one of the most active, organized, and studied movements in Brazil. Hundreds of theses, dissertations, books, and articles in many disciplines, such as history, geography, sociology, anthropology, political science, psychology, education, and social service, have looked at its educational program, communication, leadership formation, internal social relations, gender relations, symbolic aspects of its *mística* and other rituals, collective action repertoires, relations with the state, and many other aspects. Social anthropology and rural sociology research has produced interesting results in the MST's repertoires of collective action and its interactions with the state (Sigaud 2005; Chaves 2000; Rosa 2004, 2011; Medeiros 2000, 2004), this chapter's subjects. I rely chiefly on this literature to discuss the transition process.

The first section discusses the dynamics inside the PT during its first years of government and some of the segmenting that took place inside the party and in social movements allied with the PT. The second section briefly reviews the history and internal organization of the MST and analyzes its main type of collective action, land occupation, during the transition period. The third section presents land reform legislation and land reform policies after 2003, showing how they affected the MST's collective actions and its relation with the state during the transition. The last section presents interviews conducted with the MST's national leaders and shows how these leaders framed the collective action and relation with the government during the transition process.

Political Transition to PT Government

Understanding the political transition to PT government is paramount for understanding social movements' actions in Brazil after 2003. Unlike the transition from authoritarian regime to democracy in Brazil in 1985,[1] there is not much research on social movement activities during the political transition to the PT government.[2]

Assessing social movement actions in this period is relevant inasmuch as the PT is a party that historically has had social movement as an important part of its political outlook. In addition, as Alfredo Wagner Almeida (2008) points out, both the democratic transition in the 1980s and the transition to the PT in 2003 were watersheds for social movements in Brazil. The first one acknowledged new social identities—landless workers, indigenous population, and *quilombolas* (slave descendants)—and included them in the Constitution as having rights. Political pressure by social movements outside the Congress, through protest actions and demonstrations, and inside led to their inclusion. Political dispute in Congress among members allied with the left and social movements and members allied with the right characterized the discussion and voting on the constitutional text of 1988. In 2003, with the PT's victory, social movements were again able to influence public policies and specific legislation, as this was a "moment of possibilities" (Almeida 2008).

The FHC government (1995–2002) was marked by a great number of reforms, which included stabilization of the economy through fiscal adjustment and privatization of large national companies. After eight years of Partido da Social Democracia Brasileira (PSDB; Brazilian Social Democracy Party) government, the PT candidate, Luis Inácio Lula da Silva, won the 2002 elections.

This was real change in the Brazilian political process—not because democratic procedures had changed but because of the social origins of Lula, who came from the working class. In Brazilian history there had never been a president with such a profile. The composition of government also saw significant change: cabinet ministers came from the labor movement and other social movements.

The PT's victory in a presidential election was another first. The party, formed in 1980, had in its initial composition leftist intellectuals, progressive Catholics, and members of the Central Única dos Trabalhadores (CUT; Unified Workers' Central). The PT took under its wing social movements from sectors other than the labor movement, and they were an important part of its base. Over the two decades after its founding the party went through many changes, and by 2003 it had formed a wider range of alliances. In addition to traditional left alliances, the PT had allied with center parties such as the Partido Liberal (PL; Liberal Party) and the Partido do Movimento Democrático Brasileiro (PMDB; Brazilian Democratic Movement Party). The PMDB had been allied with PSDB until the 2002 elections, but after the elections, the PMDB allied with the PT and received leadership of three ministries and also the senate.

The alliance with the PMDB gave a more complex character to the new government. The PT government had made compromises with leftist groups to gain autonomy from international forces, establish a more sovereign position in relation to international financial organizations, and eradicate inequality through, for example, agrarian and tax reforms (Frigotto 2004). But after the PMDB alliance, Lula's government negotiated with the International Monetary Fund on structural and fiscal measures that the PT had called neoliberal until then; gave more autonomy to Brazil's Central Bank; and increased retirement age and set a ceiling for public worker retirement. The social security reforms on retirement had been attacked by the PT before winning the election, and the PT's later approval of the reforms was very controversial. Some PT legislators voted against them and then left the party after the reforms passed.

As it became more clear that Lula's government was not adopting the left's projects (Leher 2006), factions inside the party[3] took positions on the political path the new government was taking. Their positions had a significant impact on social mobilization.

The position taken by the majority of the PT was that the economic crisis inherited from the previous government justified continuing with the same economic policy so as to gain the market's confidence. The PT's left and movements such as the MST and União Nacional dos Estudantes (UNE; Students National Union), along with CUT's left, believed that the correlation of forces[4] in Lula's government favored the right and that pulling it back to the left would require mass mobilization by social organizations. The view of the Ação Popular Socialista (APS; Popular Socialist Action) was that the government had taken such a strong turn to the right that it would brook no dispute from critics. Believing they could not change the course of the PT from within, the APS and some other leftist groups left the PT and created a new party, the Partido Socialismo e Liberdade (PSOL; Socialism and Liberty Party).

These different positions, first expressed during CUT's Eighth Congress in 2003 (Leher 2006), affected social movement collective actions. After the defection of the APS and the creation of the small but vigorous PSOL, the party took an increasingly combative position against the PT government and instigated a number of protest actions in the first three years of the Lula government (OSAL 2006).

That many social organizations mobilized to press the government into a turn toward the left did not imply opposition to the government, as the APS position did. Despite their disagreements with the government, the social organizations that believed they needed to mobilize did not want to fracture the party. They wanted to give more power and legitimacy to the leftists in the government coalition, taking power away from the rightists and giving a more prominent position to the traditional left agenda. Underlying this strategy was the premise that they faced a government in dispute (between the left and right forces of the political alliance) and that social mobilization was fundamental to bringing the correlation of forces in the government coalition back to the left. This interpretation of those first years of the PT government is evident in the following words of the MST's leader and cofounder, João Pedro Stédile:

> We're living in a complex transition period of intense and growing dispute. . . . We face the question of whether we should not only advance agrarian reform but also pursue more general social development. These reforms would be possible only with a social fight and mobilization that gives rise to a new mass movement capable of fundamentally altering society in a way that guarantees that the government adopt the economic model originally proposed by the PT. (2004: 33–34)[5]

OSAL data show social mobilization increased during the first three years of Lula's government, but especially in 2004 and 2005. I highlight three significant collective action moments of this period. The first is a public workers strike called by CUT in response to the social security reforms in 2003. This was the first big strike experienced by the new government. CUT was not unified as to whether to strike, and a large sector of CUT did not approve of it.[6]

Another social organization trying to move the government toward the left was the Coordenaçao dos Movimentos Sociais (CMS; Social Movements' Coordination), formed of social, religious, labor, and student organizations, including CUT, the MST, UNE, the Comissão Pastoral da Terra (CPT; Pastoral Land Commission), União Brasileira dos Estudantes Secundaristas (UBES; Brazilian Union of High School Students), Conferência Nacional dos Bispos do Brasil (CNBB; Brazilian National Conference of Bishops), Conselho Indigenista Missionário (Cimi; Indigenous Missionary Council), Movimento dos Trabalhadores Sem Teto (MTST; Homeless Workers Movement), and another thirty-five organizations. CMS carried out joint and coordinated protest actions within different social sectors. The most important moment for CMS mobilization came in 2005. Three years after the new government took power a corruption scandal that involved the highest PT leaders erupted. Some legislators were being paid large amounts of money by party leaders who were also ministers in the cabinet to vote for PT legislation. The scandal, widely covered by the media and gleefully used by the opposition, resulted in the resignation of the president's chief of staff (ministro da casa civil), José Dirceu—one of the PT's oldest and most influential leaders.

CMS mobilized in defense of the president and against destabilization attempts by the opposition. The CMS organizations, believing that mass mobilization could bring the correlation of forces in the government coalition back to the left, published a "Letter to the Brazilian People": "We urge the democratic and popular forces to mobilize in order to carry out street manifestations and protests, and work to promote the true changes that the people and the country need" (National Coordination of Social Movements 2005: 3).

As for the PSOL and other leftist groups who had left the PT to oppose it, they sponsored protests against the government, such as the ones called by ANDES (Sindicato Nacional dos Docentes das Instituições de Ensino Superior; National Union of Teachers in Higher Education Institutions) (OSAL 2006).

The last important mobilization carried out in the first three years of Lula's government that I highlight is the land occupation campaign, with 461 occupations in 2004 (Comissão Pastoral de Terra 2011), led by the MST and by other rural movements. The purpose of this campaign was to pressure the government into fulfilling promises to landless families. In 2005 the MST marched from the city of Goiânia to the capital Brasília (a distance of two hundred kilometers) in support of the settlement of 430,000 families under the II Plano Nacional de Reforma Agrária (II PNRA; Second National Plan for Agrarian Reform), which was enacted in 2003 and defined agrarian reform policies (see Ministério do Desenvovimento Agrário 2003).

The following section discusses the MST and its collective actions during the political transition. As the most prominent social movement in Brazilian political context in that period, in terms of national mobilization capacity, understanding the MST is essential to understanding social movement activities in Brazil during the transition to the PT government.

The MST as a Collective Actor

According to OSAL data the organization that carried out the most collective actions of protest in Brazil during the transition period was the MST. A national movement today, it was created in 1984 at the first National Meeting of Landless Rural Workers in the state of Paraná. Among the participants of this meeting were leaders from other social movements, the rural labor movement, and the Catholic Church.

The MST's origins have to do with the rural modernization of 1970s Brazil, when small farmers were forced to leave their lands. This happened mainly in the state of Rio Grande do Sul, where over one thousand *colono* (European descendant) families were evicted from indigenous reserves where they had been living and farming for years. These farmers and CPT members obstructed public roads, demonstrated in front of banks and governmental land agency headquarters, and most importantly, occupied land.

During the 1990s the MST spread to twenty-four (out of twenty-seven) Brazilian states, gathering not only rural landless workers but also rural expropriated workers living in shantytowns and urban workers in precarious living conditions in big cities. Because the movement originated in a region of Brazil with many Italian and German *colonos*, who used an agricultural production process different from most of the country, that process was not easily adapted to other Brazilian regions. Some regions, marked by a "secular tradition of subordination to the figure of the boss" (Medeiros 2000: 40), had great difficulty adapting to the collective production model proposed by the MST.

Another important MST antecedent is its link to the Catholic Church through the CPT and liberation theology.[7] During the authoritarian regime the CPT, created in 1975 by the Catholic National Conference of Bishops of Brazil, was an important channel for political organization among rural workers. Other channels, such as political parties and trade unions, were being persecuted by the military regime, making the church important to political education and organization in both urban and rural areas during the 1970s (Sader 1988; Doimo 1995). In rural areas political education and organizations activities were coordinated mainly by CPT agents who had legitimacy because of their connection to the church. They informed people of existing laws and their rights and advised them about the country's politics (Novaes 1995).

The CPT provides more than support, however; it also is active in rural mobilization. The CPT provides assistance to rural social organizations, including information it gathers from every state in Brazil and publishes in annual reports. The CPT also engages in collective actions such as land occupations in the northeastern region of Brazil. Between 2000 and 2005 it carried out approximately one hundred land occupations (Silva and Fernandes 2006).

Elements of the Catholic tradition are present in some MST actions, such as vigils, pressing for release of imprisoned leaders, and religious festivals related to the land (*romarias da terra*). Vigils in Brazil are traditionally linked to religious meetings for prayer and Bible studies, but the MST uses them as collective action. *Romarias da terra* organized by the CPT include MST activists and have a protest element but are essentially religious festivals.

Education and literacy are paramount in the MST: "In the movement, every landless person must be studying, no matter if it's in a formal course, secondary school, or elementary school" (dos Santos 2008). A Marxist orientation underlies this promotion of education. According to one of the members of the MST's National Formation Sector, "Marxism is the key to open the doors to our revolutionary praxis" (Pizetta 2007: 246).

The movement leadership is organized nationally in a vertical system, starting at the local level with settlement and encampment coordinators and moving progressively higher to regional, state, and national coordinators. Settlements are the result of agrarian reform policies; they are created by the state and managed by rural social movements. Encampments are established and populated by families participating in land occupations that pressure the state into relinquishing that land.

The MST meets at a national congress every five years and deliberates its general goals. Annual meetings more specifically define the movement's platform, taking into account political, economic, and social context. The National Direction committee defines the movement's political line. It is composed of twenty-one members elected for two years through secret voting during annual meetings. National Coordination is the central executive body. It is the public face of the movement and responsible for implementing national congress and annual meeting decisions. National coordinators are elected in state meetings, by National Direction members, and by delegates from every MST sector, or branch. Two coordinators are elected for each state. The movement consists of sectors responsible for specific areas: production, health, gender, communications, education, youth, finance, human rights, and international relations, among others (Mirza 2006).

The movement has engaged in different kinds of collective action since its creation. It uses repertoires, or performances, that connect at least two specific actors: the claimer and the object of claim (Tilly 2006). Performances may become routine actions that are shared and exercised in an interactive process between social actors and the state.

The MST has many repertoires of collective claiming: petitions, obstruction of roads, public demonstrations, marching, vigils and *romarias da terra*, and occupation of public buildings, usually the headquarters of the national agency responsible for implementing land reform policies, the Instituto Nacional de Colonização e Reforma Agrária (INCRA; National Institute for Colonization and Agrarian Reform). The most important type of collective action by the MST is that for agrarian reform, using land occupation and encampment.

MST encampments follow particular rules: tents are grouped symmetrically and constructed of black canvas and wood, the movement's red flag is in a central camp area, and occupants must observe certain rules for living together in the encampment. These symbolic elements (Sigaud 2005) have become permanent characteristics of the movement's repertoire of land occupation. This repertoire has antecedents in land occupations of the early 1960s (Sigaud, Rosa, and Ernandez 2010).

In 1962 President João Goulart (1961–1964) created governmental institutions for agrarian reform that expropriated large properties. After the military coup in 1964 many of the properties were returned to their previous owners, and some who had participated in these actions were arrested and tortured (Sigaud, Rosa, and Ernandez 2010). After the coup, land occupations nearly disappeared. In 1978, as the end of the military regime drew near and repression eased, land occupation returned when the *colonos* in Rio Grande do Sul mentioned above were expelled from their lands, homes, and livelihoods. Some of them, later supported by the CPT and some trade unions, engaged in land occupations. These occupations were attended by many of the people later present at the meeting that created the MST in 1984.

Agrarian reform settlements are usually created on properties that have been occupied and on which families are encamped. The encampment pressures the government into expropriating the land. Once the land is expropriated the encamped families are registered in the agrarian reform national program, and if they meet all criteria they receive a portion of the land inside the settlement. Hence, the implementation of land reform policies depends on social movement actions. The state not only recognizes and legitimizes social movements directed toward agrarian reform (Sigaud 2005; Rosa 2011) but also needs them in order to identify and organize the public benefiting from the movements. In the following section I present land reform legislation and policies during the FHC government and during the first years of Lula's government and argue that governmental actions were important for defining land occupation as a collective action repertoire of the MST (Tilly 2006).

Agrarian Reform Legislation

One of the first laws concerning agrarian reform in Brazil was approved in 1964. It defines land reform as "the group of measures promoting land distribution through modifications in its ownership and use, to achieve social justice and productivity increase" (Estatuto da Terra [Land Statute], Law no. 4,504, 1964). This law was approved in the first year of the military regime, and twenty years later, when the regime ended, only forty-nine agrarian reform settlements had been created (INCRA 2000).

In 1985 the first National Plan of Agrarian Reform (Decree no. 91,766) was formulated. Its goal was to settle 1.4 million families, but it ended up settling fewer than 90,000 (INCRA 2000). Article 184 of the new democratic constitution approved in 1988 stated that the state has the prerogative of "expropriating, in social interest and for agrarian reform, the rural property that does not fulfill its social function or that is unproductive, through just and previous indemnification." A property fulfills its social function when it is used adequately and rationally, preserves the environment and makes adequate use of natural resources, follows labor legislation, and favors the well-being of owners and workers. The Constitution also stipulates that small properties are not subject to expropriation for agrarian reform purposes and neither are large productive properties.

As a result of landowners' activism[8] during its drafting, the Constitution does not define "productive" property. This made it impossible to execute the expropriation of unproductive properties for agrarian reform purposes. Not until 1993 did a supplementary law define a productive property: one that, if exploited economically, achieves simultaneous degrees of land use and efficiency according to federal indexes (Law no. 8,629).

The federal department producing the indexes and implementing agrarian reform policies, INCRA, was created in 1970. During the military regime most of its work was, rather than agrarian reform, colonization of remote regions of Brazil but especially the northern region, which was a project of the military regime. After the democratic transition INCRA functions were directed to agrarian reform as well, and the first National Plan for Land Reform was instituted in 1985.

Since 1999 INCRA has been attached to the Ministério do Desenvolvimento Agrário (MDA; Ministry of Agrarian Development) and has two main divisions that implement agrarian reform policies: one obtains land, and one develops settlements. For a property to be expropriated for agrarian reform purposes, the first division assesses whether the property is productive and fulfills its social function. If it is not or does not, then INCRA creates an agrarian reform settlement, giving the former owner indemnification.

Other forms of obtaining land for family settlements do not entail expropriation. One is the use of public lands. This form of obtaining land was used extensively in Lula's government and is now being used in Dilma Rousseff's government. A criticism of it is that it does not change the concentration of land ownership. Another way to obtain land is if the owner is willing to sell. The World Bank encouraged buying from willing sellers in Brazil during the 1990s as an option for avoiding the conflict and disruption brought by occupation and expropriation. In this form property is purchased at market prices from owners willing to sell, and families are settled on it. The families, as a consortium, buy the land with a loan from the national government (initially the World Bank also provided money), which has a twenty-year term, interest rates of 4 to 6 percent, and also pays start-up costs. Lula's government kept this alternative program of agrarian reform after making some changes to fix problems (Sauer and Pereira 2006).

After obtaining a property, INCRA selects families to settle on it according to certain criteria: income, previous property ownership, number of children, single parent, employment, and others. However, the agency works with social movements in that process, inasmuch as families making claims for land are usually already in encampments there that are coordinated by social movement leaders. Therefore, when INCRA workers arrive to register families for a settlement, the families encamped there are the ones most eligible.

INCRA's settlement development division offers technical assistance and individual loans to the families. Some of the loans these families can access are for initial establishment, land production costs, and house construction. The development division also constructs infrastructure (roads, water supply, waste disposal system) and oversees the implementation of the Programa Nacional de Educação na Reforma Agrária (PRONERA; National Program for Education in Agrarian Reform), in cooperation with social movements.

Agrarian Reform Policies in the 1990s and Land Occupation

Land reform policies during the 1990s significantly increased the number of family settlements compared to previous decades. From 1985 to 1994—from the democratic transition, when the first National Plan for Agrarian Reform was launched, until the beginning of the FHC government—89,945 families were settled (INCRA 2010). During the FHC government (1995–2002), 524,380 families were settled under the agrarian reform program (Ministério do Desenvovimento Agrário 2003).[9]

Land distribution increased during FHC's government after two collective actions in which police killed workers. Police killed nineteen workers during a road blockage organized by the MST in the state of Pará at Eldorado dos Carajás in April 1996. In 1995 in the state of Rondônia at Corumbiara, during a land occupation and encampment organized by landless workers, the landowner along with his employees and the police killed twelve workers. Both events had international repercussions and were widely broadcast by the Brazilian media. They also generated an increase in protest and land occupation by the MST and other rural organizations (Ondetti 2006). To diminish rural conflict and violence, the government increased family settlements, believing that quickly establishing agrarian reform settlements for claimant families would prevent violence (Fernandes 2003; Sauer and Pereira 2006). The governmental policy of increasing settlements contributed to land occupation becoming a repertoire used by rural social movements in their claim for agrarian reform.

> The dynamic of occupations results from state policy. Without that state policy, movements would not have been able to offer hope to its target public and would have had difficulty attracting people to occupy land. They also would not have themselves strengthened and multiplied. (Sigaud 2005: 272)

Massive creation of agrarian reform settlements during the FHC government had some effects for the MST: the considerable increase in the movement's base and a concomitant boost in land occupations. Collective land occupation and encampment began to seem to people to be a valid way to shift land ownership to rural people (Medeiros 2000), and there was a growing disposition for participating in organizations, such as the MST, that engaged in these collective actions.

Land occupation diffused to other rural movements and rural trade unions desiring agrarian reform and became their main form of action. Marcelo Rosa (2004) shows how this collective action repertoire was gradually adopted by rural trade unions in Pernambuco, who added agrarian reform claims to their agendas. The author argues that many other social movements, including trade unions and MST dissidents, also adopted the same repertoire and format, evidence that there is a specific form to claim for agrarian reform and that it is land occupation by movements (Rosa 2004, 2011).

Understanding the consolidation of this collective action repertoire as the result of an interaction of social movements with the state requires also considering how the movement's actions influenced the politics adopted by the government. Were it not for the conflict generated by the movements' land occupations, the government would not have created as many agrarian reform settlements as it did. The movements, generating conflict and demanding government action, brought the state into the center of the scene (Rosa 2004). Furthermore, as explained at the end of the last section, government implementation of agrarian reform policies is highly dependent on social movements, which identify and organize the public that will benefit from agrarian reform. Through participation in the movement do people construct their identity of landless worker. And this is the identity recognized and legitimized by the state when it formulates and implements land reform policies.

Movements' collective actions indicate which properties should be expropriated, establishing an expropriation agenda, and their internal organization and identity construction policy define which families can participate as beneficiaries. An indication that social movements have been guiding agrarian reform policy is that, between 1986 and 1997 in fourteen of the most populous states of Brazil[10] and out of the total settlements created by INCRA, 77 percent originated from land occupations (Silva and Fernandes 2006).

Some critics (see, for example, Sauer and Pereira 2006) point out that agrarian reform policies during FHC's government had serious deficiencies. Many family settlements were made quickly, lines of credit were insufficient and badly applied, technical assistance was insufficient, and the program's market orientation—linked to compromises with the World Bank for loans for agrarian reform programs—did not meet rural workers' needs. Some of these family settlements failed to develop as a productive or even self-sustaining enterprise.

MST Actions during the Transition Period

In the face of the MST's growth during the 1990s and of the increasing mobilization in the form of collective land occupation, the FHC government decided to follow a less tolerant policy toward the MST and most importantly toward land occupation actions—this happened mostly in the last two years of the FHC government. Following a more aggressive rhetoric that framed the movement as radical, rowdy, undemocratic, and politically opportunistic came judicial action constraining the MST's actions. Governmental actions in the symbolic field complemented and legitimated actions in the material field.

In its escalation in repression and criminalization of the MST, the most significant form of material constraint by the government was Bill no. 2,183-56, which was issued in 2000 and eventually became a law. It criminalized land occupations. Under this law occupied properties could not be inspected by INCRA for two years, which meant that the land could not be expropriated during this period. The law's language could be interpreted as saying that people who engage in land occupations would be permanently excluded from governmental programs of agrarian reform. This constraint significantly reduced occupations, which fell from 581 in 1999 to 393 in 2000 and to 194 in 2001. Along with this law, policing of protests increased (della Porta 1996), along with arrests, and a specialized branch of the federal police was created to deal specifically with land occupations. The movement also radicalized its actions by occupying personal property of the president's in 2002. FHC's government also significantly reduced INCRA's budget.

With the transition to Lula's government official rhetoric significantly changed. The movement's collective action was spoken of as land occupation and not land invasion. The MST's actions, such as rural education, were frequently recognized, and its collective actions were framed as a natural element of democratic participation. However, along with this legitimizing rhetoric was a subtle but effective form of framing land occupations and INCRA building occupations as democratic but unnecessary, because the government was committed to and carrying out agrarian reform.

In terms of material actions a new National Plan for Agrarian Reform (II PNRA) was formulated and launched in 2003. One of the plan's goals was to settle 920,000 families before 2007. Other goals were the improvement and development of existing settlements, promoting gender equality, and guaranteeing rights for traditional communities such as *quilombolas* and riverine populations (Ministério do Desenvovimento Agrário 2003).

As discussed in the first section, Lula's coalition government had moved to the right, and budgets were small for the MDA and INCRA. In contrast, the budget for the Ministério da Agricultura, Pecuária e Abastecimento (MAPA; Ministry of Agriculture, Livestock and Provision)—overseeing large-scale agricultural producers of exports—was more than three times the size of the agrarian reform budget. Many analysts (see Sampaio 2005a) and social movement leaders (see Santos 2008) see this discrepancy as evidence that the agrarian reform project was being put aside by Lula's government. The goals established by the plan could not be achieved with insufficient funds. Rather than the 920,000 in five years (2003–2007), only 614,000 families were settled during the whole period of Lula's government (2003–2010) (INCRA 2010). With fewer occupations occurring, the MST lost support, and government poverty and hunger relief programs and Brazil's improved economic situation meant there were fewer impoverished and miserable people in urban and rural areas in need of the MST.

The political transition ushered in a new phase for the MDA and INCRA. After being almost dismantled in the last few years of the FHC government, they reorganized internally and strengthened relations to rural social movements. They were now directed by former social movement leaders and PT cadres, leading to cooperation in policies' implementation. This meant rural social movements more actively participated in agrarian reform policies. In 2003 and 2004, the first two years of Lula's government, land occupation increased significantly compared to previous years, as Table 6.1 shows, and the MST participation in land occupations also increased but did not reach the level it had had in 2000. This lower level in the rate of MST participation continued after 2005, in part because of growth of other rural social movements and rural labor movements and the departure of dissidents who left the MST and created new social movements. (For an analysis of this fragmentation in Pernambuco, see Rosa 2011.)

The first years of Lula's government saw more participation of rural social movements in formulating and implementing agrarian reform policies but also disappointment, as some MST leaders argue, over unmet expectations for budget and priority for agrarian reform. Despite the disappointments MST land occupations continued strong in the first years of Lula's government. These three simultaneous processes cannot be reconciled, and it is not possible to frame the MST case into dichotomist institutionalization versus collective action mobilization or co-optation versus autonomy.

How the MST's leaders make sense of this complex political transition process is the subject of the following section. I interviewed MST national and regional leaders. The discussion that follows is organized around two central questions: How do leaders frame the movement's collective actions of land occupation, and how do they frame the relation between the movement and the state during the transition period?

TABLE 6.1   NUMBER OF LAND OCCUPATIONS
DURING THE TRANSITION

Year	Number of land occupations	MST's participation in occupations (%)
2000	393	72.52
2001	194	42.26
2002	184	53.26
2003	391	56.97
2004	461	57.04
2005	437	58.12

Source: Comissão Pastoral de Terra 2010.

Political Transition and the MST's Frames

The notion of frame in social movement theory was developed in the 1980s by D. Snow, E. Rochford, S. Worden, and R. Benford (1986). Their article "Frame Alignment Processes, Micromobilization, and Movement Participation" tries to establish, within frame alignment, a conceptual bridge between social psychology and resource mobilization theory explanations for the participation in social movements. The authors refer to Erving Goffman's work in *Frame Analysis* (1974) as a theoretical and conceptual basis for the analysis of social movements such as religious, peace, and neighborhood movements in the United States.

The frame alignment concept with which the authors work and the use they make of that concept throughout their analysis distances them from Goffman's perspective in many ways. Goffman referred to frame as the form individuals use to organize their experiences in order to seize their position and determine their actions in specific situations. The focus is on the experience structure that will build the frame and on the identification of the specific frame as determinant of social actions.

In social movement literature, the focus is on the strategic and external actions of building interpretative frames by social movement organizations to achieve specific ends such as participation in mobilizations, support from the external public, and membership expansion. These frames are forged through what Snow and colleagues call "tasks of micromobilization" (1986: 464) that depend on the public targeted. And those frames achieve more or less success with how closely they approach the interests, values, and beliefs of individuals, establishing a connection to their interpretative orientations.

The focus on social movement organizations' strategic actions, constitutive elements of frames forged by them, and the effects these frames have on mobilization is in line with Snow and colleagues' (1986) underlying premise: frame alignment is a necessary condition for mobilization. Frame alignment to mobilization occurs in three stages. In the diagnostic stage social actors recognize certain events as problems, in the prognostic stage they define strategies; and in the motivational stage they are motivated to act on their diagnosis and prognosis (Snow and Benford 1998). Years after their first, 1986, publication, Benford and Snow (2000) reviewed the literature on framing to examine its utility for studying social movement dynamics. They argue that frame alignment, along with resource mobilization processes and political opportunities, is central to the comprehension of social movement character and trajectory.

Land Occupation and Collective Identity

When asked how they would evaluate the MST land occupations, MST leaders responded that it was the main form of struggle used by the movement:

> We continue to insist that the form of fight with more impact is still
> the land occupation. . . . If it is a massive occupation—a nonmassive

occupation alters nothing. Now, when it is a massive occupation, it makes, in effect, a difference. (Misnerovicz 2008)

Leaders justified land occupation as the most important collective action repertoire from the standpoint of its capacity to reduce social injustice and concentration of land ownership in Brazil. Therefore, references to the immediate necessities of poor rural workers were frequent:

> When you realize that families do not have access to land, when you realize that the right to have a piece of land to farm and live on is being denied to these families, . . . you cannot close your eyes, and you cannot wait. That's why, every year, in April, we generally do our mass actions. . . . Our land occupations are one of the most legitimate actions to protest against big enterprises, against land monopoly, against the advance of transnational enterprises that invade our country, because there [in other countries] lands are expensive, and here lands are cheap and fertile and have cheap labor. Therefore, the actions we consider the most legitimate, which, in fact, demonstrate the symbol of territorial conquest, are land occupation. (Souza 2008)

In this quotation, land occupation legitimacy is also framed according to the broader agenda of the movement. The reference to "transnational enterprises that invade our country" can be understood by looking at the leading position that the MST has in Via Campesina, an international organization composed of social movements and NGOs that advocate sustainable and family-farm-based agriculture. In coordination with Via Campesina's goals, the MST has included in its agenda the fight against genetic modification of crops and transnational companies that pollute the environment and appropriate national land that should undergo land reform. This strategy frames transnational companies and genetically modified agriculture, along with capitalism and international capital, as land reform enemies. Thus, land occupation is also justified by the need to protect the country from foreign and national enterprises that pollute the environment and concentrate land and wealth.

Leaders' evaluations of land occupation also establish a connection between this type of repertoire and collective identity construction, which is "an interactive process through which several individuals or groups define the meaning of their actions and the field of opportunities and constraints for such an action" (Melucci 1996: 67). This process, constantly negotiated and constructed, involves the definition of a goal or a meaning to the action, the means to achieve it, and the external environment in which the action will take place.

Alberto Melucci's (1996) definition places collective action and collective identity as parallel processes, inasmuch as the former is understood as a constant construction of an idea of "we" and the latter is part of that construction. Social movement theory has addressed the collective identity dimension of mobilization mainly by analyzing how collective identity construction arrives at mobilization. However, as Donatella della Porta and Mario Diani argue, "it is through action that certain feelings of belonging come to be either reinforced or weakened. In other words, the evolution of collective action produces and encourages continuous redefinitions of identity" (2006: 93).

MST leaders assign a place inside the movement's dynamic to land occupation and also give it an external meaning. Land occupation is framed, on one hand, as legitimate action as seen from outside—that is, its external representation. But on the other hand, land occupation is framed in terms of collective identity construction, or given internal meaning. The following quotation elucidates the connection land occupation has to the movement's collective identity construction.

> My participation in the movement happens exactly through one of the main forms of struggle that continues to be very current, the land occupation. In '91, when I participated in the first land occupation in Palmeira, Rio Grande do Sul, it was a very big occupation. It was, in fact, a very important moment that marked me. . . . We always used to say that the occupation is the moment of baptism. One who participates in an occupation is baptized from the symbolic standpoint of participation in the movement. (Misnerovicz 2008)

If participating in a land occupation is a "moment of baptism," it is also the initial moment of identification with the movement, of belonging to that collectivity, and therefore is part of the construction of the landless worker identity, which defines the "we" of MST members, as well as of other rural worker movements that fight for agrarian reform. As argued by Rosa (2011), landless worker is currently the category the Brazilian government uses when creating public policies for this specific public; this is, to a large extent, the result of the MST's actions.

Land occupation has an internal symbolic dimension fundamental to the movement's dynamic of collective identity construction. Therefore, this is a case in which collective action is one of the causes of collective identity construction and not the other way around. Along with the symbolic meaning that land occupation has in the internal dynamics of the movement, there is also an external symbolic meaning from the standpoint of relations with the state. As Lygia Sigaud (2005) argues, land occupation and encampment are the symbolic language recognized by the Brazilian government as the legitimate form of making claims in agrarian reform. And this is the result of the long-term interaction between rural social movements and the state.

Relations with the State and Political Opportunities during the Transition

When asked how they would evaluate the movement's relation with the state, the MST leaders framed it as a dichotomy between a bourgeois state and provider state. When asked specifically about the transition period, they divided it into two different moments, one of expectation and one of deception. While trying to justify the movement's alignment with the PT despite the deception and the lack of priority given to agrarian reform, leaders stressed that there was a difference in meaning between *state* and *government*—governments change and inherit a preexisting state of regulations and bureaucracies that possibly conflict with the new government's inclinations—and mentioned the coalitional character of the government.

In calling the state bourgeois, leaders are accusing it of being allied to financial capital and thus opposed to the movement's position. In calling it a provider state, they identify it as an institution to which the movement directs its political action and that must answer the movement's claims. Therefore, MST statements on the rights that the state should guarantee to poor rural families appear next to statements in which the state is framed as a bourgeois state and thus contrary to the interests of the MST:

> Actually, we always do some protest to claim something, in our case, from the state. There is no possibility of negotiation with the state without protest. . . . And everyone who doesn't have a place to work, who doesn't have a place to live, has to go after these things. The state has to answer.
>
> I think that the state is fulfilling its duty, that today more than ever, and much more than in the last two years, it is guaranteeing that no one messes with anything that could harm the bourgeoisie. The role of the bourgeois state, such as the one we have today, is to guarantee that the bourgeoisie remains intact, and ultimately . . . , it's not our national bourgeoisie but the international financial capital that dominates Brazil today that says what Brazil can or cannot do. (Rodrigues 2008).

The following statement also shows how the MST's leaders framed the dispute inside the government and the lack of priority given to the agrarian reform program as a difference between *state* and *government*. The idea expressed here is that the government was favorable to agrarian reform, but its efforts were hindered by the structure of the state:

> Land structure doesn't alter, precisely because the state is organized so as to defend the current structure. And always, because movements and organizations struggle, organize themselves, and fight in an organized way, the state reacts to defend this structure. So we suffer this state offensive on many fronts: in repression, in criminalization, in rights exclusion, in the difficulty to move forward. This is a form of the state authorizing conservative forces to act while having state protection, so this actually has been the role of the state, despite the fact that in many cases we have a government open to dialogue. However, the state hasn't

changed; governments change, but the state still remains the same. You cannot change the state in ways that answer to our interests. On the contrary, each time it creates more obstacles. (Misnerovicz 2008)

Leaders refer to two different moments in the political transition and in the position of the movement. The first is the initial interpretation of the new government as a moment of increased political opportunity for the movement's claims. This interpretation had a mobilizing effect, and land occupations increased compared to 2002, as illustrated in the following quotation, which references the period between the elections (October 2002) and the beginning of the PT government (January 2003):

In this period especially, there was the construction of the National Plan of Agrarian Reform. That was a very mobilizing element, because there was a historic promise, both from the PT and from the president, that once elected, agrarian reform would be one of the great priorities—ultimately, that it would be inside the actions of the government. So this plan was very mobilizing and we counted on its fulfillment. This expectation meant that millions of landless workers engaged in land occupations, organized camps in roadways, etcetera. (dos Santos 2008)

As this statement from national leader Marina dos Santos shows, this first moment of transition was framed as an opening in political opportunity, or an external factor facilitating social movement mobilization. Sidney Tarrow defines political opportunities as "consistent—but not necessarily formal, permanent, or national—dimensions of the political struggle that encourage people to engage in contentious politics" (1998: 19). Political constraints can also discourage or constrain mobilization, and those "factors—like repression, but also like authorities' capacity to present a solid front to insurgents—. . . discourage contention" (21).

Neither political opportunities nor political constraints are characteristics of movements; they are external and can be used strategically by those movements. Some opportunities might be stable, such as state structures, political cleavages, repression capacity (Tarrow 1998), political institutions and political culture (della Porta and Diani 2006). Other factors might be less stable, such as electoral preferences, elite division, and party alignment (della Porta and Diani 2006). In this structural explanation for mobilization "people engage in contentious politics when patterns of political opportunities and constraints change" (Tarrow 1998: 19). On these occasions, strategically using collective action repertoires opens new opportunities. A critique of this structural model of political opportunities is that it does not consider the cognitive dimension and the interpretative frames for perceiving certain factors as political opportunities (Goodwin and Jasper 2004). It is only through the attribution of meaning to objective conditions and to the external environment that absences and deprivations are perceived as needs and certain actions are considered as desirable for a collectivity (Sader 1988).

Hence, after their initial interpretation of circumstances as favorable for agrarian reform, the MST's leaders—along with the PT's left, as discussed above—changed their view to one in which agrarian reform was not being given the expected priority during the first years of Lula's government. Their frame of this has a nuance of deception, which appears in leaders' interviews immediately after a reference to the hope they had had:

> It began to be clear that agrarian reform was not a priority in this government. This was a demobilizing element, right, . . . because there was not that hope anymore that existed in the beginning [of Lula's government] that millions of families would be settled, millions of people would have access to land. Then this was generating a picture of internal demobilization, both inside MST and inside other rural social movements. (dos Santos 2008)

> Our biggest limit from the standpoint of achievements is related to conquering the land. There was a reduction in the number of expropriated lands and family settlements. This today is our greatest limitation because of many factors. But the main one is that the federal government retreated from the land expropriation actions. But we believe that these fights are important, to encourage the base, to maintain the discussion and the struggle disposition. In spite of not getting what we expected from the government, and in spite of the deception by the government, we won't give up the fight. (Misnerovicz 2008)

Governmental policy toward agrarian reform and government deception did not lead to open opposition by the movement or to fewer mobilizations and land occupations in the first years of Lula's government. The MST's position has to be understood in the broader context of the CMS and of the PT's left, which framed it as political dispute between leftist and rightist streams of the government coalition—in which the correlation of forces was favoring the rightist stream.

In analyzing how the relation with political parties affects social movements' political opportunities and mobilization, della Porta and Diani argue that "leaving aside the question of their openness to influence by social movements, participation by left-wing parties in government would appear to have a negative effect on collective mobilization because it seems to discourage from actual protest those who are potentially more protest-prone" (2006: 217). However, in the case of the MST this correlation is more complex. During the first three years of Lula's government, land occupation action increased. But land occupation has a deeper symbolic meaning for the movement; it is more than a mobilization repertoire. It also is the movement's most important ritual of collective identity construction and therefore has an internal significance that is the basis for the movement's self-definition.

The influence that the MST and other rural movements have on defining and implementing land reform policies did not start with the PT government, but it was intensified in 2003, as movement leaders took INCRA and MDA posts. Notwithstanding this greater participation in policy definition, mobilizations did not decrease during the first years of PT government. In President Lula's first term (2003–2006) numbers of land occupations continued high, and during the second term (2007–2010) they started to decrease.[11] One of the most important factors that explain this fall in land occupations is the economy's improvement during the second term, which reduced the number of poor families.

Therefore, before concluding that the PT government had a negative effect on the MST's collective mobilizations of land occupation, consider what mobilization has done for the MST's collective identity construction and what effect mobilization has had on interaction with the state, now that land occupation and encampment for agrarian reform are recognized by the state (Sigaud 2005).

Conclusion

The transition to PT government in 2003 was an unprecedented event in Brazilian politics, particularly from the standpoint of the social movement sector. The party had been historically allied with many social movements from different sectors. As soon as the party assumed the presidency, members of these movements began to fill important governmental and political posts. What happened to the social movement sector and its mobilization during the political transition?

In this chapter I analyze the MST, the most active social movement in Brazil during the transition period. The movement is a historical ally of the PT and, as part of CMS, defended increasing mobilizations and protests during the first years of Lula's government as a strategy to move the coalition government back toward the left.

The MST's protest activity declined during the last years of the FHC government because of the 2000 law that criminalized land occupation. In the first year of PT government, land occupations increased significantly, from 184 to 391. In the following year (2004) this number went to 461. Interviews with MST leaders showed that the transition was framed as a political opportunity; many families were hopeful and joined land occupations and, therefore, participated in the movement. However, soon after the PT assumed the presidency it became clear it was following a different direction than the one expected by the movement and that agrarian reform goals established in 2003 would not be achieved. MST leaders framed this as a deception.

This governmental deception and shift to the right, however, did not lead to the MST opposing Lula's government. The MST is part of the government and retains leverage in state institutions responsible for agrarian reform policies, which include infrastructure, credit, education, and technical assistance programs. The MST, along with other rural social movements, still has a significant role in the formulation and implementation of those policies.

The political transition had no significant effect on the MST's paramount collective action repertoire. Land occupations continued as the most frequent form of claiming for agrarian reform and were used also by many other rural organizations. Land occupation is thus a rigid repertoire of collective action (Tilly 2006) and has important symbolic meaning in movements' relations with the state, which recognizes it as a legitimate form of claiming for land (Sigaud 2005). The internal meaning of land occupation to the movement is constitutive of its very organization and of the identity of its members. As national leader Valdir Misnerovicz points out, land occupation is a "moment of baptism from the standpoint of participation in the movement."

From this I make three conclusions. First, the transition to the leftist PT government did not lead immediately to a decline in the MST's mobilization activities. Second, the movement intensified protests in the two first years of the PT government because MST leadership saw increased political opportunity. When movement leadership discovered that the government was retreating on land expropriation for agrarian reform after 2003, that did not lead to a reduction in land occupation. Third, MST activities after the transition transcend dualities such as radicalization versus institutionalization, autonomy versus co-optation, or mobilization versus demobilization.

Since 2003 MST leaders have occupied high governmental positions in which they formulate and implement public policies. But the MST has maintained collective land occupation as a central and strategic element. Furthermore, rural movements such as the MST can significantly influence governmental agrarian reform policies, especially by land occupations. Land occupation sets in motion governmental actions and public policies, beginning with land expropriation and continuing with housing construction, lending for building and planting, education, and technical assistance. All these policies are implemented in strict cooperation with social movements and local organizations.

Brazilian authors criticize transitology literature[12] for not paying enough attention to social movements during the transition to democracy in Brazil in 1985 and for giving a leading role to political elites (Vitullo 2006; Avritzer 2002). Other authors hold that democracy consolidation is a necessary condition for procedural democracy and do not agree with the focus this literature gives to procedural democracy (Reis and Cheibub 1993). Authors who call attention to the importance of expanding democracy by making it more open to civil society participation in deliberative spheres also criticize transitology literature (Avritzer 2002). Consolidation implies construction of a democratic, rather than authoritarian, political culture (Dagnino, Olvera, and Panfichi 2006; Alvarez, Dagnino, and Escobar 2000; Avritzer 1995). Literature on democracy consolidation in the more than thirty years since the transition to democracy in Brazil contains many studies of and theories on deliberative and participatory democracy experiences. The most studied is the participatory governmental budget process, but there are hundreds of studies on other experiences, such as conferences and councils, that include civil society participation in public policy formulation.

The MST participation experience in agrarian reform policies does not fit any of the categories studied so far in the participatory democracy literature. In spite of the intense participation of rural social movements in agrarian reform policies, taking part in participatory arenas has never been an important strategy for the movement. Even though it did not prioritize institutional participative spheres but rather had land occupation is its chief action, the MST has had an important role in consolidating democracy in Brazil. As Donatella della Porta and Frederico Rossi argue in Chapter 1, democracy "cannot be consolidated without the universal and effective application of citizenship rights, which transcend voting. At this stage, movements in many countries claim rights for those excluded by low-intensity democracies and ask for a more inclusive democracy." In this view it is possible to assess the importance of the MST in struggling for social rights for rural populations in Brazil. Many of the social rights that families settled through the agrarian reform program currently have, such as land, housing, and financial assistance, are the result of the MST's and other rural social movement's actions.

NOTES

1. A military coup in 1964 expelled the elected president João Goulart. A massive mobilization (Diretas Já [Direct Elections Now]) began pressing in 1983 for direct elections. The Congress decided not to approve a constitutional amendment for direct and democratic election, and in 1985, after twenty years of military government, the Congress elected a civil president, Tancredo Neves, one of the leaders of the mobilization. However, Neves died before assuming the presidency, and his vice president, José Sarney, a former leader in the military regime, became president. In 1988 a new constitution was approved and direct elections were held in 1989. All political parties in existence in 1964 were outlawed by the military regime, and two new parties were created: Aliança Renovadora Nacional (ARENA; Renewing National Alliance), the government party, and the Movimento Democrático Brasileiro (MDB; Brazilian Democratic Movement), the opposition party. Neves came from the MDB and was the leader of the opposition movement (Diretas Já), and Sarney came from ARENA and was a former supporter of the military regime. By the end of the military regime those two parties were extinct, and new parties were created. The most important of them were the PMDB, which came from the former MDB; the Partido da Social Democracia Brasileira (PSDB; Brazilian Social Democracy Party), a dissident group from the PMDB and the party of President Fernando Henrique Cardoso; the Partido da Frente Liberal (PFL; Liberal Front Party), a right-wing party that came from the former ARENA and later changed its name to Democratas (DEM; Democrats); and the PT. As of 2014, the PSDB and the DEM are allied and are the opposition to the government coalition that includes the PT and the PMDB.

2. Social movement activity in Brazil during the democratic transition has been extensively studied from other perspectives. Eder Sader (1988) studied São Paulo workers' political engagement in organizations such as trade unions, the Catholic Church, and neighborhood associations. Ana Maria Doimo (1995) examined urban social movements linked to housing, health, transportation, unemployment, and so on, in Brazil during the democratic transition and found that they faced the dilemma of choosing autonomy—independence from the state had been their position during the authoritarian regime—or integration and institutionalization in a now-democratic state. The church had a definitive role in the organization and support of social movements. Lygia Sigaud's (1980) studies of rural worker organizations in Pernambuco and their mobilization in the late 1970s is an important reference for studies on rural movements and rural trade unions in northeastern Brazil. During the metallurgy factory worker strikes in 1979, when 180,000 thousand workers went on strike in São Paulo, 100,000 rural workers struck in Pernambuco—a much less publicized and remembered fact. Other important studies of Brazilian social movements during democratic transition are Viola, Scherer-Warren, and Krischke 1989; Dagnino 1994; Moisés 1982; and Gohn 1995.

3. Since its creation many different factions have constituted the PT. Until 1993 the strongest and biggest was the Articulação (Articulation). In 1993, arguing that Articulação had moved to the right, leftist dissidents created the Articulação de Esquerda (Left Articulation) within the PT, and Articulação lost its majority. Rightists in the PT allied with parties more to the center in Brazilian politics and continued to win internal PT elections, thus keeping its majority position until 2005. The opposition to the majority was PT's left, composed of the Articulaçao de Esquerda and other factions. One of the strongest factions inside the PT is the Democracia Socialista (DS; Socialist Democracy), which has a Trotskyist orientation and has held the Ministry of Agrarian Development (responsible for land reform issues) since 2003. Another important left opposition faction was the Ação Popular Socialista (APS; Popular Socialist Action). The APS left the PT in the third year of Lula's government and created a new party, the Partido Socialismo e Liberdade (PSOL; Socialism and Liberty Party). Part of the PSOL along with other dissident left forces created a new trade union, Coordenação Nacional de Lutas (Conlutas; National Struggles Coordination) as an alternative to CUT unionism. In 2005, during a political crisis (discussed later), the PT reorganized internally, and there was no majority faction until 2007. After that year's internal elections the rightists, with some new allies, reestablished their majority and changed their name from Articulação to Construindo um Novo Brasil (CNB; Building a New Brazil). This is currently the majority inside the PT. Both Lula and Dilma Rouseff belong to this faction.

4. The concept of a "correlation of forces" was used by Italian philosopher Antonio Gramsci and is reproduced frequently by the Brazilian left to refer to the power relations inside a coalition that can change the direction of its action toward the left or right.

5. All translations are mine.

6. I do not analyze CUT during the transition period. OSAL data show that protests organized by CUT after 2003 decreased when compared to the preceding three years. After having always been at odds with the government, CUT achieved its strongest position in its history in Lula's government: the three first ministers of Work were former CUTs leaders, as was the president.

7. Liberation theology grew out of a reorientation by the Catholic Church, defined by the Second Vatican Council in 1965, to promote active participation in communitarian groups. The Second General Latin American Episcopal Conference in Colombia in 1969 supported liberation theology. The conclusions of this conference (the Medellín

Declaration) call for a stronger presence of the church in Latin America and understanding the Latin American people. The conclusions of Medellín are that salvation does not happen individually but through the construction of communities and thus apply to the formation of ecclesiastic communities. From these conclusions also came recommendations to study religion among the common people and spread the evangelic word. Another conclusion was the need for formation of as many ecclesiastic communities in parishes as possible, especially in rural areas and among marginalized urban populations (Sader 1988: 155).

8. In 1985 a group of landowners founded the União Democrática Ruralista (UDR; Ruralist Democratic Union) as a response to landless workers' organizations—mainly the MST at that time. One of the purposes of UDR was to prevent inclusion in the constitution of agrarian reform clauses allowing expropriation of large productive properties. They held protests but also had help from deputies and senators inside Congress during the constitutional process who prevented such legislation. In the 1990s, while the MST was increasing its land occupation actions, UDR was also active in defending property rights. It still has today strong representation in Congress.

9. Other sources give a different number. For example, the DATALUTA project from the Universidade Estadual Paulista (UNESP; Paulista State University), lists 393,842 families as being settled during FHC's government (1995–2002) (*DATALUTA* 2011).

10. These states are São Paulo, Rio de Janeiro, Minas Gerais, Espírito Santo, Rio Grande do Sul, Paraná, Santa Catarina, Ceará, Alagoas, Sergipe, Pernambuco, Goiás, Mato Grosso, and Mato Grosso do Sul.

11. The numbers for this period are 461 in 2004, 437 in 2005, 384 in 2006, 364 in 2007, 252 in 2008, 290 in 2009, and 180 in 2010 (Comissão Pastoral de Terra 2011).

12. *Transitology* is a term created by Philippe Schmitter to refer to democratization as a transactional process among mostly elites, with only a nod to movements, unions, and protest (O'Donnell, Schmitter, and Whitehead 1988; Linz and Stepan 1999).

REFERENCES

Almeida, Alfredo Wagner. 2008. *Terras de quilombo, terras indígenas, "babaçuais livres," "castanhais do povo," faixinais e fundos de pasto: Terras tradicionalmente ocupadas* [Quilombo Lands, Indigenous Lands, "Free Babaçuais," "People's Castanhais," Faxinais and Pasture Funds: Traditionally Occupied Lands]. Manaus, Brazil: Universidade Federal do Amazonas.

Alvarez, Sonia, Evelina Dagnino, and Arturo Escobar, eds. 2000. *Cultura e política nos movimentos sociais latino-americanos: Novas leituras* [Culture and Politics in Latin American Social Movements: New Readings]. Belo Horizonte, Brazil: Editora da Universidade Federal de Minas Gerais.

Avritzer, Leonardo. 1995. "Cultura política, atores sociais e Democratização: Uma crítica às teorias da transição para a democracia" [Political Culture, Social Actors and Democratizations: A Critic to Democratic Transition Theories]. *Revista Brasileira de Ciência Sociais* [Brazilian Journal of Social Sciences], no. 28: 70–87.

———. 2002. *Democracy and the Public Space in Latin America*. Princeton, NJ: Princeton University Press.

Benford, R., and Snow, D. 2000. "Framing Processes and Social Movements: An Overview and Assessment." *Annual Review of Sociology* 26:611–639.

Bill no. 2,183-56. 2000. Available at http://www.planalto.gov.br/ccivil_03/MPV/2183-56 .htm.

Decree no. 91,766: I National Plan of Agrarian Reform. 1985. Available at http://
    www2.camara.gov.br/legin/fed/decret/1980-1987/decreto-91766-10-outubro
    -1985-441738-publicacaooriginal-1-pe.html.
Chaves, Christine. 2000. *A Marcha Nacional dos Sem-Terra: Um estudo sobre a fabricação
    do social* [National Landless March: A Study of the Fabrication of the Social]. Rio de
    Janeiro: Relume-Dumará.
Comissão Pastoral de Terra [Pastoral Land Commission]. 2011. *Conflitos no campo,
    Brasil 2010* [Conflicts in the Countryside, Brazil 2010]. Goiânia, Brazil: CPT.
Dagnino, Evelina. 1994. *Os Anos 90: Política e Sociedade no Brasil* [The '90s: Politics and
    Society in Brazil]. São Paulo: Brasiliense.
Dagnino, Evelina, Alberto Olvera, and Aldo Panfichi, eds. 2006. *A Disputa pela
    construção democrática na América Latina* [The Dispute for the Democratic
    Construction in Latin America]. São Paulo: Paz e Terra.
DATALUTA 2011: Banco de dados da luta pela terra: Brasil [DATALUTA 2011: Database
    of the Struggle for Land: Brazil]. Available at http://www.lagea.ig.ufu.br/rededata
    luta/relatorios/brasil/dataluta_brasil_2011.pdf.
della Porta, D. 1996. "Social Movements and the State: Thoughts on the Policing of
    Protest." In *Comparative Perspective on Social Movements: Political Opportunities,
    Mobilizing Structures, and Cultural Framings*, edited by Doug McAdam and John
    McCarthy, 62–92. Cambridge: Cambridge University Press.
della Porta, D., and Mario Diani. 2006. *Social Movements: An Introduction.* Malden, MA:
    Blackwell.
Doimo, Ana Maria. 1995. *A voz e a vez do popular: Movimentos sociais pós-70 no Brasil*
    [The Voice and the Time of the Popular: Social Movements Post-'70s in Brazil]. Rio
    de Janeiro: Relume Dumará.
dos Santos, Marina. 2008. Interview by the author, December 2. Brasília, Brazil.
Fernandes, B. M. 2003. "O MST e os desafios para a realização da reforma agrária no
    governo Lula" [The MST and the Challenges to the Achievement of the Agrarian
    Reform in Lula's Government]. *Observatório Social de América Latina* [Social
    Observatory of Latin America] 11:31–40.
Frigotto, Gaudêncio. 2004. "Brasil e a política econômico-social: Entre o medo e a espe-
    rança" [Brazil and the Socioeconomic Politics: Between Hope and Fear]. *Obser-
    vatório Social de América Latina* 14:95–105.
Goffman, Erving. 1974. *Frame Analysis: An Essay on the Organization of Experience.*
    Boston: Northeastern University Press.
Gohn, Maria da Glória. 1995. *Movimentos e Lutas Sociais na Historia do Brasil*
    [Movements and Social Struggle in Brazil's History]. São Paulo: Loyola.
Goodwin, J., and J. Jasper. 2004. "Trouble in Paradigms." In *Rethinking Social Move-
    ments: Structure, Meaning, and Emotion*, edited by J. Goodwin and J. Jasper, 75–97.
    Lanham, MD: Rowman and Littlefield.
INCRA. 2000. *Relatório de Atividades: INCRA, 30 anos* [Report of Activities: INCRA,
    30 Years]. Brasília: Gráfica Guarany.
———. 2010. "Publicação Especial do Instituto Nacional de Colonização e Reforma
    Agrária" [Special Publication of the National Institute of Colonization and Agrarian
    Reform], no. 2. Available at http://www.incra.gov.br/media/servicos/publicacao/
    livros_revistas_e_cartilhas/jornal_incra_27_01_2011.pdf.
Law no. 4,504: Estatuto da Terra [Land Statute]. 1964. Available at http://www.planalto
    .gov.br/ccivil_03/Leis/L4504.htm.
Law no. 8,629. 1993. Available at http://www.planalto.gov.br/ccivil_03/leis/L8629.htm.

Leher, Roberto. 2006. "Región Sur: O governo Lula e os conflitos sociais no Brasil" [Southern Region: The Lula Government and Social Conflicts in Brazil]. *Observatório Social de América Latina* [Social Observatory of Latin America] 10:81–129.

Linz, J., and A. Stepan. 1999. *A transição e consolidação da democracia: A experiência do Sul da Europa e da América do Sul* [Transition and Consolidation of Democracy: The Experience of Southern Europe and South America]. São Paulo: Paz e Terra.

Medeiros, Leonilde. 2000. "Conflictos sociales rurales en el Brasil contemporaneo" [Rural Social Conflicts in Contemporary Brazil]. *Observatório Social de América Latina* [Social Observatory of Latin America] 1 (2): 37–44.

———. 2004. "As novas faces do rural e a luta por terra no Brasil contemporâneo" [The New Faces of the Rural and the Struggle for Land in Contemporary Brazil]. *Nomadas* 20:210–219.

Melucci, Alberto. 1996. *Challenging Codes: Collective Action in the Information Age.* Cambridge: Cambridge University Press.

Ministério do Desenvovimento Agrário [Ministry of Agrarian Development]. 2003. "II Plano Nacional de Reforma Agrária: Paz, produção e qualidade de vida no meio rural" [Second National Plan of Agrarian Reform: Peace, Production and Quality in the Rural Area]. Available at http://sistemas.mda.gov.br/arquivos/PNRA_2004.pdf.

Mirza, Christian Adel. 2006. *Movimientos sociales y sistemas políticos en América Latina* [Social Movements and Political Systems in Latin America]. Buenos Aires: Conselho Latino Americano de Ciências Sociais.

Misnerovicz, Valdir. 2008. Interview by the author, November 11. Brazil.

Moisés, José. 1982. *Lições de liberdade e de opressão: Os trabalhadores e a luta pela democracia* [Lessons of Liberty and Oppression: The Workers and the Struggle for Democracy]. Rio de Janeiro: Paz e Terra.

National Coordination of Social Movements. 2005. "Carta ao Povo Brasileiro" [Letter to the Brazilian People]. *Revista Espaço Aberto* [Open Space Journal], no. 50 (July).

Novaes, Regina. 1995. "Raíces y alas: Cambios y constantes en las comunidades de base" [Roots and Wings: Changes and Constants in Grassroots Communities]. *Nueva Sociedad* [New Society], no. 136: 70–81.

O'Donnell, Guillermo A., Philippe C. Schmitter, and Laurence Whitehead. 1988. *Transições do regime autoritário: America Latina* [Transitions from an Authoritarian Regime: Latin America]. São Paulo: Vértice.

Ondetti, Gabriel. 2006. "Repression, Opportunity, and Protest: Explaining the Takeoff of Brazil's Landless Movement." *Latin American Politics and Society* 48 (2): 61–94.

OSAL (Observatório Social de América Latina). 2000–2006. "Brasil: Cronología del conflicto social" [Brazil: Chronology of Social Conflict]. *Observatório Social de América Latina* [Social Observatory of Latin America] 1–18. Available at http://www.clacso.org.ar/institucional/1h.php.

Pizetta, Adelar João. 2007. "A formação política no MST: Um processo em construção" [Political Formation in the MST: An Ongoing Process]. *Observatório Social de América Latina*, no. 22: 241–250.

Reis, E. P., and J. B. Cheibub. 1993. "Pobreza, desigualdade e consolidação democrática" [Poverty, Inequality and Democratic Consolidation]. *Dados* [Data] 36 (2): 233–260.

Rodrigues, Inês. 2008. Interview by the author, September 5. Porto Alegre, Brazil.

Rosa, Marcelo. 2004. "As novas faces do sindicalismo rural brasileiro: A reforma agrária e as tradições sindicais na Zona da Mata de Pernambuco" [The New Faces of Brazilian Unionism: Agrarian Reform and Union Traditions in Pernambucos's Zona da Mata]. *Dados* [Data] 47 (3): 473–503.

————. 2011. *O Engenho dos Movimentos: Reforma agrarian e significação social na zona canavieira de Pernambuco* [The Ingenuity of Movements: Agrarian Reform and Social Meaning in the Sugar Cane Zone of Pernambuco]. Rio de Janeiro: Garamond.

Sader, Eder. 1988. *Quando novos personagens entram em cena: Experiências, falas e lutas dos trabalhadores da grande São Paulo (1970–1980)* [When New Actors Enter the Scene: Experiences, Speeches and Workers' Struggles in the Great São Paulo (1970–1980)]. Rio de Janeiro: Paz e Terra.

Sampaio, Plínio. 2005a. "Brasil: As esperanças não vingaram" [Brazil: Unattained Expectations]. *Observatório Social de América Latina* [Social Observatory of Latin America] 18:69–80.

————. 2005b. "La reforma agraria en América Latina: Una revolución frustrada" [The Agrarian Reform in Latin America: A Frustrated Revolution]. *Observatório Social de América Latina* [Social Observatory of Latin America] 16:15–22.

Santos, Boaventura de Souza. 2002. *Democratizar a democracia: Os caminhos da democracia participativa* [To Democratize the Democracy: The Paths to Participatory Democracy]. Rio de Janeiro: Civilização Brasileira.

Sauer, Sérgio, and João Pereira, eds. 2006. *Capturando a terra: Banco Mundial, políticas fundiárias neoliberais e reforma agrária de mercado* [Capturing the Land: World Bank, Neoliberal Land Policies and Market-Oriented Agrarian Reform]. São Paulo: Editora Expressão Popular.

Sigaud, Lygia. 1980. *Greve nos engenhos* [Strike on the Sugar Cane Mills]. Rio de Janeiro: Paz e Terra.

————. 2005. "As condições de possibilidade das ocupações de terra" [The Conditions of Possibility of Land Occupation]. *Revista Tempo Social* [Social Time Journal] 17 (1): 255–280.

Sigaud, L. M., Marcelo Rosa, and Marcelo Ernandez. 2010. *Ocupações e acampamentos: Sociogênese das mobilizações por reforma agrarian no Brasil* [Occupations and Encampments: Sociogenesis of Agrarian Reform Mobilizations in Brazil]. Rio de Janeiro: Garamond.

Silva, A. A. da, and B. M. Fernandes. 2006. "Ocupações de terras, 2000–2005: Movimentos socioterritoriais e espacialização da luta pela terra" [Land Occupations, 2000–2005: Socioterritorial Movements and Land Struggle Spatialization]. In *Conflitos no campo, Brasil 2005*, edited by CPT, 96–108. Goiânia, Brazil: CPT. Available at http://www .cptnacional.org.br/index.php/component/jdownloads/finish/43/245?Itemid=23.

Snow, D., and D. Benford. 1998. "Ideology, Frame Resonance and Participant Mobilization." In International Social Movements Research, vol. 1, *From Structure to Action: Comparing Social Movements Research across Cultures*, edited by B. Klandermans, H. Krieski, and S. Tarrow, 197–217. Greenwich: JAI Press.

Snow, D., E. Rochford, S. Worden, and R. Benford. 1986. "Frame Alignment Processes, Micromobilization, and Movement Participation." *American Sociological Review* 51 (4): 464–481.

Souza, João Luis Vieira de. 2008. Interview by the author, December 1. Brasília, Brazil.

Stedile, J. 2004. "El MST y las Disputas por Alternativas em Brasil" [The MST and the Disputes for Alternatives in Brazil]. *Observatório Social de América Latina* [Social Observatory of Latin America], no. 13: 1–10.

Tarrow, Sidney. 1998. *Power in Movement: Social Movements, Collective Action and Politics*. Cambridge: Cambridge University Press.

Tilly, C. 2006. *Regimes and Repertoires*. Chicago: University of Chicago Press.

Viola, E. J., Ilse Scherer-Warren, and P. J. Krischke, eds. 1989. *Crise Politica, Movimentos Sociais e Cidadania* [Political Crisis, Social Movements and Citizenship]. Florianópolis, Brazil: Universidade Federal de Santa Catarina.

Vitullo, Gabriel. 2006. "As teorias da democratização frente às democracias latino-americanas" [The Democratization Theories across Latin American Democracies]. *Opinião Pública* [Public Opinion] 12:348–377.

7

Democratization and the Revitalization of Popular Movements in Central America

PAUL ALMEIDA

emocratization largely occurred in Central America at the end of the twentieth century. The region also experienced two waves of antineoliberal protest during this democratic transition. Beginning in the late 1990s, the region's fifty million inhabitants experienced an upsurge in popular movement activity against economic policies directly related to economic globalization. Examples of this wave of contention include the campaigns against new sales taxes and free trade in Guatemala; mobilizations against privatization and free trade in Honduras, Costa Rica, and El Salvador; struggles against the pension system and labor reforms in Panama; and major protests against consumer price hikes in Nicaragua. More than any other social grievance or issue, economic liberalization measures motivated the largest mass mobilizations in the region over the past two decades (Almeida 2014). These struggles are characterized by a more open political context in which traditional social sectors enter coalitions with emerging and novel social organizations with new collective identities (Johnston, Laraña, and Gusfield 1994).[1] This chapter examines the conditions associated with this more recent rise in antiglobalization protest in the region and its timing and compares these trends to first-wave antineoliberal protest in the 1980s and early 1990s. Particular attention is given to the processes of democratization and organizational formation and the threats associated with economic globalization that eventuate in a revitalized social movement sector during periods of political transition.

Central American Democratization

Samuel Huntington (1991) marks the beginning of global democratization as the mid-1970s as does John Markoff (1996). With the notable exception of Costa

Rica, democracy arrived relatively late to Central America. El Salvador, Guatemala, Honduras, and Nicaragua did not begin to democratize until the 1980s. Panama underwent a democratic transition in the 1990s, and civil wars in El Salvador, Guatemala, and Nicaragua did not end until the early to mid-1990s (Sojo 1999). Hence, until the 1990s, in all countries on the isthmus except Costa Rica, social struggles either focused directly on the authoritarian nature of the state or were hindered in civil society organizing.

In El Salvador, until 1991 left-of-center political parties participated in elections on a very limited basis (Artiga-González 2004). Full legalization of a broader array of political parties was not achieved until the 1994 elections (Wood 2005). In this period of democratic transition and post-civil-war reconstruction, many of the social movement campaigns in El Salvador concentrated on issues left over from the civil war, such as land titles, human rights, and compensation for former soldiers and paramilitary participants (Almeida 2008b). A parallel process took place in Guatemala (Brett 2008), where post-civil-war presidential and parliamentary elections did not take place until late 1999. Honduras began a slow process of democratization in the mid-1980s. Nicaragua maintained a socialist government in the 1980s but imposed certain democratic curtailments (e.g., curfews in conflict zones) while fighting a counterinsurgent war sponsored by the Reagan administration in the United States. Nicaragua did not reach a definitive peace and multiparty elections until 1990. Panama held its first postauthoritarian presidential elections in 1994.

Democratization is characterized by consecutive multiparty elections in which the state allows a wide spectrum of political forces to participate and compete (Diamond 1999). A consolidated democracy also tolerates the formation and expansion of associations in civil society (Foweraker and Landman 1997). Some perspectives expect democratization to increase social movement mobilization since there are fewer constraints and obstacles to mobilize (Tilly 2004). Such formulations suggest that state repression lessens in that the government is more accountable for overly coercive behavior and officeholders can be replaced in elections. Civil society actors also have greater success expectations (Klandermans 1997) in that state institutions are *relatively* more open and willing to at least listen to popular grievances. Such signaling by the state provides incentives to campaign organizers to invest precious resources and time in nonviolent collective action. The emergence and legalization of oppositional political parties during a democratic transition also increases the ability of activists to organize on a national level and support new constituencies, which may include social movements.

Other perspectives predict a reduction in social movement mobilization in the streets because more institutionalized actors, such as political parties and state agencies, take over in democratic contexts (Hipsher 1998), reducing the need for mass collective action that deploys nonroutine strategies. There does seem to be some evidence for this demobilization trend in the early days of Latin American democratization and in Central America in particular. Indeed, James Dunkerley's (1994) seminal synthesis of the entire region characterizes the political climate of the early 1990s as a "pacification" of mass opposition by domestic and international elites. However, once a democratic transition combines with the economic threats of globalization, a new upsurge in collective action becomes a heightened possibility (Almeida 2010a). I explore this issue in more detail below. Especially noteworthy is the growth and revitalization of civic organizations with the advent of democratization.

Organizational Formation and Expansion

Democratization allows a greater variety of organizations to form for several reasons. The state permits the existence of more organizations in civil society under democratization, often by providing legal recognition or nonprofit status (in the case of nongovernmental organizations). Older civic organizations left over from the authoritarian period find they have more freedom to organize. These include key social sectors such as labor unions, the educational sector (including teachers, students, and employees in high schools and universities), and rural groups such as agricultural cooperatives. At the same time, these traditional sectors that expanded during state-led development need to adapt their strategies of collective action and organizing in the new context of democratization (Almeida and Johnston 2006). Such recalibrations probably cause a lag effect in the pace of civic organizations employing novel strategies while they learn the new political environment.

New social actors emerged as global democracy advanced, such as nongovernmental organizations (NGOs), which are diverse in their memberships, identities, and missions. My emphasis here is on NGOs that at times join with the social movement sector, although their daily concerns may not involve manifest social movement struggles. NGOs advocate for women, the environment, community health, human rights, ethnic minority rights, community development, and many other interests. NGOs have facilitated many campaigns against globalization in Central America, and the NGO sector in the region experienced massive growth into the 1990s (Bradshaw and Schafer 2000).

New social movements also mushroomed in recent decades. These newer movements in Central America include environmental struggles, battles for the recognition of gay rights, and a vibrant and autonomous women's movement. Though at times these newer social movements may receive financial and technical support from NGOs, they are distinguishable from nonprofit organizations by their goals and forms of mobilization. New social movement perspectives emphasize the uniqueness of collective struggles, as well as identity and cultural issues, and go beyond the state-power and economic exclusion themes of classic social movements (Armstrong and Bernstein 2008). An interesting process in Central America involves the large coalitions that have formed in antineoliberal policy campaigns that include new social movements.

Political parties have also served as mobilizing organizations in the movements against globalization throughout Latin America (Van Cott 2005). In nondemocratic contexts, oppositional political parties are often underground (Schock 2005). Once liberalization begins, especially in a democratic transition, oppositional political parties may play crucial roles in the social movement sector (Keck 1992). In the era of globalization, the traditional structures used to coordinate social movements, such as labor unions and agricultural cooperatives and associations, have greatly weakened. Political parties organized on a national scale or across several regions provide the only organizational structures available in many communities (Almeida 2010b). Opposition parties need to build their electoral base in new democracies as well. Taking up social movement demands against unpopular policies offers one major avenue for an oppositional political party to build up its base of support (Stearns and Almeida 2004). This worked especially well in Ecuador and Bolivia in the late 1990s and early 2000s when unpopular neoliberal policies such as privatization and subsidy cuts were taken up by leftist and indigenous political parties to expand their base (Assies and Salman 2003; Yashar 2005).

In summary, new alliances emerged between traditional social movements, NGOs, new social movements, and political parties in the 1990s. These groupings provide the baseline organizational infrastructure in Central America in the period of globalization. Nonetheless, there is substantial variation between countries in the importance of each of these mobilizing collectivities. The variations affect the level of mass mobilization against the tide of the economic threats of neoliberalism.

Economic Threats of Globalization

One school of globalization theory finds heightened levels of social anomie and individualism with the spread of a consumer society model in Latin America (see Arce and Bellinger 2007 for a critique of this literature). As elsewhere in the more developed part of the global periphery, Central America has experienced a rapid spread of mall culture and the idolization of mass consumption lifestyles in major urban centers as a by-product of cultural globalization (Robinson 2008). Such perspectives predict that social solidarity and collective action campaigns will be more difficult to mount in an expanding culture of consumerist individualism (Crook el al. 1992). However, political-cultural frameworks of this particular variety fail to explain the upswing in mass mobilization in the region with the *deepening* of globalization over the past fifteen years.

Economic globalization entered Central America via the debt crisis of the early 1980s. Central American states made agreements with international financial institutions that required restructuring their national economies into a more outward orientation (see Figure 7.1). Each structural adjustment agreement between a Central American government and the International Monetary Fund (IMF) or the World Bank represents a shift in economic policy away from state-led development toward more free market reforms (Walton and Ragin 1990). The first-generation structural adjustment reforms in the 1980s included

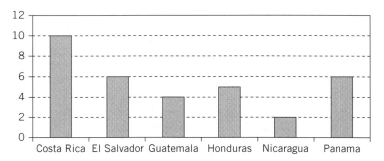

Figure 7.1 Number of International Monetary Fund structural adjustment agreements in Central America, 1981–1994. *(Source: Compiled from Green 2003)*

new sales taxes, currency devaluations, a reduction on import tariffs, wage freezes, and subsidy cuts on basic mass consumption items (cooking oil, electricity, transportation) and agricultural inputs (Green 2003).

In the mid-1980s, these first-phase economic changes at times resulted in protests, riots, and mass marches. However, the campaigns were usually not sustained for more than a month—the lack of democracy in most of the region and other issues predominated. These first-wave protests were often led by relatively narrow coalitions of students and urban workers. The debt crisis lingered into the 1990s. The external debt of each Central American country increased dramatically between 1980 and the early 1990s. Between 1980 and 1995, Costa Rica's external debt grew from $2.7 billion to $3.8 billion. In this same period, the external debt of El Salvador, Guatemala, Honduras, Nicaragua, and Panama more than doubled (Almeida 2007: 126). The international financial institutions, along with the U.S. Agency for International Development (USAID), formulated a new round of structural adjustment programs that relied heavily on the privatization of public infrastructure, utilities, and services (Chong and López de Silanes 2005). By the mid-1990s, all Central American republics were pressured to reform their national pension programs and privatize key components of their infrastructure, including power distribution, telecommunications, national postal service, water administration, social security and health care systems, and ports (Almeida 2014).

In the 1990s, the overwhelming majority of political elites governing in the region ideologically subscribed to market liberalization (Robinson 2003) and obliged the international financial institutions by attempting to push the reforms rapidly through their respective national legislatures (Haglund 2010). These second-generation reforms emerged in a context of greater democracy and much more societal experience with neoliberal measures, resulting in the largest sustained outbursts of mass mobilization in decades by the late 1990s and early 2000s. Figure 7.2 compares two phases of structural adjustment (1980–1995) and (1996–2004) with respect to major mass mobilizations countering economic reforms in Central American countries.

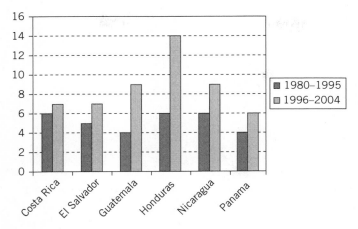

Figure 7.2 Number of Antiglobalization protests of ten thousand or more people in Central America. *(Source: Almeida 2007; Walton 1987; data from various sources in LexisNexis Academic Universe, "World News" section, 1980–2004)*

First-Wave Campaigns against Economic Liberalization, 1980–1995

In the 1980s, a wide variety of political environments existed in Central America. The Salvadoran and Guatemalan governments engaged in counterinsurgency operations, and the Nicaraguan government attempted to consolidate its popular revolution while a counterrevolutionary army infiltrated its borders (Horton 1998). General Manuel Noriega governed Panama as a quasi-corporatist military regime, and Honduras was slowly transitioning to civilian rule after decades of military control. In this same period, Costa Rica expanded the scope of its long-enduring democracy by legalizing leftist political parties in the mid-1970s (Salom 1987). Hence, when Central American governments enacted the first stabilization policies in the early to mid-1980s, the popular reactions were relatively weak. Only in democratic Costa Rica were there sustained campaigns to resist agricultural adjustments (Edelman 1999) and an IMF program to raise electricity rates (Alvarenga 2005). In El Salvador, activists organized mass marches against a currency devaluation in 1986, and in Guatemala and Panama, short-term movements arose against price increases (Walton 1987) and labor flexibility laws (Almeida 2014). However, it was not until the late 1990s that massive sustained antiglobalization campaigns emerged in the region more frequently, demonstrating a revitalization of the region's social movement sector.

In the late 1990s, several campaigns surfaced against globalization. Many of these campaigns were unsuccessful in stopping the impending neoliberal measures, but they often led to stronger mobilizations in future rounds of collective action against similar neoliberal policies in the early 2000s (Almeida

2008a) that resulted in reactivation of social movements across the isthmus. Democratization, the expansion of civic organizations, and economic threats were key ingredients in each of the campaigns. Below, I sketch major first-wave antiglobalization campaigns (1980–1995) in each Central American country.

Costa Rica

Costa Rica was the first country to enter a serious debt crisis in the early 1980s and the first to manifest signs of popular movement activity related to globalization processes (Rovira Mas 1987). The early resistance had two distinct centers of struggle: the small-farmer sector and the urban sector. The peasant struggle waged pitched battles over declining agricultural credit, and the urban struggle focused on consumer prices that rose after a loss of state subsidies.

The peasant struggle began in the early 1980s with the formation of two new agricultural associations: Unión Nacional de Pequeños y Medianos Productores Agropecuarios (UPANACIONAL; National Union of Small and Medium Agricultural Producers) and Unión de Pequeños Agricultores de la Región Atlántica (UPAGRA; Atlantic Region Union of Small Farmers). Thousands of small farmers in the central valley of Costa Rica formed UPANACIONAL in 1981 (Edelman 1999). In December 1981, UPANACIONAL coordinated roadblocks with five thousand small farmers on eight highways to demand price controls on agricultural inputs (Edelman 1999: 94). UPANACIONAL and UPAGRA engaged in several skirmishes throughout the 1980s for access to low-priced agricultural inputs and the avoidance of cheap agricultural imports. In addition, after the country signed its first full-fledged structural adjustment program in 1985, peasant associations held mass marches in the capital in 1986 and 1987 against further removal of subsidies in the agricultural sector. In June 1988, several agricultural associations simultaneously blocked roads to protest the government's neoliberal agricultural policies when low-interest credit dried up for future planting seasons (Edelman 1999: 94).

In the urban sector, price-increase protests against electricity peaked in 1983. They were led by a coalition of neighborhood associations, the Communist Party (Vanguardia Popular), and labor unions (Alvarenga 2005). The next major struggles over globalization did not take place until 1995, against pension system reform affecting public sector educators.[2] The IMF and World Bank pressured the Costa Rican state to raise the retirement age of educators to reduce its domestic fiscal deficit. Teachers formed a coalition with public sector workers to attempt to defeat the new pension law and other planned privatizations and layoffs in the public sector (Almeida 2008a). The movement peaked in July and August 1995, convoking two massive street marches with tens of thousands of participants, but in the end failed to reverse the reforms (Almeida and Walker 2007).

El Salvador

El Salvador's early resistance to economic liberalization occurred in 1985 when mass demonstrations broke out between May and July against continuing government austerity. In February 1986 more mass demonstrations took place, sponsored by the newly formed Unidad Nacional de Trabajadores Salvadoreños (UNTS; National Unity of Salvadoran Workers), against President José Napoleón Duarte's *paquete* (austerity package) that devalued the Salvadoran national currency (the colón). These mass actions were the largest since the massive state repression of the early 1980s (Almeida 2008b). In 1995, President Calderon Sol of the neoliberal ARENA party initiated a state modernization program that included privatization of telecommunications, pensions, and electricity and mass layoffs in the public sector. These economic measures were met with popular resistance and strikes in each of the affected sectors, but the campaigns failed to create a unified opposition. As a result of the lack of unity and labor union support from the public, the government pushed through all its privatization programs.

Guatemala and Honduras

Guatemala was also rocked by first-generation economic liberalization reforms in September 1985. Rioting and looting took place in the capital while teachers and public sector employees engaged in strikes and job actions against an IMF austerity program that encouraged budget cuts and new taxes. In these events, up to ten people were killed and one thousand arrested. In the end the government decided to roll back bus fare increases, control prices of basic foods, and give government sector workers a slight raise (Walton 1987).

In Honduras major popular protest occurred in 1990 under newly elected President Callejas against his Law of Economic Reorganization—referred to on the streets as the *paquetazo* (massive austerity package or measure). The organizational basis of the mobilizations occurred in 1989 with the formation of the Platform of Struggle to Democratize Honduras (Plataforma de Lucha para la Democratización de Honduras)—the broadest coalition of oppositional groups to form in Honduras in decades (Posas 2003). Several mass demonstrations and strikes took place against the economic reforms in 1990 and 1991, including strikes by banana plantation workers, health sector workers, and other public sector labor unions such as postal workers, energy sector workers, and public works employees (Sosa 2010). The 1990 and 1991 mobilizations against free market reforms represented some of the first large-scale protests against privatization in the region, including the selling off of state lands and the reversal of agrarian reform. By 1993, Eugenio Sosa (2010) contends, President Callejas successfully demobilized the popular movement via a mix of state modernization, co-optation, and repression.

Nicaragua

During most of the 1980s, the Sandinista ruling party maintained close connections to state unions and civil society associations. In the late 1980s, the Sandinista government implemented several austerity measures because of growing indebtedness and a trade embargo instituted by the Reagan-Bush administrations. The first signs of mass resistance to austerity measures erupted immediately after the Sandinista party relinquished executive power in the presidential elections of February 1990. A new labor organization was created to resist the austerity measures implemented by the recently elected Chamorro administration—the Frente Nacional de Trabajadores (FNT; National Workers' Front). The FNT was largely composed of state sector unions and small farmers affiliated with the Sandinista party.

Between 1990 and 1992, the FNT launched several campaigns to resist the austerity measures of Chamorro, who was facing a $10 billion foreign debt, the largest in Central America. Most of the campaigns focused on preventing mass layoffs in the government sphere, the closing of state institutions, and salary freezes. Many of the campaigns reached several cities and were marred by violence from both police and, less frequently, the protesters. The other major campaign of the early to mid-1990s occurred in the university community over cuts to the postsecondary-education budget (Almeida and Walker 2007). These protests erupted between 1992 and 1996 and involved thousands of university students and employees (Palazio Galo, n.d.). In addition, two major teacher strikes led by the Asociación Nacional de Educadores de Nicaragua (ANDEN; National Association of Nicaraguan Educators) took place in 1994 and 1995 over government austerity programs that froze public educator wages.

Panama

Panama also experienced austerity protests in 1983 and 1985. In these years the IMF and World Bank demanded that the Panamanian government freeze wages in the public sector and cut subsidies to basic industries. A general strike broke out in Panama City and Colón in October 1983 (Walton 1987). A massive campaign against an austerity package (Law 46) was launched in late 1984 by a coalition of professional associations (teachers and doctors) and university students called the Coordinadora Cívica Nacional (COCINA; National Civil Coordinator). A general strike and mass mobilizations of up to tens of thousands of demonstrators took place in November and December 1984, resulting in the Barletta government's cancellation of the austerity measures (Beluche 1994). Mass demonstrations and strikes also exploded in September 1985. A final first-generation antiausterity campaign occurred in Panama in 1995 against newly imposed labor flexibility laws, which weakened labor union rights. Led by the militant construction workers' union Sindicato Único Nacional de Trabajadores de la Industria de la Construcción y Similares (SUNTRACS; National Union of

Construction Workers and Related Industries), forty-nine labor unions held a monthlong strike in August 1995 striving to turn back the new labor measures. This was a particularly violent conflict between the government and labor organizations in which three hundred protest participants were arrested and four labor unionists were killed.

In sum, the participants in the first-generation campaigns against economic liberalization in Central America failed to sustain mobilizations and hold together broad coalitions. Governments in the region were just commencing democratization processes, especially after 1990 (with the exception of Costa Rica). The lack of democratization greatly hampered the formation of organizations and coalitions that could freely exercise rights of association and public assembly. Each affected social sector struggled against the relatively new threats of economic adjustment in largely independent ways. A long-term collective consciousness based on experiences of several rounds of economic reforms had yet to congeal with the subaltern classes. These conditions slowly changed by the late 1990s.

Second-Wave Popular Movements against Globalization, 1996–2011

As Central America remained in a debt crisis with governments that subscribed to a neoliberal ideology in the 1990s, a new generation of economic reforms slowly worked its way through the legislative pipeline. The second-generation reforms were characterized by privatization of basic services, infrastructure, and utilities (Edwards 1995; Kaufman and Nelson 2004). In the mid-2000s, Central American governments added free trade agreements to the list of neoliberal reforms. Unlike the 1980s, when much of the region was still embroiled in violent civil conflicts and authoritarian regimes, these second-generation reforms occurred in a climate of greater democratization. This particular combination of second-generation economic reform and greater civil society space for mobilizing proved especially volatile. The protests of the campaigns enumerated below had more diversity in participants, a greater number of them, and wider geographical reach, and were longer sustained than the first wave of protests in the 1980s and early 1990s. And at times they were more successful—a clear sign of revitalization of the social movement sector throughout the region.

Costa Rica

Costa Rican civic organizations initiated a major campaign against the privatization of telecommunications and electricity at the beginning of 2000. The government was planning to permit private sector participation in electrical power generation and distribution and in telecommunication services with the Instituto Costarricense de Electricidad (ICE), a state monopoly. The ICE provides relatively inexpensive and accessible service to much of the national population (Haglund 2010). When plans for partial privatization worked their way through the Costa Rican legislature, a coalition materialized of state sector workers (especially in the ICE), university and high school students, a small leftist political party, environmentalists, community groups, and progressive elements of the Catholic Church. The coalition began holding small rallies and leafleting in January and February 2000. As the parliament neared voting on the privatization in mid-March, the movement stepped up its activities with mass marches and protests outside the legislative assembly. When the parliament approved the measure in the first round of voting, the coalition ratcheted up the pressure with a campaign of mass civil disobedience, which included labor strikes, hunger strikes, over one hundred roadblocks throughout the national territory, and the beginning phases of a general strike, until the government backed down and canceled the privatization plans in early April—resulting in a positive outcome for the movement (Almeida 2008a).

The next major round of antiglobalization protest emerged between 2004 and 2007 against the Central American Free Trade Agreement (CAFTA).[3] The coalition that prevented privatization of the ICE expanded to include more sectors from civil society. After several national days of protests and public sector strikes against CAFTA between 2004 and 2006, the anti-CAFTA coalition coordinated a massive street march of some 150,000 people on February 26, 2007 (probably the largest demonstration in modern Costa Rican history). The historic march forced the government to put CAFTA to a popular referendum in October 2007. With this, the social movement had converted to an electoral strategy. A second mass rally of 150,000 people on September 30, 2007, marked the end of the campaign. Although the mass mobilizations revitalized the Costa Rican social movement sector, the anti-CAFTA forces suffered a defeat on the measure in October 2007, when a slight majority of Costa Ricans voted in favor of the treaty in the referendum. Nonetheless, by 2014 many of the anti-CAFTA forces regrouped and put their energies and resources into the electoral process, electing several antineoliberal activists to parliament in the Frente Amplio Party.

El Salvador

The early campaigns against state modernization in the mid-1990s had failed, and Salvadoran civil society became increasingly displeased with the rising cost of living after electricity and telecommunications privatization. In 1999, the Salvadoran government targeted the public health care system for partial privatization. Public sector unions in health care, including labor associations and unions of medical doctors, organized a multisectoral campaign of resistance. The protest coalition included a wide variety of NGOs, state sector unions, and students. Marches were held in several cities between November 1999 and March 2000, and medical staff physicians held work stoppages throughout the national hospital system. The movement succeeded in temporarily halting the privatization through an accord reached with the government in March 2000.

In 2002, the Salvadoran government once again pursued privatization of the Instituto Salvadoreño del Seguro Social (ISSS; Salvadoran Social Security Institute). The coalition of opposition rematerialized and fought a ten-month-long battle against the outsourcing of medical care and coverage. This round of collective action involved national days of protest using highway blockades and several mass street marches known as *marchas blancas* (white marches) because protesters dressed in white to display their solidarity with the health care profession. Some of the *marchas blancas* reached up to 150,000 participants, making them the largest street marches since 1980. The movement achieved its main goal of preventing privatization and signed an accord with the central government in June 2003. Smaller and less efficacious protest campaigns were organized against CAFTA between 2004 and 2007 and water privatization between 2006 and 2008. As in Costa Rica, but with even more success, the antineoliberal coalition in El Salvador turned to an electoral strategy and elected the socialist Frente Farabundo Martí para la Liberación Nacional (FMLN; Farabundo Martí National Liberation Front) in 2009 and again in 2014.

Guatemala

Major campaigns against second-generation structural adjustment reforms in Guatemala, against a new sales tax hike backed by the International Monetary Fund, broke out in 2001. Between April and August 2001, mass marches were held in several cities against the new neoliberal measure. Despite mass public opposition, the government passed the sales tax law in August 2001. The Guatemalan government moved once again in 2004 to raise the sales tax. This time a coalition of labor unions, students, NGOs, and indigenous peasants formed and successfully resisted the measure by holding a short general strike and setting roadblocks in June. This same coalition resurrected itself in early 2005 to resist CAFTA. It was the second-largest sustained mobilization against CAFTA in Central America (after Costa Rica's). Throughout March 2005, students, indigenous organizations, and labor unions held several mass marches and blockaded the nation's major highways as the Guatemalan legislature debated and subsequently approved CAFTA.

Since 2005, dozens of local struggles have broken out in indigenous communities over the expansion of mining operations and the cultivation of biofuels—Guatemalan resources to be exported to global markets. Between 2005 and 2009, local grassroots movements (largely rural indigenous Mayan communities) convoked dozens of popular consultations, a type of referendum, in municipalities throughout the departments of San Marcos, Quiché, Huehuetenango, and Sololá over the incursion of open-pit mining operations in their respective regions. In each community where a consultation took place, an overwhelming majority rejected the mining plans (Véliz 2009). Local conflicts with multinational enterprises over natural resources appear to be growing in the second decade of the twenty-first century throughout the Central American isthmus.

Honduras

In the late 1990s in Honduras, a new oppositional organization formed called el Bloque Popular (the People's Bloc). The Bloque Popular is composed of university students, public sector labor unions, school teacher associations, and peasant leagues. The group engaged in several campaigns against privatization in the late 1990s and early 2000s, resulting in much more antiglobalization activity than in the 1980s. A second, broader coalition with links to the Bloque Popular formed in 2003—the Coordinadora Nacional de Resistencia Popular (CNRP; National Coordinator of Popular Resistance). The CNRP organized several mass actions between 2003 and 2006, including a colossal demonstration through the streets of Tegucigalpa in August 2003 against water privatization (an IMF-backed measure), wage freezes, and the weakening of collective labor contracts (Posas 2003).

In the second wave of protests, the Bloque Popular also tried to prevent CAFTA's ratification by the Honduran Congress by coordinating a national day of protest in February 2005. However, the Honduran legislature ratified the treaty. These same groups coalesced to oppose the June 2009 military coup in Honduras—the Frente Nacional de Resistencia Popular (FNRP; National Front of Popular Resistance). The FNRP mobilized several mass campaigns against the coup between June 2009 and July 2011. In June 2011, with the return of ousted president Manuel Zelaya, the FNRP converted to a political party, Libertad y Refundación (LIBRE). LIBRE competed in the 2013 presidential, parliamentary, and municipal elections and achieved impressive results. LIBRE became the second-largest political party in Honduras, displacing Latin America's oldest elite two-party system (Almeida 2014). Hence, a massive nationally organized socialist oppositional party was built from mobilizing in the streets against neoliberalism over the previous decade.

Nicaragua

A new civil society umbrella organization, the Coordinadora Civil (Civil Coordinator), was born in Nicaragua after the social catastrophe wrought by Hurricane Mitch in late 1998. In its first years of existence the Coordinadora focused on disaster relief issues. Eventually the NGOs constituting the Coordinadora took on consumer rights issues and free trade. Two other major civil society federations emerged in the late 1990s and early 2000s—the Red Nacional de Defensa de los Consumidores (RNDC; National Network in Defense of Consumers) and the Unión Nacional de Asociaciones de Consumidores y

Usarios (UNACU; National Union of Consumer Associations). Both federations were made up of community and municipal consumer associations from throughout the nation. Along with the Movimiento Comunal Nicaragüense (MCN; Nicaraguan Community Movement), these consumer protection groups fought several campaigns over power and water privatization and rapidly rising transportation fares and utility bills with a mixture of success and failure (Serra 2006). Finally, health care workers protested throughout the 2000s against IMF cuts in public health spending.

Panama

After a successful mass mobilization against water privatization in late 1998, two major campaigns in Panama in the 2000s against economic restructuring centered on the Panamanian Caja de Seguro Social (CSS; Panamanian Institute of Social Security Insurance), the country's national health care and pension system. In 2003, the CSS came under the threat of privatization. In September and October 2003, CSS employees, other public sector unions (including teachers), students, and construction workers launched two general strikes to protest the attempted privatization. The strikes slowed the outsourcing of government pension services and public health care. Another CSS conflict erupted in 2005 when the government approved a new law that raised the retirement age. Between April and July 2005, several mass marches took place, some reaching up to one hundred thousand participants. Students and labor unions also protested with roadblocks throughout the nation. In the end, the government of president Martin Torrijos partially conceded to the movement's demands and watered down the aggressive pension reforms.

The oppositional coalition in both phases of the conflict (2003 and 2005) maintained a delicate unity under the Frente Nacional en Defensa de Seguro Social (FRENADESSO; National Front for the Defense of Social Security) coordinating committee. FRENADESSO has now converted into an oppositional political party—the Frente Amplio por la Democracia (FAD; Broad Front for Democracy). Another major national mobilization took place in July 2010 over a new labor flexibilization law that eroded collective labor contracts for unionized workers. Mobilizations of labor on banana plantations in the Boca de Toros region and urban workers resulted in several injuries and deaths of rural indigenous unionists by state police and security forces suppressing the revolt. The antiprivatization struggles continued in Panama in the 2010s with a major uprising in the *corregimientos* of Colón Province after the neoliberal administration of Ricardo Martinelli gained passage of a law allowing the sell-off of public lands in the Panama Canal Zone in October 2012. The popular uprising garnered participation from labor unions, students, and indigenous groups around the country and forced the national parliament to overturn the privatization legislation.

Comparing the Two Protest Waves

Figure 7.2 shows that antineoliberal protest intensified markedly in the second protest wave during the late 1990s and early 2000s. The first wave is analyzed over a sixteen-year period, and the second wave includes only nine years of data analysis, from 1996 to 2004. During the early period of globalization and first-generation structural adjustment measures from 1980 to 1995, there were a reported thirty-one antiausterity protests in the region, each of over ten thousand participants. The more democratic countries in the late 1980s and early 1990s (Costa Rica, Honduras, and Nicaragua) tended to have slightly more massive antineoliberal protests in the first wave than the countries directly or nominally controlled by their respective militaries (El Salvador, Guatemala, and Panama). In the second wave of antiglobalization protest in the late 1990s and early 2000s, fifty-two major antineoliberal events with more than ten thousand people occurred. As documented above, at least another dozen major demonstrations against privatization, free trade, and labor flexibilization have taken place between 2005 and 2012 in the region. The combination of intensified globalization (as shown by market liberalization and the selling off of public infrastructure to transnational firms) and expanded democratization appears to be associated with the current upswing in mass mobilization in Central America.

Activists in the largest campaigns pieced together coalitions of NGOs, new social movements, students, public and urban labor unions, and oppositional political parties. Indigenous rural workers and peasants participated in major mobilizations in Guatemala, Honduras, and Panama. Many of these groups are beneficiaries of the democratization process because liberalizing states grant NGOs legal status (*personería jurídica*) to operate in their territorial boundaries. Legally sanctioned oppositional political parties also have motivations to mobilize constituents on the streets over unpopular economic policies to remain competitive in future electoral rounds. NGOs and new social movements coordinated critical activities in the campaigns against free trade in Guatemala, El Salvador, and Nicaragua. In the early 2000s, left-of-center political parties (even small ones that receive less than 10 percent of the national vote), boosted mass mobilizations against economic liberalization in Costa Rica, El Salvador, Guatemala, Honduras, and Nicaragua (Almeida 2012, 2014).

Although scholars characterize Central America as a homogeneous world region in terms of similar political and cultural histories (Goodwin 2001), important differences exist among countries in terms of the social groups and sectors recruited and mobilized in recent campaigns against economic liberalization. These differences are largely explained by the social and economic composition of each nation.

In Guatemala, with a near majority Mayan population, in crucial antineoliberal campaigns urban groups of public sector workers and students reached out and formed coalitions with the rural indigenous population (such as in the anti-CAFTA mobilizations). El Salvador and Nicaragua experienced large-scale revolutionary mobilization in the past with mass support and party recruitment. The revolutionary political parties surviving into the neoliberal era (i.e., the FMLN and Frente Sandinista de Liberación Nacional [FSLN; Sandinista National Liberation Front]) have used their organizational structures and membership lists to mobilize civil society against unwanted economic reforms in a more forceful fashion than other nations in the region. In Panama, the construction workers' labor union (SUNTRACS) has been prominent in the social movement sector for two decades and continues to thrive, now with over fifty thousand members in Panama's unparalleled construction of towers and skyscrapers. In the remainder of Central America, private sector unionization continues on an accelerated decline.

In short, the social sectors recruited and mobilized for antiglobalization campaigns vary by the unique cultural, political, and economic history of each country. Democratization processes facilitate the organizational formation and revitalization among particular social groupings on the basis of these distinctive national histories. Democratic practices of universal suffrage, freedom of association, and freedom of public assembly also lead to more reformist strategies of collective action (Marks, Mbaye, and Kim 2009). In countries with long-term democratic practices, such as Costa Rica, associations and civic organizations already in place (e.g., student federations, public sector labor associations, and community councils), often find themselves at the forefront of battles over free market measures. Hence, even though the entire region has witnessed massive campaigns against neoliberal reforms organized by NGOs, labor unions, new social movements, and oppositional political parties with a variety of outcomes, significant differences remain among the countries in terms of the specific social sectors and groups mobilized.

Conclusion: Democratization and Social Movement Revitalization

Two major phases of economic globalization have passed through Central America, one in the 1980s and early 1990s and the second in the late 1990s and early 2000s. The first phase of structural adjustment occurred during a period of violent conflict in the region with largely nondemocratic governments or regimes just beginning to transition to democracy (with the exception of Costa Rica). The individual protest campaigns in the 1980s and early 1990s were not as sustained as the individual campaigns in the 2000s and occurred with less frequency, leading some scholars to view the region's social opposition as disengaged or pacified by the early 1990s (Dunkerley 1994). Many of the largest second-wave austerity protests (after 1996) involved privatization and free trade agreements in the context of democratization. Civil society groups had more freedom to organize and more experience with neoliberal reforms when launching sustained campaigns of resistance. In most campaigns in the second wave, the coalition coordinating the actions evolved from the unification of already-existing civic associations, NGOs, and new social movement organizations.

In terms of magnitude, in nearly every country on the isthmus, the size of the demonstrations in the wave of opposition to economic liberalization in the late 1990s and 2000s was the largest or close to the largest in the respective nations' histories, at times mobilizing 3 to 4 percent of the entire population in a single rally (e.g., the anti-CAFTA demonstrations in Costa Rica, the pension system reform protests in Panama, and the campaigns against health care privatization in El Salvador). The evidence suggests that democratization does not simply institutionalize earlier social struggles but provides an organizational basis in civil society to launch even larger campaigns of collective opposition when faced with new economic threats and the shrinking of an already-feeble welfare state. Even though a majority of the campaigns did not achieve their main goal of turning back the neoliberal reform measures, they tended to be more successful and effective than mobilizations in the 1980s and early 1990s over similar economic issues. The magnitude and relative success of more recent mobilizations indicate a revitalization of the social movement sector in Central America.

NOTES

Acknowledgments: Early versions of this chapter were presented to audiences at the International Workshop on Social Movements in Transition, Federal University of Minas Gerais, Belo Horizonte, Brazil, November 2008; the XII Central American Sociology conference in San José, Costa Rica, August 2010; and the II National Meeting of the Honduran Sociological Association, San Pedro Sula, Honduras, May 2011. The U.S. Fulbright Program provided funding for field research for the project ("Civil Society, Globalization and Democratization in Central America," Award #8566, Council for the International Exchange of Scholars).

1. Contested local elections in Nicaragua in 2008, the difficulty of registering oppositional parties in Panama in 2009, and the military coup in Honduras in 2009 may be signs of the end of this democratic transition in Central America.

2. Smaller strikes against austerity measures and privatization were held by power and electricity workers, public universities, teachers, and National Insurance employees between 1998 and 1994.

3. In Spanish, CAFTA is referred to as the Tratado de Libre Comercio (TLC).

REFERENCES

Almeida, Paul D. 2007. "Defensive Mobilization: Popular Movements against Economic Adjustment in Latin America." *Latin American Perspectives* 34 (3): 123–139.

———. 2008a. "The Sequencing of Success: Organizing Templates and Neoliberal Policy Outcomes." *Mobilization* 13 (2): 165–187.

———. 2008b. *Waves of Protest: Popular Struggle in El Salvador, 1925–2005.* Minneapolis: University of Minnesota Press.

——. 2010a. "Globalization and Collective Action." In *Handbook of Politics: State and Society in Global Perspective*, edited by Kevin Leicht and J. Craig Jenkins, 305–326. New York: Springer.

——. 2010b. "Social Movement Partyism: Collective Action and Political Parties." In *Strategic Alliances: New Studies of Social Movement Coalitions*, edited by N. Van Dyke and H. McCammon, 170–196. Minneapolis: University of Minnesota Press.

——. 2012. "Subnational Opposition to Globalization." *Social Forces* 90 (4): 1051–1072.

——. 2014. *Mobilizing Democracy: Globalization and Citizen Protest*. Baltimore: Johns Hopkins University Press.

Almeida, Paul D., and Erica Walker. 2007. "El avance de la globalización neoliberal: Una comparación de tres campañas de movimientos populares en Centroamérica" [The Pace of Neoliberal Globalization: A Comparison of Three Campaigns in Central America]. *Revista Centroamericana de Ciencias Sociales* [Journal of Central American Social Sciences] 4 (1): 51–76.

Almeida, Paul D., and Hank Johnston. 2006. "Neoliberal Globalization and Popular Movements in Latin America." In *Latin American Social Movements: Globalization, Democratization, and Transnational Networks*, edited by H. Johnston and P. Almeida, 3–18. Lanham, MD: Rowman and Littlefield.

Alvarenga Venutolo, Patricia. 2005. *De vecinos a ciudadanos: Movimientos comunales y luchas cívicas en la historia contemporánea de Costa Rica* [From Neighbors to Citizens: Communal Movements and Civic Struggles in the Modern History of Costa Rica]. San José: Editorial de la Universidad de Costa Rica.

Arce, Moises, and Paul T. Bellinger Jr. 2007. "Low-Intensity Democracy Revisited: The Effects of Economic Liberalization on Political Activity in Latin America." *World Politics* 60:97–121.

Armstrong, Elizabeth A., and Mary Bernstein. 2008. "Culture, Power, and Institutions: A Multi-institutional Politics Approach to Social Movements." *Sociological Theory* 26:74–99.

Artiga-González, Álvaro. 2004. *Elitismo competitivo: Dos décadas de elecciones en El Salvador (1982–2003)* [Competitive Elitism: Two Decades of Elections in El Salvador (1982–2003)]. San Salvador: UCA Editores.

Assies, Willem, and Ton Salman. 2003. *Crisis in Bolivia: The Elections and Their Aftermath*. London: Institute of Latin American Studies.

Beluche, Olmedo. 1994. *Diez años de luchas políticas y sociales en Panamá (1980–1990)* [Ten Years of Political and Social Struggles in Panama (1980–1990)]. Panama City: Centro de Estudios Latinoamericanos.

Bradshaw, York W., and Mark J. Schafer. 2000. "Urbanization and Development: The Emergence of International Non-government Organizations amid Declining States." *Sociological Perspectives* 43:97–116.

Brett, Roddy. 2008. *Social Movements, Indigenous Politics and Democratization in Guatemala, 1985–1996*. Leiden: Brill.

Chong, Alberto, and Florencio López de Silanes. 2005. "The Truth about Privatization in Latin America." In *Privatization in Latin America: Myths and Realities*, edited by A. Chong and F. López de Salinas, 1–65. Stanford, CA: Stanford University Press.

Crook, Stephen, Jan Pakulski, and Malcolm Waters. 1992. *Postmodernization: Change in Advanced Society*. London: Sage.

Diamond, Larry. 1999. *Developing Democracy: Toward Consolidation*. Baltimore: Johns Hopkins University Press.

Dunkerley, James. 1994. *The Pacification of Central America: Political Change in the Isthmus, 1987–1993.* London: Verso.

Edelman, Marc. 1999. *Peasants against Globalization.* Stanford, CA: Stanford University Press.

Edwards, Sebastian. 1995. *Crisis and Reform in Latin America: From Despair to Hope.* New York: World Bank.

Foweraker, Joe, and Todd Landman. 1997. *Citizenship Rights and Social Movements: A Comparative and Statistical Analysis.* Oxford: Oxford University Press.

Goodwin, Jeff. 2001. *No Other Way Out: States and Revolutionary Movements, 1945–1991.* Cambridge: Cambridge University Press.

Green, Duncan. 2003. *Silent Revolution: The Rise and Crisis of Market Economics in Latin America.* London: Latin American Bureau.

Haglund, La Dawn. 2010. *Limiting Resources: Market-Led Reform and the Transformation of Public Goods.* State College: Pennsylvania State University Press.

Hipsher, Patricia. 1996. "Democratization and the Decline of Urban Social Movements in Chile and Spain." *Comparative Politics* 28 (3): 273–297.

Horton, Lynn. 1998. *Peasants in Arms: War and Peace in the Mountains of Nicaragua, 1979–1994.* Athens: Ohio University Press.

Huntington, Samuel P. 1991. *The Third Wave: Democratization in the Late Twentieth Century.* Norman: University of Oklahoma Press.

Jenkins, J. Craig, and Bert Klandermans. 1995. "The Politics of Social Protest." In *The Politics of Social Protest: Comparative Perspectives on States and Social Movements,* edited by J. Craig Jenkins and Bert Klandermans, 3–13. Minneapolis: University of Minnesota Press.

Johnston, Hank, Enrique Laraña, and Joseph Gusfield. 1994. "Identities, Grievances, and New Social Movements." In *New Social Movements: From Ideology to Identity,* edited by E. Laraña, H. Johnston, and J. Gusfield, 3–35. Philadelphia: Temple University Press.

Kaufman, Robert, and Joan Nelson. 2004. Introduction to *Crucial Needs, Weak Incentives: Social Sector Reform, Democratization, and Globalization in Latin America,* edited by R. Kaufman and J. Nelson, 1–19. Baltimore: Johns Hopkins University Press.

Keck, Margaret. 1992. *The Workers: Party and Democratization in Brazil.* New Haven, CT: Yale University Press.

Klandermans, Bert. 1997. *The Social Psychology of Protest.* Oxford: Blackwell.

Markoff, John. 1996. *Waves of Democracy: Social Movements and Political Change.* Thousand Oaks, CA: Pine Forge Press.

Marks, Gary, Heather Mbaye, and Hyung-min Kim. 2009. "Radicalism or Reformism? Socialist Parties before World War I." *American Sociological Review* 74:615–635.

Palazio Galo, Edgard. n.d. "Movimiento estudiantil y la autonomía universitaria . . . una historia hecha con la participación de todos" [The Student Movement and University Autonomy . . . a History Made with the Participation of All]. Unpublished manuscript. Managua, Nicaragua.

Posas, Mario. 2003. *Situación actual y desafíos del movimiento popular hondureño* [Current Context and Challenges of the Honduran Popular Movement]. Tegucigalpa, Honduras: Fundación Friedrich Ebert.

Robinson, William. 2003. *Transnational Conflicts: Central America, Social Change, and Globalization.* London: Verso.

———. 2008. *Latin America and Global Capitalism: A Critical Globalization Perspective.* Baltimore: Johns Hopkins University Press.

Rovira Mas, Jorge. 1987. *Costa Rica en los años '80* [Costa Rica in the 1980s]. San José, Costa Rica: Editorial Porvenir.

Salom, Roberto. 1987. *La Crisis de la Izquierda en Costa Rica* [The Crisis of the Left in Costa Rica]. San José, Costa Rica: Editorial Porvenir.

Schock, Kurt. 2005. *Unarmed Insurrections: People Power Movements in Nondemocracies.* Minneapolis: University of Minnesota Press.

Sojo, Carlos. 1999. *Democracias con fracturas: Gobernabilidad, reforma ccon6mica y transici6n en Centroamérica* [Democracies with Fractures: Governability, Economic Reform and Transition in Central America]. San José, Costa Rica: Facultad Latinoamericana de Ciencias Sociales.

Sosa, Eugenio. 2010. *La protesta social en Honduras: Del ajuste al golpe de estado* [Social Protest in Honduras: From Structural Adjustment to the Coup]. Tegucigalpa, Honduras: Editorial Guaymuras.

Tilly, Charles. 2004. *Social Movements, 1768–2004.* Boulder, CO: Paradigm.

Van Cott, Donna Lee. 2005. *From Movements to Parties in Latin America: The Evolution of Ethnic Politics.* Cambridge: Cambridge University Press.

Véliz, Rodrigo. 2009. *Capital y luchas: Breve análisis de la protesta y el conflicto social actual* [Capital and Struggles: A Brief Analysis of Protest and Social Conflict]. Cuaderno de Debate 10. Guatemala City, Guatemala: Facultad Latinoamericana de Ciencias Sociales.

Walton, John. 1987. "Urban Protest and the Global Political Economy: The IMF Riots." In *The Capitalist City: Global Restructuring and Community Politics*, edited by M. P. Smith and J. Feagin, 364–386. Oxford: Basil Blackwell.

Walton, John, and Charles Ragin. 1990. "Global and National Sources of Political Protest: Third World Responses to the Debt Crisis." *American Sociological Review* 55 (6): 876–890.

Walton, John, and David Seddon. 1994. "Food Riots Past and Present." In *Free Markets and Food Riots: The Politics of Global Adjustment*, edited by J. Walton and D. Seddon, 23–54. Oxford: Blackwell.

Wood, Elisabeth Jean. 2005. "Challenges to Political Democracy in El Salvador." In *The Third Wave of Democratization in Latin America: Advances and Setbacks*, edited by F. Haopian and S. Mainwaring, 179–201. Cambridge: Cambridge University Press.

Yashar, Deborah. 2005. *Contesting Citizenship in Latin America: The Rise of Indigenous Movements and the Postliberal Challenge.* Cambridge: Cambridge University Press.

8

Strategies and Mobilization Cycles of the Human Rights Movement in the Democratic Transition in Argentina

SEBASTIÁN PEREYRA

This chapter analyzes the development of the human rights movement in Argentina throughout the transition to democracy. I argue that the transition process entailed a political institutionalization of the movement. I consider institutionalization in two specific ways: (1) as recognition of the movement as a political player in national politics and (2) as the diffusion and consolidation of the movement's most important frames or discourses within society.

An important human rights movement emerged in Argentina during the last dictatorship (1976–1983). All social movements, but this one in Argentina in particular, are heterogeneous networks of activists and organizations linked by one goal, a specific set of frames and a shared sense of solidarity.

In 1983, during the final year of the military dictatorship, new conflicts appeared within the movement. Different political conceptions emerged on how to face the transition to democracy. In the following two decades, the human rights movement played an important role in the national political debate in very different areas. Whereas the first constitutional government (1983–1989) actively promoted human rights and encouraged debates on the crimes of the dictatorship, in the 1990s the debate shifted because of a new discourse of peace and forgiveness and declined, not recovering its public presence or attaining important goals until the end of the decade. Finally, the economic and political crisis in 2001 gave the organizations and the discourse on human rights visibility, allowing a true institutionalization of the movement in the democratic regime.

One might expect that the transition to democracy in Argentina would lead to demobilization of the human rights movement, whose main purpose was fighting against the dictatorship and for a subsequent shift to the rule of law. But in this chapter I show that the actions embraced by the movement following the end of the dictatorial regime varied greatly, in part because the new political context tended to overemphasize the ideological gap between movement organizations. As I show, transition to democracy did not put an end to human rights violations. On one hand, the legacy of the dictatorial regime continued to be a matter of debate and conflict; on the other hand, new violations of human rights arose during this time of democracy.

Previous studies have focused on the origins of the human rights movement in Argentina, outlined the demands it made of the dictatorship, and examined its ability to establish both its ideological grounds and main arguments in support of the new democratic administration (see, e.g., Jelin 1985; Bruno, Cavarozzi, and Palermo 1985; Calderón and Jelin 1987; Calderón 1986; Calderón, Piscitelli, and Reyna 1992; Jelin 2005). I explore the human rights movement during the first decades of the return to democracy, proposing two different approaches to account for the movement's dynamics after 1983. First, I identify the main cycles and the activities of mobilization and the development of several public courses of action so as to reconstruct the main strategies and history of the organizations comprising the human rights movement to understand their response to the new democratic administrations. Then I examine how the human rights frame was used in other mobilization processes, such as by relatives of victims of police brutality. I then examine the characteristics of this kind of protest, looking at it as another dimension of the institutionalization of the human rights movement.

From the Origins of the Human Rights Movement to Democratic Transition

The clandestine political repression unleashed during the last military dictatorship (1976–1983) was the starting point of the organization of the human rights movement in Argentina. As arrests, kidnappings, and assassinations increased, victims' relatives demanded to know their loved ones' fate.

A significant number of human rights organizations were established before the coup d'état took place (Table 8.1). However, most of the *organismos históricos* (original organizations) came into being between 1976 and 1979; others began in the first years of the transition to democracy. A final group was created during the 1990s.

In the mid-1970s, before the military dictatorship came to power, some of these organizations started addressing political violence, assuming a posture deeply rooted in human rights, particularly when rightist armed groups such as the Alianza Anticomunista Argentina (AAA; Anticommunist Argentine Alliance) began to gain ground. With the military dictatorship's amplification and systematization of repression came the emergence of new organizations made up of the relatives of victims, or "the affected" (Jelin 2005: 159).

TABLE 8.1   HUMAN RIGHTS ORGANIZATIONS IN ARGENTINA

Social movement organization	Year founded
Argentine Human Rights League Foundation (Liga Argentina por los Derechos del Hombre; LADH)	1937
Latin American Peace and Justice Service (Servicio de Paz y Justicia; SERPAJ)	1974
Permanent Assembly for Human Rights (Asamblea Permanente por los Derechos Humanos; APDH)	1975
Ecumenical Movement for Human Rights (Movimiento Ecuménico por los Derechos Humanos; MEDH)	1976
Commission of Family Members of the Disappeared and Political Prisoners (Comisión de Familiares de Desaparecidos y Presos por Razones Políticas; CFDPRP)	1976
Mothers of the Plaza de Mayo (Madres de Plaza de Mayo; MPM)	1977
Grandmothers of the Plaza de Mayo (Abuelas de Plaza de Mayo; APM)	1977
Center of Legal and Social Studies (Centro de Estudios Legales y Sociales; CELS)	1979
Association of Disappeared Ex-prisoners (Asociación de Ex-Detenidos Desaparecidos; ADD)	1984
Argentine Forensic Anthropology Team (Equipo Argentino de Antropología Forense; EAAF)	1984
Amnesty International Argentina (Amnistía Internacional Argentina; AIA)	1985
Committee against Police and Institutional Repression (Coordinadora contra la Represión Policial e Institucional; CORREPI)	1991
Sons and Daughters for Identity and Justice against Forgetfulness and Silence (Hijos e Hijas por la Identidad y la Justicia contra el Olvido y el Silencio; HIJOS)	1995
Open Memory (Memoria Abierta; MA)	1999

The main demand of the incipient movement for human rights was "truth and justice." The organizations protested against the military regime. Public demonstrations and reports of human rights violations presented before both national and international forums conveyed one overarching purpose: a request for a democratic administration in the country. A report by the Inter-American Commission on Human Rights (IACHR) published in April 1980 and the awarding of the Nobel Peace Prize to Adolfo Pérez Esquivel, leader of Servicio de Paz y Justicia (SERPAJ; Latin American Peace and Justice Service), had a profound impact worldwide and provoked major tensions nationwide (Keck and Sikkink 1998; Novaro and Palermo 2003: chap. 4; Lorenz 2011: 209).

Bringing back democracy and reestablishing constitutional rights became mainstream views and eventually undermined the legitimacy of the dictatorial system, which began losing its hold of the country following defeat in the Falkland War (1982).

From its very beginning, the organizations making up the human rights movement displayed a distinctive heterogeneity in the diverse political views of their members and whether they were directly affected by repression. This heterogeneity led to tensions, mainly related to the intensity and types of confrontation with the state each group desired, and would be the primary source of divisions and rifts in the years to come.

> In general the "non-affected" organizations sought to take advantage of the loopholes left by the political and judicial apparatus of the dictatorship, while [affected] groups such as Mothers [of the Plaza de Mayo; Madres de Plaza de Mayo] wanted to make their claim visible by all possible means, including confrontation in public, particularly in the Plaza de Mayo, and establishing symbols such as the white scarves [they wore]. (Lorenz 2011: 207)[1]

The organizations based on family ties to victims of repression became a prominent part of the movement. The relatives of the disappeared—especially the mothers and grandmothers—exhaustively sought answers from many state agencies and interacted frequently among themselves. The mobilization process began when they failed to find information through institutional channels. Activist networks developed from there, resulting in organizations and protests that became one of the symbols of resistance to the dictatorship (Navarro 2001: 291–292). Other players (like political parties and trade unions) gradually began to support the movement, adopting their methods of opposing the dictatorship but avoiding direct negotiations with it (Stepan 1986).

Human rights was the central issue of a protest based on an ethical-humanitarian demand, which itself aimed at democratization of the country and set the minimum standards for a transition to democracy (Sonoréguer 1985; Leis 1989; García Delgado and Palermo 1989).

> This fight [for human rights] intensified after the Falkland War and was certainly the most important among those arising during the transition. . . . At the same time, it also created tensions and alliances that would last for a long time in society, among interest groups, and among political parties. (Novaro and Palermo 2003: 495)

M. Novaro and V. Palermo (2003) analyze the gradual changes in points of view that led the Catholic Church, political parties, members of the judiciary system, the media, and others to denounce the violation of human rights, whereas previously they had just offered their support to the antiguerrilla struggle. By the time the regime published "Final Document on the War against Subversion and Terrorism" (Documento final sobre la guerra contra la subversión y el terrorismo) in April 1983 and passed the Pacification Law (Ley de pacificación; in effect, granting self-amnesty for its crimes) the same year, most of these players and public opinion believed that negotiations that granted amnesty were not viable, and the armed forces was unable to impose its will on the negotiation process. The political forces and leaders who forcefully rejected all negotiation with a regime on its way out had gained the upper hand (Aboy Carlés 2010: 78).

Mobilization Cycles of the Human Rights Movement during the Transition

I divide mobilization of the human rights movement during the democratic transition into three periods, or cycles, distinguished by the response of the main human rights organizations to the changing institutional contexts: (1) the first years of the transition and the establishment of a democratic human rights agenda (1983–1989), (2) abeyance and latency signaled by pardons and retreat in human rights policies (1989–2001), and (3) institutionalization of mobilization during the democratic consolidation after the 2001 crisis.

The Democratic Human Rights Agenda

The party that would win the first presidential election following the regime's ouster, maintained the same stance on human rights that it had had during the dictatorship. The newly elected president, Raúl Alfonsín (1983–1989), had participated in the human rights movement during military rule. He was also a leader in the political party that had offered support to the human rights organizations.

The human rights policy of the Alfonsín administration was based on a human rights agenda that was a source of both governmental legitimacy and citizen commitment to the new democratic system. Laws and concrete measures that reveal the importance given to human rights by the new government include the decrees 157/83 and 158/83, ordering the prosecution of members of the guerrilla organizations and the first three military juntas; law 23,040, repealing the self-amnesty law promulgated by the military dictatorship; law 23,049, reforming the Code of Military Justice; law 23,070, reducing ordinary prison sentences of political prisoners because of poor prison conditions; law 23,077, instituting stiffer penalties for attacks on constitutional and democratic order; law 23,097, toughening penalties for torture; decree 187 of December 15, 1983, creating the Comisión Nacional sobre la Desaparición de Personas (CONADEP; National Commission on Disappeared People); signing and ratifying international conventions on human rights, such as the Pact of San

José de Costa Rica and the Law for Defense of Democracy (1984); and creating in 1984 the position of undersecretary for human rights (Subsecretaría de Derechos Humanos).

However, these laws and decrees did not end discussion, becoming, in fact, the subject of lengthy discussion by human rights organizations, particularly the following:

- CONADEP's creation obviated a bicameral parliamentary commission of inquiry (Landi 1985: 28–29).
- The competence of civil courts to try the military was questioned during debates on amending the Code of Military Justice (Bruno, Cavarozzi, and Palermo 1985; Landi 1985: 29–31; Acuña and Smulovitz 1995).
- The removal of judges who had served during the dictatorship was demanded by the movement in 1984 (Brysk 1994: chap. 7).
- Some wanted to try only military leaders and others wanted to prosecute all those involved in the repression.

Government policy was generally well received by the human rights movement because it allowed prosecuting military leaders (Juntas Militares) through unprecedented legal proceedings. During the proceedings the movement maintained persistent mobilization and presence on the streets (Lorenz 2011: 210). In 1985, with the support of all the movement's organizations, those in the dictatorship and responsible for state terrorism were brought before a civil tribunal in the Juicio a la Juntas (Trial of the Dictatorship) and sentenced to prison. However, these sentences, as well as future judicial treatment of crimes committed by the dictatorship, were later subject to debate.

The government successfully developed a new narrative of the dictatorship in which the hypothesis of the internal war argument was dismissed and the military's fundamental and systematic violation of human rights was highlighted. Release of the CONADEP report concerning the human rights violations influenced public opinion and thus the debate that followed in educational, social, and political institutions and in the mass media.

In these early years of transition, a discussion began among the *organismos históricos* about unfulfilled promises of the new democratic government. These discussions divided human rights activists within almost all organizations and focused on three main aspects (Cavarozzi 1985):

1. Economic policy: Major economic reforms were expected during the first years of the democratic transition in order to reverse the neoliberal economic program of the dictatorship and its consequences of inequality.
2. The Alfonsín administration's human rights policy: Organizations that had criticized the administration for not trying all the people

involved in the crimes of the dictatorship gained adherents after the government decided not to prosecute members of the military following the Juicio a la Juntas in 1985.

3. Revolutionary groups of the 1970s: Human rights organizations had to decide whether to condemn the violent actions of revolutionary armed groups.

The Madres de Plaza de Mayo disagreed internally on how to oppose the Alfonsín government and split in 1986. The breakaway group, led by Hebe de Bonafini and similar to left-wing parties, focused on economic policy and pushed the political discussion toward justice, social inequality, and the government's unfulfilled promises (González Bombal and Sonderéguer 1987). The group took a tougher stance on specific human rights demands and economic reforms, especially opposing government downsizing and cuts in public spending. During the two-term administration of Carlos Menem (1989–1999) that followed, the group portrayed as equivalent the disappeared from the time of the dictatorship and the system's new disappeared—unemployed workers, street children, pensioners, and those whose plight was ignored (see, e.g., "Marcha" 1993)—highlighting the disastrous consequences of the wave of neoliberal policies: "impunity [of the military], unemployment, hunger, the freedom of those responsible for genocide and corrupt unions" ("Otra marcha" 1996: 5).

These debates during the years of democratic transition led many to believe the end of the democratic process was near. With the 1987 passage of the Obediencia Debida (Due Obedience) and Punto Final (Full Stop) laws and the granting of pardons (October 1989 and December 1990) to the military condemned in 1985, the historical relationship between human rights and the democratic process in Argentina had begun to fracture, and organizations showed greater ideological-political diversification.

The shift of the human rights discourse toward left-wing positions led to a view of the prevailing economic model as the archenemy. This radicalization emerged from the position some left-wing parties and trade union sectors took in the second half of the 1980s linking the recession and economic crisis to the continuation of the dictatorship's economic policies. Since 1987 the economic situation of the country had deteriorated as the Alfonsín government's economic stabilization plans failed. These failures, aggravated by external debt contracted by the military government, led to hyperinflation in 1989–1990. Hyperinflation was ending as the Menem presidency began, giving that government a boost. This first mobilization cycle ends with a progressive decline in the human rights policies set in place by the Alfonsín government. The human rights movement slowly renewed demands in a new context.

Abeyance and Retreat of Human Rights Policies

In April 1986, the Alfonsín government itself questioned the massive numbers of the military prosecuted for their involvement in the repression. By the end of that year, Congress enacted the Full Stop law, which set a deadline for cases. Even after its enactment civil-military tensions significantly increased, eventually leading to the first of the military uprisings against the democratic administration. In all, Argentina's democratic transition faced four major military uprisings: (1) the Semana Santa Rebellion (Easter Rebellion; April 14–19, 1987), (2) the uprising of Monte Caseros (January 14–18, 1988), (3) the uprisings of Campo de Mayo and Villa Martelli (November 30–December 2, 1988), and (4) the revolt of several military units, including army headquarters and the Argentine Naval Prefecture[2] (December 3, 1990).

These uprisings overlapped discussion on human rights related to restructuring of the military. From 1987 onward, the importance of human rights organizations, political parties, and the judiciary—until then key players—lessened in the discussions and policy formulation, and the Military Staff (Estado Mayor del Ejército), the executive branch, and the military rebel groups acquired a central role (Acuña and Smulovitz 1995).

The Full Stop and Due Obedience laws and the two presidential pardons entangled the human rights issue with a discourse of peace and forgiveness and redefinition of civil-military rules that had been brought in by the Menem government. "The severity of the punishment of the officers who participated in the last rebellion [of several military units in December 1990] showed the new [Menem] government's attempt to redefine the rules of its relationship with the military: crimes committed in the past would be forgiven, but present or future disobedience would be severely punished" (Acuña and Smulovitz 1995: 150–151). The human rights issue gradually became the military issue, and the priority that condemnation of dictatorship crimes had had was removed. This change had to do with concern for the continuation of democracy and stabilization of the economy, both serious problems in the late 1980s.

Visibility of human rights organizations and their ability to mobilize decreased in the early 1990s. Large demonstrations against the *indultos* (pardons) between September 1989 and December 1990 failed to stop them. The demobilization effect of the pardons was significant, and the pacification policy of the Menem government left little room for discussing the crimes of the dictatorship. Financial compensation for victims of the dictatorship, determined individually and promoted by the Menem government as a retributive measure, was a major controversy of the time. The pardons, with their closing of the judicial route, gave impulse to other issues within the movement, less visible but equally important. For this reason, the second cycle was a period of latency: the organizations continued their work but the public debate on human rights receded. The organizations transformed themselves by incorporating demands of generations new to the movement, extending the language of human rights to include new problems related to human rights, and responding to new international pressures regarding human rights (Jelin 2005).

For example, the Abuelas de Plaza de Mayo (Grandmothers of the Plaza de Mayo) was an organization formed to identify and recover children of the disappeared born in captivity and illegally adopted by members of the military.

The Grandmothers performed their task mostly outside the public eye, in contrast to the attention that human rights demonstrations had received at various times. Thus, although public attention to human rights was on the wane, the organization did important work and advanced its cause. Its work was aided by the National Committee for the Right to Identity (Comisión Nacional por el Derecho a la Identidad) and the Genetic Data Bank (Banco de Datos Genéticos), both created in 1992. As of 2009, the Grandmothers had identified about a hundred of the four hundred children whose identities had been erased and hidden.

Another example illustrates how the language of human rights was extended. Participation by provincial and federal police in kidnapping, torture, and murder had already been determined in the years of the dictatorship. A human rights organization, the Center for Legal and Social Studies (CELS), had studied the repressive apparatus of the dictatorship and the continued involvement by security forces. In the early 1990s, the center reoriented its focus to the method of operation of a police force in a democracy. The center's and others' interest in police violence led to the creation of organizations such as the Coordinadora contra la Represión Policial e Institucional (CORREPI; Coordinator against Police and Institutional Repression).

CELS was an exemplar of this extension of the human rights agenda to include new issues. Public interest on a local level and sources of funding on an international level had wearied of the crimes of the dictatorship, but CELS renewed their interest with issues like police brutality, detention conditions in prisons and in mental health institutions, and, later, economic and social rights, governmental accountability, provision of public services, immigration policies, anticrime policies, and social protest repression policies.

Meanwhile, CORREPI has been more tied to mobilization and political issues than has CELS, which developed a more legal-oriented style of intervention against police brutality. From the mid-1990s, the two organizations further differentiated, with CORREPI consolidating its militant profile and CELS developing a more professional working style.

The military pardons marked a shift toward a reconstruction of the collective memory and condemnation of state terrorism. Some human rights organizations turned to artistic expression of grievances, a deeply rooted method in the struggle for human rights, when faced with no judicial route for condemning the dictatorship's repression. During the first years of democracy, a fierce dispute raged over how to characterize state terrorism. One side invoked the so-called theory of the two demons (*teoría de los dos demonios*), which accompanied the prosecution of those involved in crimes.[3] The pardons were backed by a peace discourse that was based on similar arguments. In 1995, the Hijos e Hijas por la Identidad y la Justicia contra el Olvido y el Silencio (HIJOS; Sons and Daughters for Identity and Justice against Forgetfulness and Silence) was formed to continue and not abandon investigation of human rights violations of the dictatorship.

From the beginning, the organization combated impunity of the dictatorship for its crimes and developed a disruptive mobilization represented by *el escrache*. *Escrachar*—according to the documents of the organization—means to expose the identity and crimes of a person who wants to remain anonymous, such as those whose names had not come to light during the trials and who had continued their normal lives. Besides a judicial sentence for criminals, the mobilization's purpose was to break through indifference and reconstruct a collective memory of the dictatorship.

International pressure in the second half of the 1990s resulted in new trials and making human rights again a subject of public debate, but somehow, the new trials and discussion were still limited by the effect of the pardons (Sikkink 2008). The confession of Alfredo Scilingo, a repentant marine who exposed the methodology used by the armed forces (fuerzas armadas) to kill the detained-disappeared, helped bring human rights back into view. This confession and other causes aroused the interest of judges in Europe who considered these cases to be crimes against humanity and, therefore, revised the statute of limitations to the criminal proceedings. As crimes against humanity, the cases could be judged by judges of any country. International trials of members of the dictatorship motivated local judges to move forward on pending lawsuits.

In 1997 new cases were opened for child abduction (a crime not covered by the Due Obedience and Full Stop laws and the pardons), and several officers were arrested. Also, truth trials (*juicios de la verdad*), started by human rights organizations in 1998, focused on state responsibility for determining the whereabouts of the disappeared.

Institutionalization and the Democratic Consolidation

The retraction in public debate on human rights ends at the beginning of the new century. The 2001 crisis[4] was a time of revival of militant activity, and this activity triggered, among other things, a revaluation of the tradition of struggle for human rights. The crisis marked the end of the transition to democracy in the sense that the institutional crisis was resolved by the democratic regime. Human rights organizations denounced and condemned the political repression of the most violent moments of the crisis, and their previous political activity, social mobilization, and protest now received further appreciation (Schuster et al. 2002). Some organizations took part in forums in which political representation was debated.

With the arrival of Néstor Kirchner's government (2003–2007), the human rights movement was strengthened. Kirchner's government had a shaky electoral legitimacy: he came in second with less than 23 percent of the vote and won by default after the candidate with the most votes withdrew from second-round voting after seeing voter projections. Kirchner thus recruited support to strengthen his government, including from the human rights movement, which showed the government's strong orientation toward revitalization of and intervention in support for human rights (Lorenz 2011: 218–219). In 2003 Congress repealed the Due Obedience and Full Stop laws (law 25,779), resulting in the gradual reopening of many cases. With remorseful soldiers and a notable change in the government's attitude in the matter, several cases that had been interrupted in the 1980s were reopened. In 2001, a court declared Due Obedience and Full Stop laws unconstitutional, a decision ratified by the Supreme Court in 2005.

Much of the work by human rights organizations in recent years has to do with the recovery of collective memory, such as finding where clandestine detention centers had operated and turning them into memorials. An example is the Escuela de Suboficiales de Mecánica de la Armada (ESMA; Naval Petty Officers School of Mechanics). In 2004, the government closed the school—one of the icons of state terrorism—and dedicated it as a memorial. To this end, a commission made up of national and City of Buenos Aires governmental representatives was created to oversee the property's transformation. This project triggered discussions on the question of memory. Something similar happened with another project to create a public space of commemoration, Paseo de la Memoria (Memory Walk). New human rights organizations emerged out of these debates on memory, as they had from those on social condemnation of repression. Such was the case of Memoria Abierta (Open Memory), a foundation created in 1999 by an ensemble of organizations: Asamblea Permanente por los Derechos Humanos (APDH; Permanent Assembly for Human Rights); CELS; Historical and Social Memory Foundation (Fundación Memoria Histórica y Social); the Madres Línea Fundadora (Founding Line Mothers), a Mothers of Plaza de Mayo organization; and SERPAJ. This ensemble was conceived as a joint effort of the movements; their mission statement declared that the foundation's purpose was to ensure that any record of what happened during the last military dictatorship and its consequences is accessible for research and education. The Provincial Committee for the Memory of the Province of Buenos Aires is a public institution formed of an integration of the state and NGOs that carries out work similar to that of Memoria Abierta but has also found ways to control state violence.[5]

The passage of time will bring new debates in the human rights movement. Questions such as "What is memory?" or "How does one remember and testify?" will inevitably resurface. We will ponder again who the legitimate participants in these debates are, what their relationship with the state is, and what the state's role is. The gradual institutionalization of the human rights movement (an ongoing process subject to changes in the government) confirms its close and constant relationship with Argentina's democratic administration. This dynamic has revitalized the organizations' work and changed the way the human rights movement mobilizes against the state. In recent years the organizations have not directly confronted the state, but this does not imply that their modes of political intervention have lost their power.

The Impact of the Human Rights Frame in Argentine Society

Analyzing the institutionalization of the human rights movement requires not only considering the dynamics of its mobilization but also exploring how its frames of collective action spread. "Several analysts . . . argue that human rights organizations introduced new principles into political language and new practices into political culture" (Wappenstein 2004: 5).

In this section I analyze the increasing importance acquired by mobilization of relatives of the victims (*familiares de víctimas*). I start by exploring the mobilization process for relatives of victims of police brutality and then consider its extension to other issues with similar repertoires of social mobilization.

Origins and Characteristics of Mobilization of Victims' Relatives

As mentioned above, in the early years of the transition to democracy, some human rights organizations opened a discussion on the scope of the struggle for human rights. Should the fight be restricted to prosecuting crimes committed during the military dictatorship or should it also include violations of human rights during and after the transition to democracy? The Permanent Assembly for Human Rights, for example, published documentation of police violence and repression in democracy (Ales and Palmieri 2002). Similarly, CELS has worked on these issues since the early 1990s. Lawyers tied to human rights organizations intervened in some cases of police brutality and transformed the way these types of cases were treated. Some cases have become emblems of the organization and mobilization of victims' relatives.

Between 1987 and 1991 the first mobilizations of relatives of victims of police brutality took place, and human rights organizations consolidated and new ones emerged. Relatives included not only the parents—often the public face and spokesperson for the victim—but also neighbors, friends, lawyers, and even organizations, all combining their efforts to mobilize. Mobilizations were particularly useful in revealing illegal use of force, particularly against young people from poor neighborhoods. "The nomination of relatives does not identify any family member—in terms of ties of kinship—of a person killed by the police, but those who have converted themselves to such because of their activism and organized protest" (Pita 2010b: 324).

In high-profile cases,[6] such as the so-called massacre of Ingeniero Budge (1997) and the Bulacio case (1991), the victims' relatives challenged the lethal use of force by police,[7] thus allowing the true version of events to come to light and opening the way for judicial investigations. However, the judicial investigations are usually flawed because police officers are often investigating themselves.

Eyewitness accounts of the massacre of Ingeniero Budge (Gingold 1997) claim police opened fire on three young men who were drinking on a neighborhood corner, police behavior consistent with its past aggressions in the area.

In contrast, the first police version of events described a confrontation with criminals who were armed and opened fire on police. Family members of the victims, advised by two lawyers with backgrounds in human rights, produced new evidence collected by police from another force—that is, staff who had no links to the police involved in the incident. Merely opening an investigation caused many witnesses to lose their fears and decide to testify, contradicting the police version. In addition, the testimony revealed that police would punish youth in poor neighborhoods on the basis of complaints from neighbors and that there was a widespread perception that police abuse was only one type of illegal practice of police personnel. In this case and others, mobilization of victims' relatives was fundamental to altering the unfavorable stereotype of young people held by police and judges. Mobilization allowed other voices to be heard that provided insight into the identity and daily lives of the victims. Whether making public statements or testifying in court, family, friends, and neighbors of the victims were crucial to contradicting the police version of events.

In the case of Ingeniero Budge, family members employed diverse tactics: they conducted a public funeral; marched to the local police station; held assemblies with the participation of youth parties and human rights organizations; held public vigils to protect the witnesses, during which they banged pots and pans at seeing a suspicious vehicle; produced an informative and widely distributed newsletter; organized demonstrations to take advantage of political situations (such as political conflicts between local, provincial, and national agencies); and spoke to the press, calling the cases a continuation of the political repression and state terrorism of the dictatorship. To keep their cause in the public eye, they used cultural activism—artistic displays, concerts, commemoration of the date, building an altar at the scene in memory of the victims, and petitioning the local council to name streets after the victims.

The Impact and Scope of the Mobilization of Victims' Relatives

This organization and mobilization changed how these cases are dealt with, either directly by changing the judicial system (challenging police) or indirectly by drawing in political or other figures in the public eye. Relatives have become protagonists who deserve some response in legal, moral, or political terms. Relatives of the victims pressure police through a judicial investigation and also through administrative processing of the police involved and the politicians responsible for the situation. In this way, the two main concerns of the relatives are addressed: the judicial cause to guarantee the thoroughness and impartiality of the investigation and efforts to take the personnel involved off the street during the investigation.

Beyond the demands, lawsuits, and pressure on the justice system, the protests connected with the cases are in themselves resistance to and confrontation with the police authority. Acts of aggression and rituals of humiliation against the police show how police interventions are perceived (Pita 2010a).

The organization and mobilization of the relatives of the victims is aimed, in particular, at monitoring court cases, a task in which lawyers have a central role. "Defense attorneys . . . [for the victims say]: 'The way is not to rely on [receiving] justice but to demand it.' What they propose [is] an appropriation of institutional mechanisms: continuing to make demands before the court but also encouraging members of the Friends and Neighbors Committee to become more active and engaged" (Gingold 1991: 31–32). Monitoring of court cases and protest activities are two important control mechanisms that encourage an impartial investigation of the facts to determine responsibilities and, eventually, penalize the guilty individuals.

Those mobilization experiences have, in general, an inorganic character, following the fundamental features of what M. V. Pita calls "the world of the relatives" (*el mundo de los familiares*), referring to the relationship of relatives of victims of police brutality (2010a: 185). Some family members continued their activism beyond the isolated incidents in which they were involved, supporting others and creating a network of experience with protest.

A statistical study on national protest events of 1989–2003[8] shows the importance of relatives of victims in social mobilizations. As shown in Table 8.2, the protests organized by victims' relatives are 9 percent of the total of protests of civil society organizations, equal to the proportion held by human rights organizations, giving an idea of their relative importance. They account for 3 percent of all protests in the period.

In 1991, only 1.8 percent of protests were led by organizations of victims' relatives. That proportion rose to 8.8 percent in 1998. Although growth is not constant, these groups held increasingly more protests throughout the 1990s (see Figure 8.1).

In the early 1990s, new organizations that had emerged expressed ideological differences with human rights organizations, for example, CORREPI and

TABLE 8.2   TYPE OF CIVIL SOCIETY PROTEST
ORGANIZATION, 1989–2003

Organization membership or focus	Percentage
Neighbors	28
Students	16
Human rights organizations	9
Relatives of victims*	9
Prisoners	8
Others[†]	30
Total	100

Source: Data from Schuster et al. 2006. Total of civil society protests:
1,692 (32 percent of protests reported in the national press, 1983–2003).
* The vast majority of protests by relatives of victims relate to police
brutality, but some have different motivation (for example, traffic accidents). See Pereyra 2005.
† All types of organizations are included in this category, none of which,
taken individually, exceed 5 percent of the protests.

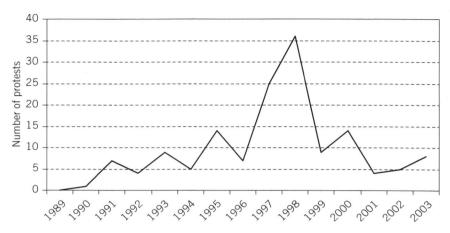

Figure 8.1 Evolution of protests by relatives of victims, 1989–2003. *(Source: Data from Grupo de Estudios sobre Protesta Social y Acción Colectiva)*

the Centro de Estudios e Investigaciones en Derechos Humanos (CEIDH; Center for Studies and Research on Human Rights).

Organizations of the relatives of the victims supported by human rights organizations also appeared, particularly after the 1992 formation of the Comisión de Familiares de Víctimas Indefensas de la Violencia Institucional (COFAVI; Committee of Relatives of Helpless Victims of Institutional Violence). But, as mentioned earlier, mobilization of victims' relatives was episodic and organization processes were mostly restricted to individual events. However, relatives of the victims expanded beyond police brutality. Recent years have seen demonstrations by relatives of victims of crime, car accidents, air accidents, abuse of drugs, and so on. In this sense, the legitimacy of the victims' relatives progressively increased.

The Programa Nacional de Lucha contra la Impunidad (PRONALCI; National Program to Combat Impunity), under the jurisdiction of the Ministry of Justice and Human Rights,[9] was created in 2003 to improve coordination among relatives and also produce analysis and recommendations. The program is composed of victims' relatives, attorneys, and other professionals who advise plaintiffs in judicial proceedings.

Organizations of victims' relatives are above all protest groups with the same legitimacy and meaning of human rights organizations. The progressive extension of their repertoire is one of the greater impacts of the movement on contemporary Argentine society.

Conclusion

What effects did the transition to democracy have on the dynamics of the human rights movement in Argentina? The answer is complex because in the last few decades of democracy, the human rights movement has followed diverse paths and seen many changes in the political sphere. However, one element prevailed beyond the comings and goings of the different events and organizations: political institutionalization.

Human rights organizations, both established and new ones that have emerged in recent years, have become recognized as legitimate political players and, as such, have a voice in public debates, the definition of policy, and so on. Institutionalization can describe the dynamics that maintain the movement through its internal differences and conflicts. Terms such as *co-optation* and *bureaucratization* tend to highlight precisely these aspects of the movement's transformation. The different organizations may have very different paths, dissimilar work styles, and even very different political stances, but they have some key features in common from the moment of their emergence.

Their institutionalization can also be analyzed from the point of view of the diffusion of collective action frames of the human rights movement. Every social movement leaves behind a set of frames and symbols that could be—often are—appropriated by future movements. Such is the case for the human rights movement in Argentina; its legacy is visible in everyday lived experiences of activists and militants of all kinds.

The human rights movement enabled protests of the relatives of victims of police brutality because it established (1) a vocabulary of human rights in contentious politics in Argentina, (2) the significance of the bond between democracy and the judicial system (the rule of law), and (3) the importance of relationships as representation criteria.

From its inception, most activity of the human rights movement has been closely related to the crimes of the military dictatorship. However, demands related to human rights have been successively reformulated with the progressive widening of the language of human rights that, in recent years, has been extended to include the most diverse grievances.

The collective action frame diversified for many reasons, and new organizations emerged as areas of interest of established organizations shifted. This process clearly shows the existence of what in the early years of the democratic transition was called a human rights culture.

NOTES

1. All translations are mine.

2. La Prefectura Naval Argentina is the nation's coast guard.

3. The theory of the two demons considers on equal terms crimes committed by guerrilla members and those committed by members of the army who occupy government positions.

4. In December 2001 a major financial crisis unfolded against a backdrop of recession and high unemployment that produced important political consequences. Popular movements called for and provided the framework for the president's resignation. A transitional government ruled during 2002 until new elections were held in 2003.

During this transition, there was a significant reorientation of economic policy that alleviated the most dramatic aspects of the crisis (Pereyra, Vommaro, and Pérez 2013).

5. See the next section. This organization is responsible for resolution 2825/06 by the Supreme Court of Buenos Aires Province, which requires judges and prosecutors of criminal jurisdiction to inform the committee of injury or death occurring in detentions.

6. For coverage of these cases, see Olivera and Tiscornia 1998; Abregú, Palmieri, and Tiscornia 1998; Centro de Estudios Legales y Sociales and Human Rights Watch 1998; Gingold 1997; Jelin 1996; Tiscornia 2008; and Pita 2004, 2010a.

7. The police version of the circumstances in which a person died is built in the absence of judges and prosecutors and in the early stages of a criminal investigation. Facts are gathered and evidence acquired to show that police coercion and force was justified. Low-income youth are generally considered dangerous by the public, which gives police some leeway to use force and encourages a reading of the police version of events as legitimate performance of duty. Needless to say, this leaves these young people vulnerable to police.

8. This was a systematic survey and statistical analysis of protest events reported in the national press performed by the Study Group on Social Protest and Collective Action of the Gino Germani Research Institute of the University of Buenos Aires. For a summary of the work and an extended discussion on the scope and criteria of the survey methodology, see Schuster et al. 2006.

9. For more on the program, see http://www.jus.gov.ar/areas-tematicas/lucha-contra-la-impunidad.aspx.

REFERENCES

Aboy Carlés, G. 2010. "Raúl Alfonsín y la fundación de la 'segunda república'" [Raúl Alfonsín and the Founding of the "Second Republic"]. In *Discutir Alfonsín* [Discuss Alfonsín], edited by R. Gargarella, M. V. Murillo, and M. Pecheny, 67–84. Buenos Aires: Siglo XXI.

Abregú, M., G. Palmieri, and S. Tiscornia. 1998. "Informe sobre la situación y los mecanismo de control de los organismos de seguridad pública interior en la República Argentina" [Report on the Status and Control Mechanism of the Homeland Security Agencies in Argentina]. In *Control Democrático en el Mantenimiento de la Seguridad Interior* [Democratic Control in Maintenance of Homeland Security], edited by Hugo Frühling, 58–97. Santiago de Chile: Centro de Estudios del Desarrollo.

Acuña, C., and C. Smulovitz. 1995. "Militares en la transición argentina: Del gobierno a la subordinación constitucional" [Argentina Military in Transition: From Government to Constitutional Subordination]. In *Juicio, castigos y memorias: Derechos humanos y justicia en la política argentina* [Judgment, Punishments and Memories: Human Rights and Justice in Argentina Politics], edited by E. Jelin, 25–52. Buenos Aires: Nueva Visión.

Ales, C., and G. Palmieri. 2002. "Crime and Human Rights in Argentina." Paper presented at the International Council on Human Rights Policy seminar "Crime: Managing Public Order in Countries in Transition," New York, October 21–22. Available at http://www.ichrp.org/files/papers/22/114_-_Argentina_-_Crime_and_Human_Rights_Palmieri__Gustavo___Ales__Cecilia__2002.pdf.

Bruno, A., M. Cavarozzi, and V. Palermo, eds. 1985. *Los derechos humanos en la democracia* [Human Rights in Democracy]. Buenos Aires: Centro Editor de América Latina.

Brysk, A. 1994. *The Politics of Human Rights in Argentina: Protest, Change, and Democ-ratization*. Stanford, CA: Stanford University Press.

Calderón, F., ed. 1986. *Los movimientos sociales ante la crisis* [Social Movements against the Crisis]. Buenos Aires: Universidad de las Naciones Unidas.

Calderón, F., and E. Jelin. 1987. *Clases y movimientos sociales en América Latina: Perspectivas y realidades* [Class and Social Movements in Latin America: Perspectives and Realities]. Buenos Aires: Centro de Estudios de Estado y Sociedad.

Calderón, F., A. Piscitelli, and J. L. Reyna. 1992. "Social Movements: Actors, Theories, Expectations." In *The Making of Social Movements in Latin America*, edited by A. Escobar and S. Alvarez, 123–161. Boulder, CO: Westview.

Cavarozzi, M. 1985. *Autoritarismo y democracia* [Authoritarianism and Democracy]. Buenos Aires: Centro Editor de América Latina.

Centro de Estudios Legales y Sociales and Human Rights Watch. 1998. *La inseguridad policial: Violencia de las fuerzas de seguridad en la Argentina* [Police Insecurity: Violence by Security Forces in Argentina]. Buenos Aires: Eudeba.

García Delgado, D., and V. Palermo. 1989. "El movimiento de los derechos humanos en la transición a la democracia en Argentina" [The Human Rights Movement in the Transition to Democracy in Argentina]. In *Los movimientos populares en América Latina* [Popular Movements in Latin America], edited by D. Camacho and R. Menjivar, 54–78. Mexico City: Universidad de las Naciones Unidas.

Gingold, L. 1991. "Crónicas de muertes anunciadas: El caso de Ingeniero Budge" [Chronicles of Announced Deaths: The Case of Ingeniero Budge]. CEDES Working Paper no. 65, Centro de Estudios de Estado y Sociedad, Buenos Aires.

———. 1997. *Memoria, moral y derecho: El caso de Ingeniero Budge (1987–1994)* [Memory, Morality and Law: The Case of Ingeniero Budge]. Mexico City: Facultad Latino-americana de Ciencias Sociales–Juan Pablos Editor.

González Bombal, M. I., and M. Sonderéguer. 1987. "Derechos humanos y democracia" [Human Rights and Democracy]. In *Movimientos sociales y democracia emergente* [Social Movements and Emerging Democracy], vol. 1, edited by E. Jelin, 34–71. Buenos Aires: Centro Editor de América Latina.

Jelin, E., ed. 1985. *Los nuevos movimientos sociales* [The New Social Movements]. 2 vols. Buenos Aires: Centro Editor de América Latina.

———. 1996. *Vida cotidiana y control institucional en la Argentina de los '90.* [Everyday Life and Institutional Control in the Argentina of the '90s]. Buenos Aires: Nuevo Hacer.

———. 2005. "Los derechos humanos entre el Estado y la sociedad" [Human Rights between the State and Society]. In *Nueva Historia Argentina*, vol. 10, *Dictadura y democracia (1976–2001)*, edited by Juan Suriano, 156–201. Buenos Aires: Editorial Sudamericana.

Keck, M. E., and K. Sikkink. 1998. *Activists beyond borders: Advocacy Networks in International Politics*. Ithaca, NY: Cornell University Press.

Landi, O. 1985. "La transición política argentina y la cuestión de los derechos humanos" [Argentina's Political Transition and the Question of Human Rights]. In *Los derechos humanos como política* [Human Rights as Politics], edited by H. Villela, 55–79. Buenos Aires: Ediciones La Aurora.

Leis, H. R. 1989. *El movimiento por los derechos humanos y la política argentina* [The Movement for Human Rights and Politics in Argentina]. 2 vols. Buenos Aires: Centro Editor de América Latina.

Lorenz, F. 2011. "Las movilizaciones por los derechos humanos (1976–2006)" [The Demonstrations for Human Rights (1976–2006)]. In *Buenos Aires: Manifestaciones, fiestas y rituales en el siglo XX* [Buenos Aires: Demonstrations, Celebrations and Rituals in the Twentieth Century], edited by M. Z. Lobato, 29–55. Buenos Aires: Editorial Biblos.

"Marcha de las madres" [March of the mothers]. 1993. *Clarín*, September 12.

Navarro, M. 2001. "The Personal Is Political: Las Madres de Plaza de Mayo." In *Power and Popular Protest. Latin American Social Movements*, edited by S. Eckstein, 241–258. Berkeley: University of California Press.

Novaro, M., and V. Palermo. 2003. *La dictadura militar (1976–1983): Del golpe de estado a la restauración democrática* [The Military Dictatorship (1976–1983): From Coup to Democracy Restoration]. Buenos Aires: Paidós.

Olivera, A., and S. Tiscornia. 1998. "Estructuras y prácticas de las policías en la Argentina: Las redes de la ilegalidad" [Structures and Practices of the Police in Argentina: The Networks of Illegality]. In *Control democrático en el mantenimiento de la seguridad interior* [Democratic Control in the Maintenance of the Interior Security], edited by H. E. Frühling, 159–205. Santiago de Chile: Centro de Estudios del Desarrollo.

"Otra marcha de las madres de Plaza de Mayo" [Another march of the mothers of Plaza de Mayo]. 1996. *Clarín*, May 12, p. 5.

Pereyra, S. 2005. "¿Cuál es el legado del movimiento de derechos humanos? El problema de la impunidad y los reclamos de justicia en los '90" [What Is the Legacy of the Human Rights Movement? The Problem of Impunity and the Demands of Justice in the '90s]. In *Tomar la palabra: Estudios sobre protesta social y acción colectiva en la Argentina contemporánea* [To Take the Floor: Studies on Social Protest and Collective Action in Contemporary Argentina], edited by F. Schuster, G. Nardacchione, S. Pereyra, and F. Naishtat, 151–192. Buenos Aires: Prometeo.

Pereyra, S., G. Vommaro, and G. Pérez, eds. 2013. *La grieta: Política, economía y cultura después de 2001* [The Crack: Politics, Economics and Culture after 2001]. Buenos Aires: Editorial Biblos.

Pita, M. V. 2004. "Violencia policial y demandas de justicia: Acerca de las formas de intervención de los familiares de víctimas en el espacio público" [Police Violence and Demands for Justice: About the Forms of Assistance from Relatives of Victims in the Public Space]. In *Burocracias y violencia: Estudios de antropología jurídica* [Bureaucracies and Violence: Studies of Legal Anthropology], edited by S. Tiscornia, 435–464. Buenos Aires: Antropofagia.

———. 2010a. *Formas de morir y formas de vivir: El activismo contra la violencia policial* [Ways to Die and Ways of Living: Activism against Police Violence]. Buenos Aires: Editores del Puerto and CELS.

———. 2010b. "Formas populares de protesta: Violencia policial y 'familiares de gatillo fácil'" [Popular Forms of Protest: Police Violence and Relatives of "Happy-Trigger" Victims]. In *Movilizaciones, protestas e identidades políticas en la Argentina del bicentenario* [Demonstrations, Protests and Political Identities in Bicentennial Argentina], edited by A. Massetti, 323–342. Buenos Aires: Nueva Trilce.

Schuster, F., G. Pérez, S. Pereyra, M. Armelino, M. Bruno, M. Larrondo, N. Patrici, P. Varela, and M. Vázquez. 2002. *La trama de la crisis: Modos y formas de protesta social a partir de los acontecimientos de diciembre de 2001* [The Plot of the Crisis: Ways and Forms of Social Protest from the Events of December 2001]. Buenos Aires: Instituto de Investigaciones Gino Germani, Facultad de Ciencias Sociales, Universidad de Buenos Aires. Available at http://webiigg.sociales.uba.ar/iigg/textos/documentos/IC3.pdf.

Schuster, F., G. Pérez, S. Pereyra, M. Armesto, M. Armelino, A. García, A. Natalucci, M. Vázquez, and P. Zipcioglu. 2006. *Transformaciones de la protesta social en Argentina 1989–2003* [Trends of the Social Protests in Argentina from 1989 to 2003]. Buenos Aires: Gino Germani Research Institute, School of Social Sciences, University of Buenos Aires. Available at http://webiigg.sociales.uba.ar/iigg/textos/documentos/dt48.pdf.

Sikkink, K. 2008. "From Pariah State to Global Human Rights Protagonist: Argentina and the Struggle for International Human Rights." *Latin American Politics and Society* 50 (1): 1–29.

Sonderéguer, M. 1985. "Aparición con vida (el movimiento de derechos humanos en Argentina)" [Live Appearance (the Human Rights Movement in Argentina)]. In *Los nuevos movimientos sociales* [The New Social Movements], vol 2, edited by E. Jelin, 21–55. Buenos Aires: Centro Editor de América Latina.

Stepan, A. 1986. "Paths toward Redemocratization: Theoretical and Comparative Considerations." In *Transitions from Authoritarian Rule: Comparative Perspectives*, vol. 3, edited by G. A. O'Donnell, P. C. Schmitter, and L. Whitehead, 64–84. Baltimore: Johns Hopkins University Press.

Tiscornia, S. 2008. *El activismo de los derechos humanos: El caso Walter Bulacio* [The Human Rights Activism: The Case of Walter Bulacio]. Buenos Aires: Editores del Puerto and CELS.

Wappenstein, S. 2004. "Re-Signifying Citizenship: Lessons from the Human Rights Movement in Argentina." Paper presented at the annual meeting of the American Sociological Association, San Francisco, August 14. Available at http://citation.allacademic.com/meta/p_mla_apa_research_citation/1/0/9/8/6/pages109862/p109862-1.php.

III

South Africa

9

Introduction

STEPHEN ELLIS

During the last quarter of the twentieth century, South Africa was home to a great number of political and social movements articulating grievances of various sorts. To many South Africans—and many foreign observers—it seemed evident that the root cause of just about every type of problem, whether or not articulated in political form, could be reduced to a single element: apartheid. Literally meaning "apartness," this was the Afrikaans word used by the National Party government after its accession to power in 1948 to designate a systematic policy of racial separation. Apartheid was a utopian vision of the radical right that aspired to manage an exceptionally complex society by dividing it into a series of separate spaces, each racially defined.

By the late 1980s, the conflict between, on the one hand, a National Party government in power for four decades, running a state that had been reorganized in line with apartheid principles, and on the other hand, a vast and disparate antiapartheid movement, seemed to offer little prospect of any negotiated solution. As the Cold War came to an end, the National Party's argument that its opponents were inspired by international communism ceased to have real purchase, either domestically or internationally. The struggle against apartheid gained public support all over the world.

Those seeking an alternative to National Party rule, whether inside or outside South Africa, were increasingly drawn to the African National Congress (ANC) as an eventual replacement. Established in 1912 as a vehicle for black South Africans of all ethnic groups to present their collective views to the country's government, the ANC had in time been transformed into a Cold War–style liberation movement. Banned by the government in 1960, it had established its headquarters outside the country. The ANC in exile opened itself by stages to

South Africans from all racial groups, diluting but never suppressing its original character as a black African organization. With strong support from the Soviet Union and its allies and from Sweden, as well as from a wide range of public opinion in all parts of the world, the ANC positioned itself as the organization destined to take over South Africa's government once apartheid had been defeated.

The most successful of the home-based organizations that challenged apartheid in the 1980s was the United Democratic Front (UDF), launched in 1983. While the UDF included many ANC members among its leaders, and while many of its adherents regarded themselves as followers of the exiled ANC, the UDF nevertheless had a character all its own. Its remarkable success, surprising even to its founders, owed a good deal to its unusual structure. It gathered under its umbrella hundreds of community organizations, religious bodies, trade unions, sporting bodies, youth organizations, and so on. It claimed to speak on behalf of two million people. As campaigns backed by the UDF shook the apartheid state during the mid-1980s, activists attached to its constituent parts tended to see their particular grievances as located within a broad ideological repertoire, including not only opposition to apartheid but also to capitalism, considered by some to be the real force shaping the South African condition. At times, UDF activists believed that they were articulating people's power, a revolutionary instrument taking the form of local assemblies and structures that replaced the legal organs of the state in townships where local authorities had been chased away and the police driven out. This contributed to the development of a distinctively South African brand of revolutionary socialist ideology. By the end of the 1980s, however, the state had reclaimed some political space by declaring a state of emergency and applying something like martial law in parts of the country. Thousands of activists were detained, and those who remained at liberty were obliged to recalibrate their ambitions. After the ANC had been unbanned in 1990, permitting the return of thousands of political exiles, the UDF dissolved itself. It was the ANC that participated in formal negotiations with the government over the country's future and that was to win the ultimate political prize in the country's first democratic elections in April 1994. A month later, Nelson Mandela was inaugurated as the country's first postapartheid president.

Interpretations of Transition

For decades, the chances of a transition from apartheid to democracy seemed so unlikely that, when the South African government unbanned the ANC, the South African Communist Party, and other banned organizations and entered negotiations that led to a legally based transfer of power, many observers regarded the transition as nothing less than miraculous.[1] These dramatic events occurred in the aftermath of the Cold War's ending, when the concept of a global wave of democratization was in vogue (Huntington 1991). In these circumstances, the process by which the apartheid state negotiated itself out of existence, to be replaced by a government led by the world's most admired politician, Nelson Mandela, indicated how even the most intractable of conflicts could find a relatively peaceful outcome.

Early attempts to describe and analyze the South African transition tended to see it in terms of the interests and aptitudes of political elites.[2] A negotiated transition, which led in the first instance to a government of national unity that included the National Party, was widely viewed as a reflection of a rational choice by South Africa's white minority, which realized that its long-term interest lay in negotiating itself out of exclusive power, while the revolutionary ANC understood that preserving the country's economic and financial infrastructure and reputation was in the interest of itself and its constituency. What seemed most in need of explanation was how such entrenched enemies could agree on a new constitution, avoiding the full-scale civil war that had seemed a real possibility.

Within quite a short time, however, new viewpoints began to emerge, in which historical details of South Africa's transition were sometimes hard to separate from an analysis of the problems that continued to face the country and its new, postapartheid government. Several studies emphasized the role of social organizations and civil society in bringing an end to apartheid, such as Ineke van Kessel's (2000) historical study of the UDF, which shows the degree to which this organization, so effective in opposing the apartheid state in the 1980s, was rooted in local grievances and local conditions. In multiple works Steven Robins (2005, 2008) notes how, ten years and more after the end of apartheid, many struggles in South Africa arose, not from disputes over questions of law or rights in the abstract, but from the specific grievances of people living in often poor communities. This perception raised questions about both the actual conditions of a major part of the population under ANC government and, implicitly at least, about the actual nature of the transition achieved in 1990–1994.

Perhaps inevitably, as South Africa's transition in time began to seem less miraculous, and as the world grew more habituated to the new environment post–Cold War, questions began to be asked about the South African achievement. Already in 1996 Michael Macdonald criticized what he considered to be an emerging consensus on the nature of South Africa's transition from apartheid. According to this author, the view was widely held that the ANC and the National Party, beginning from positions of hostility, had both been transformed by the experience of negotiation. They were said to have developed mutual trust to the extent that, discounting partisan considerations, they could agree to the promulgation of a liberal constitution that allowed a newly minted democratic government to institute its political program. Macdonald held a contrary view, maintaining that considerations of power were crucial to the eventual settlement. The South African case appeared at first glance to conform to many of the key themes conveyed by orthodox studies of transition, such as the conversion of an apparently radical opposition movement into a probusiness party that advocated fiscal conservatism and free market capitalism, especially after 1996 when the ANC, now the party of government, had chosen to implement a neoliberal economic policy that was well regarded by major business corporations that were white-dominated and identified with the old regime. To critics (e.g., Marais 1998; Gibson 2001), it appeared that while the political bargain that had been struck in the years of transition from 1990 to 1994 appeared to be eminently democratic, it was state centric and conservative in the sense of being favorable to established economic interests. Adrian Guelke (1999), referring once more in the subtitle of his book to a miracle (but this time claiming that it had been misunderstood), argued that the transition had been widely misunderstood because of excessive attention being given to the elite bargains reached during the negotiations, whereas older social and economic patterns remained pervasive.

For almost twenty years, meanwhile, a stream of local studies has tended to emphasize the relative autonomy of local actors throughout the events of the transition. In KwaZulu-Natal Province especially, where struggles during the last years of apartheid had in effect turned into a regional civil war, violence continued even after the confirmation of an elite pact between the National Party and the ANC. Local power holders, often known as warlords, followed a logic of power, position, and accumulation that was only tangentially related to events at the national level (Schuld 2013; Mathis 2013).

Overview of Part III

The three chapters in this section all address the issue of what happened to the social and political energies mobilized in the struggle against apartheid. The lines of continuity between those times and today are clear. One such trajectory is described by Steven Robins and Christopher Colvin in their analysis of forms of organization and strategies for action that have informed a wide range of movements that have come into existence in South Africa since the end of apartheid. One of the best-known and most successful of the social movements they describe is the Treatment Action Campaign (TAC), established in December 1998 to demand medical treatment for people infected with HIV. The best-known leader of the TAC, Zackie Achmat, is himself a former campaigner against apartheid, and the TAC's ability to generate support across lines of race and class by focusing on a goal of interest to people from all the country's main racial and ethnic communities is reminiscent of UDF campaigns. In addition to campaigning and demonstrating in public, the TAC has petitioned the courts and engaged with the state, reprising techniques sometimes used by the trade union movement during the last days of apartheid.

Other campaigns focusing on what is often called in South Africa service delivery—meaning infrastructure, which is often inadequate in areas of high unemployment—reject the methods used by the TAC. Some service delivery protests take the form of building barricades to disrupt traffic and impede access. This also recalls methods used in the 1980s. No one can say which of these two strategies, the collaborationist or the confrontational, is the authentic legacy of the UDF and other campaigns against apartheid, since what characterized the UDF was precisely the expansiveness that enabled it to encompass all manner of protests that had in common their opposition to policies generated by the apartheid government.

Bert Klandermans's chapter explicitly asks the question that is at the core of this book: What is the fate of movements struggling for change once a political transition has taken place? The institution of a democratically elected government in South Africa, entrusted since 1994 to a party that is consistently able to attract some two-thirds of the popular vote, provides new avenues for the representation of social and political ambitions. Klandermans's chapter is based on six broad-based surveys conducted annually between February 1995 and March 2000. The evidence suggests that during these six years South African citizens did not participate any less in politics than they had during apartheid's final years. This finding casts doubt on any suggestion that the overthrow of an authoritarian regime necessarily leads to the depoliticization of the population. How this general observation is nuanced among different segments of South Africa's population, as analyzed by race and by degree of social embeddedness, for example, is a key issue and forms the substance of the discussion. Ineke van Kessel suggests that many former UDF activists have become quite cynical about the ANC and about politics in the new South Africa more generally. However, her own observations are based on a technique quite different from the statistical analysis of thousands of responses to survey questionnaires used by Klandermans. Van Kessel's conclusions are based on her reinterviews of former UDF activists whom she first encountered twenty or more years ago. Since all in her sample are people with considerable experience, her analysis reflects the effect of aging that is not easily captured in the surveys conducted by Klandermans.

One conclusion that might be drawn about South Africa's political transition, in light of the material presented in these pages, is that many of the judgments reached in the 1990s were premature. The conclusion that the elite transition that led to the promulgation of a new constitution in 1996 was such a fine example of how elites could reach a negotiated outcome that was in their interest but also, arguably, that of the societies they represented may now be seen to have been somewhat shallow. The depth of social problems and the logic of local politics that preceded the transition have continued subsequently. In South Africa as elsewhere, a transition is more than the period between the fall of an authoritarian regime and the first democratic election subsequent to it.

Underlying any general set of questions about the nature of contestation in a changing political and social environment lie issues that are particular to South Africa. Perhaps the most basic of these is what people are really striving for when they engage in social struggles, whether in the form of social movements or in the form of explicitly political participation—for example, in political parties. UDF activists in the 1980s, influenced in part by information emanating from the ANC in exile, very often entertained ideological visions of their future expressed in forms of socialism and anticapitalism, in which participation was regarded as a supreme virtue. Perhaps unsurprisingly, looking back more than two decades later, many former activists no longer see the world in quite the same ideological terms. As Van Kessel notes, individual advancement and personal enrichment have become acceptable in governing circles, and former activists now frame their own aspirations in similar terms. Egalitarianism is no longer in fashion in South Africa, although many of the social movements studied by Robins continue to express collective goals in egalitarian form. It is clear from the new-style campaigns on service delivery that, while these are typically focused on specific issues such as the provision of sewerage and sanitation, this is no more than a specific goal derived from a more general notion of what constitutes a decent lifestyle. Much as in apartheid days, the state is ultimately held responsible for the satisfaction of these goals.

In retrospect, many activists would probably recognize that their ideas about liberation were unrealistic in the sense that this was often perceived as a climactic moment after which the world would be made anew. Few South Africans are likely to think that way today, because there is no realistic prospect of any political party other than the ANC wielding power at the national level. Perhaps what is most striking is the continuity in the preoccupations of the poor and the continuing need to struggle for these to be realized. What has changed most is the international climate in which these are expressed, together with the legitimacy of the party in power in Pretoria. The roots of inequality and injustice in South Africa being exceptionally deep, they have survived the demise of apartheid.

NOTES

1. Among many works referring in their titles to the concept of a South African miracle are Waldmeir 1997; Friedman 1994; and Sparks 2003.

2. Among leading journalistic accounts were Sparks 1995 and Waldmeir 1997. The leading theoretical treatment was Sisk 1995.

REFERENCES

Friedman, Steven. 1994. *The Small Miracle: South Africa's Negotiated Settlement.* Johannesburg: Ravan Press.

Gibson, Nigel C. 2001. "Transition from Apartheid." In *A Decade of Democracy in Africa,* edited by Stephen N. Ndegwa, 65–85. Leiden, Netherlands: Brill.

Guelke, Adrian. 1999. *South Africa in Transition: The Misunderstood Miracle.* London: Tauris.

Huntington, Samuel P. 1991. *The Third Wave: Democratization in the Late Twentieth Century.* Norman: University of Oklahoma Press.

Macdonald, Michael D. 1996. "Power Politics in the New South Africa." *Journal of Southern African Studies* 22 (2): 221–233.

Marais, Hein. 1998. *Limits to Change: The Political Economy of Transition.* Cape Town: University of Cape Town Press.

Mathis, Sarah M. 2013. "From Warlords to Freedom Fighters: Political Violence and State Formation in Umbumbulu, South Africa." *African Affairs* 112 (448): 421–439.

Robins, Steven, ed. 2005. *Limits to Liberation after Apartheid: Citizenship, Governance and Culture.* Oxford: James Currey.

———. 2008. *From Revolution to Rights in South Africa: Social Movements, NGOs and Popular Politics.* Oxford: James Currey.

Schuld, Maria. 2013. "Voting and Violence in KwaZulu-Natal's No-Go Areas: Coercive Mobilisation and Territorial Control in Post-conflict Elections." *African Journal on Conflict Resolution* 13 (1): 101–123.

Sisk, Timothy. 1995. *Democratization in South Africa: The Elusive Social Contract.* Princeton, NJ: Princeton University Press.

Sparks, Allister. 1995. *Tomorrow Is Another Country: The Inside Story of South Africa's Road to Change.* New York: Hill and Wang.

———. 2003. *Beyond the Miracle: Inside the New South Africa.* Chicago: University of Chicago Press.

van Kessel, Ineke. 2000. *"Beyond Our Wildest Dreams": The United Democratic Front and the Transformation of South Africa.* Charlottesville: University Press of Virginia.

Waldmeir, Patti. 1997. *Anatomy of a Miracle: The End of Apartheid and the Birth of the New South Africa.* London: Viking.

10

The United Democratic Front and Its Legacy after South Africa's Transition to Democracy

INEKE VAN KESSEL

The United Democratic Front (UDF) spearheaded internal resistance against apartheid in the 1980s. It was easily the most representative social movement in the history of South Africa, serving as an umbrella for a broad array of affiliated organizations, ranging from student bodies, church-based groups, trade unions, women's organizations, sports clubs, and residents' organizations. With this heterogeneous constituency, its dominant perspective envisaged postapartheid South Africa as a color-blind, participative, and egalitarian society. While the vision of a nonracial, egalitarian society was broadly shared across South Africa, member organizations maintained their own distinct character. The UDF was broadly associated with the banned African National Congress (ANC), but it did acquire an identity of its own.

After the unbanning of the ANC in 1990, South Africa entered a phase of negotiations for a new constitution that would enshrine equal civil rights for all citizens, regardless of race, class, or gender. After the first democratic election in 1994, the ANC became the ruling party, initially as the dominant force in a transitional government of national unity. For the foreseeable future, the ANC is entrenched as the ruling party of South Africa. Opposition parties stand little chance of dislocating the ANC from power, but organizations of civil society have in recent years become more vocal in criticizing the ANC for its failure to meet its promise of delivering "a better life for all," as the ANC's election slogan pledged in 1994.

The UDF disbanded in 1991, because most of its activists had flocked to the ANC as the most likely instrument for transforming South Africa and as the most promising career path from an individual perspective. Only in the Western Cape, with its large Colored population, was the dissolution of the

UDF contested. Some of the Front's affiliates, such as human rights bodies and church-based organizations, returned to their core business. From their perspective, involvement in a broad political mass movement had been an exceptional episode, a choice demanded of them in the extraordinary decade of the 1980s of mass mobilization and severe repression. Other member movements, notably youth and women, merged with the ANC Youth League and the ANC Women's League. Dozens of organizations that had had little life of their own, apart from offering a structure to be involved with the UDF, ceased to exist. Others, such as organizations of township residents, known as civic associations, were unsure about their future role.

This chapter reflects on the legacy of the UDF in postapartheid South Africa. First, I give a brief outline of the history and the main characteristics of the UDF. Next, I explore the trajectory of some social movements in postapartheid South Africa, with a focus on civic associations and social movement media. Finally, I turn to views of activists with a history of involvement in the UDF.

The findings presented in this chapter are largely derived from a wider research project, in which I revisit people and places where I initially did research in 1990–1992, during the early days of South Africa's transition to democracy (van Kessel 2000). How do former UDF activists deal with the dissonance between their previous ideals and contemporary reality? What has been the long-term impact of the UDF? How do former activists make sense of the changes in South African society: mission accomplished or vision betrayed? Are they still involved in social movement activity? Have the networks of the days of struggle survived into the period of democratic rule? Does the legacy of the UDF serve as a source of inspiration for new social movements?

What Was the UDF?

Origins

After the banning of the ANC in 1960, its leadership regrouped in exile. The armed struggle and campaigns to isolate apartheid South Africa through boycotts and sanctions dominated its strategy for the first two decades. In the 1980s, however, the leadership in exile made a strategic decision to rebuild mass-based organizations inside the country. The UDF grew out of locally based initiatives, but consultations had been made with the leadership in exile and with the ANC underground.

During the 1970s, collective protest in South Africa was located in two distinct social categories: black workers and black students. Their protest actions remained isolated phenomena rather than features of a coordinated rebellion. The 1980s, however, witnessed the growth of a broad-based social movement that mounted a sustained challenge to the apartheid state. After 1979, student activists actively sought to link up with community and worker protests.

Protest politics shifted from uncompromising noncollaborationism to a more pragmatic result-oriented approach. By taking up the bread-and-butter issues that occupied people's minds at the level of local communities, activists succeeded in broadening popular organizations and involving a wide range of ordinary residents who would otherwise have been reluctant to become involved in overtly confrontational politics.

While the ANC had been banned, some of its key documents had not been outlawed and continued to inspire antiapartheid activity. The Freedom Charter, adopted in 1955 by the ANC and its allies in the Congress Alliance, was by far the most influential document. The opening paragraph states that "South Africa belongs to all who live in it, black and white, and that no government can justly claim authority unless it is based on the will of all the people."[1] The charter set the tone for an inclusive ideology that combined racial equality with aspirations for redistribution of wealth as well as popular participation in government.

Around 1980 only churches, the emerging independent trade unions, and the racially segregated student organizations had a nationwide following. Student organizations proved important as recruiting and training grounds for activists. Secondary and tertiary students and youth in general played a crucial role in the rebellion of the 1980s. Civic associations began emerging around 1980. Civics, as they came to be known, were local neighborhood associations that took up residents' concerns such as rent, electricity, transport, safety on the streets, and education.

Since 1981 many of these organizations have become involved in discussions on the formation of a united front to counter government plans for limited constitutional reforms. The UDF was formed as an ad hoc alliance for boycotting the elections for Indian and Colored South Africans. The new constitution called for a tricameral parliament that would incorporate Indians and Coloreds in separate chambers, while whites would retain ultimate control. Africans would remain excluded from national politics: their separate ethnic national destinies were to be pursued in the context of the Bantustans, or their separate homelands. Because the government had come to accept the presence of Africans in urban areas as a permanent feature of a modern, industrialized state, urban Africans were to be given a very limited form of self-rule by elected town councils. These Black Local Authorities were made responsible for raising their own revenue. The resulting increases in rent and service charges proved instrumental in igniting the township revolts of the mid-1980s.

The main trade union movement decided against affiliating with the UDF because it wanted to maintain the autonomy of workers' organizations and take part in wider popular struggles on its own terms. The united-front formula posed the risk of workers being swamped by populist politics, as had happened to ANC-aligned unions in the 1950s. The national launch of the UDF on August 20, 1983, in Mitchell's Plain, a Colored area near Cape Town, was attended by about a thousand delegates, representing some 575 community organizations, trade unions, sporting bodies, and women's and youth organizations. Over twelve thousand people attended a simultaneous mass rally. The strength of the UDF as a front was measured at some 600 organizations and two million people.

The boycott campaigns against the tricameral elections and the municipal elections for the Black Local Authorities were a resounding success. The state's efforts to co-opt Coloreds and Indians and a small elite of urban Africans had evidently failed. Widespread school boycotts accompanied the campaigns. Parallel to election boycotts and school protests, a third source of unrest consisted of locally based community protest against increases in bus fares and rents. By the end of 1984 it was clear that South Africa had entered a phase of unrest that would be more serious than the Soweto rising of 1976.

After the successful boycott campaigns, the UDF transformed itself from an ad hoc alliance into a more permanent movement that addressed a broad range of issues. Meanwhile, dozens of townships were the scene of escalating, sometimes violent protests against the Black Local Authorities and their attempts at raising revenue to cover the costs of administration. Local protest was mostly led by civic associations. Although most civics were affiliated with the UDF, the Front had little control over local protest actions. Beginning in 1985, however, the UDF leadership began to realize more clearly the mobilizing potential of bread-and-butter issues. Civics that dealt with everyday concerns could attract large numbers of not heavily politicized township residents. But political guidance was needed to infuse local struggles with a broader meaning.

Through the UDF, disparate struggles regarding housing, transport, education, and the cost of living could be understood as part of the fight against both apartheid and capitalism. Forcing Black Local Authorities out of office presented the UDF and the civics with the challenge to provide alternative structures. Civics were thrust into a new role, for which they were hardly equipped: they had to be transformed from pressure groups into embryonic forms of local government. In numerous places, activists began to see themselves as participants in a far more ambitious project than the demolition of apartheid: the construction of a new, egalitarian, and morally just society. Civics were transformed into organs of people power.

Heavy state repression, accompanied by mass detentions, did not crush the rebellion but inspired new tactics. Consumer boycotts were introduced as a new political weapon. Successful boycott campaigns conducted by broad-based township organizations relying on participatory decision-making structures reinforced the political and moral authority of the civic and other movements that stood for an alternative social order. Conversely, coercion, intimidation, and abuse by undisciplined youth often weakened support for the boycott.

Boycotts gave ordinary people a sense of power. Many activists believed that a phase of dual power had arrived and that a revolutionary takeover was imminent. But the pattern of resistance was uneven, and coordination was lacking. Not the UDF itself, but local affiliates and people loosely associated with the UDF wielded power in the townships. More durable than the fledgling structures of people's power was the workers' power that manifested itself in a new giant federation of trade unions, the Congress of South African Trade Unions (COSATU). On December 1, 1985, over ten thousand people attended the launch of COSATU in Durban. In contrast to its predecessor, FOSATU, the leadership of the thirty-three COSATU unions held that unions ought to be involved in community struggles and the wider political arena.

People's Power

With rebellion spreading into remote corners of South Africa, boycotts flaring up intermittently, mounting international solidarity campaigns, and increasing signs of nervousness among white businesses, the UDF was confident that soon "the people" would be empowered to shape their own destiny. The year 1986 marks the high tide of "People's Power" (a commonly used slogan at the time), of the belief that representatives of the people, even the people themselves, were marching ahead and taking control of liberated areas. Defined in geographical terms, liberated areas were townships that had been liberated from the control of the apartheid state and thus became no-go areas for the police, but the term could equally apply to spheres of life where "the people" were taking over, as in schools, community media, and newly established people's courts. People's courts signified perhaps the most fundamental challenge to state authority, because they exposed the lack of legitimacy of the criminal justice system of the apartheid state. In some townships people's courts were widely appreciated for curbing crime, disciplining unruly youth, and solving domestic conflicts. But elsewhere, people's courts were resented for their harsh and arbitrary punishments. Particularly if run by youth, the courts lacked legitimacy in the eyes of older residents.

Advocates of "People's Power" envisaged a form of direct democracy, with an ongoing process of consultation and mass participation. They were quite dismissive of political pluralism and representative democracy, which was branded bourgeois democracy.

A state of emergency imposed nationwide June 12, 1986, and not lifted until 1990, amounted to virtual military rule. Dozens of national and regional UDF leaders were detained, along with twenty-five thousand other South Africans, many younger than age eighteen. Although the UDF was badly hit, the state of emergency did not bring township life back to normal. Rent boycotts continued and provided a key rallying point for township activists. Street committees organized youth brigades to prevent the eviction of rent defaulters. If electricity had been cut off, volunteers moved in to reconnect township houses. Rent boycotts acquired their own momentum. Even without the political context, this tactic had obvious advantages because it augmented family income. Consumer and bus boycotts flared up intermittently, but township residents began to show signs of exhaustion and a loss of patience with the rule of the comrades, young militants who often used heavy-handed and coercive methods. Youth organizations adapted to a semiunderground existence, but most civics ceased to function.

This period of despair and forced inactivity had a sobering effect on leading activists. When new political space opened up in 1989, they emerged from detention and hiding with a new realism. No longer intoxicated by views of imminent liberation and insurrectionary seizure of power, they set out to rebuild organizations. A series of local negotiations prepared the way for talks about the central issue of state power.

Disbanding the UDF

After the unbanning of the ANC in January 1990, the release of Nelson Mandela and his coaccused from prison, and the return of the ANC leaders from exile, UDF activists deferred to the leadership of this historic liberation movement. In the popular imagination, the ANC leaders in exile and on Robben Island had acquired the status of larger-than-life heroes. Within the UDF, three options were discussed:

1. Disband
2. Transform into a coordinating structure for organizations of civil society
3. Wait and decide later

The argument for disbanding the UDF was that the Front had served its purpose, and now the ANC should resume its rightful place. The UDF's continued existence would cause only duplication and confusion. The second option was to transform the UDF into a coordinating structure for civics, student organizations, religious bodies, and those youth and women's organizations that decided against merging with the ANC's Youth League or Women's League. This position was favored both by activists who argued that an umbrella structure was needed to exercise hegemonic control and by the proponents of an autonomous civil society. The wait-and-see option prevailed during 1990, but the UDF decided to disband in 1991, when dissolution had become a foregone conclusion because the UDF's most capable activists had been absorbed into the ANC. Paradoxically, the unbanning of the ANC had a demobilizing effect: many people believed that they could now rely on the ANC to solve their problems.

What Made the UDF a Successful Movement?

The umbrella formula of the UDF proved eminently suitable for combining a broad range of organizations committed to eliminating apartheid, from middle-class whites to township youth. The popular-front formula enabled people to identify with the banned ANC without exposing themselves to immediate state repression. It allowed organizational flexibility and accommodated a broad range of manifestations of protest and rebellion, from prayer services to chasing black mayors and chiefs out of the townships and rural villages. It configured visions of an alternative social, political, and economic order, without imposing a political orthodoxy on its heterodox following.

The UDF not only coordinated and directed internal resistance to apartheid but also provided a cultural framework that lent a wider meaning to a great variety of local struggles. By participating in rent boycotts, stay-aways (from work and school), boycotts of white-owned businesses, and school protests, people addressed their immediate concerns and also played their part in the struggle for a new society. The UDF was easily the most inclusive movement in South African history. The key to its broad appeal was the Front's ability to frame different messages for various audiences, ranging from a struggle for civil rights to a radical agenda for social transformation.

The UDF's vision was for an egalitarian, nonracial society with a strong emphasis on grassroots participation. Participation was more important than pluralism. This vision of a just society had also a strong moral component. Religious inspiration and legitimation was characteristic of many activities.

A Negotiated Outcome: Movements in Times of Transition

With the return of the ANC to the center stage of South African politics, the focus shifted from the streets to the negotiating table; the ANC simultaneously had to rebuild its party structures throughout the country. Often, UDF structures were happy to embark on their new mission of building the ANC, but occasionally UDF organizations resented being taken over by ANC newcomers. Coming from exile or prison, these newcomers were often out of touch with local conditions and sensibilities.

Agreement on an interim constitution was followed by elections in April 1994, which brought a government of national unity to power under the presidency of Nelson Mandela. The ANC had won almost two-thirds of the votes. South Africa's constitution has been widely praised as a state-of-the-art model of liberal democracy, but it is quite removed from the egalitarian, participative society envisaged by social movements in the 1980s.

How did social movement actors deal with this discrepancy between the liberal democratic state and their erstwhile ideal of an egalitarian society governed by "People's Power"? Those individuals and affiliates that became part of the ANC followed the trajectory toward institutionalization, as the ANC established itself as a centralized, hierarchical political party. Some, such as the civic associations, struggled to find a new role for themselves, while others simply folded in the early 1990s, such as those providing social movement media (e.g., newspapers). However, when the honeymoon of the Mandela presidency was over, new social movements proliferated, often building on the repertoires of popular mobilization first established by the UDF in the 1980s.

Social movements in postapartheid South Africa tend to be fragmented and more localized. At first sight, most movements seem to be single-issue oriented, but some have a wider scope than their name suggests. The Soweto Electricity Crisis Committee, formed in 2000, campaigns for the provision of electricity as a basic need as well as dealing with housing, education, health, and employment. The Anti-Privatisation Forum (APF; formed in 2000) focuses on the free provision of water as a basic necessity but uses this as a platform to proselytize a broader anticapitalist agenda.

The Rise and Decline of Civic Associations

Twenty years after the onset of South Africa's democratic transition it is becoming increasingly difficult to recall the heady atmosphere of the 1980s when civic activists saw themselves as not just representing community interests in the struggle against apartheid but also leading the way to an entirely new society. As Glenn Adler and Jonny Steinberg point out, in those days it was not uncommon "to hear civic leaders associate the apartheid regime with the liberal democratic countries of the west and to herald their own organizational ethos as the embryo of a new form of existence" (2000: 2). Civics did not perceive themselves as social movements or volunteer associations but as "mass formations" heralding a new order. Civics claimed to be "the sole and legitimate representative of the people" (7).

Concepts such as civil society or social movements did not enter the South African discourse until 1990. In the introduction to a recent volume on popular politics and resistance movements, William Beinart notes that "the term 'social movement' has entered the South African political vocabulary largely from external academic and public debate about a broader global political phenomenon" (2010: 7). The notion of a dichotomy between state and civil society was alien to the worldview of many antiapartheid activists. All were united by the imperative of overthrowing the apartheid state, but many activists in the UDF and the civics movement did not envisage liberal democracy as the desirable outcome. During the long struggle against apartheid, many activists and academics alike tended to view South Africa as a unique case. Comparative perspectives were rare. With the end of apartheid, their horizon broadened and became more open to comparative perspectives.

After the fall of the Berlin Wall, the failures of the communist states of Eastern Europe could no longer be ignored, not even by the South African Communist Party and its sympathizers, who had long regarded the German Democratic Republic in particular as a model of a people's democracy. Suddenly, "civil society," as an antidote to dictatorship, entered the vocabulary of the ANC and its allies, notably the civic associations. Ideological confusion reigned, but the demise of the communist states in Europe did not have an immediate impact in South Africa. Faced with economic stagnation in South Africa, black South Africans drew the obvious conclusion: communism had failed in Eastern Europe, but capitalism, at least as far as most blacks in South Africa were concerned, had also failed (Green 2008: 342).

How did the civics understand their role in postapartheid society? Civic activists hovered between two competing conceptions of democracy: representative democracy, based on competitive multiparty elections, and direct democracy, building on concepts of people's power, which had taken hold in the 1980s. In the eyes of many civic activists, the morally just choice was for a model of people's power, while representative democracy was seen as belonging to a world of bourgeois democracy and exploitative capitalism.

In the course of the 1980s, politicized township residents came to be imagined as a political community, a homogeneous body unified by its resistance against an external enemy. Understandably, a community under siege by brutal security forces had little time for considerations of political pluralism. However, opinions differed when it came to postliberation trajectories. Some understood the decade of the 1980s as an exceptional phase that required unity in action to defeat the common enemy. In postapartheid society, divergent interests would require distinct organizations and modes of expression. The contest in competitive elections, then, is vital to give expression to this wide range of interests and allegiances. The underlying assumption here is that there is no single and inviolable will of the people. On the other hand, many civic activists believed that the civic association was the sole legitimate representative of the people and should extend into postapartheid society. Advocates of direct democracy envisaged people's assemblies, collectively producing a single will. In the communist lexicon, "dual power" implies that organs of resistance would, after the revolution, be transformed into soviets, which would replace parliamentary representation. The establishment of alternative representative and administrative structures is then understood as not simply a matter of temporary expediency but as embryonic organs of people's power, gradually encroaching on the terrain held by the capitalist apartheid state. Yet township residents obviously have contradictory interests. Shack dwellers, backyard tenants, homeowners, hostel dwellers, and illegal immigrants have different needs and different priorities. As social differentiation increases, the divergence of interests will also increase.

It is not surprising that some civic activists wanted to carry the historical role of the civic into the future, because they had no experience with other modes of participation. They never were citizens of a pluralist representative democracy. As Steinberg points out, "To travel the path from organ of resistance, to quasi-local government, to volunteer association in the space of four years is the stuff of an identity crisis" (2000: 175).

The ANC had adopted the national democratic revolution as the characteristic for the post-1994 phase of South Africa's history. This notion was derived from the two-phase strategy the South African Communist Party had adopted to accommodate the formation of a broad alliance of forces to overthrow apartheid. After the consolidation of the national democratic revolution, the second phase—the socialist revolution—would follow. The second phase would materialize only under the leadership of the working class. This strategy is an uneasy bedfellow with the South African constitution, which enshrines liberal democracy as an end in itself, not as a stepping stone toward socialism.

A New Umbrella Structure: SANCO

It was only after the disbanding of the UDF in 1991 that an interim body, the National Interim Consultative Committee, was elected to organize the establishment of a national civic structure. The planned launch of the South African National Civic Organisation (SANCO) had to be postponed to 1992, because of lack of resources. Previously autonomous civics now became branches of SANCO, which played a central role in the negotiated reform of local government during 1992–1993 that involved an amalgamation of townships and formerly white towns. It was also closely involved in urban development initiatives (Seekings 2000: 205). As in the 1980s, civic activism and involvement was uneven, with substantial local and regional variations, but in the 1990–1993 period, the future of the civics movement seemed promising.

Dan Sandi, who was elected secretary-general of SANCO at the launch in March 1992, envisaged a shift from protest to development. The nature of development, however, was very contentious and hotly debated, as these SANCO discussion notes from 1991 show: "Another aspect of development is the increase of the national wealth in such a way that every person will have enough. While development is based on equality of opportunity and on an equal distribution of basic commodities, it cannot thrive when the total wealth of the nation is so low that if it were equally distributed, everyone would be equally impoverished."[2] The document argues emphatically for state control over the economy: "There are many aspects of development, the chief of which must necessarily be the degree of control over the wealth of the country and over the means of production, without control of the economy in the national interest, there can be little meaningful development." Advocating schemes with producer and consumer co-ops and saving clubs, the document argues that "transformation is only valid if it is carried out with the people, not for them. People cannot be developed, they can only develop themselves."

Development was both highly political and technocratic in nature, requiring expert skills and thus potentially not conducive to popular participation. This last characteristic made Gugile Nkwinti, civic activist and UDF regional secretary in the Eastern Cape, highly suspicious of suggestions to turn civics into development agencies: "Political formations tend as yet to look at development with grave suspicions, as a monster that has been introduced into our communities with a view to demobilizing and blunting the sharp edge of the masses of the people."[3]

Nkwinti's contribution is a perfect illustration of how civic activists struggled to come to terms with two competing concepts of democracy: representative, pluralist democracy and direct democracy. On the one hand, civics were celebrated as part of a vibrant and dynamic civil society that would act as a check and balance on the democratic process. On the other hand, activists like Nkwinti did not envisage civil society as a watchdog. On the contrary, social movements should exercise power themselves: "An independent and activist social movement, one that can harness and pool together most, if not all, non-party political social formations is the only mode through which people's power can be exercised in the interest of democracy itself." Nkwinti had little time for liberal democracy: "Elections in western democracies have very low polls. Posturing of charismatic candidates in the media takes the place of popular generated issues and demands."[4]

Dan Sandi, however, stated clearly that civics would not be transformed into organs of local government but would continue as independent watchdogs. Civics ought to represent all residents, irrespective of their political affiliation. Yet Sandi also envisaged "localized people's assemblies as necessary vehicles for democratic local government."[5]

Seemingly in contrast to the desire to remain a militant social movement is the often-expressed need for civics to become bureaucratic structures, with premises, equipment, workshops, training courses, transport, administrators, organizers, and fieldworkers. A substantial part of the deliberations within SANCO was devoted to the problem of how to make ends meet with limited resources.

Civics and SANCO also had to define their relationship with the ANC. During the negotiating phase, 1990–1993, the ANC and the civics movement agreed on a division of labor. The ANC would concentrate on the struggle for power over the central state, and civics would represent "the community" in the restructuring of local government and developmental issues. Although most civic leaders saw themselves as part and parcel of the liberation movement, differences arose over the future role of civics. While some civic leaders continued to see their organization as an embryonic form of local government, the ANC firmly stated that municipal administration would be the domain of representative local government with the civics serving as watchdogs.

In the final phase of negotiations, the ANC overtook SANCO in reaching a compromise that did not accommodate visions of direct democracy. At the same time, local ANC branches became more prominent in local development. Jeremy Seekings argues that the ANC was becoming more skeptical of the civics' claim to mass support, because they mostly proved unable to persuade residents to end their boycotts of rents and service charges (2000: 209).

Relationship between Civil Society and State

During 1991–1993, SANCO played a prominent role in the negotiated transformation of local government and in initiatives for urban housing and infrastructural development. But after 1993 a rapid decline set in. Civics lost influence as soon as new, democratic institutions were set up. Developmental consultations moved to new forums.

By the time of the 1994 national elections, followed by local elections in 1995 and 1996, SANCO had firmly embraced the concept of civics as watchdog bodies. SANCO now held the view that civics ought to be separate from the state: therefore, when civic leaders were elected to local or provincial or national councils, they had to resign any executive position they held in SANCO. SANCO's policy was that candidates for local elections could not run on a SANCO ticket. Thus, civic activists aspiring to serve in the local councils ran as ANC candidates and if elected, had to resign from the civic. This policy of not allowing two hats resulted in a hemorrhage of experienced civic leadership. SANCO's national executive was depleted when over half its members moved into national or provincial parliaments (Seekings 2000: 212). SANCO abandoned this policy in 1997 to allow two hats. This position remained strongly contested in Gauteng Province: If the mayor was also the chairman of the SANCO branch in town, would he march against himself?

Some civic leaders saw little or no need for a continued existence of their civic and preferred to relocate to the ANC. Also, civics were no longer the only avenue to express popular grievances: these could now be raised through elected councilors, ward committees, or other channels. Often, civics were now relegated to building the ANC at local level. Residents often were confused about the division of labor between local SANCO branches and local ANC branches. The practice of numerous ANC councilors of using a SANCO office as their constituency office did nothing to alleviate the confusion.

The role as a subordinate ally of the ANC was criticized by some civic leaders, notably Mzwanele Mayekiso, chair of the civic in Alexandra township—Johannesburg's oldest African township—and one of SANCO's main theoreticians. He blamed SANCO for having succumbed to being a lapdog rather than a watchdog (Seekings 2000: 211). After criticizing SANCO's commercial ventures, this leading exponent of the radical tradition favoring anticapitalist social movements was expelled in 1997 for alleged indiscipline.

Initially, the Reconstruction and Development Program of the ANC government seemed to offer a new role for civics as agents in a people-driven process. The program envisaged local government as the central actor in urban development, in consultation with organs of civil society. In places where civics were crucial for delivery of housing or site-and-service schemes, the leadership could derive considerable influence from its role in the allocation of sites or houses. But as the stakes became higher, contest and rivalry within or against the civic escalated (Seekings 2000: 215).

Development proved more divisive than the struggle against apartheid, in which all could unite against an external enemy. Moreover, the schedule of frequent meetings and consultations made heavy demands on volunteer activists, who also needed to provide for themselves and their families. Unsurprisingly, civic leaders demanded salaries—they were dealing every day with well-paid civil servants, NGO representatives, and private sector employees. But in an environment of massive unemployment, paid positions inevitably raised the envy of those who felt excluded.

At the national level, SANCO was gradually marginalized, in spite of its affiliation with the alliance of ANC, South African Communist Party, and COSATU, which was known as the tripartite alliance plus one. It had little influence on housing policies, although housing was one of its core concerns. The gulf between ANC and SANCO widened in 1994, when SANCO gave only lukewarm support to the Masakhane (Operation Self-Reliance) campaign. After an agreed write-off of arrears in January 1994, it was now expected that boycotts of rents and service charges would end, because the primary rationale for the boycotts had been the protest against an illegitimate state. However, even after the 1994 April elections, there was no sign of a resumption of payments. This left the ANC government in a quandary, as it could not afford to improve services and address the massive housing backlog if the culture of nonpayment persisted. SANCO president Mlungisi Hlongwane distanced the civic movement from boycott tactics. However, while SANCO paid lip service to ANC policies, branches at the local level remained strongly opposed to the eviction of nonpaying households (Seekings 2000).

Increasingly skeptical of the civics, the ANC government now instituted Reconstruction and Development Program forums comprising representatives of a broad range of civil society organizations. Other local forums mushroomed—notably the Community Policing Forums, in which community representatives liaise with the local police about safety on the streets, another key concern of the civics movement. Civic representatives complained about their marginalization. In 1997, SANCO reported a "looming breakdown" in the relationship between ANC and SANCO (Seekings 1997: 16). Conceivably, a breakdown could have opened the way for a rebirth of civics as autonomous actors of civil society, but in practice the civics have ceded this role to a new generation of social movements, such as the Soweto Electricity Crisis Committee, the APF, and the Anti-Eviction Campaign (AEC). New social struggles evolve around issues such as land, housing, health, and poor service delivery. Protests against poor service delivery focused often on water and electricity, but "service delivery" also became a catch all for everything people expected the state to deliver, from jobs to housing.

At the national level, SANCO ventured into business, a route also attempted by some of the branches. The business ventures raised the ire of its erstwhile ally COSATU, since many commercial opportunities presented themselves in privatization schemes, which were strongly opposed by COSATU (Seekings 1997: 19). COSATU has also lambasted SANCO for leaving service delivery struggles to newcomers.[6]

In one of his numerous articles on the civics movement, Jeremy Seekings argues that although South Africa experienced a general decline in civic activism, SANCO's marginalization was to a large extent of its own making (1997).

He traces how SANCO turned to business ventures after other options failed. In terms of finances, SANCO could turn to three potential sources: foreign donors, corporate sponsorship, or membership dues. After the establishment of SANCO as an umbrella organization, donor money and corporate sponsors tended to flow to the national office or the provincial offices, leaving branches with only membership dues. SANCO's target membership was about two million residents, but only a few thousand people (some five thousand) actually paid up. Donor funding, which was offered in terms of antiapartheid support, dried up after 1994 but also because SANCO proved unable to produce audited accounts. Corporate sponsorship depended on a return benefit—for example, facilitating access for urban developers. From 1997, SANCO was deeply in debt and kept afloat only by financial assistance from its business wing, SANCO Investment Holdings, and its business partner, American Insurance Group.

Trade unions fared much better than civics in navigating the transition. But unions provide indispensable services—for example, collective bargaining and individual advice and protection—and therefore workers have a strong incentive to pay membership fees. For township residents, who do not see tangible benefits of paid-up membership, the temptation to become free riders is much stronger.

Adler and Steinberg argue that giving civics another lease on life as quasi-statutory vehicles of state-driven development programs would have been ill conceived. "The struggle to install inclusive, elected governmental machinery in South Africa has been a long one. It would be ironic if South Africa were now to forfeit this victory by handing over the developmental reins to an indeterminate cluster of unelected community organizations in the name of democracy" (Adler and Steinberg 2000: 18).

Not all civics joined SANCO, because its alignment with the ANC went counter to the view that organs of civil society had to remain autonomous. In the Western Cape, the regional umbrella Cape Housing Action Committee (CAHAC) decided against joining, because it believed that civics should avoid political alignment. In the 1980s, CAHAC had been one of the core affiliates of the UDF in the Western Cape, but as civic leader Willie Simmers (2008) explained, those were exceptional times. Moreover, the view of civics as a conduit for ongoing citizen participation at local level is rather romanticized. Civic meetings attract a full house when some immediate threat has to be addressed, but between crises, township residents manifest little interest in civic matters.

The Rise and Decline of Social Movement Media

One characteristic feature of the UDF and many of its affiliates was the creative use of media, ranging from posters, T-shirts, and liberation songs to community newspapers. Alternative newspapers gave people an opportunity to shape their own news on their own terms, but the UDF could also boast a sophisticated public relations strategy. Talented UDF media activists invested lots of energy in cultivating contacts in the mainstream media. While state-controlled media such as the SABC (South African Broadcasting Corporation) were beyond their scope, they generally found a sympathetic hearing in the English liberal press; newspapers like the *Cape Times*, the *Star*, or the *Daily News*; and even in the Afrikaans newspapers.

Community newspapers like *Grassroots* and alternative weeklies like *New Nation* or *Vrye Weekblad* came to depend heavily on overseas donor money. In 1990, donor funding began drying up as reader interest in political news waned, particularly after the 1994 elections. With the exception of the *Mail and Guardian*, all alternative weeklies folded. Ventures to give papers like *South* a new lease on life by adopting a more commercially viable editorial formula failed. The vacuum was filled by commercial knock and drops (free papers full of advertising), community radio, and much later, by sensationalist tabloids like the *Sun*, featuring crime, sex, and sports rather than rent boycotts and detention without trial. Unlike the community newspapers, community radio by and large did not perceive itself as an instrument to mobilize and conscientize the masses.

While the UDF's media strategists were on the whole satisfied with the role played by the country's main newspapers, new social movements such as the APF, the AEC (established in 2000), and Abahlali baseMjondolo (AbM; "people living in shacks" in Zulu) feel marginalized in the media. Among the old media is the ubiquitous T-shirt, which no doubt owes some of its popularity to its usefulness as a free piece of clothing. When the AbM embarked on its campaign to boycott elections, its activists wore red T-shirts with the slogan "No land! No house! No vote!" (Willems 2010: 495). Apart from T-shirts, songs and dance mark most marches organized by the APF, AbM, and AEC. New is the widespread use of Internet, video, and cell phones. APF, AbM, and AEC all have their own websites, which increase their national and international visibility. E-mail distribution lists have enabled movements to circulate press statements about marches, arrests of activists, and ongoing court cases to journalists, fellow activists, and sympathizers. As in the 1980s, social movement media still benefit from assistance by sympathizers with expert knowledge, whether silkscreen printing in the 1980s or designing websites in the twenty-first century.

Wendy Willems points to the rapid proliferation of cell phones. While in 2007 only 8 percent of South Africans used the Internet, 87 percent owned a cell phone. Although most social movement activists do not have direct access to the Internet, nearly all have cell phones, which enable them to effectively mobilize their constituency. She quotes an AbM activist as saying, "Without the cellphone, there is no organization" (2010: 494).

Legacies of the UDF

Who Were the Activists?

Much of the academic discourse in South Africa in the 1980s focused on the class composition of the liberation movement. The UDF proclaimed itself a multirace and multiclass alliance, but this inclusive approach had to be reconciled with the dual principles of African leadership and working-class leadership. This issue was obviously of vital importance to those who wanted to carry the struggle beyond national liberation to socialist transformation. It was widely believed that the class base of the alliances formed in the 1980s would determine which class would rule a postapartheid society. From a radical perspective, it was of strategic interest to secure a leading role for the working class and to keep the petty bourgeoisie in check. In the influential analysis of the social composition of the liberation movement by John Saul and S. Gelb, the petty bourgeoisie are cast as potential traitor, ready to betray the revolutionary cause and to abandon their working-class allies in favor of a reformed, nonracial capitalism (1986).

Other authors took a more positive view of the petty bourgeoisie, arguing that, not the proletariat, but the aspiring middle class was the driving force in challenging the apartheid state. Tom Lodge and Bill Nasson observe that the UDF was largely a movement of the poor but that a disproportionate share of the original UDF leadership came from a radicalized middle-class intelligentsia who spoke a language quite removed from working-class experience and culture (1991: 55). However, in 1985 the profile of the regional executives became more militant and more working class, while maintaining elements of an intellectual-professional leadership such as lawyers and medical doctors.

While much of the academic analysis focused on the race-class debate, the engine of mass mobilization in the 1980s was youth. "Youth" is of course a very broad category that could include anybody between, say, twelve and thirty-five. Youth in the sense of young political activists tended to be relatively well-educated and overwhelmingly male. They were not desperate paupers but young people who were not prepared to put up with the hardships and humiliations endured by their parents. Often they were the first generation in their families to attend secondary school or tertiary education.

Unlike race, gender, and (mostly) class, youth is of course a transitory if sometimes extended phase in people's lives. At the onset of the democratic transition, many youth activists were ready to embark on the next phase in life: the time had come to establish a family, find a job, or complete their studies and settle down. The UDF was carried by the generation that reached adulthood during the 1980s. The post-1990 generation, known as born-frees, is less inclined to engage in sociopolitical activism. Social movements are about people: activism as a lifelong career is rare.

The vast majority of my informants, whom I contacted again some eighteen years after the first interviews, are no longer involved in social or political activism, and many are no longer active in the ANC. However, the social networks have largely survived, not necessarily in terms of friendship but in terms of being aware of the whereabouts of other ex-members. A sense of disillusionment is most palpable when ex-activists discuss their former comrades. Some are genuinely appalled by the ruthless power struggles. Others resent the success of their contemporaries and have exaggerated expectations of what the person on top could be doing to assist less fortunate comrades. Some were expecting to be rewarded by the ANC for their commitment and sacrifices and now feel abandoned.

From Universalism to Particularism: What Happened to Nonracialism?

The struggle against apartheid was framed in terms of universal values. The ANC in exile campaigned to have apartheid condemned as a crime against humanity. Nowadays ANC politicians make frequent recourse to the particularist values of Africanist ideologies, advocating African solutions for African problems or invoking African traditions. In the case of Zimbabwe, the call for African solutions—meant to delegitimate policy interventions from the West—often comes from the very same politicians who once campaigned for sanctions and boycotts against apartheid South Africa.

In the heated debate within the ANC about the nationalization of mines, the ANC Youth League, a fervent campaigner for nationalization, recently objected to the composition of a study group of ANC ministers with economic and financial portfolios: since Africans were in a minority in this group, it would not reflect the aspirations of the African majority. The ministers concerned were not whites but Coloreds and Indians—categories until recently accepted as black (Letsoalo 2010). In the 1980s, activists claimed their rights as South Africans and as fellow human beings. Now they invoke their Africanness as a resource, in both the ideological and the material competition.

African nationalism seems set to become the new hegemonic discourse. It may indeed provide the glue that secures the loyalty of the ANC's main constituency, but in the process another cherished principle of the liberation struggle, nonracialism, is increasingly under pressure. Numerous Colored, Indian, and white UDF activists have become disillusioned with the exclusive brand of African nationalism that has succeeded Mandela's Rainbow Nation. Often content with their careers and current status in society, they are no longer active members of the ANC. The UDF provided them with a political home, but their initial enthusiasm for the ANC was soon dampened by a sense of not belonging. In 2007, journalist Ryland Fisher, a former UDF activist in the Western Cape, published *Race*. In the introduction, he argues that issues of race, racism, and race-consciousness continue to pervade every corner of South African society. Like many Colored students of his generation, Fisher adopted the identity of black under the influence of the writings of Steve Biko.

> Recently, however, I have noticed that people who used to accept me as black now refer to me as coloured and, by that action, exclude me and others who may or may not look like me from the majority of South Africans once again. (Fisher 2007: 5)

Have the Erstwhile Ideals of a Participatory, Egalitarian Society Been Betrayed?

South Africa has become the world's most unequal society, having recently surpassed Brazil. The government's policies of Black Economic Empowerment, aimed at increasing black ownership of the economy, have created a wealthy, politically well-connected black elite and a rapidly growing black middle class, while one-third of black South Africans of working age remain unemployed. Citizen participation is no doubt more extensive than in many other parliamentary democracies, but most lines of communication amount to a top-down exercise in the management of public opinion.

As in the 1980s and early 1990s, I often encountered in my interviews in 2006–2010 a profound distrust in pluralism. ANC officials and representatives often do not see a distinction between party and state and perceive the ANC as the sole legitimate locus of power. This legitimacy is derived from its past as the liberation movement that defeated apartheid. Jonny Steinberg makes similar observations in his analysis of the civics movement when he states that the leadership of resistance in the 1980s is inclined to see itself as the "authentic" leadership, the only legitimate voice of the people (2000: 193).

ANC politicians in the rural district of Sekhukhuneland tend to view opposition as illegitimate. It is all right to have the Democratic Alliance in Cape Town—that is a thing for whites, anyway. However, in one's own district, municipality, or constituency, rival political parties such as the Pan Africanist Congress (PAC) and Azanian People's Organisation (AZAPO) ought to be silenced, sidelined, or even crushed. The distinct historical traditions in different parts of South Africa have produced different understandings of the concept of democracy. In Sekhukhuneland, the ANC has been deeply rooted for at least half a century. When I conducted my research in 1990–1991 into UDF affiliates such as the Sekhukhune Youth Organization (SEYO), I found that numerous activists had never heard of the UDF. Through their activities in youth movements, they belonged to "the organization"—and "the organization" was the ANC.

In the African township of Kagiso (west of Johannesburg), activists in the 1980s organized in a civic association, Krugersdorp Residents' Organisation (KRO), that was affiliated with the UDF, and most township activists perceived themselves as KRO activists. The Africanist tendency in Kagiso organized a rival civic association. The Western Cape lacks a strong ANC tradition, but has a long history of fragmented political opposition and religious diversity. In the 1980s, UDF activists in the Western Cape were not inclined to accommodate political rivals in the antiapartheid struggle, but nowadays most former activists here view political pluralism as an essential characteristic of constitutional democracy.

Around 1990, activists framed their aspirations in Marxist terms. Asked about his vision for South Africa, Maurice Nchabeleng, a youth leader in Sekhukhuneland, stated in 1990, "I want the dictatorship of the proletariat."

Looking back in 2007, he reformulated his ambitions at the time as "We wanted to go to the place of the whites."

Activists wanted a better life, modeled on the comfortable lifestyle of white South Africans. This aspiration was framed in the dominant discourse of the liberation struggle at that time—that is, a mix of Marxism and African nationalism. Marxism seemed to make eminent sense as an analysis of South African society and, moreover, it assured with scientific certainty that the class struggle would lead the workers to victory. Being versed in Marxism added to one's prestige as an advanced cadre.

Nowadays, getting rich and focusing on individual advancement have become acceptable aspirations in ANC circles. Former activists now frame their aspirations in the currently dominant terminology. But have the aspirations really changed? Or is it rather the mode of expression that has changed?

Egalitarian ideals are currently out of fashion. Among quite a few former activists, Margaret Thatcher's TINA policy (there is no alternative, for the free market and liberal orthodoxy) has become received wisdom. Others indeed speak of betrayal, but more often than not they feel betrayed by former comrades rather than by more abstract ANC policies. Some critics of the neoliberal order seem genuinely committed to their belief in a more just society, but quite a few just want a share of the riches. A former youth leader in Sekhukhuneland expressed his frustrations eloquently:

> Self-proclaimed communists have become capitalists. The ANC has become a bourgeois national democratic movement. Only people with money own the ANC. The SACP has become a forum for people who missed out on opportunities and positions. Some of them know nothing about communism. (M. Mabotha 2007)

Still versed in Marxism, Moss Mabotha had a ready explanation: "One's world outlook is determined by one's class position." But in spite of all his articulate criticism, the bottom line of his resentment was that he wanted to be part of the good life. He admitted to being jealous: "I also want to be rich" (2007).

Although many former activists expressed a sense of dissatisfaction, more often than not their discontent focused on former comrades in the struggle, rather than on ANC policies per se. Youth leader Silas Mabotha, who went on to become a high school principal in Sekhukhuneland, remarked that trust among former comrades has been undermined: "We cannot even advise former comrades, because they suffer from paranoia. They think you are after their job" (2006). Mabotha, reputed to have been a militant and articulate youth activist, is not today active in the ANC, "just like most of us." The ANC government, he complains, follows a capitalist agenda:

> The BEE [Black Economic Empowerment] is nothing else but building a black bourgeoisie. Unemployment is growing while some people

become superrich. We see privatization and casualization [replacement of permanent jobs by casual labor with few rights for laborers] of labor. That is not what we fought for, privatization. They are trying to do away with government altogether. (2006)

However, Mabotha also wants to share in the fruits of liberation: "We are worried that they will have run out of Mercedeses before our turn has come" (2006).

The stark increase in socioeconomic differentiation after 1994 has put considerable strain on the comrades' networks. Can solidarity networks survive when members find themselves in vastly different positions? Is jealousy perhaps a means to keep members in check and to remind them of their obligations to group members? How genuine is the commitment to socialism, now and in the past?

Authors such as Dale McKinley and Prishani Naidoo (2004), Patrick Bond (2000), and Marcelle Dawson (2010) stress the commitment to a socialist ideology in many of the new social movements, but to what extent the discourse of the activist leadership represents the sentiments of the grassroots constituency remains uncertain. In much of the criticism of the ANC government, the gross inadequacies in service delivery are blamed on its turn to neoliberalism. The implicit assumption that state-owned enterprises and strong state involvement would deliver better services to the poor remains untested. Considering the much cited lack of capacity in government, notably at the provincial and local level, it is at least doubtful that the provision of housing, water, and electricity would fare better if only the ANC had not betrayed its commitment to state planning.

Nevertheless, the problem remains: how to reconcile the current model of liberal democracy with the expectation of a (more) egalitarian or at least less unequal society? The fundamental flaw of the constitution in the view of many black South Africans is the property clause: a constitution that protects the ill-gotten gains of centuries of dispossession and apartheid lacks legitimacy. Did the Freedom Charter not promise that South Africa's national wealth, "the heritage of all South Africans, shall be restored to the people"?

Old and New Social Movements

Researching the UDF and its legacy is not only of historical interest. The UDF has become a source of inspiration for South Africans who aspire to resurrect a new broad civil-society-type movement. In an analysis of a civil society conference in October 2010, the political analyst Aubrey Matshiqi noted, "It is not uncommon these days to hear people bemoaning the fact that the United Democratic Front (UDF) was disbanded after the unbanning of the African National Congress (ANC) in 1990."

The ANC's reaction to this conference, sponsored by its ally COSATU, was marked by extreme paranoia, with ANC leaders accusing COSATU of sponsoring attempts at regime change. Matshiqi remarked that the ANC viewed the civil society venture as "an attack on the ANC and, therefore, counter-revolutionary" (2010). The incident is illustrative in two respects. It underlines that the UDF is remembered (and romanticized) as the model par excellence of popular mobilization, and it demonstrates that the ANC, carried to power on the strength of the trade union movement and popular mass movements in the 1980s, has acquired authoritarian traits that make it suspicious of spontaneity and criticism.

During the honeymoon years of Mandela's presidency, the relationship between state and civil society was largely collaborative. Former activists moved into government. Some cut their ties with their previous activist constituency, but others remained connected and responsive to grassroots concerns. For some years after 1994, there was a widespread expectation that the need for adversarial social struggle with the state was over. Social conflict was not absent, as demonstrated by strikes, contests over the demarcation of the newly formed provinces and municipalities, and anticrime protests. But in most cases there was no sustained protest. State–civil society engagements came to be largely defined by collaborative relations (Ballard, Habib, and Valodia 2006: 1).

As argued by the editors of an authoritative volume on social movements in postapartheid South Africa, the new collaborative relationship between the state, on the one hand, and the unions and civic associations, on the other, was partly facilitated by the new government's attempts to create an enabling political and financial environment. Corporatist institutions were established in which not only the unions but also NGOs and community-based organizations were represented. Public funding agencies were established to direct financial resources to the sector. Most importantly, government enabled the subcontracting of development services to civil society actors (Ballard, Habib, and Valodia 2006: 2).

For the trade unions, the honeymoon ended in 1996 when the government introduced a new economic strategy, known as GEAR (Growth, Employment, and Redistribution). GEAR focused on economic growth as the engine to increase employment opportunities and involved trade liberalization and privatization. COSATU branded GEAR as a neoliberal class project that paid only lip service to redistribution. New social movements and protests gained momentum after Mandela's presidency. Under his successor, Thabo Mbeki, the scale of social struggles became an issue of government concern as well as a topic that attracted the attention of numerous scholars, notably Bond (2000); Ashwin Desai (2002); Hein Marais (1998); Richard Ballard, Adam Habib, and Imraan Valodia (2006); and William Beinart and Marcelle Dawson (2010). Opinions differ as to the extent and contents of radical social movements in the first decade of the 2000s, compared with the 1980s. I agree with William Beinart's conclusion that the scale of popular protest in the early 2000s does not rival that of the 1970s and 1980s (2010: 3).

Some contributors to the 2010 volume Beinart and Dawson edited suggest a radicalization of ideologies and a shift from a nationalist and antiracist discourse to socialist positions. I argue that this suggestion betrays a lack of familiarity with the radical contents of the trade union movement, the civics movement, and many other UDF affiliates in the 1980s. Moreover, Marcelle Dawson, in her chapter on the APF, tends to dismiss the socialist discourse by "old" movement activists as empty rhetoric, while accepting at face value the professions of socialism by "new" movement actors (2010: 279). My own interviews with UDF activists then and now illustrate that judging the authenticity of radical discourse over time is problematic.

The Treatment Action Campaign (TAC), often hailed as the most successful of the new social movements, is neither radical nor socialist. It is a broad coalition of people and organizations from different backgrounds who have united to pursue an important but limited goal: greater access to treatment for people living with HIV/AIDS. The TAC is not overtly antagonistic to the ANC, maintains a good relationship with COSATU, and has won its most important victories through the courts. The TAC enjoys largely sympathetic coverage in the mass media and has also made use of popular television programs and new social media to spread the message.

Conversely, the APF understands its role within "a framework of fighting capitalism in the form of neo-liberalism and will not form coalitions with organizations or individuals that support neo-liberalism in any form" (McKinley and Naidoo 2004: 11). The majority of APF members have no previous history in any of the formal structures that led to its birth in 2000. In that sense, the APF is more representative of new actors than the TAC, which includes both old and new activists.

As Beinart points out, knowledge has become an ever more important resource. Social movement activity around service delivery, the environment, health, and culture "place a premium on knowledge-based politics. Ultimately, the Treatment Action Campaign (TAC) has scored its successes through the effective mobilization of scientific knowledge around the treatment of HIV/AIDS as much as its street protests and media-friendly approach" (2010: 8). Like the old movements, most new movements have links with universities or other centers of expertise to provide them with expert advice, whether legal, medical, ideological, or technical.

Unlike civic associations and youth movements, the trade union movement continued to grow after 1990. Membership of trade unions, however, offers immediate benefits, regardless of the changing political environment. Unions represent the interests of their members at the shop floor, on the level of the factory and the industry, and in regular consultation with the government. The trade union movement was firmly established when South Africa entered its phase of democratic transition. Unlike the civics movement, the trade unions did not have to invent a new legitimacy and a new role for themselves, although COSATU kept wrestling with its role in the tripartite alliance with the ANC. As Adler and Steinberg point out, labor movements were accustomed to operating in a fundamentally pluralist environment in which government's, employers', and other union federations' rights to exist were never practically disputed. Therefore, unlike the civics movement, the labor movement did not experience the transition to democracy as a "rude shock" (2000: 15).

Two decades after the onset of the democratic transition, popular protest politics remain largely localized and fragmented. The mass movements of the 1980s have lost their leadership and most gifted activists to the government and the public sector. There might be a parallel here with the United States, where the ghettos became ever more marginalized as the black middle class moved out following emancipation. In spite of all the articulate criticism about the "neoliberal onslaught" under the ANC government, no permanent or semipermanent umbrella structure frames the disparate struggles for housing, water, electricity, jobs, land, and health into a coherent alternative vision. It is true that a great variety of social movements came together at a national level at the World Conference against Racism in 2001 in Durban and again at the World Summit on Sustainable Development in 2002, but this did not result in a more permanent coalition (Ballard, Habib, and Valodia 2006: 19).

Some academics on the left signal the rise of a new militant grassroots activism with a potential to culminate in a new liberation struggle, combining forces against the "betrayal" of the revolution by the ANC government (Saul 2005: 195). In my research, I have heard ample and bitter complaints about the failures of the ANC but have seen no evidence of a broad-based sustained protest movement. This, of course, raises a new question: Why do people acquiesce? But that is the subject of another paper.[7]

NOTES

1. The full text of the charter can be found on the ANC's website at http://www.anc.org.za/show.php?id=72.

2. SANCO meeting notes, October 7, 1991, South African National Civic Organisation records, AL 3052: A1 SANCO, South African History Archives (SAHA), Johannesburg.

3. Gugile Nkwinti, "The Role and Location of the Civic Associations during and after the Transition Period: A Discussion Document," n.d. [1991?], South African National Civic Organisation records, AL 3052: A1, SAHA.

4. Ibid.

5. Dan Sandi, "What Is a Civic Association?," paper presented at Institute for a Democratic Alternative in South Africa conference, Port Elizabeth, South Africa, April 1991, South African National Civic Organisation records, AL 3052, SAHA.

6. For example, criticism came from COSATU first-deputy president Sdumo Dlamini in a speech he delivered to the SANCO Fourth Congress on December 13, 2006.

7. I have analyzed some possible explanations in van Kessel 2008.

REFERENCES

Adler, Glenn, and Jonny Steinberg, eds. 2000. *From Comrades to Citizens: The South African Civics Movement and the Transition to Democracy*. Basingstoke, UK: Macmillan.

Ballard, Richard, Adam Habib, and Imraan Valodia, eds. 2006. *Voices of Protest: Social Movements in Post-Apartheid South Africa*. Scottsville, South Africa: University of KwaZulu-Natal Press.

Beinart, William. 2010. "Popular Politics and Resistance Movements in South Africa, 1970–2008." In *Popular Politics and Resistance Movements in South Africa*, edited by William Beinart and Marcelle Dawson, 1–30. Johannesburg: Wits University Press.

Beinart, William, and Marcelle Dawson, eds. 2010. *Popular Politics and Resistance Movements in South Africa*. Johannesburg: Wits University Press.

Bond, Patrick. 2000. *Elite Transition: From Apartheid to Neoliberalism in South Africa*. London: Pluto Press.

Dawson, Marcelle. 2010. "Phansi Privatisation! Phansi! The Anti-privatisation Forum and Ideology in Social Movements." In *Popular Politics and Resistance Movements in South Africa*, edited by William Beinart and Marcelle Dawson, 266–285. Johannesburg: Wits University Press.

Desai, Ashwin. 2002. *We Are the Poors: Community Struggles in Post-apartheid South Africa*. New York: New York University Press.

Fisher, Ryland. 2007. *Race*. Johannesburg: Jacana.

Green, Pippa. 2008. *Choice, Not Fate: The Life and Times of Trevor Manuel*. Johannesburg: Penguin Books.

Letsoalo, Matuma. 2010. "Nationalisation Row Grinds On." *Mail and Guardian*, November 26.

Lodge, Tom, and Bill Nasson. 1991. *All, Here and Now: Black Politics in South Africa in the 1980s*. Cape Town: David Philip.

Mabotha, Moss. 2007. Interview by the author, March 15, Polokwane, South Africa.

Mabotha, Silas. 2006. Interview by the author, November, Apel, South Africa.

Marais, Hein. 1998. *South Africa: Limits to Change. The Political Economy of Transition*. London: Zed Books.

Matshiqi, Aubrey. 2010. "Dissecting ANC's Hostile Response to Cosatu-Sponsored Civil Society Conference." *Polity Daily News*, November 12. Available at http://www.polity.org.za/article/xxx-2010-11-03.

McKinley, Dale, and Prishani Naidoo, eds. 2004. *Mobilising for Change: The Rise of the New Social Movements in South Africa*. Vol. 5 of *Development Update*. Johannesburg: Interfund.

Nchabeleng, Maurice. 1990. Interview by the author, August, Apel, South Africa.

———. 2007. Interview by the author, March 10, Apel, South Africa.

Saul, John. 2005. *The Next Liberation Struggle: Capitalism, Socialism and Democracy in Southern Africa*. New York: Monthly Review Press.

Saul, John, and S. Gelb. 1986. *The Crisis in South Africa*. New York: Monthly Review Press.

Seekings, Jeremy. 1997. "SANCO: Strategic Dilemmas in a Democratic South Africa." *Transformation* 34:1–30.

———. 2000. "After Apartheid: Civic Organizations in the 'New' South Africa." In *From Comrades to Citizens: The South African Civics Movement and the Transition to Democracy*, edited by Glen Adler and Jonny Steinberg, 205–224. Basingstoke, UK: Macmillan.

Simmers, Willie. 2008. Interview by the author, September 17, Mitchell's Plain, South Africa.

Steinberg, Jonny. 2000. "A Place for Civics in a Liberal Democratic Polity? The Fate of Local Institutions of Resistance after Apartheid." In *From Comrades to Citizens: The South African Civics Movement and the Transition to Democracy*, edited by Glen Adler and Jonny Steinberg, 175–204. Basingstoke, UK: Macmillan.

van Kessel, Ineke. 2000. *"Beyond Our Wildest Dreams": The United Democratic Front and the Transformation of South Africa*. Charlottesville: University Press of Virginia.

———. 2008. "Post-Apartheid South Africa: Class, Culture, the Neo-patrimonial Welfare State and African Nationalism." In *Viva Africa 2008: Proceedings of the Third International Conference on African Studies*, edited by T. Machalík, K. Mildnerová, and J. Záhořík, 162–182. Pilsen, Czech Republic: Adela.

Willems, Wendy. 2010. "Social Movement Media, Post-apartheid (South Africa)." In *Encyclopedia of Social Movement Media*, edited by John Downing, 492–495. Los Angeles: Sage.

11

Movement Politics and Party Politics in Times of Democratic Transition

South Africa, 1994–2000

BERT KLANDERMANS

In 1994 free and democratic elections were held in South Africa. For the first time in the country's history every citizen could cast a vote. After decades of fierce contestation apartheid came to an end. The movement that waged the struggle all those years, the African National Congress (ANC), took office (Klandermans, Roefs, and Olivier 1998). During the era of apartheid, party politics were strictly reserved to the white population, while to the black population remained only movement politics. This changed dramatically with the new dispensation. Movement and party politics intermingled. As in every democracy, South African citizens of all walks of life now had the possibility to influence politics either through political parties or social movements or both.

In this chapter I look into the question of how political engagement of South Africa's citizens transformed with the transition. Did the blacks continue to employ movement politics to influence government, or did they shift to party politics when the ANC took office? Did the whites turn away from party politics and resort to movement politics now their people were no longer controlling the game, or did they lose their interest in politics altogether? And where do the coloreds and the Asians[1] fit in that picture? Did they coalesce with the whites or the blacks, or have they become a political force on their own? These are the kinds of questions I try to answer. I present and discuss data from a study that I and my colleagues conducted between 1995 and 2000 (Klandermans, Roefs, and Olivier 2001). We interviewed random samples of on average 2,200 South Africans each year. We asked how satisfied they were with the social and political situation in their country. We assessed grievances, social and political embeddedness in civil society, evaluation of government, patterns of identification, and engagement in party and movement politics.

Party Politics and Movement Politics

In the social science literature party politics and movement politics are treated as separate phenomena that are independent of each other. Indeed, political parties seem to be the realm of political science and social movements that of sociology. The two assumptions regarding party and movement politics encountered in the literature are the following: (1) The two reinforce each other—people who engage in one also engage in the other (see Barnes and Kaase 1979). In statistical terms one would expect a positive correlation. (2) The two alternate: movement politics compensate for failed party politics, or movements institutionalize into parties (Jenkins and Klandermans 1995)—in other words, a negative correlation. Recently, Swen Hutter (2014) proposed and found empirical support for a third option, that the two follow a logic of their own—in other words, no correlation. I hold that any kind of arrangement between movement and party politics is conceivable. Movements and parties may compete, complement each other, or act in parallel. Participation in movement and party politics often operates in tandem (Meyer and Tarrow 1998), and organizations channeling party and movement politics are intertwined (Goldstone 2003). If movements institutionalize, citizens may opt for party politics as reflected in electoral successes and declining protest activity. Conversely, if party politics fail, citizens may resort to movement politics, reflected in declining votes and rising protest activity.

Figure 11.1 summarizes the conceptual framework of the chapter. The sociopolitical context that a society provides its citizens can be characterized by a set of cleavages—such as class, race, ethnicity, religion, gender, generation, and victims of modernization and globalization. They shape the state and the political processes it encompasses (Lipset and Rokkan 1967; Kriesi et al. 1995; Hutter 2014; Jansen 2011). A society's multiorganizational field reflects the social cleavages in that society—for example, the structure of civil society, the party system, and the movement sector. The citizens who populate a society address demands to the state that are rooted in the cleavages these citizens are embedded in. In their attempts to influence politics, citizens may chose to engage in party politics, movement politics, or both. In that respect, the South African context is not different from that in any other democracy. Hence, I maintain that cleavages, multiorganizational fields, and a supply of movement and party politics shape the political landscape of the country. In the pages to come I further theorize about the reasons citizens engage in party politics and movement politics. Next I present data from research conducted between 1995 and 2000 on how engagement in politics differed between the four population groups in the country and how it changed over the first years of the transition to democracy.

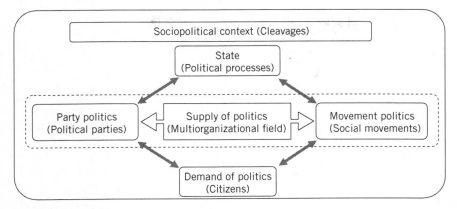

Figure 11.1 Routes to political influence.

Why People Want to Influence Politics and How

Demand of Politics

People adhere to different political leanings, have different interests and principles, are differentially embedded in society, and identify with different groups. Therefore, demand of politics in a society is not a one-dimensional story. South Africa is a divided country. The apartheid state cooked identity politics to perfection. As a consequence, during the apartheid era it made a real difference whether someone was defined as white, black, colored, or Asian. Although South African society is no longer built on the racial divide, race still very much determines where someone stands in society, even though race, class, gender, and generation are increasingly blurred. Against that background, why would South African citizens want to influence politics, and would they then engage in party politics, movement politics, or both?

As a first factor I propose grievances. A reason citizens might want to influence politics is that they are dissatisfied and aggrieved or have frustrated aspirations and believe that by engaging in party or movement politics they can make things change (Simon and Klandermans 2001). At the same time, we know that grievances and aspirations alone are not sufficient reasons for people to engage in politics. A feeling of efficacy—that is, the belief that one can exert some influence on politics—is an important moderator.

A second factor, next to grievances and efficacy, which make citizens more or less ready to engage in politics, is embeddedness in civil society. I and colleagues (2008) demonstrate elsewhere the significance of social embeddedness for political participation. The more embedded people are, the more likely they are to participate in politics. This holds for embeddedness in civil society in general and more specifically for embeddedness in political organizations. Embeddedness has a behavioral and an affective component. As for the behavioral component, people are involved in social organizations as members—active or passive—or as officials; as for the affective element, people identify more or less with the social groups they belong to—be they ethnic group, class, gender, or generation. At the same time people may display a degree of overarching, national identification. Dual identity—that is, the combination of subgroup identities with an overarching national identity—allegedly comes with fewer grievances, but if people are aggrieved, evidence suggests that they are more likely to engage in politics (Klandermans, van de Toorn, and van Stekelenburg 2008; Simon 2011).

A third reason citizens may or may not be inclined to influence politics is their evaluation of government. Robert Folger (1986) in his exposé on referent cognition theory argues that relative deprivation will not generate much resentment when it is expected to resolve in the near future. Indeed, optimism about the future (Klandermans, Roefs, and Olivier 2001) reduces people's readiness to act collectively because they feel that there is no need to. On the other hand, one may expect that trust in government encourages people to engage in politics (Giugni, McAdam, and Tilly 1999). Indeed, earlier studies found that political cynicism—the opposite of trust—both encourages and discourages political participation (Klandermans, van de Toorn, and van Stekelenburg 2008).

Supply of Politics

Grievances, efficacy, social embeddedness, and trust in government may spur citizens to engage in politics, but whether they opt for party politics, movement politics, or both depends on the supply of politics. Which parties and movement organizations prevail in their society, and to what extent do they offer opportunities to participate and influence politics? What makes people direct their political activity to party politics or movement politics? In fact, must they choose, or can they engage in party and movement politics at the same time? As indicated, evidence supports a reinforcement hypothesis—that is, people who engage in party politics are more likely to engage in movement politics as well and vice versa (a positive correlation). Other evidence supports an alternation hypothesis—that is, people who participate in the one activity participate less or not at all in the other (a negative correlation). And there is evidence supporting a separate logic hypothesis—that is, each form of participation adheres to a logic of its own (no correlation). If citizens fail to access party politics, they may resort to movement politics. On the other hand, people may see no need for movement politics when party politics work to their satisfaction, for instance, because their allies are in office (McCarthy, Rafail, and Gromis 2013). In the short term, people may spend all their energy in their party's election campaign and thus temporarily refrain from movement politics (McAdam and Tarrow 2013). Social embeddedness is a crucial factor in steering political engagement. Obviously, social embeddedness not only influences levels of involvement in politics but also sends political activity in the direction of party politics, movement politics, or both, depending on the makeup of the networks people are embedded in.

A Note on Methods

The data this chapter is based on stem from six surveys that I and colleagues conducted annually between February 1995 and March 2000.[2] The first survey was conducted in February 1995, the year after the first national democratic elections in South Africa; the last survey was conducted six years later in March 2000, nine months after the second national election in 1999. The surveys were always held at the same time of year—February or March.

Sampling: The surveys interviewed representative samples of the South African population. Every year a new probability sample was drawn by means of multistage, stratified cluster sampling. The samples totaled 2,226 (1995), 2,228 (1996), 2,220 (1997), 2,227 (1998), 2,210 (1999), and 2,666 (2000). Overall, the six samples proved to be well comparable. Comparisons over time of the four racial groups of the samples for age, sex, and education revealed that these groups were similar as far as gender was concerned but slightly different in terms of age and levels of education. However, multivariate analyses of variance (MANOVAs) with the key variables of our study as dependent variables and with age, education, and time as factors revealed no significant interactions. Hence, there was no indication that the observed differences between our samples would distort our conclusions.

Data collection: Data were collected by means of face-to-face interviews in people's homes. The interviews were carried out by trained interviewers and conducted in one of the eleven official languages. The interviews lasted thirty to forty-five minutes.

Questionnaire: The questionnaire employed in the survey contained questions regarding (1) grievances; (2) feelings of relative deprivation (individual situation or group situation); (3) social comparison (comparison of self or group with others or with other groups); (4) collective identity; (5) involvement in civil society organizations; (6) perceptions of national, provincial, and local government; (7) political interest (voting intention or party support); (8) actual participation and preparedness to take part in peaceful, militant, or violent protest; and (9) issues people would or did protest for.

Engagement in Party Politics and Movement Politics

We asked our respondents whether they would consider voting if there were elections. Close to four-fifths of our interviewees indicated that they would cast their vote. The remaining one-fifth said that they would not vote or did

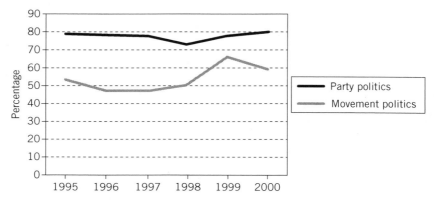

Figure 11.2 Movement politics and party politics.

not know (Figure 11.2). The year 1998 slightly deviates from that pattern, with three-quarters intending to vote compared to one-quarter who did not intend to or did not know. Also in Figure 11.2 are displayed the percentages of South Africans who indicated that they would take part in peaceful protest such as signing petitions, displaying posters, attending rallies, marching, demonstrating, painting slogans on walls, and so on. The first four years the numbers hover around 50 percent, but in 1999 the figure jumps to two-thirds and remains high in 2000. Interestingly, 1999 is an election year. As a first finding regarding my theoretical assumptions, this suggests that, if anything, party politics and movement politics reinforce each other rather than compete. The positive correlations between voting intentions and action preparedness suggest the same, although the correlations are only moderate: .18, .20, and .19 in 1995, 1996, and 1997, respectively, and even lower (.13, .15, and .12) in the last three years. This suggests that the two forms of political activity are not mutually exclusive but do not necessarily go together either. There seems to be room for the third hypothesis: movement and party politics follow their own logic. In any event, the proportion of the population engaging in politics—both party politics and movement politics—gives little indication that the transition to democracy was accompanied by depoliticization. To the contrary, voting figures remained fairly stable, while action preparedness actually increased.

Before I focus on these figures and their explanations, a short digression regarding which parties people intend to vote for and the issues they could imagine taking action for is informative. In our surveys, the vast majority of the black population intends to vote for the ANC and did indeed vote for that party in 1994 and 1999. Very few lean toward other parties, not even the Inkatha Freedom Party—ANC's competitor among the Zulu population especially in KwaZulu-Natal. Those blacks who do not intend to vote for the ANC instead abstain. White South Africans, on the other hand, rarely vote for the ANC.

TABLE 11.1   ISSUES PEOPLE MAY PROTEST FOR (%)

	1995	1996	1997	1998	1999	2000
Cost of living	16.7	16.4	26.9	22.0	13.7	12.9
Government/political issues	2.6	1.4	3.4	3.2	3.5	2.9
Work-related issues						
Job opportunities	17.6	19.1	19.5	30.3	25.3	29.9
Working conditions	1.6	1.4	1.9	1.4	4.8	4.8
Provision of public goods						
Housing	24.6	35.9	30.3	37.6	30.0	22.9
Education	13.8	15.3	10.7	26.1	14.2	13.7
Health care	3.5	7.3	4.1	8.9	7.5	4.9
Safety	13.4	11.9	15.5	33.5	26.5	32.6
Public services	1.6	1.2	2.0	1.5	20.6	12.3
Rights issues						
Human rights	8.7	8.9	11.9	6.0	7.3	10.6
Women's rights	0.8	2.4	1.6	3.2	3.6	6.1
Children's rights	3.3	5.4	9.5	9.8	8.4	9.7
N	2,226	2,228	2,200	2,227	2,210	2,666

They vote for the National Party of South Africa, the Democratic Party,[3] or one of the small conservative parties. Large portions of the white population intend to abstain from voting altogether—initially more than one-third of the white electorate, but the numbers decline to roughly one-quarter in the survey's last year. The coloreds and the Asians are torn between the ANC, the National Party or Democratic Party, and abstention.

Many of the issues our interviewees could imagine protesting for are related to the functioning of the government. Increasing proportions of the population consider protesting about the lack of delivery of public goods and services such as housing, education, health care, and crime prevention. Significant numbers also imagine participating in protest regarding rights issues (human, women's, children's; Table 11.1). These figures teach us about what people care about and what they would want to influence politics for: work, public goods, cost of living, and citizenship rights.

Movement and Party Politics

We are now ready to look in more detail into the routes people take if they want to influence politics. Table 11.2 maps the four theoretically possible patterns of political activity. Forty-five percent of our respondents reports engaging in both party politics and movement politics. Over one-tenth (12.6 percent) admits to not engaging in either form of political activity. One-third takes part in only

TABLE 11.2   MOVEMENT POLITICS AND PARTY POLITICS (%)

	Will not vote/Don't know what to vote	Will vote
Will not participate in peaceful action	12.6	33.2
Will participate in peaceful action	8.8	45.4

Note: N = 12,687.

party politics and 8.8 percent in only movement politics. As mentioned earlier, the correlation between the two political activities is modest (Pearson's *r* is .16 across the surveys).

The four racial categories differ significantly in how they engage in politics (Figure 11.3). Blacks are the most politically engaged. More than 50 percent (54.7 percent) of the black population engages in both movement and party politics, whereas not even 10 percent (7.3 percent) is involved in neither. Close to 30 percent (29.7 percent) takes part in only party politics, and 8.3 percent in only movement politics. The reverse can be observed among the whites: low levels (22.4 percent) of white citizens are involved in both party and movement politics, and high levels (26.5 percent) are not involved in either. Over two-fifths (42.5 percent) of whites engage in only party politics and 8.6 percent in only movement politics. One-third of coloreds (32.7 percent) and Asians (34.1 percent) take part in both types of political activity. One-fifth (17.4 percent and 22.1 percent, respectively) of the two groups abstains from politics altogether. The two groups differ only with regard to participation in party politics and movement politics: 40.7 percent of coloreds participated in only party politics compared to 29.7 percent of Asians. On the other hand, 14.2 percent of Asian and 9.2 percent of coloreds engaged in only movement politics.

The proportion of the population trying to influence politics fluctuates over time (Figure 11.4). Initially, a stable 15 percent of South African citizens refrained from political activity altogether. But in the election year that figure

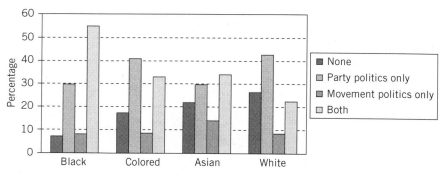

Figure 11.3 Movement and party politics by population group.

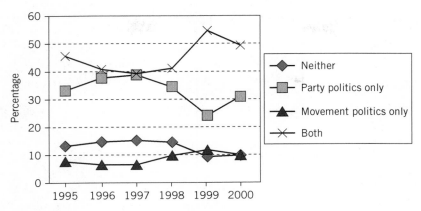

Figure 11.4 Movement and party politics by year.

dropped to 9.2 percent to remain close to that level the year after (9.9 percent). Between 1995 and 1998, the number of citizens who were involved in both movement and party politics declined from 46 percent to 40 percent but jumped to 55 percent in the election year, 1999. A year later the figure was 50 percent, still significantly higher than two years before. Obviously, the election year meant a boost in political involvement, and interestingly, involvement manifested itself in increasing numbers of citizens who engage in both party politics *and* movement politics. Paradoxically, and unlike what one would expect in an election year, this is predominantly at the expense of the proportion of the people who engage in party politics only, which declined from 39 percent in 1997 to 24 percent in 1999. The proportion of the population that participated in movement politics increased to only roughly one-tenth in 1998 and stayed at that level the last three years. In other words, party and movement politics seem to reinforce each other. Indeed, the number of citizens who engaged in movement politics increased in the election year rather than declined, while the number of those who took part only in party politics declined.

Grievances, Embeddedness, and the Evaluation of Government

What accounts for the diverging patterns of political activity? At the chapter's beginning I suggest grievances, efficacy, embeddedness, and trust in government. Table 11.3 gives the means, standard deviations, and intercorrelations of the independent variables included in the analyses: relative deprivation, influence on government, embeddedness, involvement in political parties, interest in politics, and trust in government. *Grievances* were measured as relative deprivation, or the extent to which people deem their situation worse or better than that in the past or that of others and assume that it will or will not improve in the future. The mean and median of the relative deprivation measure are beyond the midpoint of the scale, indicating that a majority of the citizens felt deprived. *Efficacy* was assessed by asking whether the interviewee believed he or she could influence government, on a seven-point scale from not at all to very much. The means and medians of influence on government were also beyond the midpoint of the scale, indicating that a majority believed they have influence on government. Embeddedness consists of social embeddedness, identity, involvement in political parties, and political interest. Social embeddedness is operationalized as the number of organizations a person is a member of. Forty-five percent of our interviewees were not a member of any organization; 28 percent were a member of one organization (often church related). The remaining 28 percent were a member of two or more organizations. Not included in Table 11.3 are the levels of identification. We constructed a dual identity measure by combining national identification and identification with one of four groups (ethnicity, class, gender, and generation—four categories relevant in the South African context).[4] A quarter (25.1 percent) of our respondents displayed a dual identity—that is, national identity in combination with identification with at least one of the four groups. One-fifth (18.2 percent) displayed only a national identity. Two-fifths (40.3 percent) of our respondents identified with only one of the subgroups, while a quarter (26.3 percent) displayed no identification with a subgroup and no national identification. Involvement in political parties concerns citizens' involvement in political parties (being active members). Fifty-six percent of our interviewees were not involved in political parties; 30 percent were passively affiliated with a political party, and the remaining 14 percent were actively involved in a political party. Interest in politics is how much people read and talk about politics. On average, our interviewees were not much interested in politics. Trust in government related to whether people trust government to act in their interest, assessed on a five-point scale from never to always. The mean and median for the trust in government measure are beyond the midpoint of the scale, indicating that a majority trust government.

TABLE 11.3   MEANS, STANDARD DEVIATIONS, AND CORRELATIONS

Variable	Mean (standard deviation)	Correlation							
		1	2	3	4	5	6	7	8
1. Relative deprivation*	3.69 (0.93)	—							
2. Influence on government*	3.86 (1.32)	−.29	—						
3. Social embeddedness†	1.12 (1.51)	−.08	.13	—					
4. Involvement in political party‡	1.55 (0.72)	−.07	.12	.46	—				
5. Interest in politics§	2.19 (1.10)	−.04	.14	.19	.23	—			
6. Trust in government§	2.82 (1.19)	−.39	.41	.08	.13	.03	—		
7. Will vote (no = 1, yes = 2)	1.78 (0.41)	−.16	.13	.10	.17	.07	.18	—	
8. Will participate in peaceful action‡	2.44 (1.16)	−.16	.19	.17	.21	.14	.19	.16	—

* Scale: 1–7; † Scale: 1–10; ‡ Scale: 1–4; § Scale: 1–5.
Note: $10,000 < n < 14,000$; all correlations are significant to $p < .05$.

TABLE 11.4   PARTY AND MOVEMENT POLITICS BY IDENTIFICATION PATTERN
(MEANS AND STANDARD DEVIATIONS)

	No group ID/ no national ID	Group ID/ no national ID	No group ID/ national ID	Group ID/ national ID
Party politics	1.75 (0.43)	1.76 (0.42)	1.80 (0.40)	1.81 (0.39)
Movement politics	2.29 (1.06)	2.48 (1.12)	2.52 (1.21)	2.68 (1.18)

The last two rows of Table 11.3 present the Pearson correlations of the independent variables with our two dependent variables (voting and taking part in peaceful action). Relative deprivation is negatively correlated with both forms of political participation. The more deprived citizens feel, the less they participate in both party politics and movement politics. Influence on government is positively correlated with both forms of participation. The more people feel that they can influence government, the more they are prepared to participate in politics. Social embeddedness, especially embeddedness in political parties, fosters both party politics and movement politics. In fact, it fosters movement politics even more than party politics. Interestingly, embeddedness in political parties reinforces movement politics more than party politics, yet another indication that movement and party politics reinforce one another. Trust in government increases participation in both party and movement politics. Thus, both forms of political participation signify feelings of trust rather than distrust. Of further interest are the negative correlations of relative deprivation with influence on and trust in government. The more deprived citizens feel, the less influence and trust in government they have, as one would expect.

Because the identification measure is a nominal scale, it could not be included in Table 11.3. A MANOVA reveals that both forms of participation vary between the different identification patterns; the differences are not very large but significant at $p < .001$ with the sizable samples (see Table 11.4). Political participation appears highest among citizens with a dual identity and lowest among those with neither national identity nor identity with any of the four subgroups.

Multivariate Analyses

So far, I have discussed only univariate analyses, except for the identification measure, but multivariate analyses are needed to estimate the unique contribution of individual factors. Table 11.5 summarizes the results of a multinomial regression analysis with political participation as dependent variable. Dummies of racial category and year of survey were entered in a first step as control variables. Because the figures for these controls reveal the patterns we know already from the zero-order relations and because they did not change the patterns of the model variables much, I did not include them in the table. In the table the means and standard deviations of the explanatory variables in the full model are given. The reference category in the regression analysis is neither party nor

TABLE 11.5   MOVEMENT AND PARTY POLITICS: MULTINOMIAL REGRESSION
(STANDARDIZED MEANS AND STANDARD DEVIATIONS)

	None	Movement politics only	Party politics only	Movement and party politics
Relative deprivation	.36 (0.97)	.22 (1.06)[ns]	.06 (1.0)**	−.20 (0.97)***
Influence on government	−.39 (0.96)	−.08 (1.02)**	−.11 (0.99)*	.19 (0.10)***
Social embeddedness	−.29 (0.65)	−.02 (0.92)***	−.09 (0.91)*	.17 (1.13)***
Involvement in political party	−.48 (0.71)	−.17 (0.93)**	−.13 (0.94)***	.21 (1.03)***
Interest in politics	−.27 (0.92)	−.06 (0.96)***	−.14 (0.99)*	.07 (0.99)***
Trust in government	−.37 (0.89)	−.27 (0.94)[ns]	−.07 (0.96)**	.25 (1.01)***

Note: $N = 8,354$. Not included are the controls racial category and year of survey. Full model Nagelkerke's $R^2 = .19$.
Reference category is none, neither party nor movement politics.
* $p < .05$; ** $p < .01$; *** $p < .001$; ns = not significant.

movement politics, hence the table shows to what extent the explanatory factors for the various participation patterns differ significantly from those of nonparticipation. The significance tests are the outcomes of the multinomial regression analysis for the full model. For clarity I present the means for the reference category as well.

Twelve percent of the variance in political participation is variation over time and by racial category.[5] Each of the three explanatory variable clusters contributes significantly to the variance explained while reducing the chi-square for time and race alone. Entering relative deprivation and influence on government into the equation increases the explained variance to 14.5 percent. Entering embeddedness next, the explained variance increases to 18.4 percent, while trust in government finally raises the explained variance to 18.9 percent. On their own the model variables explain 13.3 percent of the variance in political participation, which indicates that they account for part of the variation over time and by race. Indeed, entering the model variables reduces the chi-squares for time and especially for race, suggesting that a fair proportion of the differences in participation between the racial categories relate to differences in grievances, embeddedness, and evaluation of government among the four population groups.[6]

These global outcomes are detailed further in Table 11.5. As for feelings of relative deprivation, they reveal that respondents who participated in only movement politics were not more or less deprived than the reference category— that is, than those who took part in neither activity. Those who participated in only party politics or in both party and movement politics were *less* deprived— especially those who participated in both. Perceived influence on government is the highest among those who engage in both movement and party politics and the lowest among those who engage in neither. The other two groups are in between, but below average. Embeddedness revealed a consistent pattern: any participation profile came with more embeddedness (both social and political) than the reference category. But there is more to say about the comparison of the components of embeddedness. Social embeddedness is the least for those who engage only in party politics and the highest for those who engage in both movement and party politics. Involvement in political parties, on the other hand, is linked more to engagement in party politics and less to movement politics. However, those who participate in both movement and party politics are the most involved in political parties. Finally, interest in politics is the lowest among participants in party politics and the highest among participants in movement and party politics. Participants in only movement politics occupy an intermediate position, although more akin to those who participate in both movement and party politics. Trust in government, finally, seems more a matter of party politics. Participants in only movement politics are not so much different from those who are not engaged altogether, while participation in party politics does make a difference; the combination of movement and party politics, however, ranks the highest on trust.

In sum, people who are high on relative deprivation, low on perceived influence on government, low on both social and political embeddedness, and who experience little trust in government are most likely to abstain from any political activity. The opposite pattern appears to hold for those who engage in both party politics and movement politics. People who are low on relative deprivation, who feel they have influence on government, who are highly embedded in social and political networks, and who trust in government are likely to be actively involved in both types of political activity. The choice between movement politics or party politics seems to depend on deprivation, embeddedness, and trust as well: compared to those who engage only in party politics, participants in only movement politics feel more deprived and are more socially embedded but less interested in politics and less trustful of government.

Identity, Grievances, and Politics

A final question concerns the links between identity, grievances, and politics. As expected, relative deprivation is low among South Africans who display a dual identity. In fact, what matters is whether someone has a strong national identity, whether or not in combination with a strong subgroup identity (see Table 11.6). What interests us here is the combined working of identity and grievances on political participation. Table 11.7 exhibits the levels of participation in party politics and movement politics for different levels of relative deprivation and patterns of identification. We know already that lower levels of deprivation make political participation more likely—this holds for party politics and the combination of party and movement politics.

Table 11.7 expands the picture. Clearly, for each pattern of identification, participation declines if relative deprivation increases. This holds for both party politics and movement politics. At the same time, with one exception, the level of participation is highest for those respondents who display a dual identity and lowest for those who display neither a subgroup identity nor a national identity.

TABLE 11.6   RELATIVE DEPRIVATION BY IDENTITY PATTERN (MEANS AND
STANDARD DEVIATIONS)

	No group ID/ no national ID	Group ID/ no national ID	No group ID/ national ID	Group ID/ national ID
Relative deprivation	3.74 (0.79)	3.87 (0.96)	3.57 (0.88)	3.56 (1.00)

TABLE 11.7   PARTY POLITICS AND MOVEMENT POLITICS BY RELATIVE
DEPRIVATION AND IDENTITY PATTERN (MEANS AND STANDARD DEVIATION)

	No group ID/ no national ID	Group ID/ no national ID	No group ID/ national ID	Group ID/ national ID
Party politics by relative deprivation				
Low	1.85 (0.36)	1.86 (0.35)	1.87 (0.34)	1.88 (0.33)
Medium	1.79 (0.41)	1.81 (0.39)	1.83 (0.38)	1.84 (0.37)
High	1.71 (0.45)	1.73 (0.45)	1.79 (0.41)	1.73 (0.44)
Movement politics by relative deprivation				
Low	2.42 (0.99)	2.66 (1.03)	2.78 (1.19)	2.85 (1.17)
Medium	2.40 (1.07)	2.56 (1.08)	2.54 (1.20)	2.70 (1.16)
High	2.15 (1.06)	2.41 (1.17)	2.29 (1.17)	2.44 (1.19)

Note: N = 7,453. Party politics: main effect of identity, F = 23.18, degrees of freedom (df) = 3, $p < .001$; main effect of relative deprivation, F = 45.98, df = 2, $p < .001$. Movement politics: main effect of identity, F = 3.37, df = 3, $p < .05$; main effect of relative deprivation, F= 45.45, df = 2, $p < .001$.

The result of these two trends is that the highest level of participation in both party and movement politics is found among people with a dual identity and a low level of grievances; the lowest level of participation is among respondents without any subgroup or national identity and high levels of relative deprivation. These findings corroborate earlier findings that citizens who display a dual identity are more satisfied but are more likely to act on their grievances if they are dissatisfied.

On Population Groups

I now turn to the four population groups that have for such a long time characterized South African society—blacks, coloreds, Asians, and whites. The pattern of relationships is very similar for each of the four groups, but the absolute levels of the various independent variables are different (Table 11.8).

Relative deprivation was lowest among black citizens and highest among whites. Colored and Asian respondents occupied an intermediate position. Perceived influence on government was the highest among the black population and the lowest among the white. The colored and Asian population groups occupied a position in between. Embeddedness was high among blacks and whites and relatively low among coloreds and Asians. This holds for all separate indicators of embeddedness. Indeed, blacks and whites were the groups with

TABLE 11.8   INDEPENDENT VARIABLES VERSUS POPULATION GROUP (MEANS AND STANDARD DEVIATIONS)

	Blacks	Coloreds	Asians	Whites
Relative deprivation	3.57 (0.91)	3.76 (0.84)	3.91 (0.86)	4.14 (0.87)
Influence on government	4.04 (1.27)	3.80 (1.23)	3.73 (1.21)	3.35 (1.39)
Social embeddedness	1.27 (1.65)	0.83 (1.13)	0.63 (1.17)	0.89 (1.07)
Dual identity	28.2%	16.4%	10.4%	23.8%
No identification	22.2%	34.0%	50.0%	29.4%
Involvement in political parties	1.70 (0.76)	1.36 (0.62)	1.18 (0.50)	1.41 (0.69)
Political interest	2.25 (1.10)	2.06 (1.06)	2.39 (1.20)	2.42 (1.11)
Trust in government	2.97 (1.22)	2.71 (1.10)	2.45 (0.97)	2.30 (1.04)

Note: N = 8,354.

the highest proportion displaying a dual identity and the lowest proportion of people who did not identify with any of the four constituents (class, ethnicity, gender, or generation) or the nation. Trust in government was the highest among the black population and the lowest among the whites. The colored and Asian population groups occupied again a position in between. The combined working of these factors at the various levels created the diverging patterns of participation exhibited in Figure 11.3.

Conclusion and Discussion

The six postapartheid years between 1995 and 2000 did not make South African citizens participate less in politics—to the contrary. In that respect South Africa's modern history denies the presumption that democratization of authoritarian regimes comes with depoliticization of the population. In fact, the election year 1999 brought a boost in political activity that lasted at least until the closure of our fieldwork a year later. That year increasing numbers of South African citizens engaged in movement politics, whether in combination with party politics or at the expense of involvement only in party politics. This also denies that democratization implies institutionalization of politics as movement politics fade and transform into party politics. In this chapter I have looked into party politics and movement politics as two options citizens have at their disposal to influence the state. More specifically, I have looked into whether South African citizens intend to vote and intend to participate in peaceful collective action. Moreover, I have tried to understand how their engagement in politics— both party and movement politics—is influenced by such factors as grievances, efficacy, embeddedness, and trust in government.

Movement politics and party politics were positively correlated, although modestly. Indeed, toward the end of our study half our respondents intended to take part in both movement and party politics. Roughly one-third of the South African population engaged only in party politics, and much smaller proportions engaged only in movement politics or abstained from politics altogether. Thus, the combination of party politics and movement politics was the dominant pattern. This, however, holds only for the black population. Among whites and coloreds, only party politics was the dominant pattern, and among Asians the two activity patterns (only party politics and both party and movement politics) were more or less even. Few people were involved only in movement politics. But among nonblack citizens between one-fifth and one-quarter abstained from any political activity. All in all, there was not much reason to assume that movement and party politics are mutually exclusive or that political participation wanes during the transition to democracy. Even among the whites, for whom the levels of participation were the lowest, the tendency over the years was toward higher levels of participation rather than lower levels. It looks thus as if the black population continues to employ movement politics. On the other hand, there are no signs that the white population is turning away from party politics.

Grievances, or more specific feelings of relative deprivation, clearly influenced political participation. People were more likely to participate in political activities when they experienced low levels of relative deprivation. High levels of relative deprivation, on the other hand, reduced levels of participation, a finding that corroborates once again with that of grievances being poor predictors of political participation. Better predictors in this study as well are efficacy, embeddedness, and patterns of identification. Social and political embeddedness differentially affected movement and party politics. These patterns held for each population group, although the level of deprivation differed between the groups. Social and political embeddedness obviously reinforced political participation in both movement and party politics. Although social embeddedness seems more likely to foster movement politics and political embeddedness more likely to foster party politics, both types strongly reinforce the combined employment of movement and party politics. Positive evaluations of government also reinforce the combined use of movement and party politics. We observed lowest levels of trust among South Africans who abstained from politics altogether and highest among those who engaged in both movement and party politics. Of the two possible relations between trust in government and political participation, the positive correlation seems to be the most plausible in view of the results. The choice between movement politics or party politics seems a matter of grievances and trust in government rather than embeddedness. People who engage only in party politics are less aggrieved and trust government more than people who engage only in movement politics.

Ethnicity, class, gender, and generation refer to social cleavages that potentially divide South African society. At the same time, South Africa was involved in a nation-building project in those early days of the transition to democracy. We assessed where people fit into South Africa's social landscape, to what extent people identified with one of the four social categories, and whether they had formed an overarching national identity. Indeed, one-third of our interviewees displayed a strong national identity, and more than one-fifth had a so-called dual identity—that is, a strong subgroup identity in combination with strong national identity. Our results show that, for each type of identity, increasing levels of griev-ances resulted in lower levels of political participation, whether party politics or movement politics. Also, at each level of grievances people having a dual identity featured the highest level of political activity. This was especially true for engage-ment in movement politics whether or not in combination with party politics. These results corroborate our earlier findings with regard to dual identities.

A final observation concerns the changes in participation over time, espe-cially those in the election year. Doug McAdam and Sidney Tarrow (2013) argue that in election years political activists are sucked into the election campaign. Our findings seem to suggest the opposite. What we see is an increase in move-ment and party activities at the expense of only party activities. Admittedly, our party politics measure is a crude one. But importantly, movement activ-ity does not falter during the election year, appearing to grow. South Africa in those days of transition might have been an exception, because the country was still very much on the move and the ANC still very much acting as a movement rather than a party. Nonetheless, it is not uncommon that movement activities intensify during an election campaign as a way to put pressure on politicians. More systematic research of movement politics and party politics is needed to solve that puzzle.

NOTES

1. Black, white, colored, and Asian were the population categories distinguished by the apartheid regime.

2. A seventh survey was conducted in 1994 a few months before the first democratic elections. Because the political participation questions in that survey were different from those employed as of 1995, I report here on the six surveys conducted between 1995 and 2000.

3. During the years of our research the National Party faded away and was replaced by the Democratic Party. In 2000 the Democratic Party was renamed Democratic Alliance. A substantial part of the National Party electorate no doubt now votes for the Democratic Alliance, but after the National Party (renamed New National Party in 1997) dissolved in 2005 its remnants joined the ANC. New National Party leader Martinus van Schalkwijk became ANC minister of tourism.

4. People who chose the two highest scale points (very close or extremely close) were assumed to have identified with that category.

5. The variance was calculated using Nagelkerke's pseudo R-squared.

6. Entering the model variables in the equation reduces chi-squares for race from 1.179^3 to 385.023 and that for time from 265.793 to 208.816.

REFERENCES

Barnes, Samuel H., and Kaase Max. 1979. *Political Action: Mass Participation in Five Western Democracies*. London: Sage.

Folger, Robert. 1986. "A Referent Cognition Theory of Relative Deprivation." In *Relative Deprivation and Social Comparison: The Ontario Symposium*, vol. 4, edited by James M. Olson, C. Peter Herman, and Mark P. Zanna, 33–56. Hillsdale, NJ: Lawrence Erlbaum.

Giugni, Marco, Doug McAdam, and Charles Tilly, eds. 1999. *How Social Movements Matter*. Minneapolis: University of Minnesota Press.

Goldstone, Jack A., ed. 2003. *States, Parties, and Social Movements*. Cambridge: Cambridge University Press.

Hutter, Swen. 2014. *Protesting Culture and Economics in Western Europe: New Cleavages in Left and Right Politics*. Minneapolis: University of Minnesota Press.

Jansen, Giedo. 2011. "Social Cleavages and Political Choices: Large-Scale Comparisons of Social Class, Religion and Voting Behavior in Western Democracies." Ph.D. diss., Radboud University Nijmegen.

Jenkins, Craig, and Bert Klandermans. 1995. "The Politics of Social Protest." In *The Politics of Social Protest: Comparative Perspectives of States and Social Movements*, edited by Craig Jenkins and Bert Klandermans, 3–13. Minneapolis: University of Minnesota Press/University College of London Press.

Klandermans, Bert, Marlene Roefs, and Johan Olivier. 1998. "A Movement Takes Office." In *The Social Movement Society: Contentious Politics for a New Century*, edited by David S. Meyer and Sidney Tarrow, 173–194. Lanham: Rowman and Littlefield.

———. 2001. *The State of the People: Citizens, Civil Society and Governance in South Africa, 1994–2000*. Pretoria: Human Science Research Council.

Klandermans, Bert, Jojanneke van de Toorn, and Jacquelien van Stekelenburg. 2008. "Embeddedness and Grievances: Collective Action Participation among Immigrants." *American Sociological Review* 73:992–1012.

Kriesi, Hanspeter, Ruud Koopmans, Jan-Willem Duyvendak, and Marco G. Giugni. 1995. *The Politics of New Social Movements in Western Europe: A Comparative Analysis*. Minneapolis: University of Minnesota Press/University College of London Press.

Lipset, Seymour Martin, and Stein Rokkan. 1967. "Cleavage Structures, Party Systems, and Voter Alignments: An Introduction." In *Party Systems and Voter Alignments: Cross-National Perspectives*, edited by Seymour Marin Lipset and Stein Rokkan, 1–64. New York: Free Press.

McAdam, Doug, and Sidney Tarrow. 2013. "Social Movements and Elections: Toward a Broader Understanding of the Political Context of Contention." In *The Future of Social Movement Research*, edited by Jacquelien van Stekelenburg, Conny Roggeband, and Bert Klandermans, 325–346. Minneapolis: University of Minnesota Press.

McCarthy, John D., Patrick Rafail, and Ashley Gromis. 2013. "Recent Trends in Public Protest in the United States: The Social Movement Society Thesis Revisited." In *The Future of Social Movement Research*, edited by Jacquelien van Stekelenburg, Conny Roggeband, and Bert Klandermans, 369–396. Minneapolis: University of Minnesota Press.

Meyer, David, and Sidney Tarrow. 1998. *The Social Movement Society: Contentious Politics for a New Century*. Boulder, CO: Rowman and Littlefield.

Simon, Bernd. 2011. "Collective Identity and Political Engagement." In *Identity and Participation in Culturally Diverse Societies: A Multidisciplinary Perspective*, edited by Assaad E. Azzi, Xenia Chryssochoou, Bert Klandermans, and Bernd Simon, 137–158. Chichester, UK: Wiley-Blackwell.

Simon, Bernd, and Bert Klandermans. 2001. "Toward a Social Psychological Analysis of Politicized Collective Identity: Conceptualization, Antecedents, and Consequences." *American Psychologist* 56:319–331.

12

Social Movements after Apartheid

Rethinking Strategies and TACtics in a Time of Democratic Transition

STEVEN ROBINS
CHRISTOPHER J. COLVIN

T he transition to democracy in the early 1990s in South Africa appeared to usher in a seismic shift from the rhetoric of revolutionary socialism to a new political language of constitutionalism, rights, citizenship, and liberal democracy. One of the first significant moments in this transition was the dissolution of the influential antiapartheid social movement the United Democratic Front (UDF). The UDF, an umbrella group of antiapartheid organizations, was incorporated into the African National Congress (ANC) when the ANC was unbanned in 1990. This process of incorporation was consolidated when the ANC became the ruling party after the first democratic elections in 1994 (see Chapter 10).

With the merging of the UDF into the ANC, some political commentators predicted the depoliticization of civil society and the emergence of a disempowered and apathetic citizenry occupied only with the empty rituals of procedural democracy. It appeared as if the South African transition to democracy had precipitated a dramatic shift from revolution to rights, from radical politics to liberal reform, from mass mobilization to the mundane rituals of electoral democracy (see Robins 2008).

Like others elsewhere in the world, critics of liberalism in South Africa have argued that procedural democracy, with its fetishization of the ballot, the rule of law, and multiparty politics, threatens to erase earlier, more substantive concerns about the democraticization of everyday life, social activism, and citizen mobilization, including class-based politics of socialist and labor movements. These critics have argued that the post–Cold War period and the postmodern turn have created the conditions for the spread of ideologies of (neo)liberal individualism alongside a dizzying proliferation of identity-based and single-issue social movements that address diverse issues, often through recourse to the legal system.

Wendy Brown (1995) is one of many critics who have claimed that the turn to legal institutions to adjudicate or redress practices of discrimination and social injury threatens to undermine the emancipatory projects of social movements. For Brown, what appears under the guise of progressive politics is often an embrace of "litigation as a way of political life" (1995: ix). Brown suggests that this obsession with the law and liberal discourses of individual and group rights and responsibilities unwittingly "increases the power of the [liberal] state . . . at the expense of political freedom" (28). For Brown, this turn to the law to regulate and redress social injury obscures how domination is reproduced through the double hegemony of capitalism and the state. The result is a post-political world characterized by a retreat from collective action into a politics of individual self-interest. Similar critiques have been made in South Africa of rights-based social movements such as the Treatment Action Campaign (TAC) (see Neocosmos 2009).

Critics of liberalism conclude that a politics rooted in rights talk has contributed to fragmentation, individualization, and depoliticization. For these critics, procedural forms of liberal democracy are usually little more than the performance of the empty rituals of the ballot. They also note that these forms of procedural democracy are plagued by low voter turnout and political apathy. Within this scenario, liberal individualist conceptions of rights are seen to undermine earlier, more radical conceptions of political emancipation. Marc Edelman makes a similar argument about new social movements that have embraced political strategies that are grounded in the claims of specific groups to the protection of rights, thereby fragmenting any possibility of substantive political challenges to structural inequalities, including those between the North and the South (2001). So what do these critiques of rights, the law, and liberalism look like when viewed from the tip of Africa?

After almost two decades of democracy, community-based activism in South Africa continues to be dynamic and animated. In fact, the escalation of service delivery protests and labor strikes in recent years seems to suggest that social activism and community protests are not only alive and well after apartheid but that they are on the upsurge. In 2009 alone, there were 105 major service delivery protests, and this has only increased in recent years. In addition, the expelled former ANC Youth League activist and current leader of the Economic Freedom Fighters (EFF), Julius Malema, has appropriated the revolutionary socialist rhetoric of the Freedom Charter of the 1950s to call for the nationalization of banks, mines, and land in a quest to radicalize ANC government policy. This militancy has extended into parliament, where, in August 2014, twenty EFF members of Parliament dressed in red overalls and gumboots disrupted proceedings in the legislature in protest against President Jacob

Zuma's alleged financial mismanagement of state resources for security up-
grades at his Nkandla homestead in rural KwaZulu-Natal.

The postapartheid period has also witnessed the emergence of numerous
new social movements, including the South African Homeless People's Federation, TAC, the Concerned Citizens Forum, the Anti-Eviction Campaign (AEC),
the Anti-Privatisation Forum (APF), the Soweto Electricity Crisis Committee,
Abahlali baseMjondolo (AbM), the Landless People's Movement, the Social Justice Coalition (SJC), Equal Education (EE), Section 27, and the Right2Know
Campaign.

Although these recent movements have exhibited diverse political and
ideological orientations, it has been TAC's innovative revitalization of rights-
based activism that has most powerfully captured the imagination of South
Africans and international health and development agencies, governments,
and civil society organizations. TAC and its partner organizations (SJC, EE,
Ndifuna Ukwazi, and Section 27) could be characterized as rights-based organizations that critically engage with the state in terms of rights issues and
service delivery.

But not all civil society actors have been enamored with TAC's rights-
based approach, and critics on the left have claimed that TAC and its partner
organizations are reformist and accommodationist and that they advance the
objectives of the neoliberal postapartheid state (Neocosmos 2009). From this
perspective, movements like the AEC, the APF, and AbM have remained committed to socialist transformation and continue to regard the current state as
both neoliberal and authoritarian.

This chapter examines the ways TAC and its partner organizations have
navigated this postapartheid political landscape. It is particularly concerned
with understanding how these organizations have sought to reanimate rights-
based approaches to political mobilization in a postapartheid setting where there
are no longer clearly defined categories of villains and victims. To do so, they
have had to address a range of difficult political challenges. How do activists
animate social movements after the liberation struggle in a context in which the
state is relatively benign and progressive, promotes a rights-based constitutional
democracy, and drives massive development and welfare programs? How is it
possible in such contexts of democratic transition for social movements to critically engage the state without acting as surrogates or extensions of the state and
its (neo)liberal ideologies? And finally, how is it possible for postapartheid social
movements to engage with long-term systemic problems such as structural inequality and poverty and unequal access to education and health services? We
argue in this chapter that the strategic engagement with social audits, norms and
standards policies, litigation strategies, and rights-based approaches by TAC and
other postapartheid social movements has not, in fact, dampened community-
based activism or the political imagination in South Africa. If anything, these
strategies have complemented and reanimated collective grassroots action.

Between Revolution and Rights? Competing Visions of Social Movement Politics

In October and November 2010, Cape Town witnessed a dramatic escalation in protests over housing, toilets, and service delivery. During October alone, over twenty cars, buses, and trucks were burned in Khayelitsha. The October protests followed a declaration by a social movement of the urban poor, AbM Western Cape (AbM-WC),[1] of an informal-settlement strike that aimed to render Cape Town ungovernable. The ANC Youth League (ANCYL) in Western Cape Province jumped onto the barricades bandwagon when it claimed that it too was about to launch a fourteen-day campaign to make Cape Town ungovernable.

In response to these protests, TAC and its partner organizations, EE and SJC, strongly criticized AbM-WC and the ANCYL for causing chaos and anarchy. These protesting organizations responded that groups like TAC, EE, and SJC did not understand the depth of frustration over poor service delivery in poor communities and that their approach reflected middle-class concerns and leadership styles.

What became clear during these exchanges was that TAC and its partner organizations shared a conception of social mobilization very different from AbM's and the ANCYL's. Whereas the latter two organizations seemed to emulate the populist political style and logic of the service delivery protests that had erupted throughout South Africa's townships in recent years (Pithouse 2010; Von Holdt and Langa 2010), TAC and its allies stuck to a mode of activism that straddled both grassroots mobilization and rights-based approaches (including Constitutional Court litigation), an approach that had emerged in the course of popular struggles for AIDS treatment during the years of the Thabo Mbeki administration (Colvin and Heywood 2011).

What this also revealed was that, whereas the barricades recollected a style of resistance politics of the 1980s that involved rendering the townships ungovernable, the strategies and tactics of TAC and its allies involved critical engagement with the state in ways that reflected a major shift from apartheid-era resistance politics. For TAC and its partners, the state was indeed a legitimate and democratically elected government and it was therefore necessary to help it govern in a way that was progressive and transformative. This did not preclude resorting to street protests, civil disobedience, the courts, and the media to persuade, lobby, shame, blame, and pressure the state into responding to the needs of the poor. But it did mean working with, rather than against, the state to ensure effective service delivery. TAC activists noted that they had achieved much in the course of their campaigns for HIV treatment without ever having to burn tires or throw stones.

TAC, SJC, and EE also recognized that strategic engagement with the postapartheid state to address structural problems relating to public health, policing, housing, and sanitation required more patient, technical, and pragmatic forms of data-driven activism. In other words, they developed an activism that sought to improve state governance and service delivery at a systemic level in the long term. This contrasted starkly with the burning barricades and revolutionary rhetoric of rendering the townships ungovernable of the 1970s and 1980s. However, not all postapartheid community-based organizations shared this conception of critical engagement with the state.

In "Sometimes It Is Rational to Revolt," published in the *Cape Times* (a local Cape Town newspaper) in 2010, the activist and Rhodes University scholar Richard Pithouse argued that, in certain contexts, it makes perfect sense for poor communities to resort to forms of popular protest that include the politics of the barricades. For Pithouse, these reasons included chronic poverty, structural unemployment, poor service delivery, and state indifference to the living conditions of the poor. Pithouse's article also echoed earlier social movement theorists like Frances Fox Piven and Richard Cloward (1977) in arguing that the prioritizing of formal structures and organizational processes by nongovernmental organizations (NGOs) like TAC and SJC was precisely the way that populist energies were captured and dissipated by elites, that the emergence of organizational logics meant the end of poor people's movements. Contrary to critics of these protests, Pithouse claimed that "the riot is not inevitably antisocial and has often been precisely the collective defence of the integrity of the social" (2010: 6).

In a response to Pithouse's passionate defense of the politics of the barricades, the former antiapartheid activist Graeme Bloch (2010) argued that rights-based social movements such as TAC had demonstrated that long-term organizational building and strategizing, rather than resorts to revolutionary slogans and the romance of the barricades, are more effective in pressuring the state to respond to the needs of the poor. Pithouse and Bloch appeared to present two diametrically opposed conceptions of activism and popular politics after apartheid. They both set up a binary opposition between the barricades and rights-based approaches to social mobilization. It seemed that, at least for some activists and scholars, social movements could be categorized in terms of those committed to the revolution and those concerned with liberal reform.

What this public debate also suggested was that although TAC and its allies drew on the historical legacies of the antiapartheid struggle in terms of political culture and tactics, these have been redeployed in ways that depart from the revolutionary logic of the liberation struggle. In particular, the strategy of critical engagement with the postapartheid state draws attention to a more patient and long-term vision of politics that questions the dichotomies posited between revolution and rights, the barricades and the courts.

TAC: A Social Movement Born in a Time of Democratic Transition

TAC was established on December 10, 1998, to demand the provision of HIV treatment at a time when antiretroviral (ARV) therapy was barely available in

Africa.[2] The rank-and-file membership comprises mainly young urban Africans with secondary schooling. However, the organization also managed to attract health professionals and university students. The international face of the organization is Zackie Achmat, a fifty-something Muslim former antiapartheid and gay activist. Other TAC leaders include African men and women who joined TAC as volunteers and moved into leadership positions over time.

When TAC was founded, it was generally assumed that anti-AIDS drugs were beyond the reach of developing countries, condemning 90 percent of the world's HIV-positive population to a painful and inevitable death. While TAC's main objective has been to lobby and pressurize the South African government to provide AIDS treatment, it has been forced to engage in a much wider range of actions, including tackling the global pharmaceutical industry in the media, the courts, and the streets; fighting discrimination against HIV-positive people in schools, hospitals, and the workplace; challenging AIDS dissident science; and taking the government to court for refusing to provide Prevention of Mother-to-Child Transmission (PMTCT) programs in public health facilities.

Despite TAC's highly successful global networking, much of TAC's energy was devoted to more local matters: mobilizing poor and working-class communities, using the courts to compel the former Ministry of Health to provide ARVs at public facilities, and campaigning to protect the autonomy of scientific institutions from government interference. Although grassroots mobilization was primarily in black African working-class areas, TAC's organizational structure and support networks crossed race, class, ethnic, occupational, and educational lines. This approach to mobilization resonated with the political culture of the UDF. However, unlike the UDF, it sought to work closely with the government.

Another striking, but less visible aspect of TAC's campaigns was its capacity to build and mobilize technical knowledge and expertise. This included the use of treatment literacy practitioners (TLPs) to train people taking ARVs in the technical aspects of their disease and its treatment, the use of technical knowledge in court actions, press releases addressing technical debates around ARV drug pricing, treatment regimens, and so on. The organization was thus able to mobilize knowledge to catalyze action among stakeholders ranging from rural patients receiving treatment to high-level government officials and public health experts. Drawing on the multiracial and multiclass politics of the UDF, TAC was also able to recruit support from middle-class business professionals, health professionals, scientists, the media, trade unions, and ordinary South African citizens.

Perhaps the most distinguishing feature of TAC's mode of activism, though, was its strategic use of rights-based provisions in the South African Constitution to secure for poor people access to AIDS treatment. These legal challenges created the space for the articulation of a democratic discourse on health rights and citizenship while simultaneously blurring the boundaries between the politics of the street and the courtroom. The Constitutional Court judges could not but be influenced by growing public support for TAC, particularly as its campaigns attracted widespread media visibility and profoundly shaped public opinion through its sophisticated networking and media imaging. Through these campaigns, TAC was able to give passion and political and ethical content to the cold letter of the Constitution and the cold facts of AIDS statistics.

TAC's mode of activism could be described as grassroots globalization, or globalization from below (Appadurai 2002a, 2002b). Following the precedent of the antiapartheid divestment campaigns, TAC activism straddled local, national, and global spaces in the course of struggles for access to cheaper AIDS drugs. This was done through the courts, the Internet, and the media and by networking with South African and international civil society organizations. Widely publicized acts of civil disobedience also provided TAC with visibility within a globally connected postapartheid public sphere. The David and Goliath narrative of TAC's successful challenge to the global pharmaceutical giants captured the imagination of the international community and consolidated its ties to international NGOs and activist groups such as Oxfam, Medicins sans Frontières (Doctors without Borders), the European Coalition of Positive People, AIDS Coalition to Unleash Power (ACT UP), Treatment Action Group (TAG), and Health Gap. It seemed as if this was indeed a glimpse into what a progressive global civil society could look like.

There were a number of criticisms, however, of TAC's activist strategies. From its formation in 1998, TAC had pursued what could be considered a very narrow focus on gaining access to antiretroviral therapy (ART) for the public sector (Robins 2008). Critics accused TAC of having a too narrowly biomedical focus and political imagination despite the fairly left political perspectives of TAC's leadership. The focus on getting pills for people with HIV was also regarded by some public health activists and practitioners as an overly biomedical approach. TAC's focus on treatment access also rendered it vulnerable to critics, including President Thabo Mbeki, who claimed the organization was a front for the global pharmaceutical industry.

Despite its consistent focus on the specific issue of treatment access, though, TAC's activities brought it into contact with an extremely wide variety of actors and issues. Although the rank-and-file membership of TAC was largely black African working-class women in the townships of Cape Town, Johannesburg, and Durban, the organization was able to mobilize support in diverse communities, locally and globally, and cross (though not transcend) race, class, ethnic, generational, and educational divides. Its mobilization campaigns, which were reminiscent of UDF tactics of the 1980s, were extraordinarily successful notwithstanding concerted opposition from key health officials within the Mbeki administration and local political groups aligned with the ANC—including the South African National Civic Organisation (SANCO), ANCYL, and the Rath Foundation—that promoted alternative and denialist approaches. TAC is of course not the only civil society organization dealing with health issues. A number of small civil society health advocacy organizations take an issue-based approach to health issues, such as Epilepsy South Africa, the disability movement, and the Cancer Society. Broader initiatives such as the People's Health Movement (PHM) have also sought to address the structural causes of health and illness. However, these organizations have tended to be small and have not been visible politically, either to government or most communities. In this sense, TAC has proved exceptional in South Africa. It is not only the principal health-related social movement in South Africa but also one of the most significant social movements to emerge during the democratic transition.

Activism in the Era of ART: Xenophobic Violence and the Emergence of SJC

Once ART was introduced in the public sector in 2004, TAC still had plenty of work to do keeping pressure on government to provide ART evenly and effectively across the country. At the same time, TAC's focus started to broaden. The organization increasingly became involved in health system issues; it began to connect HIV to other conditions such as poverty, gender, and sexual violence; it intervened in public sector strikes involving health workers; and it became interested in programs that were established to train community health workers.

This broadening of TAC's scope probably reached its height during xenophobic violence in June 2008, when TAC, at least in Cape Town, became the de facto coordinator of the civil society response to the violence that resulted in sixty-two deaths and the displacement of well over thirty thousand people. TAC had been working with refugees and HIV, but the xenophobic violence of 2008 was a social and political problem of an entirely different order. Following TAC's immediate response to the refugee crisis spawned by the violence, Oxfam donated R3 million, making it possible for TAC to coordinate the civil society response to the plight of the thousands of refugees displaced by the violence (see Robins 2009).

TAC analysis of xenophobia led it to identify many of the same forms of structural violence it had identified in relation to HIV—namely, poor infrastructure, high unemployment, weak local government, and deficient service delivery. In other words, the same factors that made poor communities vulnerable to HIV made them prone to crime and everyday violence, including xenophobic violence directed at nonnationals living in these communities. To address these issues beyond the immediate response to the xenophobic violence, TAC leadership began a process that led to the formation of SJC.

The goals of SJC necessarily required a framing of social justice that was much broader and more long-term than TAC's primarily biomedical and health system focus on treatment access. As a result, SJC decided to concentrate on service delivery and infrastructural failures that were perceived to produce structural violence in townships. In the early phase of SJC, its members struggled to find a clear focus for action, and rank-and-file members in Khayelitsha were uncertain about their roles and the organization's objectives, which they initially found difficult to explain to residents. However, through ongoing meetings with branch members in Khayelitsha, it became clear that safety and security was a crosscutting concern for township residents. Through discussions with members and residents who had been assaulted and robbed while going to outside toilets at night, it became apparent that safety and sanitation concerns were also interconnected, leading to SJC's new focus on the intersection of health (sickness from poor sanitation) and safety (violent assaults because of poor access to sanitation) through the adequate provision of toilets.

Whereas SJC had previously struggled to make abstract conceptions of human rights resonate with the needs and desires of its Khayelitsha members, this clear connection between safety and sanitation allowed for a more grounded pedagogy whereby members and township residents were able to recognize that rights could be used to make claims for better access to resources and services, including policing, toilets, and improved sanitation more generally. In its focus on sanitation, safety and security, and structural violence, SJC developed a long-term strategic perspective and a patient and pragmatic approach to activism, an orientation that seemed at odds with the more short-term logics of the politics of the barricades.

Sanitation Matters: The Making of a Politics of Shit

Once safety had emerged as the key focus of SJC, the challenge was now how to make the City of Cape Town (CCT) accountable and transparent in its delivery of policing services in these poorer communities. Like TAC, SJC mobilized technical expertise to analyze crime statistics to identify the distribution of different forms of crime in Khayelitsha. An analysis of statistics from RR Section, a chronically impoverished informal settlement in Khayelitsha, revealed that gender-based violence was dramatically underreported. This was attributed to courts and police being overburdened and only homicide being routinely reported to the police. This situation of structural invisibility with respect to women and violence was identified as a serious problem that SJC had to prioritize.

SJC members began using satellite maps to show the overlay and concentration of all these problems in particular areas in Khayelitsha. These maps also led to the realization that deploying more police vehicles to the area would not necessarily be the answer because RR Section had no roads, only paths. In 2014, after many years of lobbying at the local, provincial, and national government level, SJC was successful in its call for the establishment of the Khayelitsha Commission of Inquiry into Policing. The 580-page commission report, *Towards a Safer Khayelitsha*, which was handed to Western Cape premier Helen Zille in August 2014, provided twenty recommendations on how to improve policing. The commission, chaired by retired justice Kate O'Reagan and advocate Vusi Pikoli, had generated masses of data, including statistical evidence that Khayelitsha had the lowest police-to-population ratio in the province. These kinds of findings convinced the premier and senior police that significant changes had to be introduced to improve policing in the area.

SJC's analysis of policing also raised serious questions about the accuracy of CCT's statistics, and it soon became apparent that the city did not know how many people lived in Khayelitsha. SJC's founder and then policy coordinator, Gavin Silber, also told us that whereas the CCT claimed to have achieved a ratio of five households per toilet, a more accurate figure was probably thirty households per toilet. Having this data at his disposal, Silber began a concerted process of learning all there was to know about the different types of toilets and sanitation infrastructure. SJC also launched safe toilets campaigns in response to the large numbers of children with diarrhea.

Again following TAC methodology, SJC activists sought to gather accurate data and acquire and disseminate toilet literacy as a political strategy that involved the strategic use of technical information and expertise. To achieve improved sanitation in RR Section, Silber recognized, SJC had to assist the CCT in overcoming fragmentation of its own services. The organization sought to help city officials coordinate with each other and pressured CCT to develop new policies and adhere to recognized norms and standards. These strategies were part of a war against government "poo denialism," as Silber put it. In this war, SJC deployed a diverse array of tactics, including protest, civil disobedience, social audits, litigation, engagement with the city, information dissemination, and production and analysis of technical information. In other words, this was the classic TAC activist toolkit in action.

Moreover, in the same way that Medicins sans Frontières and TAC had chosen Khayelitsha as an ART pilot site, so did SJC select RR Section as a demonstration site where it would improve safety and sanitation conditions without massive investments. The strategy was to pressure CCT to be more efficient and effective in its provision of services and to work on a small scale that involved addressing issues as they surfaced. Borrowing once more from the TAC toolkit, SJC described this process as part of a long-term process of promoting active citizenship through the grounded pedagogy of grassroots campaigns that addressed concrete issues and engaged with practical problems.

Although SJC sought to remain nonaligned in terms of party political affiliation, this was very difficult in the highly polarized political environment of Western Cape Province, with its deeply entrenched racial, ethnic, and class divides between white, colored, and Xhosa-speaking citizens. This led to a situation in which both major parties—the African National Congress (ANC) and the Democratic Alliance, the official opposition at the national level but the ruling party in Western Cape—at times accused the organization of siding with the other party.

The highly politicized environment in Khayelitsha was also exacerbated by the high stakes involved in local tendering processes. Since there were no municipal services in RR Section, all refuse removal services were outsourced and, because of lack of proper accountability, fierce competition for bids was fought out in local government structures. SJC occasionally found itself caught in the crossfire.

Although this local political landscape was very different from what TAC had had to contend with, SJC's strategies remained closely modeled on TAC's repertoire of tactics and strategies. For example, SJC instructed its lawyers to prepare a Freedom of Access to Information Act (FAIA) application to compel the city to release an embargoed report on the causes underlying the Makhaza toilet wars (see below). Other TAC-like strategies included social mobilization through branches and public protests and civil disobedience. SJC organized a mass protest at Sea Point in Cape Town's city center in which hundreds of SJC supporters queued outside public toilets to draw attention to the disparities between the massive expenditure on upgrading toilets along the promenade in Sea Point and the failure to provide adequate toilets to residents of informal settlements in Khayelitsha and elsewhere in Cape Town. Accompanying these protests were press releases, op-eds, and other publicity that ensured wide coverage of SJC and its concerns in the media.

Other TAC-like tactics included the mobilization of technical expertise in the mapping of Khayelitsha, the use of norms and standards to make claims for improved sanitation in informal settlements, requests to university-based researchers to provide evidence regarding the quality of water, and exploring technical options in terms of toilets and other sanitation infrastructure. SJC also followed TAC's approach by engaging with local government to improve service delivery and link fragmented departments dealing with sanitation.

A key difference between the challenges facing TAC and SJC, though, was that whereas TAC's fight for HIV treatment could be represented as an unambiguously righteous struggle to save lives in the face of an uncaring state and the corporate greed of the pharmaceutical industry, such moral clarity and urgency was not as self-evident when it came to the more long-term, state-driven challenges of providing jobs, housing, land, sanitation, and safety and security for its citizens. Another significant difference between the challenges facing the two organizations was that the local political terrain in which SJC operated was highly contested; SJC activists were not the only actors on the political scene. Unlike TAC activists, who primarily had to battle the state or party, SJC had to contend with turf wars with other local political actors. The following section draws attention to these local dynamics and the kinds of challenges they posed to social movements attempting to engage with more structural and systemic concerns.

Entanglements with Local Social Movement Politics: The Makhaza Toilet Wars

The issue of sanitation in poor communities was catapulted into the public arena in 2010 when the CCT erected flush toilets without walls and roofs in Makhaza Section in Khayelitsha. Although the CCT claimed that residents had agreed to enclose the toilets themselves, some local residents and ANCYL activists were enraged that residents who could not afford to enclose the toilets were in full view of the public. This precipitated widespread community mobilization and culminated in the deliberate destruction of these toilets by ANCYL activists and residents who claimed that these toilets constituted a racist attack on the dignity of black people.

The toilet wars politicized sanitation matters in ways that were unprecedented in South Africa, and sanitation problems in informal settlements achieved national media visibility. The case of the Makhaza toilets was even taken up by the South African Human Rights Commission and a delegation of high-profile public figures, including the Anglican archbishop of Cape Town, who visited Makhaza to mediate between CCT officials and the infuriated local activists and residents. These developments also led to high-level political interventions by senior ANC politicians. The onset of the toilet wars in Makhaza reaffirmed SJC activists' decision to prioritize issues of sanitation.

In September 2010, a picket of about three hundred SJC activists gathered outside the Cape Town Civic Centre to hand over a memorandum and legal application to the mayor calling on her and CCT to release its "Secret Makhaza Toilet Report," an internal investigation into the construction of controversial unenclosed toilets. In a press statement released on October 19, 2010, SJC made connections between safety and sanitation and thereby drew attention to the broader issues that SJC was concerned with:

> At present, 500 000 people in the City of Cape Town do not have access to basic sanitation, which negatively impacts on their health and safety. . . . Residents of informal settlements are routinely assaulted, robbed, raped and murdered on the often long and arduous walk to the nearest functioning toilet. People often become sick with diahorrea, gastroenteritis, and other illnesses as a result of stagnant and polluted water which is often left to gather outside their homes. Sewerage spills are often left unattended for days, weeks and even months. The SJC is working in Khayelitsha to ensure the realisation of resident's rights to safety, health, and dignity through calling for the improvement of sanitation services. (Social Justice Coalition 2010)

SJC was not the only actor on the scene, however. The toilet wars had resulted in an escalation of public protest in Khayelitsha and neighboring townships. In October 2010, AbM-WC declared an informal-settlement strike to protest, among other things, poor service delivery. AbM-WC posted the following statement on its website on October 1, 2010: "We call up on informal settlement through out the City of Cape Town to take to the street and barricade, let us make the whole City of Cape Town ungovernable, and let us create chaos throughout the City. Let us expose the fail[ure] of [the] corrupt DA and ANC led government to provide services for people residing within informal settlement" (Abahlali baseMjondolo 2010b). Meanwhile, AbM-WC activists claimed that the ANCYL was attempting to hijack AbM-WC's campaign, and when three trucks were burned on Lansdowne Road near Makhaza on November, 11, 2010, the AbM-WC leadership claimed that the ANCYL was behind it. Andile Lili, an executive member of the ANCYL's Dullah Omar region in the Western Cape, denied responsibility but claimed that his organization was about to announce the start of its own two-week campaign of protests. Lili was later to become the key leader in the "shit wars" that raged in Cape Town in 2013, when activists hurled portable toilet containers filled with feces at Cape Town's N2 highway, the Cape Town International Airport, the steps of the provincial legislature, and various other parts of the city (see Robins 2014). These poo protests targeted the portable flush toilets that the CCT was providing in informal settlements in response to what was increasingly seen as an escalating sanitation crisis in Khayelitsha and other parts of the city. Lili and the feces flingers from the urban periphery literally dragged the stench of shit from the shantytowns to Cape Town's centers of political and economic power (Robins 2014). As a local ANC branch chairperson and leader of the protests described it, the DA's portable toilets "cause a smell in the houses," and it is "unhygienic to live with poo inside the house." He added that "we want the people who are living in those nice [upper-middle-class] areas like Constantia to feel how poo can damage your life when it is next to you" (quoted in [Johannesburg] *Sunday Times*, August 18, 2013). In 2010, during the height of the open toilet wars, few Capetonians could have anticipated the next stage in the evolution of poo politics. At the time, SJC activists strongly opposed the escalation of violent protests in Khayelitsha and other areas.

The burning of tires and trucks at the barricades on Lansdowne Road during October and November 2010 drew attention to the highly contested local political environment within which SJC operated. From the perspective of an SJC activist, Sipho,[3] the young men at the barricades were being used by political and nonpolitical organizations: "These organizations like strategies of telling people to burn [tires and trucks], but people of Khayelitsha suffer from these protests. . . . TAC, since 1998, haven't burned tires and still got ARVs. When you burn tires, you get potholes in the streets; you don't get houses" (Sipho 2010).

In some cases, the differences between SJC's approach and that of the other organizations came into more direct conflict. For example, members of one of the SJC branches in Khayelitsha were chased out of a local community meeting by SANCO and street committee members. According to Sipho (2010), "Some SJC branches in other places work well with street committees, but sometimes the committees can act as gatekeepers" that seek to exclude SJC activists from meetings because they perceive SJC as intruding on their turf. Gavin Silber (2010) had a similar account of gatekeeping by SANCO leaders: "I was told I had to carry an ID with me so SANCO could identify me at any time. . . . One of our members almost got attacked by SANCO leaders for not discussing things with them." Silber told us that this gatekeeping occurred because SJC's campaigns could be construed by ward councilors and community-based politicians as a threat to local power bases and access to jobs and bidding.

During this monthlong campaign in October 2010, about twenty buses and trucks were burned in Khayelitsha alone. The nightly barricades of burning tires, trucks, buses, and garbage resulted in the disruption of the transport thoroughfare into Khayelitsha. In response to the ongoing roadblocks and burning barricades, SJC, together with the Congress of South African Trade Unions (COSATU, a major ANC-aligned affiliation of trade unions), TAC, and EE, issued a strong statement condemning the role of AbM-WC and the ANCYL in these campaigns:

> A few weeks ago Abahlali baseMjondolo Western Cape, supported by some elements of the ANC Youth League and other community organisations, called for a "general-strike of informal settlements" to bring production in factories and shops to a standstill. They proposed to make the City "ungovernable" and cause "chaos throughout the City." They openly encouraged residents to burn tyres, block roads and throw stones and rubbish. This call is immature, ignorant and shows contempt for our communities. The poor and working-class people of Khayelitsha cannot advance their struggle this way. *To build their own power they need patient organisation and unity.* (Treatment Action Campaign et al. 2010; emphasis added)

AbM-WC leaders issued press statements lambasting the four organizations that signed the statement for presenting a middle-class view and claiming to be the legitimate leaders of the poor even though they did not reside in Khayelitsha. This view was reiterated in an AbM-WC statement posted on the organization's website on October 13, 2010:

> It is legitimate to create a short period of disorder, just like a strike at a work place does, as a tactic of struggle. If TAC disagree with us on this they should engage us in a discussion of tactics rather than condemn our campaign in a way that can justify state repression. . . . We are not a professional organisation with millions of rands of donor funding that can operate in a middle class world. We are a movement of, for and by the poor. We therefore have to struggle where we are and with what we have. If that means burning tyres on Lansdowne Road then that is how we will struggle. We will not be intimidat[ed] into accepting that only the donor funded organisation know how to struggle properly. (Abahlali baseMjondolo 2010a)

This statement was followed by another response, this time from Professor Martin Legassick, a veteran activist representing the Conference of the Democratic Left and supporter of Abahlali baseMjondolo:

The Conference of the Democratic Left in the Western Cape reiterates its support for the period of action called in October by Abahlali base-Mjondolo in the Western Cape in protest at the lack of housing and service delivery. In contrast to others, we regard the tactic of direct action and civil disobedience as legitimate forms of protest under a neoliberal and pro-capitalist state. Our democracy would not have come into existence without such acts of civil disobedience on a mass scale, and sustaining and deepening democracy can also depend on such acts of civil disobedience as long as they enjoy the support of the people on the ground. We also reject the idea that has been put forward that such actions are "anarchic" or "reactionary." . . . Those that criticize the Abhalali baseMjondolo call for mass direct action pretend we live in a "normal democracy" and forget the gross inequality and violence of the current system. They also forget that this system has a name— capitalism. (Legassick 2010)

These tensions between direct action and more patient and pragmatic modes of community organizing are somewhat reminiscent of the divergent approaches of populists and "workerists" during the antiapartheid struggle (see Beinart and Dawson 2010). Whereas the workerists focused on factory-floor union issues such as wage negotiations, the populists looked to broader community mobilization and popular resistance. In the Western Cape in 2010, it seemed as if a similar tension could be identified between advocates of rights-based approaches and critical engagement with the postapartheid state, on one hand, and those organizations that believed in direct action and popular resistance, on the other.

It also appears that TAC's struggles for HIV treatment were not perceived as serious threats to local community leaders, community-based organizations, political structures, and local power brokers and gatekeepers. Although TAC had to deal with AIDS dissident and denialist groups within the administration as well as local organizations such as SANCO and the ANCYL, its public health work did not directly threaten the power base of local political actors. This was not the case when it came to SJC's involvement in sanitation matters in Khayelitsha. In fact, SJC's involvement in Khayelitsha in negotiating improved sanitation services from the local authorities was bound to pose a threat to certain local interests, including ward councilors, street committees, SANCO, and development forum leaders, as well as social movement activists from rival organizations. Despite these difficulties, by 2014, SJC had not only made significant inroads in terms of using social audits of sanitation infrastructure to lobby, pressure, and negotiate with the CCT for toilet janitors and improved sanitation services but also contributed to the establishment of the precedent-setting Khayelitsha Commission of Inquiry into Policing.

Concluding Reflections on Postapartheid Political Movements

In February 2011, we joined a group of American exchange students who visited AbM-WC in QQ Section in Khayelitsha. AbM-WC had been in the news in September and October 2010 as a result of its almost daily erection of barricades in Khayelitsha and its calls for popular protests to render Cape Town ungovernable until the city management responded to service delivery needs in informal settlements. The leader of the movement in the Western Cape, Mzonke Poni, accompanied the exchange students on a walk through QQ Section. He stopped in front of a large mound of garbage and began to speak about daily conditions in the informal settlement. He told the students how residents had to relieve themselves using buckets and plastic bags and how they would throw these bags, "flying toilets," in the direction of a wetlands area next to the settlement where it was not possible to build houses. Poni also told the students of how residents walked long distances to request to use the toilets of shebeen (bar) owners and residents who lived in the adjacent formal housing scheme called Q Section. Sometimes they were charged to use these toilets, and many residents could not afford to pay. The students were overwhelmed by both Poni's accounts of daily conditions and the pungent stench from the nearby piles of waste. Poni commented on the students' discomfort and pointed out that QQ residents have to endure this daily. Having recently visited RR Section, where SJC had managed to get CCT to improve sanitation infrastructure, we too were shocked by the sight and smell of huge heaps of uncollected garbage.

What neither the students nor we could have anticipated during our visit in February 2011 was that toilets were about to become *the* key campaign issue in the run-up to the May 2011 local government elections. Media images of unenclosed toilets in Makhaza in the Democratic Alliance–controlled CCT and in Moqhaka township in ANC-run Free State Province shocked politicians, journalists, and citizens. Notwithstanding concerted efforts by social movement activists from organizations such as SJC and Abahlali to draw attention to ongoing sanitation disasters in many informal settlements, before the outbreak of the open-toilet scandal there had been very limited public and media concern about practices of open defecation, the bucket system, or that large numbers of poor people have to use plastic bags to relieve themselves (Robins 2014). There was something about the image of the modern porcelain toilet without walls that triggered widespread shock and outrage. The open toilet became a potent political symbol and came to be interpreted as an affront to black dignity. What the escalation of the toilet wars in the run-up to 2011 elections also suggested was that the slow and patient rights-based approach of SJC had contributed to transforming sanitation into a national political issue. In addition, SJC's focus on service delivery resonated with the popular demands that animated service delivery protests. It also resonated with AbM-WC's own concerns.

The tensions between SJC and AbM-WC during the informal-settlement strike of October 2010 were read by some political commentators as a manifestation of ongoing battles between the civil society advocates of radical populism and liberal technicism. Yet as suggested above, this binary opposition seems to be overstated. The interesting question in this story of the clash between the politics of the barricades and rights talk is not so much why popular forms of resistance politics have reemerged but rather why this politics of service delivery protests and the barricades have emerged at this particular time and place. Were the barricades on Lansdowne Road in Cape Town necessarily a sign of the failure of rights-based approaches such as those used by TAC and SJC? This idea of the failure of previous political forms, and the reaching of a boiling point by the poor, was indeed a strong part of AbM-WC's self-justification and self-narrative of their emergence. What seems more directly at stake for many actors, however, is not so much the conflict between one form of political protest and another as it is that, in the toilet wars we have a political problem that is deeply entangled with local political realities in a way that the fight for ART was not.

For TAC, fighting for ART involved taking the government and the ANC leadership on, and though there were also local manifestations of that conflict, this contestation did not really involve local actors in any fundamental way. Most local councilors, activists, stakeholders, and so on, had little to do with the health system, and TAC's activism did not represent a threat to local interests and relationships. The toilet wars, however, have proved very different for a number of reasons. First, many waste services are contracted out, giving local businesses a huge stake in how services are delivered and who is held accountable. Second, SJC coming in and organizing certain communities and engaging with government around specific local issues challenges local forms of governance like SANCO and community street committees. Third, the Western Cape is a highly contested space at the local level as well. Since the ANC lost control of both local and provincial government, there have been accusations from the Democratic Alliance that certain ANC groupings in the Western Cape are trying to regain power by encouraging service delivery protests. For instance, it is widely held by the Democratic Alliance and some political commentators that the ANCYL in the Western Cape stirred up political resistance in the toilet wars for precisely such purposes.[4]

SJC has had local political challenges on its hands of the sort that TAC never had. It may be the kind of battle that health activists will increasingly encounter if they try to more directly address the structural causes of health problems. Keeping a narrow focus on a disease, or even on the health system as a state service, is likely to allow one to steer clear of many of the interests and agendas of local and national political actors. Intervening in health more broadly, however—by, for example, addressing sanitation as a public health and security issue—means new political challenges for health activists. The former ANC councilor and leader of the poo protests of 2013, Andile Lili, has now become the leader of Ses'khona Peoples Rights Movement, a Khayelitsha-based and ANC-connected social movement that has embarked on a more militant and confrontational style of sanitation activism than SJC. Ses'khona members took sanitation activism in new directions when they embarked on a campaign of dumping human waste in public places in Cape Town.

It is not clear whether the lessons of the toilet wars in Khayelitsha in 2010 and Ses'khona's poo protests of 2013 signal something broader about the current post-transition political environment. For instance, did the clash over protest tactics between AbM-WC and SJC in October 2010 highlight some of the limits of TAC's rights-based approach in poor communities? Is the rights-based approach adopted by SJC less suited to grassroots struggles for service delivery in informal settlements? Or are the creative tensions between the politics of the barricades and rights-based approaches not routinely experienced by social movements engaging in other struggles over access to housing, land, water, or electricity?

What does seem clear from the South African case is that rights talk and recourse to litigation strategies by social movements during the two decades since the transition to democracy has not contributed to either the depoliticization of civil society or the emergence of a disempowered and apathetic citizenry that is duped by the fetishization of the ballot and empty rituals of procedural democracy. If anything, the postapartheid period has witnessed a popularization of the idea of rights as legitimation for the proliferation of popular protests around issues of service delivery. South Africa's transition to democracy has not resulted in a seamless shift from revolution to rights, from populist politics to sanitation, from mass mobilization to political apathy and citizen disempowerment. Instead, the antiapartheid movement's calls for "the struggle to continue"—*a'luta continua*—seem to be very much alive and well throughout the country.

NOTES

1. AbM-WC is an affiliate of the well-established social movement of the urban poor based in Durban (see Bohmke 2009; Chance 2010). The Durban-based AbM movement has a large following and has been especially strong in Kennedy Road settlement, working with communities and nongovernmental organizations to address issues of housing, sanitation, and empowerment of the poor. The Cape Town affiliate, by contrast, was only recently established and is widely characterized as a loosely structured and thinly spread organization.

2. For a detailed account of the early history of TAC and its campaign for mother-to-child-transmission prevention program, see Treatment Action Campaign 2001.

3. "Sipho" is a pseudonym.

4. It was in this context that AbM-WC entered the fray with similar tactics of barricades and popular protest. However, AbM-WC went out of its way to dispel accusations that it was a front, or instrument, of the ANC and instead claimed it represented the poor who are oppressed and neglected by Democratic Alliance and ANC governments alike: "We are very well aware that the ANC Youth League tries to support every protest in Cape Town because they want to undermine the DA. But we know very well that the

ANC has the same policies as the DA here and we do not allow the ANC to exploit our own struggles for their own gain" (Abahlali baseMjondolo 2010a). So a great deal was at stake politically in how the toilet saga and other service delivery issues were to be addressed, challenged, and resolved.

REFERENCES

Abahlali baseMjondolo. 2010a. "Abahlali baseMjondolo of the Western Cape Replies to the Treatment Action Campaign." October 13. Available at http://archive.today/Nbcr.

———. 2010b. "Urgent Call." October 1. Available at http://abahlali.org/node/7335.

Appadurai, A. 2002a. "Grassroots Globalization and the Research Imagination." In *The Anthropology of Politics: A Reader in Ethnography, Theory and Critique*, edited by J. Vincent, 271–284. Malden, MA: Blackwell.

———. 2002b. "Deep Democracy: Urban Governmentality and the Horizon of Politics." *Public Culture* 14 (1): 21–47.

Bloch, Graeme. 2010. *Cape Times*, October 28.

Bohmke, H. 2009. "Between the Halo and the Panga: Accounts of Abahlali BaseMjondolo on 26th September." Unpublished manuscript.

Brown, W. 1995. *States of Injury: Power and Freedom in Late Modernity*. Princeton, NJ: Princeton University Press.

Chance, K. 2010. "The Work of Violence: A Timeline of Armed Attacks at Kennedy Road." Research Report No. 83, University of KwaZulu-Natal, School of Development Studies, Durban, South Africa.

Colvin, C. J., and M. Heywood. 2011. "Negotiating ARV Prices with Pharmaceutical Companies and the South African Government: A Civil Society/Legal Approach." In *Negotiating and Navigating Global Health: Case Studies in Global Health Diplomacy*, edited by Ellen Rosskam and Ilona Kikbusch, 351–372. London: Imperial College Press.

Edelman, M. 2001. "Social Movements: Changing Paradigms and Forms of Politics." *Annual Review of Anthropology* 30:285–317.

Legassick, Martin. 2010. "Conference of the Democratic Left in the Western Cape Statement of Support for the Abahlali baseMjondolo of the Western Cape Call to Action in October." Press release, October 20.

Neocosmos, M. 2009. "Civil Society, Citizenship and the Politics of the (Im)possible: Rethinking Militancy in Africa Today." *Interface: A Journal for and about Social Movements* 1 (2): 263–334.

Pithouse, R. 2010. "Sometimes It Is Rational to Revolt." *Cape Times*, October 22, p. 6.

Piven, F. F., and R. A. Cloward. 1977. *Poor People's Movements: Why They Succeed, How They Fail*. New York: Pantheon.

Robins, S. 2008. *From Revolution to Rights in South Africa: Social Movements, NGOs and Popular Politics*. Woodbridge: James Currey and University of KwaZulu-Natal Press.

———. 2009. "Humanitarian Aid Beyond 'Bare Survival': Social Movement Responses to Xenophobic Violence in South Africa." *American Ethnologist* 36 (4): 637–650.

———. 2014. "Slow Activism in Fast Times: Reflections on the Mass Media after Apartheid." *Journal for Southern African Studies* 40 (1): 91–110.

Silber, Gavin. 2010. Interview by the authors. Khayelitsha, Cape Town, June 15.

Sipho. 2010. Interview by the authors. Khayelitsha, Cape Town, June 15.

Social Justice Coalition. 2010. "SJC to Deliver Legal Application to City of Cape Town Demanding Release of Secret Makhaza Toilet Report." Press release, October 19.

Treatment Action Campaign. 2001. "Treatment Action Campaign: An Overview." Available at http://www.tac.org.za/Documents/Other/tachist.pdf.

Treatment Action Campaign, Social Justice Coalition, Equal Education, and Congress of South African Trade Unions. 2010. "Unite Poor and Working Class People in Khayelitsha through Disciplined and Sustained Organising: Reject Abahlali base Mjondolo's Call for Violence and Chaos!" Press release, October 12.

Von Holdt, K., and Langa, M. 2010. "Community Protests, Xenophobic Attacks and Violence: The Contradictions of Insurgent Citizenship." Paper presented at the "Decade of Dissent" symposium, South African Research Chair in Social Change, University of Johannesburg, November 14–16.

IV

East-Central Europe

13

Introduction

GRZEGORZ EKIERT

Transitions to democracy are times of heightened political mobilization. They give rise to social movements and transform the contours of civil society. After years or even decades of silence and quiescence, ordinary people take center stage, and mass political action escapes the confines of the infrapolitical domain (Scott 1992). Guillermo O'Donnell and Philippe Schmitter describe this as the "resurrection of civil society," a phenomenon that may

> involve the resurgence of previous political parties or the formation of new ones . . . ; the conversion of older institutions, such as trade unions, professional associations, and universities, from agents of the governmental control into instruments of the expression of interests, ideals, and rage against the regime; the emergence of grass-roots organizations articulating demands long repressed or ignored by authoritarian rule; the expression of ethical concerns by religious and spiritual groups previously noted for their prudent accommodation to the authorities; and so forth. (1986: 49)

The collapse of communist regimes in Central, Southern, and Eastern Europe was no exception to this rule. Despite the recent tendency to see these events in terms of elite bargains and leaders' decisions, or as the self-generated implosion of a system that had run out of steam (Kotkin 2009), 1989 was a time of unprecedented mass upheaval. Millions of people across the communist world took to the streets to demand political change and thousands of movements and organizations emerged to challenge communist rule (see, for example, Ash 1990; Stokes 1993; Beissinger 2002; Kenney 2003). The images of mass demonstrations on the streets of Budapest, Leipzig, or Prague; the 375-mile-long human chain of two million people across Estonia, Latvia, and Lithuania; the fall of the Berlin Wall; candlelight vigils in Sofia; the revolutionary upheaval in Romania; and hundreds of other big and small protests were transmitted by the media around the world, showing the depth and intensity of popular mobilization. Yet despite the impromptu qualities of these events, seemingly spontaneous crowds were often coordinated by preexisting networks of activists and rapidly developed organizational structures, transforming themselves from loosely organized movements and assemblies into myriad civil society organizations.

Moreover, the 1989 springtime of nations was not an entirely surprising event, as is often suggested. The collapse of communism was preceded by equally unexpected waves of contention that swept across the Soviet bloc. In several cases, only mass repressions and Soviet military interventions allowed the communist regimes to survive. The revolt in Berlin in 1953, the Hungarian revolution of 1956, the Prague Spring of 1968, and the emergence of Solidarity in Poland in 1980 were only the most spectacular instances of mass mobilization, revealing the deep currents of discontent and opposition to communist rule across the region (Kusin 1978; Ash 1985; Bernhard 1993; Ekiert 1996; Kubik 1994; Sebestyen 2007). These and other episodes of contention planted the seeds for communism's demise.

Such instances of political mobilization from below and open contention highlighted both the legitimacy deficit of these regimes and the widespread currents of everyday resistance that pervaded communist societies (Kopstein 1996). In the declining years of communist rule and especially after the Helsinki Agreements in 1975, opposition activities intensified and various social and cultural movements, as well as openly political organizations, emerged throughout the region pursuing diverse political and social agendas. It is not surprising, therefore, that expanding opportunities for political participation and collective action were eagerly embraced by millions of ordinary people when communist regimes started to crumble. Unfolding political conflicts and regime transitions spawned multitudes of new movements and organizations, transformed the institutions of the old regime and its bases of political support, and generated mass contention that rapidly diffused across the region. This snowballing wave of contention spelled the end of communism in Europe, opening new opportunities for collective action and political participation and democratizing large swatches of the former Soviet bloc.

What is surprising, however, is that as soon as the victory of opposition movements and civil society was achieved, as soon as oppressive communist regimes were gone and democracy was established or perceived as realistically reachable in many countries, the death of social movements was declared. Political activists were concerned about social passivity and the absence of sustained political mobilization. Scholars documented low trust and anemic social participation and worried about the general weakness of civil society in postcommunist countries (Ekiert and Foa 2012). Accordingly, concerns about participation deficit and political demobilization and about enfeeblement and deficiency of civil society have animated debates about democratization in the region since 1989. Paradoxically, in the wake of the democratic revolutions, the notion gained currency that communism had wiped out any traces of genuine civil society and that totalitarian legacies are particularly inhospitable to civic revival and to active, self-organized citizenry capable of defending its own interests and identities. The reconstitution of civil society and the establishment of effective democratic practices were seen as highly unlikely (Howard 2003; Bernhard and Karakoc 2007).

Ralf Dahrendorf (1990) famously argued that while building democratic institutions and market economies in postcommunist Europe can be relatively swift, rebuilding civil societies presents a much greater challenge, one that may require three generations. A few years after 1989 additional concerns about civil society were raised. John Ely, for example, noted "the disappearance of 'civil society' and the 'civic movements' initiatives and influence, and not their expansion and the constitutional rationalization of their demands." He described this as "the puzzle of the 'catch-up revolutions' of 1989–1990 in Eastern Europe" (1994: 132). Bill Lomax concluded that "in many respects, the failure to develop and strengthen civil initiatives and popular participation— the failure to create an active and independent civil society—represents a new, post-communist betrayal of the intellectuals" (1997: x). These sentiments have been echoed by political and social activists across the region (Jawlowska and Kubik 2007–2008). Yet the inauguration of democracy—with all its guarantees of political rights and freedoms, encouragement for political participation, and support for civic initiatives—should have had the opposite effect. Why would the seemingly strong, active, and mobilized civil society of the transition period that succeeded in forcing communist regimes to capitulate and relinquish political power become weak after democracy was established?

Michael Bernhard addresses this paradox in analyzing post-1989 developments in Poland:

> Whereas there is general agreement that civil society played a key role in the overthrow of communist regimes in 1989 . . . and that among communist countries Poland had the most developed civil society in the region at the time of the collapse, there is now a widespread belief that civil society in post-communist countries is weak. (1996: 309)

Bernhard points to four factors responsible in his view for the enfeeblement of mobilized civil society after 1989: political demobilization resulting from the pacted transition that privileged elite negotiations and cooperation at the expense of popular forces, collective action, and grassroots organizations; decapitation of the movements' organizational leadership through its migration to the new state bureaucracies, political parties, and democratic institutions; effects of post-totalitarianism (low social trust and aversion to formal participation in various organizational domains); and demobilizing social consequences of the ensuing economic crisis, recession, and costly economic reforms. Thus, he argues that strong civil societies that effectively challenged communist governments across the region became weak and demobilized as a result of factors inherent in the nature of the process of negotiated democratization and the cost and extent of the economic transformation that took place in the postcommunist context. In short, the specific model of political change, together with the communist legacy, explains the weakness of civil society and the extinction of social movements that had arisen to challenge communist rule.

The chapters on post-1989 East-Central Europe included in this section expand on Bernhard's analysis and shed more light on this seeming puzzle of postcommunist politics. In short, the cases of the Solidarity trade union, Polish peasant organizations, and FIDESZ in Hungary suggest a more complex answer to the question of what happened to mobilized collective actors during the transition to democracy and the consolidation of new democratic regimes. These depict a complex process of organizational conversion and institutionalization of the loosely structured movements of the transition period and their integration (often contentious) into the institutional architecture of postcommunist states and regimes in East-Central Europe. Moreover, they show the accommodation between associational structures inherited from the old regime and newly emerging civil society actors.[1] The careful analysis presented in these chapters demonstrates that the post-1989 condition was not one of postrevolutionary gloom, political demobilization, and failure to sustain broad public participation. Nor was the defeat of grassroots movements brought about by the onslaught of neoliberal policies and dire economic straits or a betrayal of democratic ideals by the winners of the transformations, as has sometimes been suggested (see, for example, Ost 2005). Instead, this was a relatively successful movement institutionalization that took place in densely organized societies and in the context of massive transformations that opened up opportunities for collective actors to integrate into rapidly changing institutions of interest representation and governance. In turn, these new democratic institutions were infused with styles of action and political practices inherited from the social movement legacy. The successful use of social movement tactics by the Hungarian FIDESZ and the inherited contentious strategies employed by Polish trade unions and peasant organizations are well documented in these chapters. This social movement inheritance had advantages and disadvantages for specific political parties and interest groups in various stages of the transformations. It is important to assess the salience of the movements' legacy for postcommunist politics: Has it declined as these countries move away from the founding moments of democracy, or has it become hybridized and routinized as a permanent element of political practices?

Seen from this perspective, post-1989 relations between prodemocracy movements and East-Central European states represent the successful institutionalization of the massive 1989–1990 wave of contention into the new institutional matrix of postcommunist states. The process involved mutual accommodation between old and new collective actors, merging of associational domains, migration of activists to formal political institutions, and diffusion of social movement practices. Such successful institutionalization, of course, was not the case in countries east of the Polish border that experienced authoritarian reversals or stalled political transformations. Successful changes were taking place in a liberal political context and were supported by political elites and accommodating state policies as well as significant external assistance. This process of institutionalization, resource conversion, and accommodation of a wide range of political practices signifies a shift from social movement politics to new civil society politics and a fundamental transformation of the institutions of interest articulation and representation and the patterns of political participation. The decline of loosely structured movements and rapid growth of civil society suggests that there is a sort of zero-sum relationship between the domain of social movements and grassroot politics and the domain of organized civil society. The quickly democratizing societies able to establish solid guaranties of civil and political rights tend to facilitate the inclusion of mobilized actors and to shift patterns of contestation and conflict from the streets to institutions of representation and governance. Conversely, when the democratization process stalls or reverses and actors of the old regime retain the upper hand, the domain of movement politics is preserved and episodic grassroots mobilizations become the norm. This argument echoes Samuel Huntington's (1968) classic claim about the relationship between institutionalization and political order.

In this brief introduction, I outline both the specific and the general contexts of the East-Central European postcommunist transitions and substantiate the argument about specific patterns of transformation in relations between mobilized social actors and state, political, and civil society institutions.

Social Movements and Opposition in East-Central Europe under the Old Regime and Beyond

The broadly conceived communist legacy (Ekiert and Hanson 2003) is the first important element in the effort to understand the relations between mobilized collective actors and the constraints and opportunities offered by the collapse of communist regimes and the ensuing democratization process. Too often, thinking about transition from communism is pervaded by totalitarian imagery, depicting a hapless and atomized society capable only of generating random and spontaneous acts of rage. Yet under the old regime, all East-Central European countries had a distinct (politicized, bureaucratized, centralized, and comprehensive) pattern of associational life and interest "representation." The presence of this type of social organization was a defining element of state socialism and one of the most fundamental institutional differences between it and other political regimes, both democratic and authoritarian (Ekiert and Kubik 2014). However, important differences among communist countries in the structure, historical continuity, and function of associations reflected contrasting historical traditions, distinct strategies of communist takeover, and diverging political developments during the communist period. As a result, the legacies of communist rule in the sphere of associational life are quite distinct in each post-communist country, and they influence their respective post-1989 civil society transformations in a specific manner.

During the communist era, particularly in its post-totalitarian phase (1956–1989), communist-controlled mass organizations underwent important transformations. The official institutional sphere experienced a gradual process of pragmatization, deideologization, and even limited pluralization (Ekiert 1991; Linz and Stepan 1996). This happened to a different degree in various countries, with Poland and Hungary leading the way. In the 1970s and 1980s, many official organizations became less ideological and acquired a degree of autonomy in managing their internal affairs; some even developed considerable lobbying capacity. Membership in many organizations during this time was becoming increasingly voluntary and entailed the provision of various special benefits and collective goods. This gradual transformation of the nature and role of mass organizations had important consequences for state-society relations and produced striking differences across the Soviet bloc, with a growing split between reformist (such as Poland or Hungary) and orthodox communist regimes. The process of diversification was accelerated in the 1980s and aided by the rise of the Solidarity movement in Poland, the deepening systemic crisis of communism, and the emerging challenge from embryonic counterhegemonic and oppositional movements and organizations across the region.

Alongside the transformation of state-controlled organizations, independent or oppositional movements and networks had emerged in many East-Central European countries already by the mid-1970s (and even earlier in Poland). Reflecting the declining intensity of political repression, growing intellectual and cultural dissent, deprivatization of religion, and increasing openness toward the West, autonomous social initiatives, human rights organizations, cultural, environmental, and religious movements were gaining ground in communist societies (Tokes 1979; Keane 1985; Ekiert 1991). The implosion of communist ideology, the emerging discourse on human rights, samizdat, and networks of independent communication provided foundations for this phenomenon (Skilling 1988; Judt 1988). In fact, the self-organization of East-Central European societies against their communist regimes provided a stimulus for the resurrection of the concept of civil society among Western researchers and ignited debate over the relationship between civil society and democracy in the social sciences during the 1980s and 1990s (Keane 1988).

By the 1980s, East-Central European communist countries, Poland in particular, had what can be described as incomplete civil societies (Ekiert and Kubik 1999; Kubik 2000), comprising a large number of associations and movements and a dense structure of organizations at various levels and in all functional domains but without autonomy, a legally defined public space, or enforceable rights and liberties. These incomplete civil societies shared many institutional characteristics across the region but also displayed some profound differences in their density, composition, normative orientation, and practices in both official and independent sectors. In all communist countries an enormous state-controlled sector comprised mass organizations, including youth organizations, trade unions, farmers' unions, professional associations, recreation and leisure organizations, sports clubs, women's organizations, and veterans' and retirees' unions. This sector was institutionally similar across the region, although formal and informal practices within these organizations, and the level of political control exercised across them, differed significantly among the Soviet bloc countries. In some countries, such as Poland and Hungary, this transformation of the formal associational sphere allowed some interest articulation and representation and redefined state-society relations. It also opened up space for independent initiatives. In other countries, these processes were less advanced and largely confined beneath a surface of organizational unity, ritualized official discourse, and conformist practices.

In Poland and to a lesser degree in Czechoslovakia and Hungary, the independent, semilegal sector of civil society became well established in the 1970s. It comprised a wide range of groups, including semiautonomous churches and religious movements, human rights organizations and illegal political opposition groups, independent artistic and cultural movements, single-issue apolitical movements (environmental, ethnic, consumer), and self-help groups. It was more diverse but also more visible and capable of influencing state policies in these three countries than in the rest of the Soviet bloc. As Figure 13.1 illustrates, these countries had a higher number of independent organizations in 1989 than other countries in the region (Pehe 1989), larger and more diverse oppositional movements, more public support for independent activities, more coordination and contacts among independent groups, and a higher number of contentious events challenging communist authorities (Bruszt et al. 2007).

In sum, under the old regime the countries of East-Central Europe had a dense associational structure composed of a diverse state-controlled sector of social and professional organizations and a very active and relatively large independent sector of political, religious, and cultural movements. These organizational resources provided solid foundations for the mass political mobilization that brought down communist regimes in 1989 and for the reformulation of civil society after 1989. The idea that civil societies in postcommunist countries were built from scratch has little merit and is patently false for Poland, where millions of people were involved not only in state-controlled organizations but also in independent movements. All these independent resources were mobilized during the time of transition. Thus, the collapse of communism was in a significant part a contentious process involving bottom-up pressure and mass mobilization generating a massive organizational reconstitution of the public

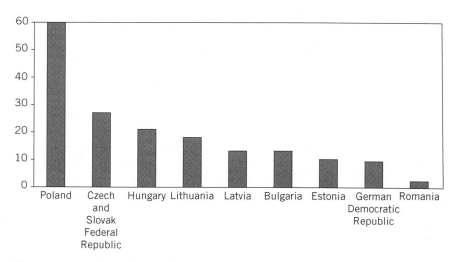

Figure 13.1 Number of independent movements in Eastern Europe, June 1989. *(Source: Pehe 1989)*

space and the associational realm. The critical element of this process was the rapid institutionalization of movements, the sectoral makeover of civil society (i.e., a shift from old to new organizations), and the fundamental transformation of relations between state and society.

The institutionalization of the 1989–1990 wave of mass mobilization involved a complex interaction among inherited communist-era associations, pre-1989 oppositional networks, and activists, as well as movements and organizations that emerged in 1989. This interaction was taking place in the context of expanding resources and opportunities for civil society organizations and ongoing transformations of the institutions of representation and governance. The result was a rapid institutionalization process that led to the conversion of loosely structured movements into a formally organized civil and political society that experienced increasing professionalization and specialization. Transformations of the organizational infrastructure of bottom-up activities were paralleled by an identity fracture. A generalized political identity, developed to challenge the communist hegemony, splintered into myriad competing identities reflecting political, social, ethnic, religious, and other cleavages specific to each society. The resulting fragmentation, specialization, and professionalization of formerly broad-based movements were without doubt disappointing for many activists. Moreover, new opportunities within the economic domain facilitated the conversion of a portion of the opposition's skills and networks from the public to the private realm.

The post-1989 process of civil society reconstruction followed two distinct, parallel developments. First, there was the reinvention and resurrection of sectors of civil society suppressed by the communist regime. This was mani-

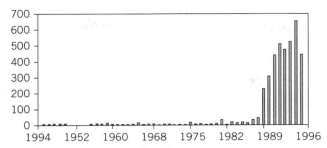

Figure 13.2 Number of registered civil society organizations in Poland.
(Source: Krasnodebska et al. 1996)

fested in massive social mobilization and the rapid emergence of a wide spectrum of new organizations and movements (mostly nongovernmental organizations [NGOs], foundations, charities, and religious and ethnic minority organizations but also employer and business associations). Figure 13.2 shows the civil society expansion in Poland.

These newcomers were by and large the organizations absent in the associational landscape inherited from the communist regime (e.g., NGOs, charities, and foundations) and nascent organizations competing directly with inherited communist-era organizations (e.g., independent trade unions or new professional associations). They had their roots in the social movements of the 1980s and the mobilizations of 1989–1990. Many of these organizations failed to secure resources and attract members and disappeared as quickly as they had emerged, especially in the sectors of civil society in which they faced competition from former communist-era organizations (e.g., labor unions, professional associations). The emerging independent sector had a different level of organizational growth and success and a different composition across the region (OECD 1994; Anheier and Seibel 1998; Kuti 1999; Mansfeldova et al. 2004; Nalecz and Bartkowski 2006), but broad similarities are obvious among East-Central European countries regarding the speed and intensity of civil society growth in the initial years of democratization.

Depending on specific circumstances across the postcommunist region (such as conflicts and wars, the quality of democracy, external support, existing traditions, and the extent of economic crisis), the emerging sectors of civil societies exhibited various institutional configurations, different balances between inherited and new organizations, contrasting styles of collective action, and various normative orientations. Moreover, different collective actors played a dominant role in shaping civil society actions and political influence. For example, trade unions were the most powerful and active organizations in Poland, while in other countries the identity-based organizations were most powerful. Finally, newly independent states employed different strategies for encouraging or discouraging activities through a variety of legal regulations and financial means, including registration procedures, tax exemptions, and

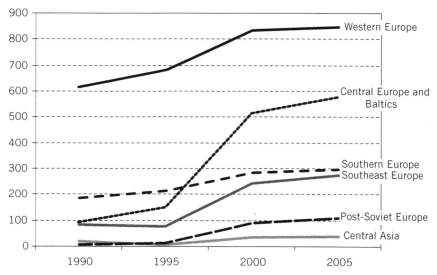

Figure 13.3 Number of international NGOs per capita. *(Source: Kaldor, Anheier, and Glasius 2003)*

subsidies (Simone 2004). State actors entered into differently structured relations with civil society actors also on local and national levels.

The end result of this organizational revolution was the emergence of a relatively robust and well-institutionalized civil society in the countries of East-Central Europe (Ekiert and Foa 2012; Ekiert and Kubik 2014). These civil societies have been rapidly converging to Western European levels, as, for example, the data on international NGOs presented in Figure 13.3 suggest.

During the first decade and a half following the collapse of communism, East-Central Europe rapidly overtook Southern Europe in terms of the density of international NGOs and is now converging on Western Europe in this regard. Meanwhile, Southeastern Europe is now approaching the consolidated democracies of Southern Europe overall in the richness and diversity of active international organizations. The data indicate not only rapid change over time but also a widening gap between regions of the former communist bloc, with a clear divide emerging between post-Soviet Europe and the other countries of the former Soviet bloc.

Moreover, the growth dynamic of these new civil societies has been fairly stable. The rates of growth in the number of organizations were highest in the first few years of transition (e.g., 400 percent increase in Poland). This robust organizational growth took place despite all the postcommunist countries experiencing dramatic transitional recessions. And while this growth leveled out around 1994, it has remained strong longitudinally. As Figure 13.4 illustrates, in Poland, on average, some four thousand new NGOs and five hundred foundations are registered every year. That fewer than 13 percent of all NGOs

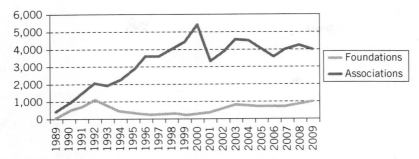

Figure 13.4 Number of new associations and foundations registered in Poland, 1989–2009. *(Source: Przewłocka 2011: 8)*

in 2006 were established before 1989 reinforces the point about the strong organizational growth of civil society in East-Central Europe.

Finally, general conditions for the creation and sustainability of civil society organizations in East-Central Europe are more conducive than in other parts of the former Soviet bloc, as suggested by the NGO Sustainability Index compiled by the U.S. Agency for International Development, presented in Figure 13.5. Note that the professional organizations of civil society, and not social movements, have been the main beneficiaries of efforts by the state and European

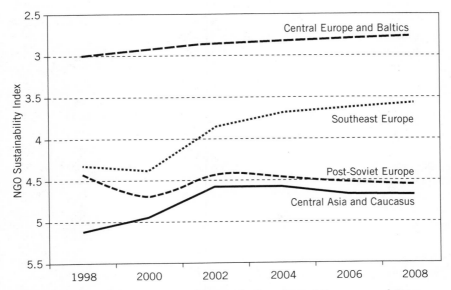

Figure 13.5 NGO Sustainability Index scores for East-Central European and Asian regions, 1998–2008. Lower scores indicate higher sustainability for the NGO sector. *(Source: USAID 2011)*

Union (EU) to facilitate civil society growth and public participation in these new democracies.

In a parallel process, the majority of formerly communist-controlled organizations experienced a complex and, by and large, successful process of reform and adaptation to new democratic conditions. They often lost a significant portion of their members and resources and frequently split into smaller organizations, changing their names, leaders, and agendas. But it should be emphasized that the majority of these organizations survived the transition to democracy and were able to protect most of the resources that they had before 1989. Many of these organizations also preserved old linkages and preferential access to various bureaucratic levels of the state administration (Fric 2008: 244–245).

This adaptation of communist-era organizations, as well as the organizational and normative reinvention of new sectors of civil society, was not uniform across the region. There were different levels of civic mobilization and political conflict during the transfer-of-power stage of democratization. In some countries the formation of a new civil society was a highly contentious process, while in others it moved along in a more orderly and subdued fashion (Ekiert and Kubik 1998). The intensity of the initial political conflict shaped the organizational landscape of new civil societies. The ratio of inherited and newly formed organizations also differed across the region. Old communist-era organizations have remained more powerful in countries where former communists managed to initially stay in power. In countries where the political opposition was successful in taking over the reins of government, two distinct patterns of adaptation resulted in either a more pluralist (Poland) or a more corporatist (Slovenia, Hungary) structuring of civil society, with other countries falling between these two antipodes. These patterns shaped the rate of civil society's organizational growth, the relation between civil society and the state, the level of competition among organizations, and the level of contention in state–civil society and business–civil society relations. The more pluralist the civil society, the more robust and active it is.

Thus, postcommunist civil society emerged from a complex institutionalization and recombination process involving the internal transformations of communist-era associations, the institutionalization of social movements, the emergence of new sectors of civil society, and interactions between old and new organizations and between them and newly democratic states. David Stark (1996) introduced the concept of recombination for analyzing processes of economic and institutional transformation in the region, but it fits equally well for other institutional domains. What happened in the social movement and associational domains may be called recombined institutionalization. This peculiar nature of civil society reformulation created a range of civil society types that were highly diversified, variously networked, and unequal in distribution of resources and influence. In some countries organizations inherited from the old regime retained much of their resources and influence, especially in countries where new states lapsed into authoritarianism, reimposing restrictions on civil society activities and restoring state-sponsored and state-controlled associational networks. Thus, the initial outcome of civil society's resurrection and reformulation differed significantly across the region.

More importantly, the patterns of civil society's reconstitution had profound consequences for social movements and grassroots activities. In countries of East-Central Europe new civil society organizations sapped energy from the social movement domain. Emerging interests, identities, and passions could easily find space, support, and resources within the expanding domain of civil society, local self-government, and relatively open new-party systems. In many other postcommunist countries in which the process of conversion and reconstitution of civil society was constrained and limited, loosely structured social movements have remained an important political actor. Many repeated grassroots mobilizations have been followed by a demobilization cycle, as illustrated by so-called color revolutions or recent events in Ukraine. Similarly, the growing number of extremist, right-wing movements in East-Central Europe can be attributed to the political limits of institutionalization and their inability to become legitimate partners of organized civil society (Ramet 1999; Minkenberg 2002; Kopecky and Mudde 2003; Rupnik 2007).

Finally, one would expect that given the extent of the organizational density of the previous regimes, the external assistance provided for civil society building, and the competition between old and new social organizations, the process of civil society reformulation should be qualitatively different in postcommunist and postauthoritarian cases. Postcommunist civil societies should be more robust and organizationally denser than postauthoritarian civil societies in successful democratizations. One would also expect in postcommunist countries a more effective movement institutionalization and, therefore, a smaller political domain for grassroots movements and a larger civil society domain, except in countries that reverted to authoritarianism or have radical movements against the new political system. These claims still need verification.

In sum, initial democratic transformations in Central and Eastern Europe resulted in the emergence of recombined civil societies and the institutionalization and professionalization of social movements that challenged communist rule in 1989–1990. These new civil societies registered significant growth and have concurrently undergone diverse processes of transformations. The emerging trajectories of civil society transformations were shaped by the quality of democracy in individual countries, resources and strength of local civic initiatives, role of the state in financing and supporting emerging civil society sectors, quality of institutional infrastructure, and involvement of external actors. The first important distinction that needs to be made is between countries that experienced a gradual consolidation of democratic institutions and practices and countries that experienced retrenchment of liberties and freedoms and the restoration of authoritarian systems.

The quality of the public sphere and state's respect for rights and liberties is perhaps the most important parameter shaping social movement conversion and civil society reorganization. In countries that reverted to authoritarian rule, the process of institutionalization was arrested. They have incomplete civil societies facing many restrictions and constraints often akin to incomplete civil societies of late communism.[2] In such countries, loosely structured social movements capable of periodic mobilization still play an important political role. Thus, grassroots mobilization-demobilization cycles characterize the relations between state and society.

Although regime type is important, state policies vis-à-vis civil society generate a second dimension of diversity. The states in the region have been instrumental in creating political and economic conditions for social movements and civil society organizations and in providing institutional infrastructure that imposed constraints and opened opportunities for civil society actors. The legal and institutional changes regarding registration procedures, financing and taxation mechanisms, restriction of activities, and so on, pushed civil society development into diverging trajectories across the region.

A third important dimension of diversity was the preferred model and direction of domestic legal regulations concerning the civil society sector. Postcommunist countries were not uniformly influenced by the European model of state–civil society relations—a corporatist model characterized by a professionalized civil society (constituting the significant employment sector) involved in formal structures of social partnership, largely financed by the state and focused on service provision.[3] Candidate and subsequent member countries of the EU moved domestic legislation in this direction. Civil society organizations in these countries increasingly sought resources from the European Social Fund and participated in projects funded by structural funds. Thus, for East-Central European countries the EU enlargement process and EU membership provided a critical turn in the pattern of civil society transformations. Accession to the EU has strengthened civil society actors in new member states in three distinct ways: the integration process provided opportunities to civil society organizations to enter EU-supported networks, tap the significant new resources through access to EU structural and community funds, and increase its political role on the local and national levels through EU-mandated procedures that stimulate the partner role of civil society in many policy arenas (Gasior-Niemiec and Glinski 2007: 29–30).

The fourth dimension of diversity is the nature of sectoral rebalancing and diversification in civil society organizational structure, the prevailing political affiliations of civil society actors, and the prevailing action repertoires adopted by civil society leaders and organizations. Traditional sectors of civil society composed of trade unions and professional organizations inherited from the communist regime became weakened in response to structural changes in the economy and the emergence of new patterns of representation and bargaining and articulation of new identities. At the same time, the NGO sector experienced dramatic growth. The progressive professionalization of civil society drives its fragmentation and specialization. These are no longer even single-issue organizations but rather niche organizations specializing in a specific service or expertise. The sectoral composition of civil society is also shaped by the role of religion and churches, alliances with political parties, and by state support. In general, one could discern pluralist and corporatist patterns of civil society organization emerging in different postcommunist countries. In terms of the style of action it is possible to distinguish between contentious and accommodating civil societies emerging in the region (Ekiert and Kubik 1998). Finally, in terms of the political orientations of civil society actors one could distinguish between liberal and illiberal civil societies. In many countries, there has been resurgence of right-wing political movements that have limited capacity to institutionalize and integrate into the existing structure of civil society. Therefore, extremist, right-wing politics may remain a social-movement-based and weakly structured domain of political life in East-Central Europe.

Conclusion

I put forward four simple claims that are echoed and developed in the substantive chapters that follow. The first claim is an observation that the bottom-up pressure and massive popular mobilization that involved millions of people and spawned a wide variety of social movements and civil society organizations before and during 1989 was an integral and important part of transition to democracy in East-Central Europe. While elite transactions and the removal of geopolitical constraints were indispensable elements of democratization, without sustained mass pressure from below the democratization process would have stalled as it did in some other contexts, both postcommunist and postauthoritarian. Successful democratizations have at their heart a balance between top-down and bottom-up dynamics. Newly mobilized political and social movements need to be institutionalized and accommodated in the policy-making process and in governing and representative institutions to facilitate the process of democratic consolidation.

The second claim is that, to understand the role of mobilized collective actors in the collapse of communist regimes and in the postcommunist context, we need to conceptualize the process of state-society relations in terms of two fundamental shifts. They involve the transformation of state-society relations, changing the calculus of costs and rewards of individual involvement in contentious politics and the underlying organizational matrix of contention. The first shift is that from infrapolitics and everyday forms of resistance predominant during the communist period to open political participation in the newly established public sphere. In this process, practices of everyday resistance broke from the confines of the infrapolitical domain and burst into the public sphere. This transformation in the nature of oppositional political activities resulted in emergence of loosely structured movements and networks of activists who challenged communist rule and facilitated transitions to democracy. In some cases this transformation took place well before the collapse of communist regimes. In Poland, for example, the emergence of the Solidarity movement in 1980 epitomizes such a shift in political practices. "Early shifters" had distinct advantages in democracy building during and after 1989. Countries in East-Central Europe such as Poland, Hungary, and Czechoslovakia enjoyed a faster and more comprehensive democratization process than other countries of the region.

The second shift takes place after the establishment of democratic institutions and credible guaranties of civil and political rights. This shift consists of converting the loosely structured political and social movements that emerged during the regime-change period into a fully institutionalized civil society. This process takes many forms. Experienced movement activists may migrate to party politics, local government, and state bureaucracies. Others exit politics altogether, focusing instead on opportunities in the private sphere. Networks of activists and movements enter the formal civil society domain with its highly institutionalized and regulated organizations (NGOs, trade unions and professional organizations, and religious, local, and ethnic organizations, etc.). This shift displays different levels of completeness in various countries depending on the quality of newly established democratic institutions and the openness and willingness of political elites to accommodate pressures from below. It also depends on the relationship between old and new sectors of civil society. In countries of East-Central Europe there was a high degree of completeness in converting loosely structured movements into fully institutionalized organizations of civil society, but in many postcommunist countries that process was thwarted. Countries such as Ukraine experienced recurring waves of mobilization based to a large degree on informal networks of activists.

The third claim is that the associational structure inherited from the old regime played an important role in absorbing and channeling the public energy generated by democratic transformations. As these organizations changed and adapted to the new democratic environment they often lost their privileged status and resources. They were forced to compete for members, resources, and influence with newcomers to the public domain. Some countries experienced a comprehensive recombination process in which old organizations changed fundamentally and opened their doors to activists and networks looking for institutional outlets to pursue their goals and interests. Thus, they became standard tools of democratic interest representation. In other countries the transformations of the old associational sector were stifled, resulting in the survival of old corporatist arrangements and a "pillarized" (Schmitter 1997: 248) civil society.

Finally, the fourth claim is that the processes described above differ significantly among subregions of the former communist bloc. The dynamic shifts from infrapolitics to public contention and from loosely structured movements to organized civil society, sketched above and illustrated by the substantive chapters in this section of the book, reflect the experience of East-Central European countries such as Poland, Hungary, and the Czech Republic and to a lesser extent the other countries that joined the EU in 2004. The other parts of the former communist world display different patterns of transition in both political and economic dimensions and, accordingly, different patterns of relations between social movements, democratization, and politics.

NOTES

Acknowledgments: I thank George Soroka and Roberto Foa for their contributions to this chapter and Jan Kubik for our ongoing intellectual collaboration.

1. East-Central European political dynamics and patterns of transformation differ significantly from those in other parts of the former Soviet bloc because of a number of region-specific factors including levels of socioeconomic development, specific communist legacies, and European Union membership opportunity (see Ekiert, Kubik, and Vachudova 2007). Accordingly, generalizations built on East-Central European evidence cannot be readily construed as broad patterns common to all postcommunist regimes.

2. Scholars studying emerging civil society in Russia (Fish 1994; McFaul 2002) argue that initially the weakness of the Russian state contributed significantly to the organizational weakness. Subsequently, the turn to the authoritarian direction and the political and bureaucratic constraints imposed on civil society activities blocked civil society development.

3. The White Paper on European Governance adopted in 2001 provides a model of civil society–state relations: "Civil society plays an important role in giving voice to the concerns of citizens and in delivering services that meet people's needs" (see Gawin 2006: 77).

REFERENCES

Anheier, Helmut, and Wolfgang Seibel. 1998. "The Nonprofit Sector and the Transformation of Societies: A Comparative Analysis of East Germany, Poland and Hungary." In *Private Action and the Public Good*, edited by Walter Powell and Elisabeth Clemens, 177–192. New Haven, CT: Yale University Press.

Ash, Timothy Garton. 1985. *The Polish Revolution: Solidarity.* New York: Vintage Books.

———. 1990. *Magic Lantern: Revolution of '89.* New York: Random House.

Bernhard, Michael. 1993. *The Origin of Democratization in Poland.* New York: Columbia University Press.

———. 2002. *Nationalist Mobilization and the Collapse of the Soviet State.* New York: Cambridge University Press.

Bernhard, Michael, and Ekrem Karakoc. 2007. "Civil Society and Legacies of Dictatorship." *World Politics* 59:539–567.

Bruszt, Laszlo, Nauro Campos, Jan Fidrmuc, and Gerald Ronald. 2007. "Does Civil Society Development under Communism (1985–1991) Help Explain Political and Economic Performance during Transition?" Unpublished manuscript. April.

Dahrendorf, Ralph. 1990. *Reflections on the Revolution in Europe.* New York: Random House.

Ekiert, Grzegorz. 1991. "Democratization Processes in East Central Europe: A Theoretical Reconsideration." *British Journal of Political Science* 21 (3): 285–313.

———. 1996. *The State against Society.* Princeton, NJ: Princeton University Press.

Ekiert, Grzegorz, and Roberto Foa. 2012. "The Weakness of Post-Communist Civil Society Reassessed." Open Forum Paper, no. 11, Harvard University, Center for European Studies, Cambridge, MA.

Ekiert, Grzegorz, and Stephen Hanson, eds. 2003. *Capitalism and Democracy in Central and Eastern Europe.* New York: Cambridge University Press.

Ekiert, Grzegorz, and Jan Kubik. 1998. "Contentious Politics in New Democracies." *World Politics* 50 (4): 547–581.

———. 1999. *Rebellious Civil Society.* Ann Arbor: University of Michigan Press.

———. 2014. "Myths and Realities of Civil Society." *Journal of Democracy* 25 (1): 46–58.

Ekiert, Grzegorz, Jan Kubik, and Milada Vachudova. 2007. "Democracy in Postcommunist World: An Unending Quest." *East European Politics and Societies* 21 (1): 1–24.

Ely, John. 1994. "Libertarian Ecology and Civil Society." *Society and Nature* 2 (3): 98–151.

Fish, M. Steven. 1994. "Russia's Fourth Transition." *Journal of Democracy* 5:31–42.

Fric, Pavol. 2008. "The Uneasy Partnership of the State and the Third Sector in the Czech Republic." In *The Third Sector in Europe,* edited by Stephen P. Osborne, 230–255. London: Routledge.

Gasior-Niemiec, Anna, and Piotr Glinski. 2007. "Europeanization of Civil Society in Poland." *Revija za Socijalnu Politiku* [Journal of Social Policy] 14 (1): 29–47.

Gawin, Dariusz. 2006. "European Civil Society: The Citizens' or Eurocrats' Project?" In *Civil Society in the Making,* edited by Dariusz Gawin and Piotr Glinski, 77–88. Warsaw: Institute of Philosophy and Sociology, Polish Academy of Sciences.

Howard, Mark. 2003. *The Weakness of Civil Society in Postcommunist Europe.* New York: Cambridge University Press.

Huntington, Samuel. 1968. *Political Order in Changing Societies.* New Haven, CT: Yale University Press.

Jawlowska, Aldona, and Jan Kubik. 2007–2008. "Dyskusja redakcyjma 'Societas Communitas': Rozmowa o aktualnym stanie i perspektywach rozwoju aktywnosci zbiorowej w Polsce" [Discussion: Social Activism in Contemporary Poland]. *Societas/Communitas* 2 (4–5): 11–40.

Judt, Tony. 1988. "The Dilemmas of Dissidence: The Politics of Opposition in East-Central Europe." *East European Politics and Societies* 2 (2): 185–240.

Kaldor, Mary, Helmut Anheier, and Marlies Glasius, eds. 2003. *Global Civil Society 2003.* London: Oxford University Press.

Keane, John, ed. 1985. *The Power of the Powerless.* Armonk, NY: M. E. Sharpe.

Keane, John. 1988. *Civil Society and the State: New European Perspectives.* London: Verso.

Kenney, Padraic. 2003. *A Carnival of Revolution: Central Europe 1989.* Princeton, NJ: Princeton University Press.

Kopecky, Petr, and Cas Mudde. 2003. *Uncivil Society: Contentious Politics in Post-Communist Eastern Europe.* London: Routledge.

Kopstein, Jeffrey. 1996. "Chipping Away at the State: Workers Resistance and the Demise of East Germany." *World Politics* 49 (3): 391–423.

Kotkin, Stephen. 2009. *Uncivil Society: 1989 and the Implosion of Communist Establishments.* New York: Random House.

Krasnodebska, Urszula, Joanna Pucek, Grzegorz Kowalczyk, and Jan Jakub Wyganski. 1996. *Podstawowe statystyki dotyczace dzialan organizacji pozarzadowych w Polsce* [Nongovernmental Organizations in Poland: Basic Statistics]. Warsaw: Program PHARE—Dialog Spoleczny.

Kubik, Jan. 2000. "Between the State and Networks of 'Cousins': The Role of Society and Noncivil Associations in the Democratization of Poland." In *Civil Society before*

Democracy, edited by Nancy Bermeo and Philip Nord, 181–207. Lanham, MD: Rowman and Littlefield.

———. 1994. *The Power of Symbols against Symbols of Power*. University Park: Pennsylvania State University Press.

Kusin, Vladimir. 1978. *From Dubcek to Charter 77: A Study of Normalization in Czechoslovakia*. Basingstoke, UK: Palgrave Macmillan.

Kuti, Eva. 1999. "Different East European Countries at Different Crossroads." *Voluntas* 10 (1): 51–60.

Linz, Juan, and Alfred Stepan. 1996. *Problems of Democratic Transition and Consolidation*. Baltimore: Johns Hopkins University Press.

Lomax, Bill. 1997. "The Strange Death of Civil Society in Post-Communist Hungary." *Journal of Communist Studies and Transition Politics* 13 (1): 41–63.

Mansfeldova, Zdenka, Slawomir Nalecz, Annette Zimmer, and Eckhard Priller. 2004. "Civil Society in Transition: Civic Engagement and Nonprofit Organizations in Central and Eastern Europe after 1989." In *Future of Civil Society: Making Central European Nonprofit-Organizations Work*, edited by Annette Zimmer and Eckhard Priller, 99–121. Wiesbaden, Germany: Verlag fur Sozialwissenschaften.

McFaul, Michael, ed. 2002. Special issue, *Demokratizatsiya* 10 (2).

Minkenberg, Michael. 2002. "The Radical Right in Post-Socialist Central and Eastern Europe: Comparative Observations and Interpretations." *East European Politics and Societies* 16 (2): 335–362.

Nalecz, Slawomir, and Jerzy Bartkowski. 2006. "Is There Organizational Base for Civil Society in Central Eastern Europe?" In *Building Democracy and Civil Society East of the Elba*, edited by Sven Eliaeson, 163–195. London: Routledge.

O'Donnell, Guillermo, and Philippe C. Schmitter 1986. *Transitions from Authoritarian Rule: Tentative Conclusions about Uncertain Democracies*. Baltimore: Johns Hopkins University Press.

OECD (Organisation for Economic Co-operation and Development). 1994. *The Emergence of Business Associations and Chambers in the Economies in Transition: Examples from the Czech Republic, Hungary, Poland, and the Slovak Republic*. Paris: OECD.

Ost, David. 2005. *The Defeat of Solidarity*. Ithaca, NY: Cornell University Press.

Pehe, Jiri. 1989. "Annotated Survey of Independent Movements in Eastern Europe." Background report 100, June 13, Radio Free Europe, Munich, Germany.

Przewłocka, Jadwiga. 2011. *Polskie organizacje pozarzadowe: Najwazniejsz pytania, podstawowe fakty* [Polish Nongovernmental Organizations: Fundamental Questions, Basic Facts]. Warsaw: Klon/Jawor.

Ramet, Sabrina. 1999. *The Radical Right in Central and Eastern Europe since 1989*. University Park: Penn State Press.

Rupnik, Jacques. 2007. "From Democratic Fatigue to Populist Backlash." *Journal of Democracy* 18 (4): 17–25.

Schmitter, Philippe. 1997. "Civil Society East and West." In *Consolidating the Third Wave Democracies: Themes and Perspectives*, edited by Larry Diamond, Marc Plattner, Yun-han Chu, and Hung-mao Tien, 239–262. Baltimore: Johns Hopkins University Press.

Scott, James C. 1992. *Domination and Arts of Resistance*. New Haven, CT: Yale University Press.

Sebestyen, Victor. 2007. *Twelve Days: The Story of the 1956 Hungarian Revolution*. New York: Vintage Books.

Simone, Karla W. 2004. "Tax Laws and Tax Preferences." In *Future of Civil Society: Making Central European Nonprofit-Organizations Work*, edited by Annette Zimmer and Eckhard Priller, 147–168. Wiesbaden, Germany: VS Verlag fur Sozialwissenschaften.

Skilling, Gordon H. 1989. *Samizdat and an Independent Society in Central and Eastern Europe*. Columbus: Ohio State University Press.

Stark, David. 1996. "Recombinant Property in East European Capitalism." *American Journal of Sociology* 101 (4): 993–1027.

Stokes, Gale. 1993. *The Walls Came Tumbling Down*. New York: Oxford University Press.

Tokes, Rudolf. 1979. *Opposition in Eastern Europe, 1968–1978*. Baltimore: Johns Hopkins University Press.

USAID. 2011. *2010 NGO Sustainability Index for Central and Eastern Europe and Eurasia*. Washington, DC: USAID.

14

From Anticommunist Dissident Movement to Governing Party

The Transformations of Fidesz in Hungary

MÁTÉ SZABÓ

The general elections in Hungary in the spring of 2010 were an overwhelming victory for the Fidesz-MPSZ[1] party (see Figures 14.1 and 14.2). The party won more than two-thirds of the seats in parliament, giving it an absolute majority and final say on all political questions, including changing the constitution, which it did in April 2011.

Fidesz began in the Budapest samizdat-opposition scene of the 1980s, emerging from a radical, anticommunist student movement. It became a political party in 1988, during the transition to democracy, and used its protest culture to become a mobilizing party after the transition (Bozóki 1992). Its past as a former underground group with active protest roots enabled Fidesz to adapt as political opportunities changed. To gain its election victory in 2010, it revitalized its mobilizing strategies and frames and used civic networks (Bozóki 1988). As the party in power, Fidesz has continued to use a mobilizing party strategy that it used, though differently, while an opposition party.

A hybrid organization—a political party in parliament and a government with civic and protest facets—combines elements of organization and mobilization and framing of parties, civic organizations, and protest movements. I give a summary of Fidesz's transformation and revivals over the last twenty years from a suppressed underground, informal group to the governing party with huge political support from voters.

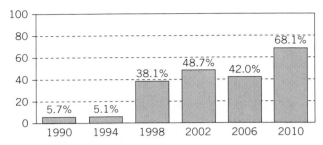

Figure 14.1 Fidesz results in national elections. *(Source: Compiled from National Election Office data at http://www.valasztas.hu)*

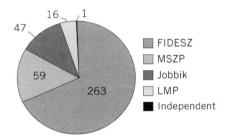

Figure 14.2 Results of 2010 elections, number of parliamentary representatives (total = 386). *(Source: Compiled from National Election Office data at http://www.valasztas.hu/en/parval2010/298/298_0_index.html)*

A Hybrid Party

In Hungary, a 1989 law allowed political parties to exist (Körösényi, Tóth, and Török 2009). The network of independent groups that existed before the transition became political parties, civil society organizations, and protest movements during and after the transition. The roles of parties, civic organizations, and protest movements differ in a pluralist democracy from their roles in a communist state. New characteristics of civic activism emerged out of the pluralistic structural opportunities of the new political system that came after the communist leader János Kádár left office. In the new constitutional democracy, public mobilization and protest were transformed to legally and constitutionally regulated political institutions. With the freedom to associate and gather, legal and public networking, mobilization, and nonviolent protests became widely accepted forms of political action. Before transition, autonomous groups, especially those protesting against the existing regime, were suppressed or controlled as much as possible by the powerful communist party state. Dissent was not allowed in the state-owned and state-controlled monopolist and centralized media and in the official science and culture institutions. Movement organization and mobilization was forbidden. Framing discourses were marginalized to the private communication of underground networks and Western-based media like Radio Free Europe and journals smuggled into the country.

Fidesz, outlawed as a protest movement in the Kádár era, preserved its dissident and clandestine political tradition and its experience as a form of identity after the transition (Machos 1992). The party retained its strong anticommunism, popular mobilizing strategy from its past as a suppressed underground movement. Its leading activists, later top government leaders (such as the current prime minister, Viktor Orbán), were in the underground of the 1980s. Being outlawed in the communist system had long-lasting effects on them. The myths, symbols, and fights of the suppressed protest movements, all based on a fundamental rejection of communism, have been kept alive in the new political culture and remain in the current goals and strategies of Fidesz.

During the 1990s most Fidesz leaders had a past of pre-1989 activism. But after 1989 Fidesz supporters started coming from every political generation and group—including former communists—and a new generation of professional activists became dominant, although the goals and the culture of the anticommunist heritage from before the regime change were preserved. This shift from an old to a new generation was accelerated by the development of Fidesz into the leading and unifying force of the center right, whose main enemy became the reformed Socialist Party. The sharp left-right division preserved the feeling in Fidesz of being a resistance culture against former communists, identified by Fidesz as Fidesz's main enemy in the electoral arena, the Hungarian Socialist Party (Körösényi, Tóth, and Török 2009). Although civic protest did not lose its importance for Fidesz after 1989, protest has become only one form of its political activities.

After 1989, pragmatic and policy-issue-oriented approaches dominated. From 1988 to 2010 six national and local elections and a period of Fidesz government transformed the former student group into a center-right party in a political-administrative system of representation and governance (Körösényi, Tóth, and Török 2009). PR work, fund-raising, national and international networking, professional education, development of the organization, and campaigning and voter mobilization became priorities among Fidesz activists and required professionally trained employees. At the beginning of the twentieth century Max Weber and Robert Michels analyzed the transformation of modern social movements into political parties and their bureaucratization and professionalization (Tarrow 1994). Later social research differentiating among organizational structures, goals, and programs challenged the Weber-Michels paradigm that the stabilization and longer-lasting organizational success of a party require that it give up radical goals and become part of the establishment (Zald 1990). According to these later findings, professional bureaucratic party organizations may preserve radical goals and a conflict-oriented culture from its past as a social movement, which describes the development of Fidesz in Hungary.

The Three Faces of Fidesz: Dissident Movement, Political Party, and Mobilizing-Populist Party

Fidesz development had six stages:

1. A dissident movement between 1988 and 1990
2. A political party established in 1990 in a growing multiparty system and rejecting mobilizing strategy in 1992
3. The leading force of the center-right between 1992 and 1998, the year it won the election
4. A top-down mobilizing party in popular government campaigns between 1998 and 2002
5. After the 2002 elections, which Fidesz lost, the leading mobilizing party of the right-wing opposition, especially after the 2006 autumn riots
6. The party in power as of 2010

The mobilization of 2002–2010 is different from that of 1988–1992, because it is based on a nationwide organizational network, a former governing party's material and personnel resources, a new type of political orientation, and a civil society with a system of political pluralism (Ekiert and Kubik 1998). In 1988–1992, there was a transition of social, economic, and political systems; roles of parties and movements were changing in a unified civil society supporting democratic transition beyond authoritarianism (Ekiert 1991). Thus, the development of FIDESZ into Fidesz-MPSZ is a change from bottom-up to top-down strategies of mobilization, from a social movement to a party, from civil to political, from nongovernmental organization (NGO) to a position in government. The organization and strategy of Fidesz in 1988 was an avant-garde in the system transition, and later it followed the models of right-wing and center parties in Europe.

Fidesz as a Dissident Movement

Hungary's protest tradition before 1989 consisted chiefly of younger, urban, professional white-collar workers and students. Networks of underground dissent were mainly informally organized groupings of artists, scientists, and students concentrated in the capital, Budapest, and in some bigger university towns such as Pecs and Szeged (Schöpflin 1979).

The proportion of youth protesting in Hungary was one of the highest among the Central-European communist countries (Ramet 1991) and clearly dominated protest actions in 1980s Hungary for the environment, peace, and human rights. Some were expelled from their university, had visas revoked, were forced to enter military service, or experienced some other, milder form of government repression (Haraszti 1990; Miszlivetz 1989). These youth were following the tradition of protest of the Hungarian revolutions of 1848 and 1956, when youth and students initiated actions (Tőkés 1998).

Hungarian protesters shared many characteristics—commitment to peace, ecology, and human rights (Pollack and Wielghos 2004)—with those in the new social movements and Green parties in the 1980s in Western Europe (Judt 1988; Ramet 1991), but goals and cultures were different. The Western movements of the 1980s were allies of left-libertarian parties, had social goals that included gay and squatter rights (Larana 1994), and criticized the market economy and bureaucracy. The social activism in former Eastern Bloc countries rejected the planned-economy and bureaucratic-gerontocratic communist structure (Máté Szabó 1991; Knabe 1988). Eastern activists had moved from alternative Marxism to liberalism; the Western from the New Left to alternative ecology and peace movements. Eastern movements preferred a market economy and representative democracy; Western autonomous movements criticized the consumer society and Western values and institutions.

Fidesz was a movement established during the Eastern Bloc's last days that advanced Western values of a market economy and human rights and opposed the leftist ideology of the former communist regime. Fidesz never had the trade-unionist character of the Solidarity movement in Poland (Arato 1992; Ekiert and Kubik 1998), instead promoting national identity and self-determination over the forced communist internationalism of the Eastern Bloc. Fidesz rejected communist internationalism but embraced rights for the two to three million Hungarian minorities living in surrounding countries—Czechoslovakia, Yugoslavia, and Romania were former Hungarian territories divided after World War I into new states. Thus, nationalism, national minorities, and self-determination shaped the Fidesz political universe—a very different one from the cosmopolitanism and global solidarity of Western new social movements concerned with the rights of indigenous people everywhere and with the rights of immigrants (Joppke 1994).

In 1992, under its popular leader Viktor Orbán, FIDESZ gave up its protest strategy to take a right-wing, proestablishment orientation and in 1993 abolished its former upper age limit of thirty-five (Mudde and Kopecky 2002, 2003). The party lost its provocative and protest character, and groups unwilling to abandon their underground identity left or were pushed out by the center-oriented mainstream.

Fidesz as a Political Party Searching for a Position and Identity

Among the parties in Hungary's first parliament (1990–1994), Fidesz was the most active in protests between 1989 and 1994 (Machos 1993), but its events are concentrated in the first three years, 1989–1991, after which it did not protest. Party strategy had changed and youth and alternative movements had been pushed out of Fidesz leading positions. Fidesz activities were concentrated exclusively in parliament, and it tried to escape its past by conforming with accepted political behavior of the new institutions. Fidesz did not participate in the campaigns of the liberal Szabad Demokraták Szövetsége (SZDSZ; Alliance of Free Democrats) and Magyar Szocialista Párt (MSZP; Hungarian Socialist Party) against the Christian-democratic government led by the Magyar Demokrata Fórum (MDF; Hungarian Democratic Forum) (Bozóki 1999–2000).

With its original age limit of thirty-five, Fidesz had institutionalized a new political generation of the Hungarian opposition. It had been strongly affiliated with students and ecology and peace movement activists. The SZDSZ, in contrast, was formed of older generations from the liberal groups and of some veterans of the 1956 revolution and out of the traditions of Hungarian dissent, such as the Budapest School of Georg Lukács and opposition to repression of civil rights in the 1970s and its later samizdats (Kende and Smolar 1989). The different political traditions moved the two parties in different directions: SZDSZ remained more liberal, and Fidesz sought alliances with nationalist parties in a pragmatic quest for power. SZDSZ had a strong tendency toward social liberalism, and Fidesz merged liberal conservatism with alternative viewpoints (e.g., ecology, feminism, youth movement) and then with Hungarian nationalism and its Third Way political alliance. The two parties had both come from anticommunist protest movements, but their political values increasingly diverged, even as the age difference narrowed after Fidesz ended its age limit. In SZDSZ, the generation of founders, with their political culture of a clandestine underground movement, was pushed out of the leadership and replaced with more professional technocrats without underground backgrounds. In Fidesz, its founding fathers remained in the core group of party leadership (Csizmadia 1995), but they themselves had become professionalized politicians and technocrats.

Both parties also experienced internal differentiation and conflict among intraparty groups with different values and strategies. In Fidesz from the beginning, there was an internal division between "movementists," who pushed for social engagement, direct democracy, civil rights activism, and the peace and ecology campaigns of social movements, and technocrats, who supported professionalization, a market economy, and representative democracy and were led by Viktor Orbán. The pragmatic and power-oriented technocrats prevailed in 1993, with the majority supporting Orbán. Orbán had been arguing for political parties to have a political monopoly in parliamentary politics, and he criticized both left and right extraparliamentary movements for competing with political parties for a presence in the Hungarian political scene.

SZDSZ also had internal debates and leadership conflicts over movement versus party, but in its case, technocrats lost their positions, and SZDSZ preserved its openness toward social movements and political protest. The so-called taxi-driver blockade, a three-day nationwide street blockade by taxi drivers and their supporters against a sudden large increase in fuel prices by the government in October 1990, made the two parties' differences clear. Fidesz rejected the drivers' demands, but the leaders of SZDSZ joined them in their demands. This type of extraparliamentary engagement was preserved in SZDSZ but diminished in Fidesz during 1990–1994 (Bozóki 1992).

Fidesz, after its strategic reorientation in 1992–1993, increasingly supported church and nation (Mudde and Kopecky 2002; Falk 2003) and grew from an alternative party in 1988 to a liberal party in 1992 and from a liberal to a center-right, Christian populist party between 1992 and 1998, when it changed its name to Fidesz-MPP (Magyar Polgári Párt; Hungarian Citizens' Party). It also changed its character internationally, quitting the European Convention of Liberal Parties and becoming a member of the Christian Democrats. Its alliances changed: Fidesz had backed the SZDSZ, but after SZDSZ joined the Socialist parties in 1994–1998 in a governing coalition, Fidesz allied with right-wing opposition parties.

From Fidesz to Fidesz-MPP: Gaining the Leadership of the Center Right

At the general elections in 1994, Fidesz won 7 percent of the seats and sent only twenty representatives to parliament (see Figure 14.1). In the wake of the party's failure in the elections, the entire party leadership resigned, although Orbán had been reelected again as party chairman. The party analyzed its loss in the document "From Opposition into Opposition."

At Fidesz's Seventh Party Congress in late April 1995 in Budapest, the delegates changed the name of the party to Fidesz–Hungarian Civic Party and adopted the declaration "For a Civic Hungary," which stated that Fidesz was a liberal civic party. Orbán, elected as party chairman for the third consecutive time, proposed a three-party alliance between Fidesz, MDF, and the Keresztény Demokrata Néppart (KDNP; Christian Democratic People's Party), believing that was the only viable alternative to the MSZP-SZDSZ coalition, which had an overwhelming 72 percent majority in the parliament.

Orbán and the chairman of MDF started negotiations on their parties' cooperation in May. In September KDNP disbanded, and the number of Fidesz parliamentarians increased by fourteen (thirteen from the disbanded KDNP plus one former MDF member). With its thirty-four members of parliament, Fidesz had become the biggest opposition party and entitled to one of the vice-chairmanships of parliament. In October, the Fidesz National Board adopted a resolution calling on Fidesz to conclude an agreement with MDF, which would make its position in next year's general elections much stronger. This agreement was signed at the end of the year. Fidesz reached a similar agreement with the group that had left KDNP, the Hungarian Christian Democratic Alliance (MKDSZ), which shared candidates with Fidesz.

At a meeting of the party's regional leaders in mid-December, Orbán declared that the conditions for cooperation between civic political forces had been fulfilled and that the flagship of this cooperation was Fidesz.

Fidesz as a Mobilizing Party

Political protest in 1989 related to the regime change. In the election years of 1990, 1994, and 1998, when political issues were part of the campaigns, protests diminished (Körösényi, Tóth, and Török 2009).The election years 2002 and 2006, with their polarization of the progovernment and antigovernment initiatives and organizations, were peak points of protest from the right, which accused the left of manipulating parliamentarism and constitutionalism for its own purposes and framed the electoral victories of the left and liberals as a conspiracy of communism and capitalism.

Hungarian communists remained politically influential by transforming their political power into economic and social power with the country's marketization and privatization. Continuity with the communist past was symbolized for them by the governments led by the MSZP in 1994–1998 and 2002 (Körösényi, Tóth, and Török 2009). Demand for replacing the "communist criminals" in official positions was highest in 1989, when the communists were still in power and the *nomenklatura* were in place. Along with institutional restructuring and changing political elites, this demand diminished but did not completely disappear, gaining momentum in 2002 and 2006 after left-liberal electoral victories. Fidesz-MPP was supported by right-wing protesters demanding review of election results and punishment for communist criminals. Their protests challenged governments of MSZP and SZDSZ in 2002 and 2006, calling them communist.

The 2002 election brought the MSZP-SZDSZ social-liberal coalition to power. The Fidesz ability to quickly put on a new face as circumstances required was called on to develop a new image and organization after its defeat. Fidesz-MPP opened up to citizen's initiatives (Citizens' Circles) from the right, which called for at least a recount of votes and at most that the new government resign and new elections be held. In 1992, Fidesz had criticized the mobilization strategy of SZDSZ and its protest against the government; in 2002, Fidesz-MPP adopted a new mobilization strategy that shared some of SZDSZ's 1992 strategy and was more accommodating of civil society to regain its position after its electoral failure against the left and liberals.

From Government to Opposition

The defeat in the 2002 elections made Fidesz-MPP again a mobilizing party. The Fidesz-MPP strategy was to target and challenge the communists who came back to political power in 2002 and regain its 1988–1990 image as an anticommunist dissent movement.

Fidesz-MPP as the governing party of a center-right coalition had acted like a populist government, stressing its national and popular (Glenn 2001; Mény and Surel 2002) character and holding meetings in small, unknown villages. Prime Minister Orbán had acted as though he had a direct link with supporting masses. After the Fidesz government's defeat, in his annual State of the Nation speech in February 2005, Fidesz chairman Orbán called for a "consultation," and a National Consultation Body was set up in March, consisting of conservative intellectuals. The consultation team toured Hungary throughout the summer and sent questionnaires to every citizen in the country to gauge their opinions on social and legal issues. This direct appeal to citizens was a favored mobilizing method of Fidesz and sees much use today.

The president's term ended in 2005 and in accordance with the Constitution the parliament was to elect a new one. Tensions within the governing social liberal coalition (which had only a ten-seat majority in the parliament) and other problems led to a victory by the opposition. In the third and final round of voting, a candidate who was not a politician but a professor of law, former underground green activist, and Catholic received the necessary support from Fidesz members, and in August László Sólyom took office as president of Hungary. Sólyom was nominated by an environmental NGO, Védegylet (Association to Defend), and in the popular vote of Fidesz supporters he received the majority of the vote.

Viktor Orbán was reelected as chairman of Fidesz June 11, 2005, and continued his campaigns to win popular favor. Civic Governance 2006, a Fidesz program, held conferences on new government policies after winning elections in 2005–2006. In the 2006 campaign, the party emphasized its pragmatic nature. Fidesz and MDF did not continue as a coalition in the 2006 campaign, and MDF distanced itself from Fidesz, which now needed a new ally as the 2006 elections came closer. Fidesz opted for the reorganized KDNP, and the parties' respective leaders signed a cooperation agreement. The two parties put up a joint list for the coming elections. MDF had separate candidates throughout the country.

Fidesz held its nineteenth congress in March 2006, and chairman Viktor Orbán was unanimously elected to lead the party and be its candidate for prime minister. The Fidesz platform was also adopted, and Orbán announced that the party would host a grand rally in Kossuth Square April 1, a week before the first round of elections. On election day a big crowd gathered before the parliament building and conservative intellectuals, artists, and athletes lined up to demonstrate their support for Fidesz.

In the first round, the Socialists led with 43.2 percent of votes cast; Fidesz obtained 42.0 percent, SZDSZ 6.5 percent, and MDF 5.0 percent. Fidesz had two weeks before the second round to refine its strategy to replace the Socialist government. Talks were initiated with MDF, but its leader, Ibolya Dávid, refused to aid Orbán. On April 23, after the second round, the Socialist-liberal government remained in office.

Return to Mobilizing Roots

A mobilizing populist style, following the concept of Yves Mény and Yves Surel (2002) but ignoring the wide range of meanings of *populism*, was gaining momentum in the political culture of Fidesz-MPP and its supporters (Márton Szabó 2006):

- Orienting toward antiestablishment, antielite, anti-political-class rhetoric
- Standing with the people to retain their national and rural plus ethnic community identity against the cosmopolitan Socialist-liberal parties and their allies
- Accusing institutional processes, such as elections and parliamentarism, of ignoring the popular will for reviewing election results in 2002 and 2006
- Organizing a Hungarian Citizen's Alliance (Magyar Polgári Szövetség)—and changing its name to Fidesz-MPSZ—with the nation and civil society, in which national and religious symbols play a role; establishing hegemony beyond the sphere of politics and society with cultural and social community building
- Remaking the party to give momentum to the spontaneously developed civic initiatives (Citizens' Circles, 2002–2005), on the one hand, and a political alliance of the center-right parties led by Fidesz-MPSZ, on the other

This mobilizing populism emerged partly by recalling former experiences, structures, and traditions of anticommunist dissent or by referring to Western center-right party models in Germany (Christian Democratic Union [CDU], called a *Volkspartei*, or a catch-all party) and Italy (Forza Italia). Using the Western model synthesized these elements into a unique political strategy and new, innovative organizational forms within Fidesz. At its 2003 conference the party adopted a new name—Fidesz–Hungarian Citizens' Alliance (Fidesz–Magyar Polgári Szövetség)—that reflected its reincarnation as a hybrid of civil society, the governing party of the nation, and a coalition of center-right parties under the strong-leadership democracy model of Viktor Orbán. In 2006, a right-wing popular mobilization, supported by Fidesz, against the reelected Socialist-liberal government and its prime minister, Ferenc Gyurcsány, resulted in violent riots. Fidesz tried to take the lead in opposing restitution of communism in its competition with the right-wing group Jobbik (Movement for a Better Hungary) in the extraparliamentary arena and also in parliament after the 2010 elections.

Against the Socialist-Liberal Government and the Crusade against Prime Minister Ferenc Gyurcsány

In the 2006 campaign, Fidesz did not repeat its political mobilization of 2002, instead merely adopting existing civic initiatives without even putting its own stamp on them. Fidesz lost that election, and the Socialist-liberal coalition was reelected. A few months after the election, on September 18, 2006, a tape recording of Prime Minister Ferenc Gyurcsány privately addressing the leaders of the Hungarian Socialist Party at the government-owned elite resort Balatonőszöd was released. In the "speech from Őszöd" (az őszödi beszéd), the prime minister criticized his own party's economic policy and said their campaign platform had been a lie, in the sense that it could not be implemented because of EU restrictions on further government debt in Hungary in 2006.

Approximately ten thousand people gathered in Kossuth Square in Budapest in front of the Hungarian Parliament. They marched to the nearby Hungarian state television headquarters to broadcast their demand for the resignation of the government and other radical and basic changes in Hungarian politics and society. The government rejected the demand and police tried to remove the protesters from the building. Thousands of demonstrators started a "siege and battle," in which rioters severely damaged the building and television equipment, that lasted till morning. The battle ended when the weak police force withdrew.

In the following days, confrontations and battles between police and demonstrators took place in the streets of Budapest. A demonstration in Kossuth Square was a permanent fixture until October 23, when police broke it up in preparation for celebration in the parliament of the fiftieth anniversary of the Hungarian Revolution by invited guests of the government. Fidesz had supported the permanent demonstration by sending speakers almost every day, but it rejected street violence and the illegal demonstrations, as did other parties of the parliament.

Break up of the Kossuth Square demonstration resulted in a wave of rioting elsewhere in Budapest during the October 23 celebrations. At an official mass gathering of Fidesz in the heart of Budapest, thousands of demonstrators fought police, built barricades on the Pest side of the city at Erzsébet Bridge, and later burned the barricades. (Erzsébet Bridge was the site of a traffic block on July 4, 2002, when demonstrators rejected the electoral victory of the Socialist-liberal coalition because of alleged manipulation by the Socialist Party). Police cordons closed off Kossuth Square until March 17, 2007, when massive criticism led the Budapest police to reopen the square to demonstrations. Fidesz parliament members, led by Viktor Orbán, removed the police fence February 1, 2007, to show their support for human rights.

The riots that started September 18, 2006, resulted in unprecedented material losses and personal injury. Police and demonstrators both suffered severe injuries. Private and public property was damaged, and tourism and business in Budapest were affected. Political actors and political institutions lost prestige, and Hungary lost its image of a peaceful and orderly place for investment and tourism. The global media had expected celebrations of the Hungarian Revolution but saw instead street fighting between authorities and citizens in Budapest.

Results of the 2010 Election

The Hungarian electoral system's majoritarian character helped Fidesz-MPSZ take the leading role of the right, despite competition from the extreme rightist party, Jobbik, which was the only relevant challenger from the right to Fidesz in the 2010 spring parliamentary elections. The left's Hungarian Socialist Party had no chance after the "speech from Őszöd" and police brutalities in the resulting mass demonstrations.

In the first round of the election, Fidesz-MPSZ and its allies won a simple majority of seats. In the second round, Fidesz and KDNP candidates won enough seats to achieve the two-thirds supermajority required to modify major laws and the country's constitution. The two major parties of the 1989–1990 regime change, the conservative MDF and the liberal SZDSZ, lost all their seats. Voters were influenced by the high unemployment rate—nearly 11 percent in March 2010. The Socialist MSZP (in the ruling coalition with SZDSZ) was further damaged by a series of corruption scandals involving its members and officials. Consequently, the opposing Fidesz-MPSZ-KDNP campaigned under the slogan "The time has come!" It promised to create one million jobs over ten years, boost lending, support small business, cut taxes, and punish crimes committed by communists (from the first communist dictator in 1947 to the last Socialist prime minister in 2009). Other major contenders included the rightwing Jobbik and Politics Can Be Different (LMP), a Green-liberal party founded in February 2009 out of Védegylet, the NGO that had backed László Sólyom, president from 2005 to 2011.

The participation of Jobbik (founded in 2003, it won nearly 15 percent of the vote in the European Parliament elections of June 2009) in the 2010 elections caused much controversy. Jobbik used anti-Roma and anti-Semitic rhetoric, and party leader Gábor Vona argued that "Hungary belongs to the Hungarians." Both Fidesz-MPSZ-KDNP and MSZP refused to enter a coalition with Jobbik.

The 2010 election brought a brand-new situation to Hungarian politics. Fidesz won all categories of voter: gender, location, age, educational level, and so on. The landslide resulted partly from how seats are distributed in the Hungarian electoral system, which favors the winner and puts other parties at a disadvantage, which makes them even weaker. This system, instituted in 1989, was meant to make a strong and stable governing majority possible. But in 2010, it led to a two-thirds majority of Fidesz.

The Wildflower Occupies the Flowerpot

The most successful political party in Hungary in twenty-five years combines the tradition of anticommunist dissent with new forms of populism from Western democracies. Since taking power in 2010, Fidesz has balanced populist mobilization with crisis management and the requirements of EU membership. It mobilized voters by promising to control the nation's economy, but it must also meet the EU's demand that Hungary be a stable and reliable member and support an austerity program. Voters are hoping that Fidesz can complete the transformation to a market economy, liberal democracy, and welfare state (Offe 1994), despite its conflicting roles as "friend of the people" and austerity management agent of the European crisis.

Fidesz, an outlawed protest movement of the Kádár communist era, has preserved its outlawed and clandestine political tradition and identity. It retains its strong anticommunism, popular mobilizing strategy and hatred for the agents of the communist past. Its leading activists, including its current and eternal prime minister Viktor Orbán, were socialized in the underground of the 1980s. Being outlawed in the communist system produced long-lasting effects on them. The myths, fights, and symbols of the suppressed protest movements still live in the goals and strategies of the current political culture of Fidesz-MPSZ: fighting communist crime, emancipating the country from the past, and being radical populists and searching for an alternative third way for fiscal policy.

The former protest movement had transformed into a party of the new parliament in 1990. Fidesz was a minority party with liberal affiliations. However, as Hungarian liberals moved into a governing alliance with the successor to the communist party, Fidesz moved to become the leading force of the center right. A competition among five center-right parties made Fidesz the leader of a center-right government (1998–2002). While the Socialists and liberals governed twice (2002–2010), Fidesz has become the chief mobilizing populist party within both parliamentary and extraparliamentary spheres. The economic crisis together with the protests it mobilized helped the Fidesz-KDNP alliance gain a two-thirds majority in the 2010 elections.

The tradition of being an underground political movement gives Fidesz in its role as the Hungarian government an innovative and provocative style of communication and action. "Actors make rules; rules make actors" is a leading idea of transition literature on the role of social movements in regime changes and democratization processes. The informal protest movements of the transition influenced the rules of the new democracy, which now has to obey those same rules. Protest movements become institutionalized as the political parties they back gain power. In this way "movementist" parties may emerge or reemerge, as Fidesz did in Hungary as a crisis manager of the economic and fiscal challenges of the first decade of the twenty-first century.

Hungary's EU governance was managed by a former underground protest movement between 2010 and 2014 that was sometimes an enfant terrible to the governments of the EU countries. Its main achievements—a Hungarian constitution and new basic laws—mirror a type of movement fundamentalism from the pre-1989 underground. The Brussels-led EU institutions and policies are provoking Fidesz in the same way that the Moscow-based Eastern Bloc did. Orbán organized rallies and mass demonstrations to support establishing Hungarian national days on March 15 and October 23. Many analysts have compared him to the late Hugo Chávez of Venezuela, although minus Chávez's left-wing vocabulary. This right-wing populism of the Fidesz Hungarian government has been harshly criticized by international organizations and in Europe, especially by the European Parliament, which passed resolutions against it. Fidesz has remained faithful to the anticommunism and popular mobilization of its movement roots, but its scope has expanded from a microlevel student community to a macrolevel, nationwide mobilizing party.

NOTES

Acknowledgments: I thank Dr. Ágnes Lux of the Eötvös Loránd University Faculty of Law and State Sciences, Institute of Political Science, for her kind help in preparing this manuscript. The research was supported by and realized under the framework of TÁMOP 4.2.4. A/2-11-1-2012-0001 "National Excellence Program—Elaborating and Operating an Inland Student and Researcher Personal Support System," a key project subsidized by the European Union and cofinanced by the European Social Fund.

1. Fiatal Demokraták Szövetsége (Alliance of Young Democrats) called itself FIDESZ in the 1990 and 1994 elections but changed its name in 1998 to Fidesz–Magyar Polgári Párt (Fidesz-MPP; Fidesz–Hungarian Citizens' Party). At the May 2003 national party assembly the name changed again, to Fidesz–Magyar Polgári Szövetség (Fidesz-MPSZ; Fidesz–Hungarian Citizens' Alliance). Within the alliance are different social and political organizations, among them the Christian Democratic Party (KDNP), which was an autonomous party but now is a satellite organization of Fidesz, despite having a leadership of its own, members in the parliament, and positions in the government. Currently, the alliance is one political unit with organizational differentiation.

REFERENCES

Arato, Andrew. 1992. "Civil Society in Emerging Democracies: Poland and Hungary." In *From Leninism to Freedom*, edited by M. L. Nugent, 127–153. Boulder, CO: Westview.
Bozóki, András. 1988. "Critical Movements and Ideologies in Hungary." *Südosteuropa* 42 (7–8): 377–388.
———, ed. 1992. *Tiszta lappal: A FIDESZ a magyar politikában, 1988–1991* [A White Sheet: The Start of FIDESZ in Hungarian Politics, 1988–1991]. Budapest: FIDESZ.
Csizmadia, Ervin. 1995. *A magyar demokratikus ellenzék* [The Democratic Opposition in Hungary]. 3 vols. Budapest: T-Twins.
Ekiert, Grzegorz. 1991. "Democratic Processes in East Central Europe." *British Journal of Political Science* 21 (3): 285–315.
Ekiert, Grzegorz, and Jan Kubik. 1998. "Contentious Politics in New Democracies: East Germany, Hungary, Poland, and Slovakia, 1989–1993." *World Politics* 50 (4): 507–547.
Falk, Barbara J. 2003. *The Dilemmas of Dissidence in East Central Europe.* Budapest: Central European University Press.
Glenn, John K., III. 2001. *Framing Democracy: Civil Society and Civic Movements in Eastern Europe.* Stanford, CA: Stanford University Press.
Haraszti, Miklós. 1990. "The Beginning of Civil Society: The Independent Peace Movement and the Danube Movement in Hungary." In *In Search of Civil Society*, edited by Vladimir Tismaneanu, 71–88. New York: Routledge.

Joppke, Christian. 1994. "Revision, Dissidence, Nationalism: Opposition in Leninist Regimes." *British Journal of Sociology* 45 (4): 542–561.

Kende, Pierre, and Aleksandr Smolar. 1989. *Die Rolle oppositioneller Gruppen am Vorabend der Demokratisierung in Polen und Ungarn (1987–1989)* [The Role of Oppositional Groups in the Beginnings of Democratization in Poland and Hungary]. Cologne: INDEX.

Knabe, Hubertus. 1988. "Neue soziale Bewegungen im Sozialismus" [New Social Movements in Socialism]. *Kölner Zeitschrift für Soziologie und Sozialpsychologie* [Cologne Journal of Sociology and Social Psychology] 40:551–569.

Körösényi, András, Csaba Tóth, and Gábor Török. 2009. *The Hungarian Political System.* Budapest: Hungarian Center for Democracy Studies Foundation.

Larana, Enrique, Hank Johnston, and Robert Gusfield, eds. 1994. *New Social Movements.* Philadelphia: Temple University Press.

Machos, Csilla. 1992. "Von der 'alten' zur 'neuen' ungarischen Opposition: Demokratische Charta '91" [From the "Old" to "New" Hungarian Opposition: Democratic Charter '91]. *Berliner Debatte Initial* [Berliner Initial Debate], no. 4: 57–68.

———. 1993. "FIDESZ—Der Bund Junger Demokraten: Zum Porträt einer Generationspartei" [FIDESZ—the Young Band of Democrats: A Portrait of One Generation's Party]. *Südosteuropa* 47 (1): 1–26.

Mény, Yves, and Yves Surel, eds. 2002. *Democracies and the Populist Challenge.* New York: Palgrave.

Miszlivetz, Ferenc. 1989. "Emerging Grassroots Movements in Eastern Europe: Toward a Civil Society?" In *State and Civil Society,* edited by Vera Gáthy, 99–113. Budapest: Ventura.

Mudde, Cas, and Peter Kopecky. 2002. "The Two Sides of Euroscepticism: Party Positions on European Integration in East Central Europe." *European Union Politics* 2 (3): 297–326.

———, eds. 2003. *Uncivil Society? Contentious Politics in Eastern Europe.* London: Routledge.

Offe, Claus. 1994. *Der Tunnel am Ende des Lichts: Erkundungen der politischen Transformation in Neuen Osten* [The Tunnel at the End of the Light: Explorations of Political Transformation in the New East]. Frankfurt: Campus.

Pollack, Detlef, and Jan Wielghos, eds. 2004. *Dissent and Opposition in Communist Eastern Europe: Origins of Civil Society and Democratic Transition.* Aldershot, UK: Ashgate.

Ramet, Sabrina P. 1991. *Social Currents in Eastern Europe.* Durham, NC: Duke University Press.

Schöpflin, George. 1979. "Opposition and Para-opposition: Critical Currents in Hungary, 1968–1978." In *Opposition in Eastern Europe,* edited by R. Tőkés, 142–187. London: Macmillan.

Szabó, Máté. 1991. "Changing Patterns within the Mobilization of Alternative Movements in Hungary." In *Democracy and Political Transformation,* edited by G. Szoboszlai, 310–325. Budapest: Hungarian Political Science Association.

Szabó, Márton, ed. 2006. *Fideszvalóság* [The Reality of Fidesz]. Budapest: L'Harmattan.

Tarrow, Sidney. 1994. *Power in Movement.* Cambridge, MA: Cambridge University Press.

Tőkés, Rudolf L. 1998. *Hungary's Negotiated Revolution: Economic Reform, Social Change and Political Succession, 1957–1990.* Cambridge, MA: Cambridge University Press.

Zald, Mayer N., and John D. McCarthy, eds. 1990. *Social Movements in an Organizational Society.* London: Transaction.

15

Defending Interests

Polish Farmers' Protests under Postcommunism

GRZEGORZ FORYŚ
KRZYSZTOF GORLACH

The changing economic, political, and social reality in Poland after 1989 created an environment for development of society as a whole, as well as its individual segments. The radical institutional change aimed to implement the principles of free market economy, liberal democracy, and a framework for civil society. The changes have brought new opportunities for development but also a whole range of threats. The most potent threat, from the viewpoint of individuals and social groups, seems to be of an economic nature. The attainment of political and economic independence, freedom for economic initiatives, and unlimited opportunities for participation in civic affairs caused all sectors of society to simultaneously lose their sense of economic security. Moreover, the political and economic changes created a visible division between those who took advantage of the completed transformation and those who mostly paid for the transformation. Such a situation might have been conducive to social mobilization and created a social base for democracy, yet it also resulted in the escalation of conflict between the state and some social groups afflicted by the negative effects of reforms. Such a conflict is conducive to social protests, which are a form of defense of interests on the part of groups that do not derive profits from the undertaken reforms. These groups might also treat these protests as a kind of political participation. Thus, protest seems to be a significant factor in democratic consolidation. Social protests have always had an essential impact on the shape of the Polish political system. In bygone times they helped trigger change and, as a result, the disintegration of the communist system (see Ekiert 1994). Currently, protests influence the process of consolidating democracy in Poland.

The new opportunities strongly affected farmers' households. Changes toward modernization unlocked farm-selection mechanisms, contributing to greater opportunities and diversity in terms of development and participation in a market economy. Many traditional farms were unable to develop under the new circumstances of the market economy. Others, merging into the modernization process, had to face the reality of rough market competition. Extensive changes left their mark not only on the structure of the farms but also in the minds of their owners. Adapting to the new conditions, people living in the country were forced to abandon traditional country values (land as a sacred value, strong connections between family and farm, etc.) and follow only the economic forecasts. The guiding principle used to be to maintain the farm at any price, but this principle was no longer required. Now the only criterion for keeping the farm in existence was whether the farm could turn a profit. The destruction of the traditional rural farming class accelerated at an unbelievable pace and continues to accelerate to this day.

As has been stressed before:

> At first glance, these "family farmers" might be expected to be the most likely supporters of the movement towards an economic system based on private ownership and free markets. This large community of more than 2 million land-owning households seemed a natural ally for a government seeking support in the early stages of the transformation and appeared to be the best prepared to meet the demands of the private market. This was not a hope expressed only by politicians. Social scientists (e.g., Cohen 1992) also reasoned in the same way as they pointed to privately held farm land, a rudimentary agricultural market infrastructure, and a collective memory of entrepreneurship. Actual developments, however, were quite different. (Gorlach and Mooney 1998: 263)

Therefore, we decided to look at farmers' activities in the period of post-communist transformation. We wanted to describe how they collectively tried to defend their interests. What are the major characteristics of their protests? Should they be treated—as Karl Marx once described them—as a "sack of potatoes" or "collective inactors" (Zhou 1993: 66) or, quite to the contrary, as important social actors contributing their own collective action in the democratic transition?

Farmers' Protests in Poland: Theoretical Perspectives and Historical Contexts

Exclusive and Inclusive Approaches to the Waves of Protest

The analysis of social movements in the theoretical perspective is based on the following assumptions. First, social movements are not isolated episodes; they have a tendency to form in clusters and, as a result, make bigger waves of protest than they would in isolation. The literature on social movements shows two fundamental approaches. The first one is restrictive and exclusive, in which waves of protests "[have] strong expansion and contraction of the magnitude of protest, extend over a longer period of time, encompass large parts of the social movement sector, and affect most national territory" (Kriesi et al. 1995: 113). Such a restrictive definition can sometimes turn against its users. The authors of this approach devote a lot of time to explaining why many protests of increased number and intensification do not meet these criteria. Consequently, they focus their analyses on large-scale protest waves, whose intensity, scope, and longevity force members of the national polity to take sides (113). In this perspective, as the authors state, "protest waves occupy an intermediary position between routine protests and revolutions; unlike routine protests, protest waves shake the foundations of the polity; unlike revolutions, they ultimately cause only limited damage" (113). In the sociological literature R. Koopmans has a less restrictive approach. He "distinguishe[s] protest waves as periods of intense and widespread contention from times of normal politics—essentially an empirical observation rather than a theoretical assumption" (2011: 41).

How one approaches the waves of protests determines the way of looking into more particular problems and the additional issues that relate to them. The exclusive perspective concentrates on characteristics such as mechanism of emergence, expansion, and discontinuation of the waves of protests. Within this perspective several controversies have appeared regarding the effect of the politics of the state authorities on the protests or the role of the competition of social movement organizations in the protest dynamics. After analyzing several societies, we define a pattern of protest methods and their changes that agrees with H. Kriesi and colleagues: "Seeds of institutionalization and radicalization [are] planted by the growing involvement of professional SMOs [social movement organizations] and external allies on the one hand, and the increasing repression of confrontational actions on the other" (1995: 122). That is, organizations are behind more protests, and protests become more radical or even slip into terrorism. The balance of external and internal factors determines the dynamics of protests. External factors include the repressive politics of state authorities and changes to the openness of the political system and protesters' chances of succeeding. Internal factors are the innovative forms of protests, their level of militancy, the scale of participation in social movements, and the support they can generate from nonparticipants.

Kriesi and colleagues' analytical perspective encompasses a relatively narrow area of interest. However, these authors collected material describing four societies of Western Europe—Federal Republic of Germany, the Netherlands, Switzerland, and France—and situations occurring in the United States and Italy, which allows making broad comparisons. The new social movements mentioned above are not the subject of our interest. First, our research subject is only one society (Polish society). Additionally, our analysis focuses on the actions of just one social category (farmers). We are interested in protests that in the sociological literature are not defined as new social movements. Quite the opposite, we study movements focused on defending a group's own interest. Finally, we are particularly interested in very specific periods of the history of Polish society, such as the political transformation of 1989 and social reforms that accompanied it. These periods indicate an unstable sociopolitical system, and thus Koopmans's inclusive concept of waves of protest describes them (2011: 41). As Koopmans emphasizes, differences between normal politics and intensified protests might be treated as "unequal distribution of contention over time and space [that] hinges on the self-reinforcing dynamics [of] political stability and instability" (2011: 41).

This analytical perspective creates opportunities for wider observation that is not limited by the dynamics of protests but treats protests as leading to a democratic consolidation of a society undergoing rapid, broad, and radical social changes.

Historical Perspective of Polish Transformation

Investigators focusing on the early stages of Poland's transformation stressed the relatively unclear character of group interests presented by major actors at that time. As Claus Offe points out, the "most conspicuous distinguishing characteristic is indeed the lack of any elaborated theoretical assumptions and normative arguments addressing the questions of who is to carry out which actions under what circumstances and with what aims" (1992: 11–12). Similarly, David Ost notes, "Social groups in post-communist society do not have a clear sense of what is in their interest and what is not" (1991: 3). Others argue, "Ost's point may not hold as well for Poland's farmers as for the wider population" (Gorlach and Mooney 1998: 263). Polish farmers might have had a well-developed sense of their interests as a result of their experience under communism, when they had to struggle with collectivization. During the late 1940s and early 1950s, peasant tradition and culture became their "weapons of the weak" (Scott 1985, 1990) against the enforced collectivization, which increased in the mid-1950s. The collectivization was followed by more sophisticated efforts from communist authorities to favor the socialized sector of agriculture—namely, collective and state farms. Certain economic measures were used to push private farmers to the collective sectors, leading to the policy of "growth without development" (Kuczyński 1981: 47). J. Wilkin writes, "The determined struggle of the peasants to survive, as well as the weaknesses of collective forms of agriculture, enabled peasants to force through greater changes in the socialist economic system than other social groups" (1988: 8). One change, in 1983, was really spectacular, not only in an economic interest sense but also in a symbolic one: an amendment to the constitution of communist Poland that treated family farms as an "equal [compared to other types of ownership] part of the national economy" (for a more detailed analysis, see Gorlach and Mooney 1998: 265–270). Polish peasants emerged from the communist period as a peculiar group. They did not experience the Western-type farmerization because of the nature of the communist economy and communist government policies of constant attempts at collectivization and programs of growth without development. On the other hand, they did not experience the extended collectivization that transformed the majority of peasants in other Eastern European countries in the Soviet bloc into working labor on state and collective farms (for a more detailed analysis, see Gorlach 2001: 51–78).

Because of "path dependency," or the claim that societies and particular social groups are not "starting from scratch" and find materials to build a new order in the ruins of the old one, we provide a historical perspective for considering the mobilization of farmers to protect their interests (Stark 1992: 4). Similarly, theorists of social movements claim that existing networks, preexisting organizations and institutions—such as the separate political party, even under communism, that Polish farmers had—and other material and symbolic resources might be used to organize social protests and efforts to defend particular interests (Tilly 1978; also see della Porta and Diani 2006). Zjednoczone Stronnictwo Ludowe (ZSL; United Peasant Party), as it was called under communism, was of course controlled by the leading communist party, Polska Zjednoczona Partia Robotnicza (PZPR; Polish United Workers' Party). However, it was based on the long, rich tradition of the peasant political movement that began as long ago as the end of the nineteenth century, and its role became more important in the 1980s, when delegitimization of communist rule resulted from the Solidarity revolution in 1980–1981 and there was a subsequent period of martial law (Korboński 1990). Farmers became very much involved in politics during the Solidarity revolution, forming three different organizations based on a variety of economic interests and regional networks.

In 1981, after a few months of intensive efforts, all the organizations were united under the Independent Self-governing Trade Union of Individual Farmers "Solidarity" (for a more detailed analysis, see Gorlach 1989; Gorlach and Mooney 1998: 268–269). Farmers' tendency to form organizations has increased since 1989 as a result of changing political opportunities. We argue that this tendency should be treated as not only a product of emerging democracy and the political ambitions of particular leaders or political groupings but also of differing perceptions of economic and social interests as presented by rural and agricultural social actors. To systematize this picture of the social and political rural stage, we employ two basic criteria to characterize the main messages of farmers' organizations: symbolic political issues (communist, solidarity, and postsolidarity) and socioeconomic programs (farmerization, the third-way approach, and fossilization). "Farmerization" means the emphasis on market forces and the perception of large and modern farms being the future of Polish agriculture. In sharp contrast, "fossilization" stresses the advantage of backwardness in postcommunist peasant agriculture in Poland. It describes the rather small and traditional farms, using more traditional (and often, more environmentally friendly) methods of production, that form the core of fu-

TABLE 15.1   PEASANT ORGANIZATIONS AND THEIR CHARACTERISTICS

| | Socioeconomic programs | | |
Symbolic politics (ethos)	Farmerization	Third way	Fossilization
Solidarity	SL-CH	PSL-PL NSZZ RI "Solidarity"	—
Postcommunist	—	PSL	KZRKiOR
Post-solidarity	—	—	Samoobrona

Source: Based on data from Gorlach and Mooney 1998: 277.
Note: SL-CH, Stronnictwo Ludowo-Chłopskie (Folk Peasant Party); PSL-PL, Polskie Stronnictwo Ludowe–Porozumienie Ludowe (Polish Peasants' Party–People's Agreement); NSZZ RI "Solidarity," Niezależny Samorządny Związek Zawodowy Rolników Indywidualnych "Solidarność" (Independent Self-Governing Trade Union of Individual Farmers "Solidarity"; KZRKiOR, Krajowy Związek Rolników Kółek i Organizacji Rolniczych (National Union of Farmers, Circles and Farmers Organizations).

ture Polish agriculture. The "third way" combines farmerization and fossilization, meaning that the future of Polish agriculture lies in its marketization and strict regulation, protecting farmers from the excesses of pure market forces (for a more detailed presentation, see Gorlach and Mooney 1998: 274–280). In Table 15.1 we present the political stage of rural (peasant) organizations after the political breakthrough of 1989. We refer to the symbolic politics (ethos) as the ideological origin of particular organizations and the second characteristic, or variable, as the main ideas of the socioeconomic programs of organizations in our investigation.

We agree that social protests are important in consolidating democracy (Ekiert and Kubik 1999: 183). Moreover, social protests have been treated as a legitimate method of political participation in contemporary democracies, and their role increases along with growing difficulties and deficits of representative democracy and its institutional arrangements (della Porta and Diani 2006). However, the literature on postcommunist transformation and consolidation and discussions of social protests in Poland, in our opinion, have not taken into consideration the specificity of farmers' protests and thus lack an analytical perspective. Therefore, we focus on farmers because of their peculiar history in Poland under communism, as mentioned earlier. Moreover, we extend the analysis beyond the period under Grzegorz Ekiert and Jan Kubik's investigation (1999) and cover the period 1997–2001 to form a broader historical perspective (see also Foryś 2008) and focus exclusively on farmers' protests.[1] We chose the period from 1997 to 2001 because that is when the second set of reforms (after the Balcerowicz Plan) were implemented by the coalition government headed by Jerzy Buzek and formed of the conservative (Akcja Wyborcza "Solidarność") and liberal (Unia Wolnosci) parties. The reforms in 1997–2001 resulted in similar discontent as that under the Balcerowicz Plan and caused the financial situation to deteriorate. The agricultural boom collapsed and farm incomes declined, leading to the second wave of farmers' protests.

In our examination we did not use the classic method for analyzing protest events, which takes into account only single protests. The units of analysis in the fifty-eight cases we analyze are single protests, series of protests, and protest campaigns. We include series of protests and protest campaigns for two reasons. First, such an approach was used by Ekiert and Kubik (1999), and we therefore used the same units of analysis, and second, we could not obtain complete information from newspaper accounts on all single protests, which were sometimes eclipsed by series of protests and protest campaigns.

Characteristics of Farmers' Protests

Number of Farmers' Protests

One of the most basic characteristics of farmers' protests in Poland is their number. The total number of all protests, of any type, in 1989–1993 was 1,476, with 112 of them (7.6 percent) being protests in which farmers participated. In individual years the percentage of farmers' protests were, respectively, 4.5 percent in 1989 (at the start of the transformation process), 11.1 percent in 1990 (the year of the Balcerowicz Plan), 6.5 percent in 1991, 6.7 percent in 1992, and 9.6 percent in 1993 (Table 15.2).

As can be seen in Table 15.3, the percentage of the total number of social protests, excluding farmer protests, remained virtually unchanged throughout this period, standing at around 20 percent. Protests by farmers were quite different from protests by other social groups. The lowest farmer protest activity took place in 1989; however, most farmers' protests in this year occurred in its second half. A significant increase in protests among farmers happened the next year, when the Balcerowicz Plan, with its negative consequences, especially

TABLE 15.2   COMPARISON OF FARMERS' AND NONFARMERS' PROTESTS BY YEAR, 1989–1993

	Percentage of total yearly protests (number of protests)					
Protesters	1989	1990	1991	1992	1993	Average (total)
Nonfarmers	95.5 (300)	88.9 (272)	93.5 (273)	93.3 (293)	90.4 (226)	92.4 (1,364)
Farmers	4.5 (14)	11.1 (34)	6.5 (19)	6.7 (21)	9.6 (24)	7.6 (112)
Total	100.0 (314)	100.0 (306)	100.0 (292)	100.0 (314)	100.0 (250)	100.0 (1,476)

Source: Based on data from Ekiert and Kubik 1999.

TABLE 15.3   COMPARISON OF FARMERS' AND NONFARMERS' PROTESTS FOR ALL YEARS, 1989–1993

	Percentage of total protests for all years (number of protests)					
Protesters	1989	1990	1991	1992	1993	Total
Nonfarmers	21.9 (300)	19.9 (272)	20.0 (273)	21.5 (293)	16.7 (226)	100.0 (1,364)
Farmers	12.5 (14)	30.4 (34)	16.9 (19)	18.8 (21)	21.4 (24)	100.0 (112)

Source: Based on data from Ekiert and Kubik 1999.

for agriculture, was put into practice. A significant decline in farmer protest activity the following year proved to be temporary, and protests started again after 1992.

During 1997–2001, the number of protests with farmer participation was 58: 12 in 1997, or 20.7 percent; 17 in 1998, or 29.3 percent; 13 in 1999, or 22.4 percent; 12 in 2000, or 20.4 percent; and 4 in 2001, or 6.9 percent.[2] Unfortunately, because we lack data regarding the total number of protests of all types in Poland during that time, we cannot make a comparison for 1989–1993. However, some conclusions can still be drawn by taking the number of protests into account: relatively little protest activity occurred at the beginning and end of 1997–2001, and maximum mobilization occurred in 1998 and 1999. In terms of the percentage of farmers' protests, 1998 was similar to 1990. In 1990 and 1998 the biggest numbers of farmers' protests were reported.

Types and Ranges of Farmers' Protests

The farmers' protests in the first period, 1989–1993, which has a broader point of reference to the actions of all protests, seem to be marginal actions compared to all of the country's protests as a whole. As it turns out, this is not quite true. A significant proportion took place as a simultaneous series of protests or protest campaigns and thus were hidden, even though they involved a few thousand to several thousand protesters around the country (Table 15.4).

These data show us a significant feature of farmers' protests: a salient tendency for single protests to dominate during the entire period. However, by examining the series of protests and protest campaigns categories, we can also see increasing frequency in these categories of protests in all cases. It is visible in the 1997–2001 period (especially 1998 and 1999). This demonstrates a special

TABLE 15.4   TYPES OF FARMERS' PROTEST EVENTS, 1989–1993 AND 1997–2001

	Percentage of total yearly events (number of events)					
Type	*1989*	*1990*	*1991*	*1992*	*1993*	*Average (total)*
Single protest	57.1	88.2	84.2	61.9	87.5	75.8
Series of protests	28.6	5.9	—	9.5	4.2	9.6
Protest campaign	14.3	5.9	15.8	28.6	8.3	14.6
Total	100.0 (14)	100.0 (34)	100.0 (19)	100.0 (21)	100.0 (24)	100.0 (112)
	1997	*1998*	*1999*	*2000*	*2001*	*Average (total)*
Single protest	75.0	52.9	46.1	50.0	75.0	59.8
Series of protests	16.7	5.9	38.5	50.0	25.0	27.2
Protest campaign	8.3	41.2	15.4	—	—	13.0
Total	100.0 (12)	100.0 (17)	100.0 (13)	100.0 (12)	100.0 (4)	100.0 (58)

Source: Based on data from Ekiert and Kubik 1999.

mobilization among farmers, visible in 1989, when the Balcerowicz economic plan brought negative consequences to farm households.

When looking at the types of protest actions in the first period, single protests dominated. In turn, this dominance of single-event protests might appear to reflect the weakness of farmer mobilization compared to other social groups. However, examining the total contribution of these single-event protests shows that the resulting contribution (to all farmer protests) is smaller than the same figure among protests of other social groups and compares at 75.8 percent to 81.4 percent. For farmers, the figures were 9.6 percent for series of protests and 14.6 percent for protest campaigns, and in the whole population of protests (encompassing other social groups as well as farmers) they were 7.3 percent and 11.3 percent, respectively (Ekiert and Kubik 1999: 117). These figures confirm the increased mobilization potential of farmers as well as their greater level of organization, resulting in a higher proportion of protest campaigns.

For comparison, similar characteristics of the period 1997–2001 reflected the trends in 1989–1993 that can be described as a kind of professionalization of farmers' protests. This professionalization stemmed from growth in the percentage of protest series and campaigns. The protesters had to mobilize considerable material, organizational, and human resources.

The territorial scope of the protests is another indication of the intensity and strength of the protests and level of protesters' mobilization (Table 15.5). We make a closer comparison between the farmers' protests and the actions

TABLE 15.5   GEOGRAPHIC RANGE OF FARMERS' PROTESTS, 1989–1993 AND 1997–2001

	Percentage of total yearly protests (number of protests)					
Range	1989	1990	1991	1992	1993	Average (total)
Local	42.9	73.4	52.6	47.6	79.2	59.1
Regional	14.2	14.8	10.6	23.8	4.2	13.5
Nationwide	35.8	11.8	36.8	23.8	16.6	25.0
Unknown location	7.1	—	—	4.8	—	2.4
Total	100.0 (14)	100.0 (34)	100.0 (19)	100.0 (21)	100.0 (24)	100.0 (112)
	1997	1998	1999	2000	2001	Average (total)
Local	58.3	70.6	69.2	66.7	100.0	73.0
Regional	16.7	5.9	7.7	8.3	—	7.7
Nationwide	25.0	23.5	23.1	25.0	—	19.3
Unknown location	—	—	—	—	—	—
Total	100.0 (12)	100.0 (17)	100.0 (13)	100.0 (12)	100.0 (4)	100.0 (58)

Source: Based on data from Ekiert and Kubik 1999.

taken by groups of all social categories using the analysis of Ekiert and Kubik (1999: 120–121).

In 1989–1993, local and nationwide protests dominated. Together, they represent over 80 percent of the protest instances that occurred over those five years. A relatively small number of regional protests were noted in 1989–1993, with the exception of 1992, when the regional and nationwide protest numbers were comparable. The similarity might be explained by the conflict that arose between the leaders of organizations. Consequent to the conflict, the Samoobrona (Self-defense) party, which began as a farmers' trade union and since 1992 has been a political party, became independent. This independence actually made the party less mobilized and thus it had less of an influence on the main government institutions. The dominant role that local protests played in 1989–1993 also presented a high potential for opportunities to mobilize compared to the opportunities of other social groups. Nevertheless, the preponderance of local protests shows that farmers were facing the basic problem of mobilizing their resources to enter the nationwide scene. A quick appraisal shows that the farmers appear to have undertaken protest actions of such a magnitude, not because the lack of available resources forced them to, but because resources were sufficient to achieve certain goals.

A polarization of the protest actions in terms of their range began to take place. Just as in the first period, local and national protest actions dominated, while the regional activities lost strength. Such a pattern of domination, apparent in both periods, can be explained by regional protests requiring significant effort from the protesters. The amount of effort made, such as mobilizing the relevant human and organizational resources, does not necessarily correlate with the likelihood of fulfillment of demands. The percentage of nationwide actions continuing at a similar level in subsequent years is what makes the second period (1997–2001) different. This is another argument supporting the claim that there was a professionalization of protests, which gained strength in the second period. The only exception was in 2001, in which only local protests took place. Local protests by farmers had their culmination point in 1998–1999. The events of 2001 confirm the eventual decline in farmers' protests. The number of nationwide protests in the second period indicates that the mobilization potential of the protesters was well formed and remained stable. Only the number of local and regional protests changed.

We now investigate the characteristic intensity of the protests, with intensity defined as the number of days of protests in the different periods. The total number of days of farm protests in the first period was 739 (Ekiert and Kubik 1999: 121), while the second period saw only 224 days (our data). Of course, since there were nearly 50 percent fewer protest events in 1997–2001 compared to 1989–1993, it is naturally somewhat difficult to compare these figures. Better conclusions can be drawn by taking the average length of protest times from both periods into consideration. The average duration of protest actions during 1989–1993 was 6.5 days (Ekiert and Kubik 1999: 121). In 1997–2001 it grew to 9 days (our data). The second period is thus characterized by more radical farmers' actions. The quantity and, perhaps above all, the quality of the protest actions were stronger and more intense in 1997–2001. On the one hand, the government had become increasingly resistant to the demands of protesting farmers. On the other hand, farmers began to realize that to achieve their goals they would have to show greater determination and take more radical actions.

Theory suggests that an important sign that mobilization of resources is available to protesting groups is when they start to use their own organizational structures. If the group does not have its own organizational structure, it creates one or uses that of other groups. All such techniques are aimed at increasing the efficiency of achieving the group's goals. They are also indicators for the researcher of the path the protesters followed. A conclusion drawn from the protest characteristics listed in Tables 15.4 and 15.5 is that professionalization of these activities must also be taken into consideration. The statistics of the farmers' protests reflect organization, which professionalized the groups and their actions.

Organizers of Farmers' Protests

The 1989–1993 period reveals three major changes in the organizational aspect of the protests. The first change is a systematic decrease in the percentage of spontaneous—planned by individual farmers without the formal participation of an organization—protests and a corresponding increase in organized protest. In 1992 there were no spontaneous protests, which may be particularly significant (see Table 15.6). Some spontaneous activities likely occurred, but they were probably marginal, and information about them was not included in the newspaper sources used in this study. This, of course, is only a supposition.

The second change also appeared in 1992. As can be seen, there was a new entity in the group of organizations, Samoobrona, which immediately took the lead in initiating protest actions and which may explain the lack of spontaneous protests that year. In years that organizations initiated more protest actions, spontaneous protests declined. In earlier years of the discussed period,

TABLE 15.6   ORGANIZERS OF FARMERS' PROTESTS, 1989–1993

Organization	Percentage of total yearly protests (number of protests)					
	1989	1990	1991	1992	1993	Average (total)
Farmers Solidarity	28.6	29.4	36.8	38.1	33.3	33.2
Samoobrona	—	—	—	57.1	33.3	18.1
Others	14.3	17.6	26.4	4.8	25.0	17.6
Spontaneous	57.1	53.0	36.8	—	8.4	31.1
Total	100.0 (14)	100.0 (34)	100.0 (19)	100.0 (21)	100.0 (24)	100.0 (112)

Source: Based on data from Ekiert and Kubik 1999.

organized protests had been growing. In 1992, with Samoobrona's arrival, participation by other organizations significantly dropped, and a kind of polarization of protests between two organizations took place. The two organizations were NSZZ RI "Solidarność" (Independent Self-governing Trade Union of Individual Farmers "Solidarity"), established in 1981, and Samoobrona. Throughout the whole period (except for trailing Samoobrona's lead in 1992 and a tie with Samoobrona in 1993), however, Farmers Solidarity held the leadership in number of protests.

The third change was how protest actions under Samoobrona differed from previous actions. With time, Samoobrona became a permanent part of the political scene, in the form of a political party with representatives in parliament. Ekiert and Kubik in their analysis completely ignore Samoobrona's evolution, even stating that no organization was created, despite their initial hypotheses. They note, "We [also] hypothesized that we would find a large number of organizations created as a result of the collective protest actions. None of these hypotheses, however, were confirmed" (1999: 125). The establishment of Samoobrona contradicted their observation. They analyzed the protests of all social groups simultaneously and noted that the nearly 1,500 actions of social groups could have weakened the effect that Samoobrona had built up. On the other hand, the explanation of Ekiert and Kubik confirms the assumption contained in this study, that farmers' protests must be analyzed separately. The specificity of the farmers' protest dynamics and occurrences associated with them allow this. As it turns out, Samoobrona was a perfect example of an organization developed on the wave of farmers' protests.

Somewhat similar trends in organization participation in animating protests occurred in both periods. In 1989–1993, Farmers Solidarity played the dominant role for the first years, but its role then declined in 1993. In 1997–2001, Farmers Solidarity again had the dominant role in the first years but that role declined beginning in 1999.

In 1989–1993, spontaneous protests were the second-largest category (nearly one-third of all events). By 1997–2001, spontaneous protests were by far the smallest category (just over one-tenth of all protests), confirming the institutionalization of collective farmers' protest actions. The first period was marked by a continuously declining growth rate. In the second period, there was a noticeable decline in the years 1998–2000, with increases at the beginning and end of the period (see Table 15.7).

We explain these different patterns of growth in two ways. First, in the early years, protesters believed that only a coordinated, organized action would bring desired results. Over time, a learning process achieved through common acting, which is emphasized in the theory of new social movements, took place (Ekiert and Kubik 1999: 47). Second, the appearance of Samoobrona in 1992 increased competition among organizations fighting for influence in the farmers' domain, thus the organizations could not afford to be indifferent to any collective protest actions.

TABLE 15.7   ORGANIZERS OF FARMERS' PROTESTS, 1997–2001

	Percentage of total yearly protests (number of protests)					
Organization	1997	1998	1999	2000	2001	Average (total)
Farmers Solidarity	50.0	50.0	32.0	20.0	28.6	36.1
Samoobrona	—	18.2	32.0	40.0	14.3	20.9
Others	16.7	22.7	32.0	33.3	42.8	29.5
Spontaneous	33.3	9.1	4.0	6.7	14.3	13.5
Total	100.0 (12)	100.0 (22)	100.0 (25)	100.0 (15)	100.0 (7)	100.0 (81)

The numbers of spontaneous protests in 1997–2001 clearly formed part of a broader phenomenon, a wave of protests. At the beginning there was a relatively large number of spontaneous protests. The wave rose to a maximum intensity and then began to fade as the result of the organizational mobilization of protesters. Later, in the descent phase of the wave, spontaneous protests began to intensify again. As the basic demands of organizations began to be realized, the organizations became less interested in supporting the protests. This was especially true for those less spectacular, single actions involving a small number of protesters. This confirms the way that single types of protest actions during this period worked (see Table 15.4), which coincides with the way spontaneous actions were carried out. The increase in the proportion of single protests was accompanied by the increase in the percentage of spontaneous protest actions.

Economic Reasons for Farmers' Protests

Although change in political opportunities associated with the beginning of democratization of Poland's political system contributed to the form and scale of farmers' protests, that change did not directly cause the protests. The direct cause of the farmers' protests was economic deprivation. The data in Tables 15.8 and 15.9 show changes in household incomes of individual social groups for 1989–1994 and 1996–2001. The vast majority of Polish society experienced at least economic inconvenience, but farmers saw the greatest impact. In both time periods, similar trends were present.

In the first period, 1989–1994, farmers' incomes saw very large declines in 1990–1992, obviously associated with implementation of the first phase of the economic reforms. Although other social groups saw similar declines, farmers and farmers/workers (those who had a small farm and also worked in a factory)[3] suffered the most. The main reason for the reduction of farm income was reduction in prices of agricultural products. Prices in 1989 were lower by more than 7 percent compared with 1988, and in 1992 prices were lower by about 25 percent compared to 1990. These decreases dramatically affected agricultural consumption and investment. A rapid collapse occurred in 1990, when consumption was

TABLE 15.8   CHANGES IN REAL INCOME (PER CAPITA)
IN FAMILIES, 1989–1994 (%)

	Type of family			
Year	Workers	Farmers	Farmers/ workers	Retired
1989	100	100	100	100
1990	66	75	71	72
1991	66	62	60	90
1992	66	57	52	73
1993	67	64	59	87
1994	77	72	70	101

Source: Based on data from Dziurda 1993; Central Statistical Office 1994, 1995.

TABLE 15.9   CHANGES IN REAL INCOME (PER CAPITA)
IN FAMILIES, 1996–2001 (%)

	Type of family			
Year	Workers	Farmers	Entrepreneurs	Retired
1996	100	100	100	100
1997	116	110	115	119
1998	138	118	134	137
1999	149	119	147	148
2000	166	133	163	153
2001	172	144	166	167

Source: Compiled from data in the 1997–2002 editions of the Central Statistical
Office's *Statistical Yearbook of Poland.*

less than half compared to 1989, and the biggest collapse concerned consumer expenses (Central Statistical Office 1994: 440, table 28).

Table 15.3 shows the number of farmers' protests in each year in 1989–1993. Most protest activity coincides with deepening declines in farmers' income. This is very clear in 1990 (thirty-four protests and a 25 percent loss of income compared with the previous year). In 1992 and early 1993, when there was a culmination of protests and a drop in incomes to their lowest level since 1989, there was another decline. In 1993 farmers' earnings slightly increased. The increase in farmers' protests in 1993, however, was a consequence of income having reached its lowest level just a year prior. This is explained by half the protests taking place in the first three months of 1993. The increase in protest activity during this period was a further culmination of activities that had actually begun the previous November.

Starting in 1993, however, farmers' income grew but still lagged behind incomes of other social groups. Other farmer-related economic indicators—mainly investments in farm improvements—also grew, as a result of government policy becoming more protectionist. The policy came out of the new coalition of Sojusz Lewicy Demokratycznej (SLD; Left Democratic Alliance), itself a coalition of leftist parties formed in 1999, and Polskie Stronnictwo Ludowe (PSL; Polish Peasants Party), an agrarian party established in 1895 and restored in 1989. Clear upward trends in farmers' income, however, slowed again in 1998–1999. This again underscores the strongly negative financial state of the farmers compared to other social groups. The incomes of other groups continued their upward trend. By the end of the 1996–2001 period, the incomes of other social groups had increased much more than that of agricultural households. Also, growth in other economic indicators, such as investments in farming and prices of agricultural products, stagnated, and the total collapse of the desired growth had to be dealt with. In fact, throughout 1997–2001 (except for a minimal increase in 1999 of 2.2 percent over the previous year) there were declines in investments in farm improvements.

During both 1989–1993 and 1997–2001 the sense of economic deprivation felt by the rural community was objective, as opposed to the subjective feeling of other social groups. This is incompatible with the opinion of Ekiert and Kubik, who, in analyzing the application of the theory of deprivation for their analysis of protest activity of certain social groups in Poland, said that "the wages in this [nonindustrial public] sector in 1993, *relative* to the wages of the industrial sector, were at their lowest since 1989. But if we include 1994 in the analysis, the theory fails: during this year, the wage gap between these two groups increased over the previous year, yet the magnitude of protests among the nonindustrial public sector employees was nowhere near its 1993 level" (1999: 152; emphasis in original). But it is possible that in the case of farmers' protests in the first and second periods, this theory does apply. It should also be added that Ekiert and Kubik, when analyzing all social protests in Poland in 1989–1993, did not believe that the economic factor was so important in triggering these actions. For them the improvement in objective economic indicators did not mean elimination of the subjective sense of deprivation of many social groups. Yet in the case of farmers, as it turns out, there was a close correlation between the objective worsening of their situation and a subjective feeling of deprivation. Farmers turned to protesting because they had real, financially related reasons for doing so. Figures 15.1 and 15.2 illustrate this correlation between the worsening of farmers' economic situation and their protest activities.

The correlation between the increase in the number of protests and the economic recession in agriculture was particularly visible in the 1989–1993 period; in the 1997–2001 period protests increased even while farmers' household incomes were experiencing stagnation (1998–1999). One farmer said, "I have a big farm. We got a loan and built a new cowshed. And now we have empty pockets. We pay 1,000 zlotys every month to repay the loan. At any time we could lose our possessions. The majority of us are in a similar position" ("Policja" 1999: 4). As the minister of agriculture said, "The biggest problems are found with owners of large farms who have taken out loans. The price of agricultural products dropped, thus farmers' income decreased, and they had problems with repaying their debts" (Wyrobec 1999: 29).

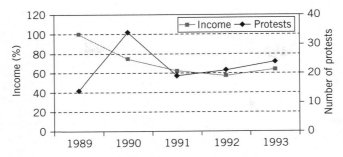

Figure 15.1 Income and number of farm protests, 1989–1993.

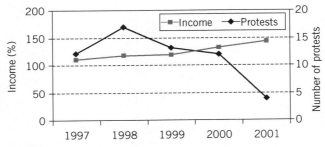

Figure 15.2 Income and number of farm protests, 1997–2001.

Protesters' Demands and Targets

The vast majority of the demands by protesting farmers in 1989–1993 related to their economic situation. Such demands (the material compensation and economic changes categories in Table 15.10) made up 82.5 percent of all reported demands over the whole period. Demands for material compensation substantially increased in 1989, the first wave of protests, as a direct response to the inconvenience caused by the ongoing transformation. This increase indicates a defensive response to the government's policy of intervention. Farmers were asking for price subsidies on agricultural products, low-rate investment loans, and cheaper fuel. Farmers expected the government to take direct and simple actions to compensate them for the effects of the prior government reforms. The government subsequently withdrew from intervention in the economy, including agriculture. The same response was visible in the category of economic changes too. Within this category farmers expected institutional changes in the economy of agriculture (such as debt cancellation for farmers, agencies for restructuring and modernization of agriculture, a ban on the import of agricultural products, and state protectionism in agriculture).

Moreover, particularly in 1989, the demands had a kind of class character and were limited to problems related to a particular category and its interests. In other words, the demands reported were made by the protesters on behalf of

TABLE 15.10   DEMANDS AND GRIEVANCES IN FARMERS' PROTESTS, 1989–1993

	Percentage of total yearly demands (number of demands)					
Type of demand	1989	1990	1991	1992	1993	Average (total)
Material compensation	57.1	26.5	15.8	42.9	32.1	34.9
Economic changes	39.6	29.9	52.1	52.3	64.3	47.6
Political changes	3.3	17.6	10.9	—	3.6	7.1
Changes in specific policies	—	26.0	5.3	—	—	6.3
Unknown demand	—	—	15.9	4.8	—	4.1
Total	100.0 (65)	100.0 (90)	100.0 (47)	100.0 (19)	100.0 (28)	100.0 (249)

Source: Based on data from Ekiert and Kubik 1999.

the protesters. This relationship is shown by the largest percentage of material compensation demands being in that year; 1992 came in second. In 1989, protesters were reacting to the profound economic changes. In 1992, the increase in demands can be explained, we believe, by the arrival of Samoobrona on the union scene. Samoobrona's demands and populist program dominated in 1992 as an organizer of protest actions by farmers. But Samoobrona's presence also led to a rebound in the number of demands for material compensation.

There was a relatively small proportion of political demands in 1989–1993. Demands to dismiss political or government officeholders related mostly to the economy. However, because of limited data, Table 15.10 shows only two years' (1990 and 1991) demands related to changes in certain policy areas: in 1990 there were many reported demands of an economic nature and for changes in the growing protectionist nature of government policy, at least in the area of agriculture. Nonetheless, there was some sense of a return to the rules of real socialism, so it cannot be definitively claimed that the protests had an antisystem nature. The demands were not the expression of a total negation of democracy and free markets. Farmers were aware of the new reality of opportunities available to them, but they did not necessarily agree to bear the economic risks and consequences caused by the implementation of the rules governing that reality. In this sense, that aspect of farmers' protests differed slightly from the characteristics of protests of other social groups. The fundamental differences were that in the case of protests by other social groups, the share of economic demands was noticeably smaller than in the farmers' protest groups. Economic demands made up "only" 57.5 percent (Ekiert and Kubik 1999: 131) of the cause of protests by other protest groups. Farmers' protests based on economic demands were 82.5 percent (material compensation and economic changes; see Table 15.10). Included within the economic demands of all the protests reported by Ekiert and Kubik were demands of a political nature as well. Political demands towered over the share of economic demands and amounted among other social groups to 30.3 percent (1999: 131). Likewise, this was shown in the proportion of economic demands in individual years of the first protest wave within all social groups. Just as in the case of farmers' protests, economic demands of other social groups dominated in 1989 (66.7 percent), but the order in subsequent years was different. In the case of farmers' protests, the proportion of economic demands increased in 1992 and 1993 and decreased in 1990–1991, while for protests overall, the trend was the opposite. There were increases in 1991 (62.2. percent), and declines in subsequent years. This comparison reveals the diversity of farmers' protests against the backdrop of protests by other social groups.

The observed trends concerning the inclusion of individual categories of claims by farmers and all social categories may indicate the presence of two differentiating factors in the timing of the protests. First, the vast dominance in economic demands among farmers occurred mainly because of the collapse of farm incomes. In other social groups this factor was also dominant, but its pressure was not so significant because the decrease in incomes was not so severe. Second, we believe that the different growth of economic demands between groups in individual years can be explained by the protests becoming more politically oriented in all social groups in 1991–1993. Ekiert and Kubik also emphasize this political influence (see 1999: 132). This was the reason for the decreasing number of economic demands. However, farmers' protests, as is clear from the pattern of the protests, underwent a sort of "economization." Economic factors became increasingly important in the years after the protests for the owners of large farms, but this is speculation in the absence of data for 1989–1993.

Another element present in the farmers' demands was a growing ability to articulate the needs for overall economic changes in agriculture. This could indicate a gradual maturation in the consciousness of farmers that simple material compensation cannot solve the growing problems of agriculture. The ability to articulate significant modifications needed in agricultural policy was also seen as necessary. Later years, especially 1994–1997, would confirm this observation. Agricultural policy in 1994–1997 left behind neoliberal principles and increased government participation in a return to protectionist policies in agriculture. Furthermore, in a sense, agricultural policy in 1994–1997 was a result of the first wave of protests. Lack of data prohibits a definitive comparison of farmers' demands with the demands of other social categories during the second wave of protests. Trends in farmer demands in 1997–2001 are shown in Table 15.11.

The second wave was characterized by a strong dominance in the demands for changes to economic policy. There were fewer demands concerning material compensation, although the sum of these two categories (material compensation and economic changes) amounted to 74.1 percent of all protest demands. In the following years there was decreasing inclusion of material compensation demands. To some extent, this was a result of the actions undertaken by the coalition government of 1993–1997. The coalition of SLD and PSL did indeed start changing the course of liberal agricultural policy. During the next economic collapse, especially 1998–1999, it appeared that Polish agriculture required

TABLE 15.11   DEMANDS AND GRIEVANCES IN FARMERS' PROTESTS, 1997–2001

| Type of demand | *Percentage of total yearly demands (number of demands)* | | | | | |
	1997	*1998*	*1999*	*2000*	*2001*	*Average (total)*
Material compensation	20.0	12.8	14.9	13.3	—	12.2
Economic changes	52.0	61.7	48.9	66.7	80.0	61.9
Political changes	12.0	6.4	19.1	6.7	20.0	12.8
Changes in specific policies	8.0	2.1	4.2	13.3	—	5.5
Unknown demand	8.0	17.0	12.9	—	—	7.6
Total	100.0 (25)	100.0 (47)	100.0 (47)	100.0 (30)	100.0 (5)	100.0 (154)

long-term reforms to ensure stability and predictable conditions. The main expectations, and the fight for economic changes related to them, focused on two issues that were especially evident during 1997–1999: first, the introduction of a duty on imported agricultural products, especially grain, from abroad and, second, market stability and the ability to profit from agricultural production by establishing minimum prices.

Compared with material compensation and economic changes, political demands were rather modest in 1997–2001 although more than material compensation alone. The vast majority of the demands concerned resignation of people occupying leading positions (Prime Minister Jerzy Buzek, Minister of Finance Leszek Balcerowicz) or resignation of the entire government and dissolution of the parliament. The political demand, which competed to some extent with the demand for resignations, was to increase protesters' influence on political decisions. But overall, farmers' protests were about economics, in contrast with the protests of other social groups, which were more political, according to Ekiert and Kubik (1999).

The previous demands of protesters were clearly defined. They addressed individual people, political and economic institutions, and organizations both Polish and international. We examine indirect and direct targets of protest actions in both periods.[4] Tables 15.12 and 15.13 show indirect and direct targets of farmers' protests. Both help us consider the changing nature of protests in the globalization and Europeanization of the public scene in Poland after 1989.

The percentages of protest issues in the first wave of protests show that the country's central institutions (government, parliament, office of the president, and individual ministries) dominated. A significant part of the direct issues were made up of regional and local institutions. In our opinion, however, such issues were exceptions to the rule, resulting from particular types of assumptions. First, we noted that as percentages of protests aimed at local and regional institutions increased, protests directed at central institutions dropped. Therefore, the recipient of the demands shifted from a higher to a lower institutional level. With this shift came a decreased mobilization potential of protesters that

TABLE 15.12 DIRECT AND INDIRECT TARGETS OF PROTESTS, 1989–1993

	Percentage of total yearly targets (number of targets)					
Direct targets	*1989*	*1990*	*1991*	*1992*	*1993*	*Average (total)*
Central institutions of the state	50.0	47.1	45.5	66.7	58.3	53.5
Regional and local institutions	8.3	38.2	36.4	20.0	16.7	23.9
Other	41.7	8.8	4.5	—	20.8	15.2
Unknown target	—	5.9	13.6	13.3	4.2	7.4
Total	100.0 (24)	100.0 (51)	100.0 (22)	100.0 (26)	100.0 (53)	100.0 (176)
Indirect targets						
Central institutions of the state	64.0	70.6	83.0	90.5	87.5	79.1
Regional and local institutions	—	3.0	4.3	—	—	1.5
Foreign proprietors and institutions	28.6	8.7	10.6	—	—	9.6
Other	7.4	17.7	2.1	9.5	12.5	9.8
Total	100.0 (14)	100.0 (101)	100.0 (47)	100.0 (81)	100.0 (263)	100.0 (506)

Source: Based on data from Ekiert and Kubik 1999.

TABLE 15.13 DIRECT AND INDIRECT TARGETS OF PROTESTS, 1997–2001

	Percentage of total yearly targets (number of targets)					
Direct targets	*1997*	*1998*	*1999*	*2000*	*2001*	*Average (total)*
Central institutions of the state	65.0	60.0	61.3	50.0	100.0	67.2
Regional and local institutions	15.0	12.5	12.9	10.0	—	10.1
Other	20.0	27.5	25.8	40.0	—	22.7
Total	100.0 (20)	100.0 (40)	100.0 (31)	100.0 (20)	100.0 (7)	100.0 (118)
Indirect targets						
Central institutions of the state	72.2	100.0	91.7	93.8	85.7	88.7
Regional and local institutions	11.1	—	4.2	—	—	3.0
Other	16.7	—	4.2	6.3	14.3	8.3
Total	100.0 (18)	100.0 (24)	100.0 (24)	100.0 (16)	100.0 (7)	100.0 (89)

was not necessarily expressed by a decrease in the number of protests (most protests took place in 1990). Instead, a single type of protest action—local—predominated in 1990–1991, when a marked increase in local and regional protests occurred, during which the respective entities ended up being the receivers of the demands. For the majority of the protesters, these institutions were considered the only available targets at that time for receiving their protest actions and list of demands.

The targeting of the government, parliament, president, individual ministries, and so on, in direct protest actions depended primarily on the mobilizing potential of the protesters, assuming they acted in a rational way and always articulated demands directly against the entity with the highest executive power for the realization of those demands. The highest power will always lie in national institutions, which means it will always be necessary to have significant resources. In practice, this meant organizing protests mostly in Warsaw and, to achieve the desired effect, involving a large number of protesters. Since there was not an overabundance of protesters in the capital, it was decided to undertake smaller-scale actions directed at state representatives in the field.

These demands seem to confirm the statistics pertaining to the targeted receivers of all demands during 1989–1993. The participation of what may be considered average-level state representatives in the field was comparable to the minimum amount of participation by the central institutions. The targeted recipient is also a factor to be taken into consideration by protesters aiming for the desired result. It was definitely expected that the government and its institutions could offer a guarantee for executing the demands. Almost 80 percent of the targets of farmers' and other social groups' protests were central institutions, mainly the government and individual ministries. Slightly more than 9 percent of farmers' and other groups' protest targets were regional and local levels of institutions (Ekiert and Kubik 1999: 135).

Trends observed during the second wave of protests are presented in Table 15.13. These trends confirm the primary regularity observed in the earlier period. However, a detailed analysis of individual categories shows several differences between the two waves. Before presenting these differences, it is worth looking at the years 1997–2001, which deal with the main targets of protest actions.

Protests for improving conditions with central institutions as direct targets occurred more often during the second wave than the first, making up more than 60 percent of these. They remained close to 60 percent for the period, with the exception of 2000 and 2001. A decline to 50 percent in 2000 saw a corresponding increase in another category. The year 2001 was marked by a significant increase over the average, which was caused by all the actions that year for improving conditions were conducted in Warsaw (the capital). The central institutions were nearby, which allowed the demands to be made directly to the representatives. These representatives did not necessarily act as the main recipients in each case. It was a fairly unusual situation, as in the previous period and in the earlier years of the second wave of protests, because in each case, a greater proportion of central government institutions were the main targets of protest. An exception to this rule was seen in 2001, when the protesters, in some cases, gave the government an intermediary role in conflicts or somehow bypassed the main recipient, thinking that the government would be a stronger guarantor of their demands.

Conclusion

The mobilization potential of farmers was greater than that of other social categories and was accompanied by a higher level of organization of the protest actions. They had greater participation in protest campaigns and series of protests. This is clearly visible only for 1989–1993 and may only be assumed for the years 1997–2001. However, throughout the entire time frame under investigation, farmers have actively been trying to defend their economic interests by protesting existing policies and challenging the state.

Activities aimed at improving agricultural conditions led to emergence of new organizational entities. Samoobrona's emergence and subsequent career has confirmed the specificity of the farmers' protests.

The demands of the farmers were related to their economic situation. That formed also the peculiar organization of farmers' protests along the lines of producers of particular goods. Modernization of many farms and their connection to the market resulted in the weakening of farmers' solidarity and the emergence of branch group interests.

With the increased organization of protests (as with farmers' protests) the diversity of the methods of protest decreased. Moreover, the tendency toward the institutionalization of protests has also been confirmed. For example, we observed that organizations' role grew in initiating and carrying out protest actions, spontaneous protest actions decreased, and cooperation between the rural organizations increased. The involvement of farmer organizations in such activities constitutes a major resource for farmers. Moreover, the processes that led to established organizations becoming more involved in the protest movement were the same ones that led to the professionalization and routinization of protests. The professionalization was expressed primarily by the increase in the percentage of actions that were a series of protests and protest campaigns. This increase also showed the increased mobilization of protesters, because these actions required the involvement of considerable human and organizational resources.

Appearance of organizations ready to initiate and lead protest actions was not the only sign of institutionalization; cooperation was another. Organizations' initial mistrust for each other during the first wave of protest and intense rivalry became close cooperation in 1997–2001. Protesters also developed repertoires of protests. The second wave of rural protest exhibited repertoires of long-lasting actions (blockades of roads, demonstrations, and vandalism).

Institutionalization was also apparent in the interactive aspect of protest action. Internally, farmers' organizations cooperated among themselves; externally, they formed a permanent way of reaching a compromise between themselves and the state. Negotiations were a road to it. In this way farmers' problems and farms entered the forum of conventional politics and in the process were pulled into the mainstream of the contemporary political debate.

Farmers' protests showed that they are capable of affecting government policy and are a significant political force that can independently influence policy in Poland. Thanks to the peculiar dynamics of farmers' protests, they had a chance to develop. Both the institutionalization and professionalization of farmers' protests demonstrate, we believe, democratic consolidation in the postcommunist transition in Poland. At the same time, they show the process of modernization, not only for many of the farms but also their owners through their public participation in democratic society, such as protest activities. Polish peasants became transformed into modern farmers by the democratic transition. However, at the same time, farmers should be treated not as a Marxian "sack of potatoes" or "collective inactors" (Zhou 1993: 66) but as one of the architects of the new democratic order in contemporary Poland.

NOTES

Acknowledgments: We express our gratitude to Grzegorz Ekiert and Jan Kubik for giving us access to their database of social protests in Poland from 1989 to 1993.

1. We gathered material using the protest events analysis method, accepted by researchers for studying collective actions, protests, and social movements and which gathers information about protests from newspapers, police statistics, and movement documents. The method provides the most extensive and systematic sets of data on protests and both qualitative and quantitative aspects of protest actions. Our analysis is based on information contained in the two national daily newspapers, *Gazeta Wyborcza* and *Rzeczpospolita* (1997–2001). These newspapers are the biggest, most comprehensive, and most detailed in Poland. We took into consideration, among other things, characteristics of protests such as type of protest (single, series of protests, protest campaign), number of participants, range, organizer, type of demands, addressee of demands, and duration. With the consent of Grzegorz Ekiert and Jan Kubik, we also used accumulated data from their research (1989–1993), which was funded by the Program for the Study of Germany and Europe, administered by the Center for European Studies at Harvard University. This allowed us to gather information about rural protests in the fullest possible way. For more on the protest events analysis method, see Tilly 1995; Tarrow 1989; Koopmans and Ruimann 1999; and Ekiert and Kubik 1999.

2. These fifty-eight protest events comprise single protests, series of protests (different protest actions undertaken by various collective actors at the same time that articulate the same or similar demands), and protest campaigns (protest actions officially coordinated by one decision-making center).

3. This category disappeared after the fall of communism, which explains its absence in the data used for Table 15.9.

4. Indirect targets of protests were perceived by protesters as the reason for their problems and the entities capable of resolving these problems. Because protesters often

did not have the resources to act against these targets, direct targets, who were in direct contact with protesters, were sometimes a substitute.

REFERENCES

Central Statistical Office. 1994. *Statistical Yearbook of Poland, 1993*. Warsaw: Central Statistical Office.

———. 1995. *Statistical Yearbook of Poland, 1994*. Warsaw: Central Statistical Office.

———. 1997–2002. *Statistical Yearbook of Poland*. Warsaw: Central Statistical Office.

Cohen, S. 1992. "Staggering toward Democracy: Russia's Future Is Far from Certain; A Roundtable Discussion." *Harvard International Review* 15 (2): 14–17.

della Porta, D., and M. Diani. 2006. *Social Movements*. Oxford: Wiley-Blackwell.

Dziurda, M. 1993. "Dochód na głowę: Na łeb, na szyję" [Per Capita Income: The Rapid Decline]. *Tygodnik Solidarność* [Weekly Magazine Solidarity], no. 27: 2.

Ekiert, G. 1994. "Protest jako forma życia publicznego w Polsce postkomunistycznej 1989–1992" [Protest as a Form of Public Life in Postcommunist Poland 1989–1992]. In *Studia Socjologiczne* [Sociological Studies], no. 2: 5–31.

Ekiert, G., and J. Kubik. 1999. *Rebellious Civil Society: Popular Protest and Democratic Consolidation in Poland, 1989–1993*. Ann Arbor: University of Michigan Press.

Foryś, G. 2008. *Dynamika sporu: Protesty rolników w III Rzeczpospolitej* [The Dynamic of Contention: Farmers' Protests in Poland]. Warsaw: Scholar.

Gorlach, K. 1989. "On Repressive Tolerance: State and Peasant Farm in Poland." *Sociologia Ruralis* [Rural Sociology] 26 (1): 23–33.

———. 2001. *Świat na progu domu* [World on the Doorstep of Home]. Kraków: Uniwersytet Jagiellonski.

Gorlach, K., and P. H. Mooney. 1998. "Defending Class Interests: Polish Peasants in the First Years of Transformation." In *Theorising Transition: The Political Economy of Post-Communist Transformation*, edited by J. Pickles and A. Smith, 262–283. London: Routledge.

Koopmans, R. 2011. "Protest in Times and Space: The Evolution of Waves of Contention." In *The Blackwell Companion to Social Movements*, 2nd ed., edited by D. Snow, S. Soule, and H. Kriesi, 19–46. Malden, MA: Blackwell.

Koopmans, R., and D. Rucht. 1999. "Introduction to Special Issue: Protest Event Analysis—Where to Now?" *Mobilization* 4 (2): 123–130.

Korboński, A. 1990. "Soldiers and Peasants: Polish Agriculture after Martial Law." In *Communist Agriculture: Farming in the Soviet Union and Eastern Europe*, edited by K. E. Wadekin, 263–278. London: Routledge.

Kriesi, H., R. Koopmans, J. W. Dyvendak, and M. Giugni. 1995. *New Social Movements in Western Europe: A Comparative Analysis*. London: University College London Press.

Kuczyński, W. 1981. *Po wielkim skoku* [After a Great Leap]. Warsaw: Państwowe Wydawnictwo Ekonomiczne.

Offe, C. 1992. "Democratisation, Privatisation, Constitutionalisation." Paper presented at the Post-Socialism: Problems and Prospects conference, Charlotte Mason College, Ambleside, Cumbria, UK, July.

Ost, D. 1991. *Solidarity and the Politics of Antipolitics: Opposition and Reform in Poland since 1968*. Philadelphia: Temple University Press.

"Policja usuwa blokady" [Police Remove Blockades], 1999. *Rzeczpospolita* [The Republic], January 26, p. 4.

Scott, J. C. 1985. *Weapons of the Weak: Everyday Forms of Peasant Resistance.* New Haven, CT: Yale University Press.

———. 1990. *Domination and the Arts of Resistance: Hidden Transcripts.* New Haven, CT: Yale University Press.

Stark, D. 1992. "Path Dependence and Privatization Strategies in East Central Europe." *East European Politics and Society* 6 (1): 17–54.

Tarrow, S. 1989. *Democracy and Disorder: Protest and Politics in Italy, 1965–1975.* Oxford: Clarendon Press.

Tilly, C. 1978. *From Mobilization to Revolution.* New York: Random House.

———. 1995. *Popular Contention in Great Britain 1758–1834.* Cambridge, MA: Harvard University Press.

Wilkin, J., ed. 1988. *Gospodarka chłopska w systemie gospodarki socjalistycznej* [Peasant Economy in a Socialist State]. Warsaw: Warsaw University Press.

Wyrobec, P. 1999. "Dlaczego dotować" [Why We Should Subsidize]. *Gazeta Wyborcza* [Electoral Gazette], January 26, p. 29.

Zhou, X. 1993. "Unorganized Interests and Collective Action in Communist China." *American Sociological Review* 58:54–73.

16

From Total Movement to Interest Group

Labor and Democratization in Poland

MICHAŁ WENZEL

W orkers were the driving force of postwar history in Poland, and political change was a direct result of labor protests. The systemic transition was achieved by the Solidarity movement, which united workers and intellectuals and was a mass phenomenon unique in recent history. At the movement's peak, every third adult Pole belonged to it. When it was banned, it went underground and led a cross section of the population in the struggle for democracy and freedom. It managed to combine far-reaching political goals with nonviolent methods, assuring a peaceful transition process.

After the system changed, the movement disbanded. It split into separate groups pursuing different interests, and most former members stopped identifying with it. It was an inevitable process: the changing roles of organized labor are related to the changing systemic constraints of the former and current system. The former authoritarian socialism had been unique in its degree of political control over the economy, which forced the opposition to act as a "total" movement, one pursuing a wide range of goals. Liberal democracy rendered such a model obsolete. The decoupling of political and economic power exposed internal contradictions within the unitary social movement. Interests of different economic categories started to diverge, and the common front of workers, intellectuals, and oppositional ideological groups crumbled. Unions started to act as an interest group for their members, and they often clashed with their former allies.

Some argue (see Ost 2005) that the Solidarity movement abandoned its base during transition, betrayed its goals, and helped implement a socioeconomic system inconsistent with the interests of the workers who constituted the core of its membership. I argue that the opposite is true. The movement was an active participant in the transformation processes, and it defended the workers' interests vigorously and effectively. Its decomposition was a key element in assuring effective transformation from the unitary, monistic system into a pluralist one. To oppose the monoparty, Solidarity pursued a broad-front strategy. In power, it did not strive for monopoly. Perhaps this is its longest-lasting legacy for the new order.

This chapter starts with a brief consideration of conceptual challenges related to comparing social movements in authoritarian and democratic regimes. It describes the trajectory of labor activism in pre- and post-transition. It documents the micro-level union participation in transition on the basis of protest activities during the time of the reforms. Finally, new forms of activism and new, post-transition challenges are considered.

Social Movements under Transition as a Research Problem

The study of the role of civil society and social movements in democratization processes necessarily includes the social, political, and economic context in which they functioned. One of the defining characteristics of the state under authoritarian socialism was the level of control: it controlled not only the political process but the nonpolitical associations as well, and it owned most enterprises. It was, ultimately, the employer to most employees. The ruling party not only set the economic policy but was involved in microregulating enterprises on a day-to-day basis. This political-economic setting conditioned the composition of the democratic movement and the direction of its actions. The Solidarity movement, by far the most numerous and the one with the biggest impact on the regime change, was formed as a trade union. In the former system, performing union roles entailed setting political (democratic) goals as well. It was impossible to improve the working and material conditions of employees without introducing sweeping reforms within the political system.

The democratic movement under the new democratic capitalist system was, again, largely conditioned by the political-economic change taking place during the transition years. The democratic transformation was accompanied by an extensive economic reform. Its core tenet was the reduction in state ownership of enterprises. Numerous state enterprises were privatized and some even went bankrupt. By the end of the twentieth century, most employees had a private employer, and most of the enterprises formed after the transition were not unionized. In these circumstances, the old Solidarity movement found it hard to sustain its mode of functioning. Economic and political power was no longer located in one hand, and the state would not and could not address the economic problems of employees of troubled enterprises. Solidarity, however, for a long time tried to operate in a way similar to the pretransformation period: to articulate a mix of ideological-political and economic demands. In the post-transformation years, it lost most of its members and societal support. After initial attempts to continue as a national movement, it restricted itself to articulating the narrow economic goals of employees within the state sector.

Spontaneous social activity (i.e., collective action that is not a routine or legally prescribed behavior of a social or political organization) under authoritarian socialism took the form of protest actions: strikes and street demonstrations. A study of protest is a study of what is considered proper in a given context: what is legitimate and conventional (Kubik 2008: 43). Movements that had defined themselves under the former regime struggled to find a function for themselves in an open political system because of the changing nature of what was legal and legitimate. The limits of legality were extended, and unconventional and illegitimate methods might have become ineffective.

The difference between pre- and post-transformation patterns of mass mobilization is manifested in the motivation behind the decision to participate in group activity. In general, participants need to see a stake in the actions they take. Selective incentives obtained by individuals are much better at encouraging participation than collective benefits or public goods (Olson 1965). Determining the correspondence between group interest and political outcomes is possible in an open political economic system, in which the level of interest articulation is directly linked to policies determined by the democratic process in which interest mediation is institutionalized. Under state socialism, the correspondence was unclear, because the authorities made decisions in a top-down authoritarian manner. Moreover, even if a movement was successful and managed to extract concessions from the authorities, the economic outcome of the resulting policies was unclear. For instance, the 1989 reform was supported by the workforce of big industrial enterprises, such as shipyards, but the abolishment of state socialism initiated events that would render shipyards useless and consequently bankrupt.

The open political and economic system introduced during the transformation made possible influencing policy making both through routine (e.g., the Tripartite Commission) and unconventional (e.g., protest) activity and allowed the calculation of costs and benefits from participation. Such a calculation was a significant motive for organizing, but it does not explain the variance in activities. In the case of social movements, as opposed to interest groups, the motive for joining is not the calculation of marginal benefits but a cluster of different motives (Kubik 2008). In the transformation years, a key factor in determining which organization a person joined was the identity inherited from the past system: whether a person had sympathized with the government or the opposition.

Democratization and a market economy changed the political opportunity structure, under which movements operate: formal institutional structure of the political system, informal practice toward protesting groups, and "configuration of power apparatus, directly impacting its opponents" (Kriesi 1996: 160).

The political opportunity structure required a change in tactic (from unconventional to conventional) and a shift in focus (from the state to a diverse set of targets: state, state enterprise, private enterprise). Social movements are vehicles for contentious mass mobilization (Tarrow 1998: 4). A movement emerges, develops, and disappears in continuous interaction with various actors in public life, and the government is its main adversary. Protests and social movements are calculated political strategies, employed when other models of interaction with the government failed (Tilly 1978). Because independent social activism was not allowed in authoritarian state socialism, interest articulation necessarily took noninstitutional forms, such as illegal strikes and demonstrations. Institutional interest resolution resulted in a shift of focus for the protest activity. The state was no longer responsible for the totality of decisions, hence multiple targets emerged.

The pre- and post-transformation period require a slightly different conceptual framework for describing social bottom-up activity. Conflict resolution becomes institutionalized. Whereas activism during state socialism can be analyzed as social movement, the post-transformation period is usually conceived of as civil society, or interest group expression. The former framework puts a stress on contentiousness and unconventionality; the latter foregrounds the institutional role of nongovernmental organizations (NGOs) or interest groups as mediators between the individual and the state.

Are trade unions a civil society organization? The question is whether organizing employees can be construed as a civic activity. The concept of civil society seems to have a different meaning when used in relation to authoritarian and democratic regimes. Under an authoritarian-state socialist system, both illegal economic activity and organizing employees in an enterprise bear the marks of civil activity: they happen at the grass roots, are beyond the bounds of the state, and involve locally organized communities. Consequently, proponents and theoreticians of civil society see the gray economic zone of the real socialist period as an asset in the transformation process and the emergence of free trade unions as the paradigmatic form of organization on the micro level (see Rychard 1993). E. Gellner believes independent civil activity cannot be analytically differentiated from the enterprise relations: "The unification of the economy in one single organisation and its fusion with the political and ideological hierarchy is not merely most inefficient: it also leads . . . to totalitarianism. . . . To allow an independent economic zone is to leave an enormous breach in the authoritarian system, given the importance of the economy. To deprive civil society of an independent economic basis is to throttle it, given the inevitability of political centralisation" (1994: 164).

The market economy provides a different setting. The economic and the political are increasingly separated, and trade unions become an interest group. Their goals are narrowed to the economic interest articulation. The other aims of a total movement are serviced by other types of organizations.

Postwar Working-Class Mobilization: 1956–1980

Paradoxically, the nominally Marxist state was undone by the class it purported to represent. The mass opposition movement that negotiated democratic change in 1989 was the final stage in a long line of development of working-class protest movements. The post–World War II years in Poland (1944–1989) were characterized by high levels of spontaneous protest activity. The subperiods of the People's Republic were bound by mass worker unrest, which triggered changes in the power elites and altered the political direction of the country. In the Marxist state, the economic and political demands were inextricably linked, because the economy was under strong political control at all levels, from the central government to the workplace; enterprises were, in fact, governed by a double executive, the nominal manager and the Communist Party committee overseeing the enterprise. As a result, any dispute, even when apparently devoid of political context, gained a political dimension. Party officials were involved in solving labor disputes. Consequently, economic demands instantly became political: they required the decision of the political (party) apparatus and were perceived as a threat by its leaders.

The first wave of postwar labor protests started after stringent restrictions, in force during postwar Stalinism, were eased in the mid-1950s. The industrialization taking place in 1949–1955 required a great deal of sacrifice from employees, and the standard of living did not rise correspondingly. The brutal methods of enforcing production plans, combined with continuing poverty, led to workers' frustration. In the USSR, after Stalin's death, Stalinism was condemned and the reign of terror was gradually eased. The political climate became milder. In these circumstances, a dispute over pay erupted in a heavy machinery plant in Poznan in western Poland. Officials at first agreed to concessions but later withdrew from the agreement. The news about the withdrawal caused street protests and riots. The demonstration was repressed by the army. According to different estimates, 60–80 people died, about 600 were wounded, and 250 were arrested.

These events triggered a political change from totalitarianism to an authoritarian system. In industrial relations, a significant but temporary change was the creation of workers' councils (*rady robotnicze*) in November 1956 (see Ost and Wenzel 2009). They were a means of assuring the direct participation of workers in the decision-making process in enterprises. The task of workers' councils was the comanagement of enterprises, in particular consulting on economic plans, setting the direction of enterprise development, deciding on allocation of profits, and setting output norms and pay rates. The functions were wide ranging and overlapped (e.g., in matters of pay and profit allocation) with those of official trade unions. This achievement was, however, short lived: they were effectively dissolved about a year later.

The next juncture in Polish political history was also caused by labor protests. Again, it happened in conditions of political instability. The party leadership was weakened by student protests in March 1968, which were followed by an anti-Semitic purge: Jews in official positions were exposed, labeled Zionists, and forced to emigrate. The political instability was coupled with a long-lasting stagnation in living standards and a sense that this was not about to change. In December 1970, street protests erupted in several cities on the Polish coast: Gdańsk, Gdynia, Szczecin, and Elblag. Industrial workers went on strike and protested on the streets. The party Central Committee resorted to force. The army and police were sent to control the riots and opened fire on protesting workers. At least thirty-nine people were killed, over one thousand were wounded, and three thousand were arrested (see Eisler 2000).

The workers' protests were, again, followed by a change in political leadership. In contrast to the previous period, the Edward Gierek leadership introduced measures to improve living standards. The indirect achievement of the protesting workers consisted of liberalization and changes in redistribution, which increased consumption. The basic principles of the political and economic system, however, did not change.

The origins of the Solidarity trade union (and movement) can be traced to the mid-1970s, when the Komitet Obrony Robotników (KOR; Committee for the Defense of Workers) was formed in response to government persecution of workers involved in the 1976 strike wave. Strikes were triggered by the same proximate cause as the 1970 wave: a sharp rise in the price of meat. News of the price hikes pushed workers in industrial plants in the cities of Radom and Ursus (now a Warsaw suburb) to go on strike. Apparently, the protests were spontaneous. The demonstrations were harshly repressed by the police, and massive arrests followed. KOR consisted of a group of activists, mostly intellectuals from Warsaw, some of them long-term opposition activists. Their best-known leader was Jacek Kuroń. KOR demanded "re-employment for strike participants . . . , amnesty to those convicted for protest participation . . . , full disclosure of information about protests and methods used to suppress them . . . , [and] trial for those responsible for torture and the beating of workers" (Kuroń 2009: 410). It supported workers legally and materially. It was especially active in alerting Western public opinion about these events and about other human rights violations of the Polish regime.

The formation of KOR was a harbinger of the Solidarity movement in two important aspects: it acted openly, and it was an attempt to form a class alliance between intellectuals and workers. One of the most important achievements of KOR was its legality tactic: conducting oppositional activity without openly violating the law. That was possible only if activists acted openly, which they did, abandoning the clandestine tactics used previously by some of them. Obviously, acting openly exposed them to easy persecution: a life of a long string of arrests and prison sentences (see Kuroń 2009: 412–440). However, their actions had a broad popular appeal for workers otherwise uninterested in politics and were strongly publicized by both the underground press and foreign radio stations that transmitted in Polish, such as Radio Free Europe.

The other innovative move was the alliance between intellectuals and workers: intelligentsia offered help for workers for the causes important for the workers (living and working conditions, recourse to the law, etc.). Previous working-class protests were largely met with indifference by intellectuals, partly because their demands were rather less important for white-collar workers than blue-collar workers (protests were almost always triggered by rises in food prices). On the other hand, when students protested in 1968 over freedom of speech, they were not supported by workers. KOR was an attempt to bridge this gap. Its core founders were later among key advisers to Solidarity and acted in opposition until the end of authoritarian socialism.

Social Movement as an Agent of Democratization: 1980–1989

The beginning of the democratic transition can be traced to a large (by far the largest in the postwar period) strike wave in the summer of 1980. The strike activity was most intense in the biggest cities, in the large industrial plants. The early locations of mass strikes were shipyards (Gdańsk, Gdynia, and Szczecin) and coal mines, but the protests spread around the whole country. Social and economic instability reached such a magnitude that the government was forced to offer genuine concessions. Crucially, political change was introduced in addition to economic benefits for the protesting workers. In particular, the right to form free, independent trade unions was recognized. For the first time, employees could organize and be independent of political control.

On the basis of the Gdańsk agreement between the strike committee and the representatives of the government, the Solidarity trade union was formed. Its original structure was territorial, rather than sectoral. In a short time, it reached a membership of eight to nine million, in a country of thirty-six million people. While it represented people of all walks of life, its core constituency was young manual workers in the production industry (Wenzel 2009).

To call Solidarity a trade union is misleading; it was much more than that. Solidarity was a broad social movement that represented or sought to represent not only employees but all sections of the society. It had at least three different goals during the early period: national liberation (asserting national values, including religious symbolism), workers' rights (asserting social-egalitarian values), and liberation of the society (asserting liberal-democratic values). In the interpretation proposed by Alain Touraine, Solidarity was acting for class, nation, and democracy. According to Touraine, "They wanted to drive the Party from their lives, and to limit it to its proper functions within the state, so that a free society might once more exist" (1983: 56). The early congruence of class, national, and democratic-social aspects was made possible by existence of a common adversary, the Communist Party.

Put another way, Solidarity was a total movement in that it encompassed a cross section of society and strived to transform the whole of the institutional sphere, on both a micro and a macro level. The years 1980–1981 were a period of activity by numerous civil society organizations, some of them acting officially, some unofficially. Solidarity was the largest and best known, and independent organizations frequently claimed some sort of affinity with it, even if they did not have direct ties to it. For instance, the newly formed Independent Students' Union and the Writers' Union had, among their leaders, Solidarity activists. The groups formed in opposition to the existing official organizations, and, similarly to Solidarity, had liberalization as their goal.

Liberalization ended with the introduction of martial law in 1981. Power was seized by the military, and the official body governing the country for over a year was the Military Council of National Revival. For the next seven and a half years (1982–1989), both Solidarity and other independent organizations and associations went underground. Although illegal, they maintained a relatively high level of activity, spreading information about the actions of the movement, about the abuse of political and employee rights by the authorities, and so on. Toward this aim, Solidarity established newsletters, a network of distribution for them, and a radio station. It had connections to the Polish-language sections of European and American radio broadcasters, such as Radio Free Europe and the BBC. The information was collected through the network of Solidarity activists and sympathizers. Other forms of activity were protests: strikes and demonstrations. Data indicate that large numbers of activists participated: according to a survey that asked about past activities, 7 percent of adults were members of clandestine structures, 5 percent went on strike at one time or another during the 1980s, and 3 percent illegally demonstrated (Wenzel 2010). While the retrospective character of the survey may not provide absolute precision in the true numbers, survey results indicate there was a broad circle of potential participants in protest activities. Self-organization, even in illegal and potentially dangerous forms, was not unusual during the autocratic regime.

Both demonstrations and strikes often had noneconomic demands: democratization, liberalization, and the release of political prisoners. In recent research, the goals of the Solidarity trade union in 1980–1981 were enumerated. The most important were freedom, civil rights, and equal rights for every citizen. Ranked only fourth was the first economic goal: adequate pay and working conditions (Roguska 2010). This does not mean that employees in Poland had an unusual hierarchy of needs, a sort of inverted Maslowian pyramid with economic needs last in line. Rather, the hierarchy of goals reflected an accurate assessment of the mechanisms of the economy and the state. In a state where the economy was subject to political control, changing economic conditions necessarily implied political change: abandoning party (and during martial law, military) control over enterprises and the economy.

From Total Movement to Interest Groups: The Trajectory of the Labor Movement during the Transition, 1989–2004

With the onset of transition, the internal contradictions of the oppositional movement began to appear. In opposition, Solidarity was a loose coalition of different ideological and interest groups: workers, liberal intellectuals, Roman Catholic Church–affiliated ideologues, nationalist activists, emerging private-sector entrepreneurs, and others. Organizations bore the name "Solidarity" but had no relation to the core group around Lech Wałęsa, the union president. For instance, there was a militant Solidarity (Solidarność Walcząca), which espoused violent methods. In 1989, the contradictory goals and roles became apparent. The political arm of the oppositional side maintained the Solidarity name but called itself Citizens' Committees with Lech Wałęsa, acknowledging the dual character of the movement: on the one hand, it was a trade union representing employees, and on the other hand, it was a representation of democratic social forces with noneconomic goals. At the time of transition, this difference was named: two entities were formed, both bearing the Solidarity name (Wenzel 1998). A clear separation of the two in terms of organization, goals, and also the symbolic sphere took several more years.

Transition was negotiated during the so-called Round Table negotiations, in which reformist leaders of the Communist Party negotiated with the leaders of the unofficial, illegal Solidarity and the official trade unions. Partners negotiated the transformation of the political system. The goal was, eventually, full democracy. As a result of the agreement, competitive elections were held. Solidarity won and took the government. It introduced a far-reaching program of economic reform (the so-called shock therapy), which involved mass privatization, liberalization of foreign trade, and introducing market prices (Balcerowicz 1992).

Solidarity faced a diverse set of challenges. On the one hand, it legitimized the new system. Many leading activists were in government, and the reforms were associated in public opinion with the Solidarity movement. It put a protective umbrella over systemic reform to shield it from popular dissatisfaction: leaders explained reforms publicly, rationalized the need for austerity measures, and warned about the danger of abandoning the path to reform. Some critics claim that Solidarity abandoned its principles and membership base then (e.g., Ost 2005). On the other hand, the bargaining power of employees in general was eroded by the political rivalry of trade unions, or their "conflicting pluralism," as J. Gardawski calls it (2003).

The thesis that Solidarity (and possibly other unions) acted against its base at the beginning of the transformation comes from the early period of the transformation. Economic reform was imposed in purely top-down mode, with no social consultation process. Such a rapid procedure was justified by the critical state of the economy (hyperinflation). Although the Solidarity trade union did not participate in the reform design, it initially supported it, and the negative consequences were attributed to the Solidarity people, whether union activists or intellectuals associated with the movement.

Conflicting pluralism, on the other hand, originated in the 1980s, when Solidarity was banned. A government-sponsored trade union was formed to attract former Solidarity activists. It was called the Ogólnopolskie Porozumienie Związków Zawodowych (OPZZ; All-Poland Alliance of Trade Unions). Although it was sponsored by the party, it was to a large degree independent, unlike the official unions in earlier periods. This union played an independent role during the transition Round Table negotiations. During the transition, it allied with the post-Communist left-wing party (Sojusz Lewicy Demokratycznej [SLD]; Alliance of the Democratic Left). At the same time, the Solidarity trade union allied with right-wing parties formed by former underground oppositional activists. Subsequently, it formed a political grouping in which it had a controlling stake, called the Akcja Wyborcza Solidarność (AWS; Solidarity Electoral Action). In 1989–2005, the right-wing and left-wing governments alternated. It meant that one of the big trade unions (Solidarity or OPZZ) was always tied to government. This gives rise to the co-optation hypothesis: political involvement demobilized activists and prevented them from acting in the interests of their members.

The goal of the analysis that follows is to verify hypotheses about the role of trade unions on the ground (in enterprises, institutions, on the streets), rather than among the elites, during the transition. The OPZZ and Solidarity leaders supported "their" governments and opposed the competing union. Did this co-optation extend to the level of ordinary members?

A related issue is the range of tactics: whether the unions continued the tactics from the 1980s and to what extent (and when) they adapted to the institutional framework of democratic capitalism. How did the methods change in the 1990s? Before 1989, strikes, disruptive demonstrations, and street protests were practically the only method available for articulating interests. After 1989, the open sociopolitical system provided a wide range of institutional channels.

For the analysis, data from projects recording all protest events occurring within the country are used (see the details under "Appendix: Data Source" later in the chapter). The trends in indicators are first presented, and then two hypotheses are tested on case studies.

The Dynamics of Protest

Protest intensity in Poland is related to the stage of transformation.[1] In the first years, the number of protests was high. It peaked in 1998 and fell after 2002 (Table 16.1). The waves of protest were strongest during the radical reform of the economy and the state.

Trade unions were by far the most active organizers of protest events (Table 16.2). The Solidarity trade union was the most involved and active union.

TABLE 16.1   NUMBER OF PROTESTS, 1989–2004

Year	Number of protests
1989	313
1990	307
1991	292
1992	308
1993	256
1994	260
1995	185
1996	308
1997	236
1998	368
1999	185
2000	277
2001	146
2002	230
2003	162
2004	187

TABLE 16.2   NUMBER OF ORGANIZATIONS LEADING OR SPONSORING MAIN PROTEST EVENTS, 1989–2004

	1989	1990	1991	1992	1993	1994	1995	1996
Trade unions	95	84	162	205	163	77	46	105
Professional organizations	4	12	14	9	8	7	5	37
Political parties	20	29	5	16	12	18	26	13
Youth organizations	11	11	5	4	6	3	13	17

	1997	1998	1999	2000	2001	2002	2003	2004
Trade unions	83	117	60	65	29	64	85	24
Professional organizations	46	15	19	14	1	8	30	10
Political parties	19	27	17	17	7	10	15	9
Youth organizations	15	9	4	12	0	3	6	6

The second-most-common category of events is spontaneous protests that have no clear organizational sponsor. Perhaps surprisingly, events organized by farmers' unions, which were well-publicized and became springboards for spectacular political careers (the Samoobrona, "Self-defense," leader Andrzej Lepper being the best example) were not numerous.

In 1999–2004, the number of events organized by unions slowly declined, reaching a low point in 2004. Political parties, as protest organizers, also diminished in importance. The declining role of political parties is related to the change in demands: political demands became far less frequent (see Table 16.7 later in the chapter).

TABLE 16.3   NUMBER OF EVENTS ORGANIZED BY SOME PROTESTING
GROUPS, 1989–2004

Group	1989	1990	1991	1992	1993	1994	1995	1996
Workers	112	35	113	131	88	117	66	148
Farmers	14	34	20	21	27	17	9	3
Service industry employees	44	14	23	31	9	0	11	14
Youth/students	35	44	24	34	17	9	32	38

Group	1997	1998	1999	2000	2001	2002	2003	2004
Workers	123	207	67	106	44	92	73	40
Farmers	14	29	15	23	6	19	6	5
Service industry employees	9	8	11	3	0	7	2	1
Youth/students	30	20	14	21	21	17	15	22

On the other hand, a rise occurred in the number of events organized by professional associations, including of the teaching and medical professions, during 1996–1997. This may be an indicator of the debates surrounding the impending reforms in the educational and medical fields, which changed the working conditions for these professions.

Workers in the production industry are by far the most common participants (Table 16.3). Young people were relatively active throughout the transformation period as well. The analysis of the trends reveals notable covariance between the waves of events staged by certain groups and the stages of transformation. Events staged by workers rose in importance throughout the 1990s, but this trend ended in 1999–2000, and since then, the number has continued to fall. In 2004 the second-lowest number of events with workers' participation was recorded. This is a reflection of the falling number of controversial privatization cases and also, perhaps, the diminishing role of the government in managing the economy. The state has largely shed its role as owner and manager and restricted itself to that of regulator.

Farmers were exceptionally active in the first years of the transformation and again in 1997–2000. They were the first casualties of the shock therapy. State-owned farms went bankrupt at the beginning of the 1990s and their employees largely became redundant, their situation aggravated by residence in areas of very high unemployment. Private farmers also suffered from very high interest rates. Loans became too expensive, and many fell into the debt trap. The 1998–2000 intensification of rural protest coincides with the turn-of-the-century economic crisis. It brought into public life Samoobrona, the radical-populist farmers' union and political party.

Public sector employees and health care specialists were especially active in 1996–1997. At that time, the early preparations for the 1998–1999 reforms might

TABLE 16.4 MOST COMMON METHODS OF PROTEST, 1989–2004 (NUMBER OF EVENTS)

Method of protest	1989	1990	1991	1992	1993	1994	1995	1996
Strike	159	43	92	74	64	11	25	30
Demonstration/ march/rally	61	108	83	115	70	50	87	89
Open letters/appeals	39	37	77	80	83	89	59	91

Method of protest	1997	1998	1999	2000	2001	2002	2003	2004
Strike	47	36	24	16	8	13	14	8
Demonstration/ march/rally	84	93	46	92	72	76	84	81
Open letters/appeals	71	109	33	77	20	76	30	47

have already contributed to mobilizing people and generating protests among those who concluded that their basic interests were threatened.

In the beginning of the transformation, strikes were the most common method of protest. However, their frequency gradually decreased after 1993; they were the most common method in 1989 but the fifth most common in 2004—less common than demonstrations, open letters, pickets, and symbolic manifestations. This finding is consistent with the diminishing of organized labor as a significant force. Demonstrations and open letters and appeals became the most common methods from the early 1990s (Table 16.4). Disruptive or violent methods (road blockades, occupation of buildings, riots, etc.) were less common.

Changing Goals, Changing Tactics: Labor Mobilization during the Reforms

G. Ekiert and J. Kubik made an in-depth analysis of the initial period of transformation, 1989–1993. They concluded that

the high level and specific features of protest in Poland typify two important, though contradictory, features of the Polish post-communist situation. On the one hand, the high magnitude of the protest [compared with other post-communist countries] reflected institutional chaos, particularly the lack of well-defined and routinely accepted channels of interest articulation and mediation. . . . High magnitude of protest demonstrated . . . disappointment with the inaccessibility of the state and the ineffectiveness of political parties. On the other hand, the high institutionalisation of protest activities meant that they became the routine mode of political participation and, rather than undermining democratic consolidation, they enhanced it. (1999: 196)

The authors note that these features can be attributed to two institutional factors, one structural and one historical: "The countries with [a structure of] corporatist institutions will experience different patterns of state-society interactions than countries without it" (Ekiert and Kubik 1999: 197). Corporatist institutions were introduced in Poland in 1994 but never really took off. In the 1990s they were periodically boycotted by either of the big trade unions (OPZZ or Solidarity). A parliamentary act giving the Tripartite Commission legal foundation was passed in 2001, but divisions among peak union structures and the weakness of social partners contributed to limiting its role (Gardawski 2009: 492–494). Historically, "Poles are more likely to resort to contentious collective action as a means of political participation than other Central Europeans," and "it is also a legacy of many decades of protest in Poland" (197). Strikes, demonstrations, and various forms of industrial action were the dominant mode of articulating interests under the former system, and this tradition survived transformation. As it happened, however, by only several years.

To test the validity of these conclusions in the subsequent stages of systemic transformation, I chose two periods for detailed comparison. They are November 1997 through December 1998 and November 2001 through December 2002. Each period was the initial fourteen months of government led by AWS (1997–1998) and the post-Communist SLD (2001–2002). In many respects, they provide a controlled environment (context) for studying protest activities. Both of these governments were formed by political parties with close ties to trade unions: AWS had ties to the Solidarity trade union, and SLD had ties to the OPZZ trade union. Both unions had members in their respective parliamentary representation and in government, and they were roughly equal in size.

Their government agenda was different, however. The AWS government formed in 1997 proposed a reform program that entailed an overhaul of the health system, local government, social security, and education. It was the so-called four reforms program, prepared in 1998 and implemented in 1999. Reforms were designed to change (1) health care, by replacing the centralized state system with a publicly funded but independent system of financing; (2) local government, by decentralizing it and creating additional levels; (3) pensions, by replacing the state pay-as-you-go pension system with a mixed system in which individual pension funds with obligatory membership would cover part of the pension; and (4) the educational system, by creating an additional level of schooling and new types of schools. The SLD government formed in 2001 did not introduce major reforms.

The analysis of differences in response to different agendas tests several hypotheses. It is evident from Table 16.1 that 1998 was a year of particularly numerous protests. I posit the following:

1. High protest incidence was caused by the implemented and planned reform changes. The Solidarity trade union was an active participant in negotiating the reform. Because of its legacy as a total movement,

its activists might have had noneconomic goals, in addition to purely economic.

2. There would be co-optation: unions unrelated to the governing party would be relatively more active during each period. Since there was personal involvement of union leaders in party structures, especially strong in the case of Solidarity, power in the hands of the party to which a union has ties would have a detrimental effect on its readiness to protest.

Below are tables with numbers of events in subcategories. As shown in Table 16.5, the total number of events in 2001–2002 was only 62 percent of the 1997–1998 value. The trade-union-organized events in 2001–2002 were half as numerous (52 percent) as in 2001–2002. The decrease in number of union protests does not explain the whole variance, because the number of nonunion events also fell. Political affiliation does not influence protest activity. Both Solidarity and other unions were more active in 1997–1998 than in 2001–2002.

The number of events in state enterprises (including schools and hospitals) fell in 2001–2002 compared with 1997–1998 (Table 16.6). The drop is

TABLE 16.5   NUMBER OF PROTEST ACTIVITIES DURING THE INITIAL FOURTEEN MONTHS OF THE AWS AND SLD GOVERNMENTS, RESPECTIVELY

	Organizer			
Government	Trade unions (excluding Solidarity)	Solidarity	All trade union organized*	Total protests of any organizer
AWS (1997–1998)	63	66	107	403
SLD (2001–2002)	44	24	56	249

* Number does not double-count events organized by both Solidarity and other trade unions.

TABLE 16.6   NUMBER OF PROTEST ACTIVITIES DURING THE INITIAL FOURTEEN MONTHS OF THE AWS AND SLD GOVERNMENTS, RESPECTIVELY, IN ENTERPRISE BY TYPE OF OWNERSHIP

	Location			
Government	State enterprise	Private enterprise	Public institution	Total protests of any organizer
AWS (1997–1998)				
Nonunion	31	15	10	296
Union	32	19	2	107
Total	63	34	12	403
SLD (2001–2002)				
Nonunion	15	9	3	193
Union	5	13	0	56
Total	20	22	3	249

particularly strong with regard to union-led events. For private enterprises, the number decreased as well.

The structure of demands changed (Tables 16.7 and 16.8). Economic demands are slightly more frequent in 2001–2002, in spite of the overall drop in the number of events. Both pay increase demands and other economic demands increased, while noneconomic protests decreased. In particular, political protests were much more frequent in 1997–1998. This category encompasses events in which workers took issue with structural changes in enterprises, including demanding removal of unacceptable management.

In state enterprises, all types of protests diminished in number, including economic (Table 16.8). One explanation is that many state enterprises, in which unions were strong, were privatized. The tradition of protest, which determined many events in the early years of transformation, led to strikes in large

TABLE 16.7   TYPES OF DEMANDS EXPRESSED IN PROTEST ACTIVITIES DURING THE INITIAL FOURTEEN MONTHS OF THE AWS AND SLD GOVERNMENTS, RESPECTIVELY (NUMBER)

Type of demand	Government	
	AWS (1997–1998)	SLD (2001–2002)
Pay increase	43	48
Economic (excluding pay)	66	79
Political	139	88
Ecological	20	14
Religious	6	3

TABLE 16.8   TYPES OF DEMANDS IN ENTERPRISES BY TYPE OF OWNERSHIP (NUMBER)

Type of demand and enterprise	Government	
	AWS (1997–1998)	SLD (2001–2002)
Pay increase		
State enterprise	14	9
Private enterprise	10	12
Public institution	1	1
Economic (excluding pay)		
State enterprise	20	3
Private enterprise	5	8
Public institution	1	1
Political		
State enterprise	26	5
Private enterprise	4	6

Note: Total numbers of events differ between Tables 16.7 and 16.8 because Table 16.8 does not contain data on events at noninstitutional locations (e.g., street protests) and unknown locations.

state-owned enterprises. The transition from state to private enterprise is often a transition from a unionized to a nonunionized workplace (Wenzel 2009), and unions find it much more difficult to stage protests there. Another major reason may be that the economic situation of enterprises stabilized.

Qualitative analysis of demands from this period indicates that a large number of them were (directly or indirectly) related to the reforms, especially in health and education. The health care reform in particular was far reaching: it changed from a state-funded system to one receiving public financing through independent sources. The health service facilities were to be operated by local government. Education reform created a new type of school and changed the age of transition from one level to the next. Both reforms tried to address existing grievances about public sector services, but they created new sources of discontent by upsetting the status quo. Examples of protests directly connected to reforms are physicians' protests about contract conditions, nurses' demands for guarantees against layoffs, and teachers' demands to retain a school in their locality. The introduction of health care reforms resulted in a high degree of insecurity among educational and health care employees. The government's restructuring plans were not always explicit about employment levels and working conditions in the new institutions. Nurses in particular had believed themselves underpaid for a long time, and the reform additionally threatened (in their opinion) their job security. The reform triggered a wave of nurses' protests (often large and disruptive) that lasted for the whole term of the Jerzy Buzek government.

In other cases, protest events were indirectly linked to reforms. For instance, administrative reform changed the number of districts (*voivodships*) from forty-nine to sixteen. A protest by local administration employees in a *voivodship* capital that was to be demoted as a result of reform, even if the protest was not concerned with the reform, was connected with it in an indirect way: the environment for it (the office where it was staged) would disappear in the reformed structure.

The expectations about the role of unions in the reform process are partially confirmed. Union activity was higher during the reform period, when more was at stake. Reforms determined power relations and material conditions of employees in the reformed system for years to come. Solidarity and other unions were active participants and took part in structuring the reform. However, the co-optation hypothesis does not hold. Political affiliation is not related to protest activity. Solidarity did not offer any break to the government formed by the political party formed by Solidarity. This was partly due to the bottom-up, decentralized nature of many events.

Post-transition Mobilization: New Forms of Activism

At the turn of the twenty-first century, forms of mass mobilization inherited from the former political and economic system were gradually becoming outdated. Trade unions were instrumental in changing the system, and they were vocal actors in the early period of transformation; they were also significant participants in the reform process in late 1990s. By the end of the twentieth century, the basic features of the new system were firmly in place. The transition period ended in many spheres of the economy and state:[2] the constitution was accepted, state institutions were set. Privatization slowed down, although in 2000–2010 several large-scale privatization projects were prepared or completed, such as in the energy sector. Trade unions declined in membership in the transition years 1989–2001, and then membership stabilized at a low level. Currently, 15 percent of employees belong to them (Wenzel 2009).

It is fairly well established (Bernhard and Karakoc 2007; Kramer 2002) that civil society in Eastern Europe is weak relative to Western European countries. Different commonly used measures confirm this finding. It is, however, argued by some sociologists that these indicators do not capture the specificity of Polish or Eastern European civil society, because they tend to focus on established formal organizations, rather than informal networks that constitute civil society's core in the region. NGOs may be unpopular, and they are associated in the public opinion with state institutions, to which they are often tied. However, low membership in such organizations does not mean that citizens are inactive. They operate through informal or semiformal networks, dubbed "homemade civil society" in a recent study (Giza-Poleszczuk 2009).

I make another argument here. Findings about civil society in Eastern Europe are static; they do not take into account the dynamics of the society. They are a snapshot of the region at a very specific point in time: in the midst of a radical transition. Perhaps low levels of activity are because of temporary factors related to systemic change and not to any deeper cultural or institutional reasons. If so, we can expect activity to grow in the post-transition period, in a stable institutional setting.

The accession to the European Union ended the transition period. The system consolidated, and the country's acceptance into the European Union was a visible sign of its viability. In many ways, it was a symbolic end of the systemic change. A new set of challenges gained in relevance. The focus of social activity shifted, becoming less economic, as described above. With diminishing anxiety about day-to-day material concerns, issues related to lifestyle, self-realization, and an improving social and ecological environment have gained in importance. As survival concerns diminished (Wciórka 2008), sensitivity to issues of social cohesion and social quality came into the foreground.

To test the above statements, I use data on membership in civil society organizations in Poland, collected in public opinion surveys conducted by the Centrum Badania Opinii Społecznej (CBOS; Public Opinion Research Center) in Warsaw. The surveys took place in 1998–2010, so they cover both the late transition period and the first decade of the twenty-first century. In the surveys, respondents were asked if they were active in different types of organizations. By *active*, "devoting one's free time without pay" was meant. Twenty-nine different types of organizations were listed, both formal and informal to account for noninstitutionalized civic activity (see Boguszewski 2010).

The years 1998–2008 were relatively stable in terms of civic activity (Table 16.9). The number of activists fluctuated, but the changes were minor. On the other hand, after 2008 activity increased: the proportion of Poles active in NGOs rose by 8 percentage points.

The figures for civil society activity for 2010 confirm the weakening of trade unions in terms of social engagement (Table 16.10). After 2008, the number of activists in civil society organizations rose for almost all types of organizations, and it fell for only one: unions. Activism in educational committees, sports'

TABLE 16.9   CIVIC ACTIVITY, 1998–2010

	1998	1999	2002	2004	2006	2008	2010
Number of adults	1,167	1,522	973	1,057	1,007	890	1,052
Inactive (%)	77	76	79	76	77	80	72
Active (%)	23	24	21	24	23	20	28

Source: Boguszewski 2010.

TABLE 16.10   CIVIC ACTIVITY IN CIVIL SOCIETY ORGANIZATIONS

Organization	Percentage of volunteers						
	1998	1999	2002	2004	2006	2008	2010
Educational groups, PTAs, school foundations	4.5	5.5	3.2	4.2	4.8	4.8	8.0
Sports clubs	2.2	3.1	2.7	4.8	3.5	2.8	5.8
Children's charities	1.2	2.9	1.0	2.4	3.5	2.4	5.1
Church and religious organizations	3.6	3.9	2.0	3.9	3.4	2.8	4.5
Charities (not for children)	1.5	2.8	1.3	2.4	2.1	2.4	4.0
Anglers', hunters', and gardeners' clubs	2.4	3.1	1.8	2.9	2.5	1.6	3.3
Youth and students' organizations	1.5	2.0	2.1	2.3	2.3	1.8	3.2
Volunteer fire fighters	3.0	2.0	3.0	2.2	3.4	1.4	2.7
Artistic (choir, musical band, theater group)	0.9	1.8	0.9	1.9	1.6	0.8	2.6
Self-help (e.g., AA)	0.6	1.1	0.4	1.0	1.3	0.8	2.5
Scientific associations	0.6	1.4	0.8	1.4	1.2	0.5	2.3
Animal protection groups	1.1	1.1	0.7	0.8	1.6	0.3	2.3
Trade unions	3.2	4.8	3.3	3.8	3.9	3.2	2.1
Regional associations, town and local culture clubs	0.7	0.8	0.4	0.6	0.8	1.0	1.9
Seniors' and pensioners' clubs	1.4	1.4	1.2	1.8	1.8	1.2	1.8
Countryside and tourists' associations	1.6	2.0	0.6	1.3	0.9	1.1	1.7
Health care foundations	0.7	1.2	0.6	0.8	1.5	0.9	1.7
Local government on lowest level (neighborhood council)	1.0	1.2	0.3	1.0	1.2	0.9	1.6
Hobby clubs	0.5	0.7	0.7	1.2	0.7	1.0	1.5
Environmental organizations	0.9	1.5	0.3	1.2	1.8	0.9	1.5

Source: Boguszewski 2010.

associations, charities, youth organizations, and so on, increased significantly. Activism in animal protection groups increased sevenfold compared with the previous period, signifying the increased (although still low) importance of environmental issues.

How can this increase in activism be interpreted? Involvement grew, but it differed from the activism in the early transformation years. Data appear to indicate an upsurge in activity related to pursuing self-realization and environmental goals. Growing educational awareness is reflected in the increased importance of education-related formal and informal pressure groups. Increase in social responsibility is manifested by the doubling of the number of individuals involved in charitable work. One might hypothesize that harbingers of postmaterialist orientations as understood by R. Inglehart are appearing (see Abramson and Inglehart 1995). Consistent with the materialist versus postmaterialist value-shift hypothesis, the involvement related to postmaterialist values should be increasing in importance.

The change signaled here is recent and has yet to be independently confirmed by other data sources and with other methods. However, it is consistent with the conclusions drawn from the analysis of the protest data. The disappearance of the transformation-era model was evident, and improvement in the economic standard of living and institutional stability of 2005–2010 provided opportunities for pursuing goals higher in the Maslowian hierarchy.

Summary and Conclusion

The revolutionary reforms introduced in 1989 and 1990 changed economic, social, and political life. They created a new system that was consolidated before or around the time Poland entered the EU. The Solidarity movement was the key actor in introducing the systemic change, and both Solidarity and other unions were active, on-the-ground participants in negotiating the reforms: in enterprises, institutions, and communities. They even contributed to the change of value orientations. However, economists, sociologists, and political scientists detect the end of the transformation period. The models of social mobilization dominant in the time of systemic change are slowly becoming outdated.

Data on protests in 1989–2004 provide evidence of these trends. From 1989 to 2004 protest intensity diminished. The further from the commencement of the 1989 reforms, the less mobilization was recorded. This trend was particularly pronounced in economic demands. At the beginning of the transformation, the stakes were higher, as new rules were, to some extent, negotiated. At the grass-roots level, the outcomes of market reform and property transformation for enterprises were unclear, and power and ownership could be changed by collective action. As the situation stabilized, such motives lost their relevance. Another wave of protests in the second half of the 1990s confirms this observation. As the major reforms of the state were introduced, for many groups the stakes rose again and some of their members engaged in collective action. Trade unions were active participants in the micro-level socioeconomic transformation, as much as they were at the macro level.

The high prevalence and often-disruptive nature of protests in the 1990s was attributed (Ekiert and Kubik 1999) to limited state capacity to accommodate societal grievances. They were expressed in extrainstitutional forms because of the absence of legitimate and conventional channels, such as tri- or bilateral dialogue, employee representation in enterprises, and collective bargaining agreements. Their weakness was partially from the competition between two major unions: the "conflicting pluralism" (Gardawski 2003). Moreover, the existing institutions changed rapidly, often breaking continuity and being unaccountable for the actions undertaken by previous incumbents. Consolidation of the institutional order is another factor contributing to the diminishing prevalence of protest activities. Trade unions had many roles in the early economic transformation: Solidarity provided a protective shield at the national level for the reforms in their first months; at the enterprise level, it often participated in selecting new management. In the following years, Solidarity ceased to be the key actor, and all unions lost members. This loss coincided with the decrease in the number of labor-sponsored protest events.

The primary goal of the activists and ordinary members of the Solidarity movement under communism was a free, pluralist society. This aim united people of different ideologies, worldviews, and interests. It was articulated by the leaders of the movement: leadership and membership were united in this respect. Solidarity gained power, and it fulfilled these goals by splitting into a variety of groups. One of them is the trade union that bears the same name. Unions have become institutionalized, and their goals narrowed to the economic sphere. However, the disappearance of old forms of activism does not mean that the society is passive. It becomes fragmented and pluralized in a changed political setting. New civil society is emerging, untouched by the legacies of the former system.

Appendix: Data Source

The analysis is based on data from research that collected information reported in the media about all protest events taking place in Poland and Hungary from 1989 to 2004 and in Taiwan and South Korea from 1987 to 2004. A protest event is collective action to articulate grievances and demands in a way that is not a routine or legally prescribed behavior of a social or political organization. Certain kinds of action that are constitutionally or legally guaranteed, such as strikes, rallies, or demonstrations, are considered protest events because of their radical and disruptive nature. The data provide information about the number and frequency of all such protest events during the political and economic transitions and about many dimensions of protest events, including participants, their demands, targets of protest actions, and strategies. The responses of the state and other political actors to protest events are recorded as well. Two national-level newspapers were chosen as data sources in Poland: *Gazeta Wyborcza* and *Rzeczpospolita*. They were continuously published during the entire period under study, which ensures data comparability. Trained coders entered media reports about protest events using a web-based data-entry protocol. The project was originally designed by Grzegorz Ekiert and Jan Kubik. The data collection for its second round (1994–2004) in Poland was coordinated by Michał Wenzel and Jan Kubik.

Data collection for 2004–2010 was made possible by research grant awarded by the National Science Center in Poland (grant number N N116 791840).

NOTES

1. The information in this section was first presented in Wenzel and Kubik 2009.
2. According to the World Bank, Poland is not an economy in transition any longer. See Cabaj, Morawski, and Słojawska 2008. Dariusz Rosati, former member of the Board for Monetary Policy, claims that the EU accession process ended the transformation period. See Rosati 2002.

REFERENCES

Abramson, P. R., and R. Inglehart. 1995. *Value Change in Global Perspective*. Ann Arbor: University of Michigan Press.

Balcerowicz, L. 1992. *800 dni: Szok kontrolowany* [800 Days: A Controlled Shock]. Warsaw: BGW.

Bernhard, M., and E. Karakoc. 2007. "Civil Society and the Legacies of Dictatorship." *World Politics* 59 (July): 539–567.

Boguszewski, R. 2010. "Aktywność Polaków w organizacjach obywatelskich w latach 1998–2010" [Poles' Civic Activity in 1998–2010]. Research report BS/16/2010, Centrum Badania Opinii Społecznej, Warsaw.

Cabaj, J., I. Morawski, and A. Słojawska. 2008. "Koniec transformacji" [End of Transformation]. *Rzeczpospolita*, May 14.

Eisler, J., ed. 2000. *Grudzień 1970 w dokumentach MSW* [December 1970 in the Documents of the Ministry of the Interior]. Warsaw: Instytut Pamięci Narodowej, Komisja Ścigania Zbrodni Przeciwko Narodowi Polskiemu, DW Bellona.

Ekiert, G., and J. Kubik. 1999. *Rebellious Civil Society*. Ann Arbor: University of Michigan Press.

Gardawski, J. 2003. *Konfliktowy pluralizm polskich związków zawodowych* [Conflicting Pluralism of Polish Trade Unions]. Warsaw: Fundacja imienia Friedricha Eberta.

———. 2009. "Ewolucja polskich związków zawodowych" [Evolution of Polish Trade Unions]. In *Polacy pracujący a kryzys fordyzmu* [Working Poles and the Crisis of Fordism], edited by J. Gardawski, 459–532. Warsaw: Scholar.

Gellner, E. 1994. *Conditions of Liberty: Civil Society and Its Rivals*. London: Hamish Hamilton.

Giza-Poleszczuk, A. 2009. "Trzeci sektor, instytucje publiczne i chałupnicze społeczeństwo obywatelskie" [Third Sector, Public Institutions and Homemade Civil Society]. Paper presented at the "Poland after Twenty Years of Freedom" conference, University of Warsaw, May 22–23.

Inglehart, R. 2008. "Changing Values among Western Publics from 1970 to 2006." *West European Politics* 31 (1–2): 130–146.

Kramer, M. 2002. "Collective Protests and Democratization in Poland, 1989–1993: Was Civil Society Really 'Rebellious?'" *Communist and Post-Communist Studies* 35:213–221.

Kriesi, H. 1996. "The Organizational Structure of New Social Movements in a Political Context." In *Comparative Perspectives on Social Movements: Political Opportunities, Mobilizing Structures and Cultural Framing*, edited by D. McAdam, J. J. McCarthy, and M. N. Zald, 152–184. Cambridge: Cambridge University Press.

Kubik, J. 2008. "Polityka kontestacji, protest, ruchy społeczne: logika rozwoju teorii" [Politics of Contestation, Protest and Social Movements: The Logic of Theory Development]. *Societas/Communitas* 4–5:1–82.

Kuroń, J. 2009. *Autobiografia* [Autobiography]. Warsaw: Krytyka Polityczna.

Olson, M. 1965. *The Logic of Collective Action: Public Goods and the Theory of Groups.* Cambridge: Harvard University Press.

Ost, D. 2005. *The Defeat of Solidarity: Anger and Politics in Post-communist Europe.* Ithaca, NY: Cornell University Press.

Ost, D., and Wenzel, M. 2009. "Trade Unionism in Poland since 1945." In *Trade Unionism since 1945: Towards a Global History*, edited by C. Phelan, 261–290. Bern: Peter Lang.

Roguska, B. 2010. "Oceny historycznego znaczenia NSZZ Solidarność" [Evaluation of Historical Significance of Solidarity Trade Union]. In *Solidarność: Doświadczenie, pamięć i dziedzictwo* [Solidarity: Experience, Memory and Legacy], edited by M. Grabowska, 62–79. Opinie i diagnozy 16. Warsaw: Centrum Badania Opinii Społecznej.

Rosati, D. 2002. *Nowa Europa: Raport z transformacji* [New Europe: Report from the Transformation]. Warsaw: Instytut Wschodni.

Rychard, A. 1993. *Reform, Adaptation and Breakthrough.* Warsaw: IFiS.

Tarrow, S. 1998. *Power in Movement: Collective Action, Social Movements and Politics.* Cambridge: Cambridge University Press.

Tilly, C. 1978. *From Mobilization to Revolution.* New York: McGraw-Hill.

Touraine, A. 1983. *Solidarity.* Cambridge: Cambridge University Press.

Wciórka, B. 2008. "Samopoczucie Polaków w latach, 1988–2008" [Subjective Well-Being of Poles, 1988–2008]. Research report, Centrum Badania Opinii Społecznej, Warsaw.

Wenzel, M. 1998. "Solidarity and Akcja Wyborcza 'Solidarność': An Attempt at Reviving the Legend." *Communist and Post-Communist Studies* 31 (2): 139–156.

———. 2009. "Związki zawodowe w badaniach CBOS, 1980–2008" [Trade Unions in CBOS research, 1980–2008]. In *Polacy pracujący a kryzys fordyzmu* [Working Poles and the Crisis of Fordism], edited by J. Gardawski, 533–550. Warsaw: Scholar.

———. 2010. "Doświadczenia z okresu stanu wojennego i podziemnej Solidarności" [Experience from the Martial Law and Underground Solidarity]. In *Solidarność: Doświadczenie, pamięć i dziedzictwo* [Solidarity: Experience, Memory and Legacy], edited by M. Grabowska, 28–38. Opinie i diagnozy 16. Warsaw: Centrum Badania Opinii Społecznej.

Wenzel, Michał, and Jan Kubik. 2009. "Civil Society in Poland: Case Study." Paper presented at "The Logic of Civil Society in New Democracies: East Asia and East Europe" conference, Taipei, June 5–7.

Contributors

Paul Almeida is an associate professor of sociology and serves as the chair of the Social Sciences Graduate Group at the University of California–Merced. His work analyzes civil society responses to political and economic transitions in the developing world. Almeida's research has appeared in the *American Journal of Sociology, Mobilization, Social Forces, Social Problems,* and other scholarly outlets. He is the author of *Waves of Protest: Popular Struggle in El Salvador* (University of Minnesota Press, 2008) and *Mobilizing Democracy: Globalization and Citizen Protest* (Johns Hopkins University Press, 2014).

Christopher J. Colvin is a medical anthropologist with a doctorate in social anthropology and a master of public health in epidemiology. His research focuses on how communities, civil society, and the state engage with each other around health and understand their respective roles, responsibilities, and capacities in improving public health. He has examined HIV and gender transformation, task shifting to support antiretroviral therapy and Prevention of Mother-to-Child Transmission programs, community participation in health governance, AIDS activism and global health diplomacy, and health system reform to address the HIV and tuberculosis epidemics. He is also interested in ways to better integrate social science evidence into health policy making. He recently contributed several systematic reviews of qualitative evidence to the World Health Organization's first set of official guidelines to formally incorporate qualitative evidence.

Alison Dahl Crossley is a postdoctoral research fellow at the Clayman Institute for Gender Research at Stanford University. She is studying contemporary feminist mobilization among U.S. college students. She holds a master of arts and doctorate in sociology with a doctoral emphasis in feminist studies from the University of California–Santa Barbara and a master of arts in media and communications from Goldsmiths College, University of London.

Donatella della Porta is professor of sociology in the Department of Political and Social Sciences at the European University Institute, where she directs the Center on Social Movement Studies (Cosmos). She also directs a major European Research Council (ERC) project, Mobilizing for Democracy, studying civil society participation in democratization processes in Europe, the Middle East, Asia, and Latin America. Among her very recent publications are *Mobilizing for Democracy* (Oxford University Press, 2014), *Can Democracy Be Saved?* (Polity Press, 2013), *Clandestine Political Violence* (Cambridge University Press, 2013, edited with D. Snow, B. Klandermans, and D. McAdam), *Blackwell Encyclopedia on Social and Political Movements* (Blackwell, 2013), *Mobilizing on the Extreme Right* (Oxford University Press, 2012, with M. Caiani and C. Wagemann), *Meeting Democracy* (Cambridge University Press, 2012, edited with D. Rucht), *The Hidden Order of Corruption* (Ashgate, 2012, with A. Vannucci). In 2011, she received the Mattei Dogan Prize for distinguished achievements in the field of political sociology.

Grzegorz Ekiert is professor of government at Harvard University, director of Minda de Gunzburg Center for European Studies, and senior scholar at the Harvard Academy for International and Area Studies. His teaching and research interests focus on comparative politics, regime change and democratization, civil society and social movements, and East European politics and societies. His current projects explore civil society development in new democracies in Central Europe and East Asia and patterns of political and economic transformations in the postcommunist world.

Stephen Ellis is the Desmond Tutu Chair Holder in the Faculty of Social Sciences at the VU University Amsterdam and a senior researcher at the Afrika Studiecentrum in Leiden, Netherlands. He has been the editor of the newsletter *Africa Confidential* and a past editor of *African Affairs*, the journal of Britain's Royal African Society. In 2003–2004 he was director of the Africa program at the International Crisis Group. His most recent book is *External Mission: The ANC in Exile, 1960–1990* (Hurst, 2013).

Olivier Fillieule is research director at the Centre National de la Recherche Scientifique and professor of political sociology at the International Institute of Political and International Relations of the University of Lausanne. He is a member of Centre de Recherche sur l'Action Politique de l'Université de Lausanne. A list of his research interests and publications is available on his personal website: http://people.unil.ch/olivierfillieule.

Grzegorz Foryś attended Jagiellonian University in Kraków, Poland, as an undergraduate and then earned a doctorate in sociology there in 2006. He is an assistant professor at the Pedagogical University of Kraków. His research interests are social movements, political sociology, and social change. He has recently been investigating the role of different social movements in promoting multifunctional rural development in Europe and especially in Poland from the perspective of political science.

Krzysztof Gorlach received his undergraduate degree in sociology from Jagiellonian University in Kraków, Poland, and his doctorate in sociology from there. He is a full professor of sociology at Jagiellonian University. His research has investigated rural sociology, social movements, social class, and mobility, as well as political sociology. He earned the Kościuszko Foundation Fellowship, Senior Fulbright Research Fellowship, Colleges of Cambridge and Oxford Hospitalities Scheme, and Andrew W. Mellon Fellowship. He was a visiting fellow at the University of Wisconsin–Madison; Oxford University, and the Institute of Human Sciences in Vienna.

Ineke van Kessel is a senior researcher with the African Studies Centre in Leiden, Netherlands. Trained as a historian, she has also worked as a journalist. Her main research interests are social and political movements in contemporary South Africa and the historical relations between the Netherlands and Africa's Gold Coast (present-day Ghana). Her publications include *"Beyond Our Wildest Dreams": The United Democratic Front and the Transformation of South Africa* (University Press of Virginia, 2000), *Merchants, Missionaries and Migrants: 300 years of Dutch-Ghanaian Relations* (KIT/Sub-Saharan, 2002), *Movers and Shakers: Social Movements in Africa* (Brill, 2009, edited with Stephen Ellis).

Bert Klandermans is professor in applied social psychology at the VU University, Amsterdam. He is the author of the now classic *Social Psychology of Protest* (Blackwell, 1997). He is the editor and coauthor (with Suzanne Staggenborg) of *Methods of Social Movement Research* (University of Minnesota Press, 2002), and with Conny Roggeband he edited the *Handbook of Social Movements across Disciplines* (Springer, 2007). He is the editor of *Social Movements, Protest, and Contention*, the prestigious book series of the University of Minnesota Press. He is coeditor of Blackwell-Wiley's *Encyclopedia of Social Movements* and *The Future of Social Movement Research: Dynamics, Mechanisms, and Processes* (University of Minnesota Press, 2013). In 2013 he received a prestigious Advanced Investigator Grant from the European Research Council to study movement and party politics, as well as the Harold Lasswell Award for lifetime achievement of the International Society of Political Psychology. In 2014 he received the John D. McCarthy Lifetime Achievement Award from Notre Dame University.

Camila Penna holds a doctorate in sociology and is an associate professor at the University of Brasília, Brazil. She has published articles on social movements and state relations and on social and political theory. Her dissertation, "Social Movement Activity in the Transition to PT Government: The Case of MST in Brazil," is an ethnographical study of the National Institute of Colonization an Agrarian Reform (INCRA), Brazil's agrarian reform agency. Her work addresses the interaction between the agency's civil servants, social movement activists, the Workers' Party, and other political actors and stakeholders in Brazil's agrarian reform policies.

Sebastián Pereyra holds a doctorate in sociology from the École des Hautes Études en Sciences Sociales in Paris. He is a researcher at the Argentinean Scientific and Technological Council (CONICET) and is assistant professor in contemporary social theory at the Instituto de Altos Estudios Sociales, Universidad Nacional de San Martín of Argentina. He has specialized in social movements and public problems. His most recent book is *Política y transparencia: La corrupción como problema público* (Siglo Veintiuno Editores, 2013). He is editor of volumes on social protest and social movements in Argentina; he has also published articles in social science journals from Argentina, Brazil, México, and France, among others.

Steven Robins is a professor in the Department of Sociology and Social Anthropology at the University of Stellenbosch, South Africa. His book *From Revolution to Rights in South Africa: Social Movements and Popular Politics* (James Currey, 2008) examines globally connected social movements, nongovernmental organizations, and community-based organizations that address access to AIDS treatment, land, and housing. He is editor of *Limits to Liberation after Apartheid: Citizenship, Governance and Culture* (James Currey, Ohio University Press, and David Philip, 2005) and (with Nick Shepherd) of *New South African Keywords* (Jacana and Ohio University Press, 2008). He is currently working on issues relating to social movements involved in community-based struggles over access to improved public education, health, and sanitation in informal settlements.

Federico M. Rossi received his doctorate from the European University Institute, Florence, and is a postdoctoral fellow at Tulane University. His research focuses on trade unions, social movements, democratization and contentious politics, and youth political participation. He has published his work in *Desarrollo Económico, European Review of Latin American and Caribbean Studies, International Sociology, Latin American Politics and Society, Latin American Perspectives, Mobilization,* and *Social Movement Studies,* among others. He is the author of *La participación de las juventudes hoy: La condición juvenil y la redefinición del involucramiento político y social* (Prometeo, 2009) and coeditor with Marisa von Bülow of a forthcoming book (*Mobilization Series on Social Movements, Protest, and Culture,* Ashgate) that provides a perspective from Latin America on theory building in social movement studies.

Ton Salman studied philosophy and anthropology and received his doctorate in 1993 for research on grassroots organizations in Chile under Pinochet. He specializes on Latin America (mainly Bolivia, Ecuador, and Chile) with emphasis on social movements, democratization, urban culture, and citizenship. Currently he is working on projects dedicated to the anthropologizing of citizenship research in Latin America, the search for a new democracy in Bolivia, and questions of statutory versus communal administration of justice. In addition to many journal articles, he is author (with Willem Assies) of *Crisis in Bolivia: The Elections of 2002 and Their Aftermath* (Institute of Latin American Studies, 2004) and editor (with Willem Assies and Marco Calderón) of *Ciudadania, cultura política y reforma del Estado en América Latina* (El Colegio de Michoacán, 2002). He was a research fellow at the Center for Latin American Research and Documentation (CEDLA) and Institute for Development Research Amsterdam (InDRA) (both at the University of Amsterdam); the Latin American Faculty of Social Sciences (FLACSO) in Quito, Ecuador; the Center for Bolivian Strategic Research (PIEB) in La Paz, Bolivia; the Academy of Christian Humanism University (UAHC) and Alberto Hurtado University, in Santiago, Chile; and El Colegio de Michoacán in Zamora, Mexico; among others. He is a member of the Research School for Resource Studies for Development (CERES) and an associate professor in the Department of Social and Cultural Anthropology at the VU University, Amsterdam.

Máté Szabó is a professor of political science in the Institute of Political Science at the University Eötvös Loránd, Budapest, Hungary. He was a fellow of the Alexander von Humboldt Foundation in Germany, and was a visiting fellow of the Netherlands Institute of Advanced Studies, Wassenaar, and of the European University Institute, Florence. He specializes in civil society, social movements and political protest, and theory of law and politics. He has published more than three hundred articles. He was ombudsman of Hungary and parliamentary commissioner for human rights in 2007–2013.

Verta Taylor is professor of sociology at the University of California–Santa Barbara. Her current research focuses on same-sex marriage, the gay and lesbian movement, and queer identities. Her books include *Drag Queens at the 801 Cabaret* (with Leila Rupp; University of Chicago Press, 2003); *Rock-a-By Baby: Feminism, Self-help and Postpartum Depression* (Routledge, 1996); *Survival in the Doldrums: The American Women's Rights Movement, 1945 to the 1960s* (with Leila Rupp; Oxford University Press, 1987); *The Marrying Kind? Debating Same-Sex Marriage in the Gay and Lesbian Movement* (with Mary Bernstein; University of Minnesota Press, 2013); and *Feminist Frontiers* (with Nancy Whittier and Leila Rupp; McGraw-Hill, 2012). Taylor was the 2011 recipient of the American Sociological Association's Jessie Bernard Award for her research on gender, the 2008 John D. McCarthy Lifetime Achievement Award for her scholarship on social movements, and the 2008 Simon and Gagnon Award for her career of scholarship in sexualities.

Cornelis van Stralen is professor of Psychology and Health Policies in the Graduate Program of Psychology at the Federal University of Minas Gerais in Brazil, where he is also a researcher in the Center of Collective Health Education. He was an activist in the struggle for health care reform and is a long-standing campaigner for publicly provided and funded universal health care in Brazil. His research and teaching focus on political participation, particularly in the health sector. He is coeditor and coauthor of *Psicologia Social: Ética, Participação Política e Inclusão Social* (Social psychology: Ethics, political participation and social inclusion; CRV, 2011) and of *Psicologia Social: Memórias, Saúde e Trabalho* (Memory, Health and Labor; ABRAPSO Press, 2004). He was president of the Brazilian Social Psychology Association (2003–2005) and the Brazilian Political Psychology Association (2005–2007), and since 2011 he has been the general secretary of the Political Psychology Association. From 2011 till 2013 he was the coordinator of the Health Policy, Planning and Management Committee of the Brazilian Association of Collective Health. He has conducted several research projects on political participation and health councils.

Michał Wenzel is assistant professor at the Center for the Study of Democracy, University of Social Sciences and Humanities (SWPS) in Warsaw, Poland. Before that, he was a researcher and analyst at CBOS Public Opinion Research Center in Warsaw. He was a postdoctoral scholar at Max Planck Institute for the Study of Societies in Cologne. He was also a visiting scholar at the University of Oxford and the University of Michigan. He has held numerous teaching positions. His interests include research methodology, empirical study of social movements, public opinion research, and political attitudes. He is a team member of Democratic Audit of Poland, a comprehensive empirical study of various aspects of democracy in Poland.

Index